LIFE IN A
COLD CLIMATE

ALSO BY LAURA THOMPSON

Agatha Christie: A Mysterious Life

*A Tale of Two Murders: Guilt, Innocence,
and the Execution of Edith Thompson*

LIFE IN A
COLD CLIMATE

Nancy Mitford

THE BIOGRAPHY

LAURA THOMPSON

PEGASUS BOOKS
NEW YORK LONDON

LIFE IN A COLD CLIMATE

Pegasus Books, Ltd.
West 37th Street, 13th Floor
New York, NY 10018

First Pegasus Books hardcover edition January 2020

ISBN: 978-1-64313-303-4

10 9 8 7 6 5 4 3 2 1

Printed in the United States of America
Distributed by W. W. Norton & Company

To my mother, with all my love

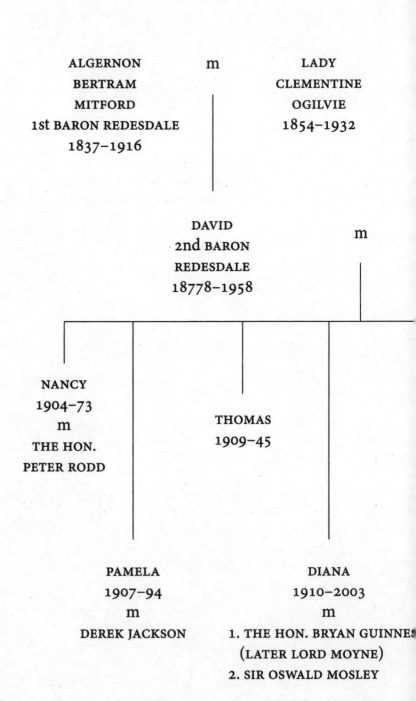

ALGERNON BERTRAM MITFORD 1st BARON REDESDALE 1837–1916 **m** LADY CLEMENTINE OGILVIE 1854–1932

DAVID 2nd BARON REDESDALE 18778–1958 **m**

NANCY 1904–73 m THE HON. PETER RODD

THOMAS 1909–45

PAMELA 1907–94 m DEREK JACKSON

DIANA 1910–2003 m
1. THE HON. BRYAN GUINNES (LATER LORD MOYNE)
2. SIR OSWALD MOSLEY

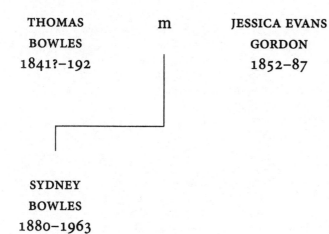

THOMAS
BOWLES
1841?–192

m

JESSICA EVANS
GORDON
1852–87

SYDNEY
BOWLES
1880–1963

UNITY
VALKYRIE
1914–48

DEBORAH
1920–2014
m
LORD
ANDREW
CAVENDISH
(11th DUKE OF
DEVONSHIRE)

JESSICA LUCY
1917–96
m
1. ESMOND ROMILLY
2. ROBERT TREUHAFT

ACKNOWLEDGMENTS

This book was written when two of Nancy's sisters were alive, and I remain hugely grateful to Lady Mosley and the Duchess of Devonshire, both of whom received me with great kindness. I shall remember our conversations with enormous pleasure. Without Lady Mosley's initial help – which was offered freely and unquestioningly, to a person of whom she knew nothing – I doubt very much that my book could have been written; I am deeply indebted to her for such generosity.

I should like to thank Alexander Mosley, who has also sadly died, and Viscount Norwich; Fran Blackwall, Peter Brook, Jacques Brousse, Lord Dulverton, Natasha Fairweather and Helen Marchant; the BBC Written Archives Centre at Caversham, which was quite wonderfully helpful to me; the Bodleian Library; Bristol University Library; Cambridge University Library; the London Library; the Public Record Office at Kew; and the Taylor Institution in Oxford for showing me the correspondence between Nancy Mitford and Theodore Besterman.

I owe a huge debt to Selina Hastings for her 1985 biography of Nancy Mitford: although our interpretations of Nancy's life differ in several ways, I could not have written my book without reference to this earlier work. I am also greatly indebted to the work of Charlotte Mosley, wonderful editor of Nancy's extensive correspondence.

My thanks to my original publishers, Headline. Lastly I am hugely grateful to all at Head of Zeus, and to my agent Georgina Capel, for enabling this book to appear in a new edition.

CHAPTER 1

The little grave at Swinbrook church is a sad sight now. One searches for many minutes, eyes wandering over the whiter tombstones, and the shock of finding it is considerable. Can this possibly be right? It is like a grave from two hundred years ago: the grave of a forgotten and anonymous person, of a poor serving girl who died alone and unlamented. It is covered with the thick damp lace of greenish moss, and there are no flowers.

On it are written, in plain script barely legible beneath the decay, the words: NANCY MITFORD, Authoress, Wife of Peter Rodd, 1904–1973. Above the words is carved a strange fat animal, which is in fact a mole taken from the Mitford family crest. Nancy disliked the sign of the cross because she thought it a symbol of cruelty. So her sister Pamela, also buried in Swinbrook churchyard, chose for her the mole, a neat eccentric image that in later life was embossed on Nancy's writing paper. An aunt of hers wrote to say how much she loved the letterhead: 'your charming little golden cunt (Glostershire of my young days for moles, few people now know what it means).' '*She's* not in the Tynan set,' Nancy had remarked. Beneath the earth, then, she may be laughing: her favourite thing in the world.

Yet as one of England's most devout Francophiles she had dreamed of a burial at Père-Lachaise cemetery, '*parmi ce peuple*' – as Napoleon put it – '*que j'ai si bien aimé.*' She called it the 'Lachaise dump', but that was just her Englishness coming out. She loved the place. What she no doubt imagined was lying in florid, elegant state between Molière, La Fontaine, Balzac and Proust: a comforting thought, as if death were merely a continuation of her glittering Parisian middle age. As in Dostoevsky's story 'Bobok', the buried people would simply carry on with the gossipy, deliciously trivial life that they had lived overground. 'We've already passed enough friends to collect a large dinner party, a large amusing dinner party', says Charles-Edouard de Valhubert in Nancy's novel *The Blessing*, as he walks among the graves with his English wife. And then: 'Is it not beautiful up on this cliff?'

Nancy dreamed of beauty around her in death. 'I've left £4000 for a tomb with angels and things', she wrote to Evelyn Waugh ten years before she died. 'Surely it's an ancient instinct to want a pretty tomb?' She also dreamed, in a way that would have amused, but irritated Waugh like a verruca, of a heaven that was really like fairyland, full of the people she had loved, along with sexy men such as Louis XV and Lord Byron – 'I look forward greatly. Oh how lovely it will be' – and with *The Lost Chord* playing. 'And an occasional nightingale.'

This was something that she said during a radio interview, and obviously it is an enchanting little conversational tease of the kind that she always adored. Yet there is a quality to her voice, as she lingers on those paradisiacal images, that reveals what was always there, and constitutes so great a part of her appeal: the yearning soul within the sophisticate's carapace: the imagination that can take illusion and make it into something real. Nancy *did* respond to that idea of heaven as fairyland. And she probably did imagine drifting into death on 'waves of bliss', like those which take Polly Hampton up the aisle in *Love in a Cold Climate*. But Polly, of course, is not really moving towards bliss. She is making a doomed and farcical marriage with that dirtiest of old men, Boy Dougdale, who has been sleeping with her mother and will later turn pederast. This is the truth, which does not mitigate one jot the shining belief in love that has impelled Polly's actions: for Nancy Mitford is at one and the same time, and in pretty well equal parts, a complete romantic and a complete realist.

So here is the grave in which she lies. Sombre, dilapidated, rooted in deep unchanging Oxfordshire. No brilliant Père-Lachaise neighbours, no sparkling subterranean *potins*, just poor brain-damaged Unity Mitford beside her, the sister who put a bullet in her head on the day that war was declared and died from its slow creep nine years later. Some way away from these two, close to Pamela, lie the Mitford parents, David and Sydney, whose only son, Tom, is commemorated by a plaque inside the church. Around that dear little stone doll's house are scattered most of the remains of that rampaging family mythology. Now birds sing above the stillness; rabbits hop softly between the tombs. It is intensely withdrawn, intensely English: a silent reminder of what lies beneath the fantastical cleverness, the Francophilia, the taste for Boucher and Boulle and *les gens du monde*.

Nancy's most famous novel, *The Pursuit of Love*, was the fourth that she wrote but the first in which her voice found full, clear expression, and this is surely because it, too, was rooted in this world, the world of damp and occasionally sunlit country, the world of calmly waiting churchyards set in England's heart, the world upon which glamour and foreignness impact like a dream of delight. Nancy's life, then, in a way. When she lay dying in her house at Versailles, whose Frenchness is as absolute as a page in the diary of Saint-Simon, she said to the Duchess of Devonshire: 'I would give anything for just *one more day's hunting*.'

'Now that's interesting, don't you think?' says her sister.[1]

Yet it all began in London, where Nancy Mitford was born on 28 November 1904. Until 1911, when the family acquired a little summer cottage in High Wycombe, she hardly left the city. This was the unflashy London of the cash-strapped gentry: of shopping at the Army and Navy Stores, of quiet back streets and confined spaces, of correctness rather than smartness. *Love in a Cold Climate*'s Lady Montdore, with her staggering house on Park Lane, her pity for 'the idea that some poor ladies have to live in Chelsea', would have thought very little of Nancy's first home: a neat stucco-faced house at Number 1 Graham Street (now Graham Terrace and now, of course, worth a fortune). Technically it was in Belgravia but it had no SW1 swank about it. Nancy later described memories of her early years as being 'shrouded in a thick mist' but even so she remembered this house as 'minute'.

In 1910 the Mitfords moved to a larger, although not grander, house at Number 49 Victoria Road, one of those long unchanging roads that lead south from Kensington High Street. And so Nancy was a London child through and through, briefly attending Francis Holland School, taking her two daily walks in parks, going to museums and theatres (where during *Peter Pan* the Mitford children shouted that no, they did not believe in fairies), gazing up at houses on whose scrubbed steps stood nannies in their shiny black straw bonnets, glimpsing through long windows the band-box smart parlourmaids and the women in their clinging, drifting skirts.

There was no indication, then, of what was to come: of the rich texture of life that would be woven as the family spread like yeast; of the secret, wild intimacy of child-hunts and Hons' cupboards and homes where 'the cruel woods crept right up to the house', as Nancy would later write in *The Pursuit of Love*. All that was like another, unimaginable world. At the start, the Mitfords were a conventional little unit. There was not much money, there was no prospect of Nancy's father inheriting the family title², and so they went about their business like any other straitened upper-class newly-weds: handsome David, working for his daily bread in Covent Garden while dreaming of striding across moors with a shotgun; serene Sydney, desultorily pushing her pretty baby's pram around pristine London squares; Lily the young nanny; Nancy the blissful sole recipient of love and attention – and then Pamela, the second child, blond and sweet and as different from her sister as two people could be.

From the moment of Pam's birth, Nancy seems to have seen her life differently. She later said that it 'threw me in a permanent rage for about twenty years'. Until 25 November 1907, a day on which she was no doubt dreaming of how she would celebrate her third birthday, life was an idyll. Thereafter it was imperfect, irrevocably different, the enchanted London skies covered with clouds. From then on, if she wanted to feed ducks on the Round Pond in Kensington Gardens, Pamela would have to do so too. If she wanted to read in the nursery, Pamela would be there 'creaking the rocking-horse'. If she wanted the attention of her nanny, Pamela's great pale eyes would claim it from her. 'Why don't you love me anymore?' Nancy was heard to say over and over again to Lily, whose treacherous arms were now bound tight around the new Mitford baby. Eventually the girl was dismissed by Sydney on the grounds that her presence was too upsetting; this may have been what Nancy – who even at three years old was no doubt very much all there – had wanted.

'Ninny' – as Lily Kersey was called – 'was quite untrained and knew nothing about babies.' So Nancy wrote in an essay about her childhood, published fifty-five years after the birth of Pamela. 'I think she was also partly responsible for my great nastiness to the others . . .' By her own admission, Nancy's memories of the past were hazy, and so in order to draw this conclusion about her first nanny she had to rely, as she said, on 'family hearsay'. All the same her sister Diana thinks that there is probably something in it. 'Simply she was the only child until she was three, and then she was jealous of the baby. Especially as the nanny was very very silly, and made a fuss of the baby and not of her. Well everybody knows not to do that now – people are so careful with their second baby, not to push the other one aside. But you see the nanny they had was aged eighteen or something, and hadn't read Freud . . . !'[3]

The shock of Pam's appearance was compounded, or possibly neutralised, by the birth of Tom in 1909 and Diana in 1910. Around this time – 'a kind of Mitford dark ages', as Nancy wrote – a woman arrived in the household known as 'the Unkind Nanny', of whom it is said that she was once found banging Nancy's head against a bedpost. Again Nancy says that she recalls nothing of this ('Did the Nanny beat us or starve us or merely refuse to laugh at our jokes? I shall never know'). And so she does not appear remotely traumatised by this demon's short reign. Yet the actions of her first, loved nanny stayed with her, even though she had to be reminded of them: 'You were terribly spoiled as a child, and by all,' her mother would later say to her. 'In fact until Pam was born you reigned supreme.' And hearing this seems to have struck, in Nancy, a reverberating chord of memory: years after the event, she decided to see its intense significance.

Rather a strange way, incidentally, for a mother to address her daughter? It certainly has an air of detachment. Yet that was quite usual between these two; with them, there was a directness unsoftened by affection, and a distance uneasily bridged by duty. Indeed the strongest feeling one gets, reading this essay on Nancy's childhood, was that its real target was not the nannies but Sydney. The point of shooting these darts at Lily Kersey and the Unkind Nanny was surely, in part at least, to make the reader wonder what kind of woman would employ such people to look after her daughter.

Nancy's dislike of her mother peeps out from between the careful barbs of her sentences, which Lady Redesdale must have read like someone picking roses without gardening gloves. Not so much when Nancy describes a 'delightful day dream' of longing to hear that her parents had gone down on a ship, leaving her to 'gather up the reins of the household in small but capable hands and boss "the others"'. That is mere childish fantasy (oddly enough it nearly happened: the Mitfords booked passages on the *Titanic* but did not take the trip). But when she writes about the sacking of the Unkind Nanny, for example, she begins to twist the knife in earnest: 'My mother retired to bed, as she often did when things became dramatic, leaving my father to perform the execution . . .' And here the blade gleams more visibly:

So what did my mother do all day? She says now, when cross-examined, that she lived for us. Perhaps she did, but nobody could say that she lived with us. It was not the custom then. I think that nothing in my life has changed more than the relationship between mothers and young children. In those days a distance was always kept. Even so she was perhaps abnormally detached. On one occasion Unity rushed into the drawing-room, where she was at the writing-table, saying: 'Muv, Muv, Decca[4] is standing on the roof – she says she's going to commit suicide!' 'Oh, poor duck', said my mother, 'I hope she won't do anything so terrible', and went on writing.

It is a good story (corroborated? Unity couldn't, and Jessica didn't) and well told in the way that Nancy steps lightly between judiciousness and condemnation. If true, it does say something about Sydney, not least that living with six daughters might lead a mother to treat them like so many tempestuous divas: let the storms break, knowing that they will blow over. Ironically, it is just the kind of reaction that Nancy would normally have admired. Yet when it came from Sydney, she elected to resent it. Later in her essay she recalls how Sydney would transfer her affections between her daughters – 'She was entirely influenced by physical beauty; those who were passing through an awkward or ugly age were less in favour than their prettier sisters' – and, again, how lethally this reads.

So it was not surprising that Lady Redesdale reacted badly when this essay appeared. 'Oh *goodness* I thought it would make you *laugh*', Nancy wrote to her mother in August 1962, after its publication in *The Sunday Times* under the title 'Mothering the Mitfords'. Clearly she was concerned, and yet in another way she was not concerned at all, else why would she have done it? She must have known exactly what she was saying, and that her mother would know it too, but she had apparently been unable to stop herself. 'All I can say is you must forgive & I'm very very sorry if you are annoyed, because I can't stop it unless I stop the whole book[5] which would cost thousands of pounds. Oh dear it has cast a cloud . . .' A couple of weeks later Nancy's fractious perturbation has increased. She sounds about fifteen years of age, as if guilt were driving her into an ever deeper tantrum; and how she must have resented this. 'But the person who appears completely vile is *me*!! . . . No more efforts at autobiography I've learnt my lesson.'

She had written about Sydney already, in a sense, when she portrayed her as Lady Alconleigh, or Aunt Sadie, in *The Pursuit of Love* and *Love in a Cold Climate*. And she used this portrait as a sort of (pretty poor) defence: 'In any case everybody knows you are Aunt Sadie who is a character in the round & is you in middle age exactly as you were.' Actually there is not much similarity between the woman described in Nancy's essay and the one in her two great novels. Sadie has charm to burn, whereas Sydney – according to this portrait, at least – had none; but then Sadie, unlike Sydney, is very much a Mitford. Like almost all of that family she is tremendously funny, even though she does not necessarily mean to be ('Always remember, children, that marriage is a very intimate relationship, it's not just sitting and chatting to a person, there are other things you know', is her way of trying to put Polly off her engagement to Boy Dougdale in *Love in a Cold Climate*). Her tremendous vagueness is not a product of innate detachment, more a poetic retreat from the demands of her relentless family. And she is generally greatly adored: her husband only wants to be with her, sensible Fanny thinks the world of her, her younger children are nearly obsessed with getting her attention.

Linda, though . . . Sadie's daughter Linda is the heroine of *The Pursuit of Love* and, as such, she inevitably holds something of Nancy's fundamental self. Somehow, no doubt without being aware of it, Nancy conveys a wariness in Linda's relationship with her mother.

When Linda takes up her life of Parisian ecstasy with her great love, Fabrice de Sauveterre, a pervasive note in the narrative – so constant as to be almost unnoticeable – is her real dread of Lady Alconleigh's disapproval:

She hadn't liked it when Linda had committed adultery with Christian, but he, at least, was English, and Linda had been properly introduced to him and knew his surname . . . how much less would Aunt Sadie like her daughter to pick up an unknown, nameless foreigner and go off to live with him in luxury . . . [Lord Alconleigh] would disown her for ever, throw her out into the snow, shoot Fabrice, or take any other violent action which might occur to him. Then something would happen to make him laugh, and all would be well again. Aunt Sadie was a different matter. She would not say very much, but she would brood over it and take it to heart, and wonder if there had not been something wrong about her method of bringing up Linda which had led to this; Linda most profoundly hoped that she would never find out.

This is infinitely more sympathetic, again, than the portrait of the real mother, but there is something similar. That delicate, sorrowing ability to induce guilt was pure Sydney, as is the very faint sense, in Aunt Sadie, of something kept hidden within herself, withdrawn even from her children; which is not quite what one wants from a mother. In some mysterious way Linda feels like a motherless child, a rootless girl. Despite her large family, despite her wild capacity for joy, there is something sad and solitary in her, and this has surely seeped into Linda from Nancy herself.

So it was as though Nancy had felt a chill coming off her mother, against which she could not warm herself. And it is all too easy to predicate from this her later failures in relationships with men – 'I think that all her love affairs were unhappy,' says her sister Diana – and the growth of her spiky carapace, her laughing defence against hurt. Easy to see a pattern established in the birth of Pamela: the definitive example of Diana's remark that 'the trouble with Nancy's life is she doesn't come *first* with anybody'.

Which sounds terribly sad, indeed quite pitiable, until one then starts to wonder how much it actually means. As Stephen Spender would later ask, in his *Listener* review of the 1985 biography of Nancy by Selina Hastings: 'how many of us can be certain that we are first with anybody?' Equal first perhaps, but being all things to another person is pretty rare. And certainly – to go back to the formative years – Nancy came equal first with her Nanny Blor, who is the heroine of her *Sunday Times* essay. Blor (real name Laura Dicks), a robust nonconformist of natural and unstinting kindness, arrived at Graham Street in 1910 as a sweet solution to the problems created by her predecessors. From the first, she gave and inspired love in equal measure. She was, says Nancy's sister Deborah, 'a complete saint'.[6]

Unlike fickle Sydney, Nanny Blor had no favourites. 'If she felt on the side of the little ones,' wrote Nancy, 'especially her own baby, Diana, against the bully that I was, she never showed it. Her fairness always amazed me, even as a child . . .' The essay is a homage to the woman who was, as will be seen, the first of several substitute mothers in Nancy's life. And the warmth with which Blor is described is perhaps the most deadly shot that Nancy aimed at her real, cool, distant mother. It was not Sydney, so the implication goes, who had 'mothered' this particular Mitford.

Of course, and this Nancy scrupulously reiterates, she grew up in the era of nannies and of parental remoteness (one might say that this era has never ended, although now it is that of childminders and working late at the office). And so it was to be expected that a child of her class and time lived in the way that she describes: 'we "came down" to see our parents finishing their breakfast and again, dressed up in party clothes, after tea . . . But we spent the major part of our lives in the nursery . . .' What is unusual is that a woman like Nancy saw this as worthy of criticism. She did not object to nannies *per se*, nor to being left alone by her parents; almost certainly she would have brought up a child of her own in this way. It is a rather more fundamental point that she seems to have been making, about the relative levels of affection that she received from her mother and from Blor. And this, yes, she did mind a good deal. Coming equal first with her nanny was a wonderful compensation, but should compensation have been necessary?

Indirectly, and perhaps unconsciously, Nancy wrote about this in her four post-war novels. She pulled the same trick that she did in 'Mothering the Mitfords', putting into each of these books an image of alternative motherhood: something warm and 'normal' and not much like Sydney. For example, the two books in which Aunt Sadie features (*The Pursuit of Love* and *Love in a Cold Climate*) also contain a woman who comes close to being the perfect mother: Fanny's Aunt Emily, sister to Sadie, an emblem of sanity who believes in education for women and in letting children develop sound instincts in an atmosphere of enlightened freedom. This is how Fanny is raised (having been abandoned by her real mother, the Bolter, the third sister, who sits in a Riviera *boîte* somewhere at the far end of the maternal spectrum). She becomes just such a mother herself, as Nancy shows in her last novel, *Don't Tell Alfred*. Fanny's three sons are disasters in various ways but her manner of dealing with them – never asking questions, guiding not pushing, hiding their worst fooleries from their father, always keeping a sense of humour – is exemplary, unremittingly kind and sensible. Nancy's approval of Emily and Fanny, of their ease with the maternal role, is ever present. It sings quietly in vignettes such as the one that shows Fanny starting every day with her son's adopted child on her bed, finding him 'delightful company; a contented, healthy baby, easily amused and anxious to please'. It is explicitly stated in the passage in *The Pursuit of Love* when Fanny is accused, by her Uncle Matthew, of becoming hideously middle-class because Emily has sent her to school: 'All the same, my aunt was right, and I knew it and she knew it.'

It is as though, having seen the ways in which – in her opinion – her own mother had gone wrong, Nancy conceived a fully rounded idea of what a mother *should* be like: and very attractive it is too. For a woman who never bore children, it is in fact remarkable how well Nancy understood motherhood. She portrays good mothers in her novels with absolute naturalness, for all the world as if she had raised a brood herself. At the same time she is wonderful at describing bad mothers, which some people think she would have been herself (children would have been 'a great pest to her', says her sister Diana). For example when Linda gives birth to a 'howling orange' in *The Pursuit of Love*, she tells Fanny that it is 'really kinder not to look' in the cradle, while Polly, in *Love in a Cold Climate*, views her pregnancy with a sort of distant horror. But then both these women have been impregnated by men whom they no longer love, which Nancy clearly sees – and probably rightly – as making a difference.

Conversely, in her novel *The Blessing*, Grace de Valhubert is so besotted with her husband that her son, Sigismond, is washed in the same happy waves of love: mother and child have a delightful relationship, a charming and funny intimacy. Nonetheless it is interesting that Nancy put a version of Nanny Blor into this novel, with whom Sigi spends much of his time while Grace concentrates on her fascinating man ('A woman who puts her husband first seldom loses him'). And Sigi is, indeed, shown to crave more attention from his parents. But his attempts to get it are comic rather than pathetic, because it is made wholly clear that there is no lack of love between Grace and her son. Nanny does not, in this case, come first.

For Nancy, of course, she did. Nancy did believe that her mother lacked love for her, and as time went on she found it more and more convenient to blame her for anything that had gone wrong in her life. For example in 1961, in a letter to Diana, she would attribute her lack of physical energy to the assertion that 'the dentist says I was starved when I was five and having our mater I guess that may be true.' (In 'Mothering the Mitfords' she wrote that Lily Kersey had 'laid the foundations for the low stamina which has always been such a handicap to me in life'; but then this, too, was an oblique attack on Sydney.) Also, more viciously, she would try to blame her mother for her own inability to have children. She claimed that Sydney had – by her own admission – employed a syphilitic nursemaid, and that this person had by some mysterious means infected Nancy and rendered her infertile. It is actually impossible to think that even Nancy believed such a story. But it was the kind of thing that she would say within the family.[7]

And it must have been hovering in her mind, along with the 'Mothering the Mitfords' essay, when Sydney died in 1963: there was painful unfinished business between mother and daughter, and no doubt for Nancy a certain amount of guilt. 'I think she probably had big regrets,' says Debo. If so, these could have dissipated her fury; instead, Nancy used them to stoke the fires of resentment. The rage that simmers beneath the ladylike prose of 'Mothering the Mitfords' was let loose after Sydney's death, to the point where, in 1971, Nancy was writing this to her sister Jessica on the subject of their mother: 'I had the greatest possible respect for her; I liked her company; but I never loved her, for the evident reason that she never loved me. I was never hugged & kissed by her as a small child – indeed I saw very little of her . . . I don't believe this really applies to you & Debo? Certainly Debo loved her & Diana did in old age but not when we first grew up. She was very cold & sarky with me. I don't reproach her for it, people have a perfect right to dislike their children . . .'

Poor Nancy – this was real and burning in her at the age of nearly sixty-seven, when the distancing process of adulthood might be thought to have intervened. She was wholly unwilling, or unable, to take a mature perspective of the kind that Jessica displayed in her reply: 'I actively loathed her as a teenager (especially as an older child, after the age of fifteen), and did not respect her. But then, after getting to re-know her I became immensely fond of her and really rather adored her. She probably didn't change, as people don't, especially after middle-age. Most likely we did.'

Yet if Nancy changed towards her mother it was to become less, rather than more, accepting. And, in her own middle age, she considered giving these feelings some sort of autobiographical expression. Back in June 1962, Nancy had told Sydney that, because she remembered so little of her early life, 'I could no more write memoirs than fly.' But although her memories were incomplete they had, as she showed in 'Mothering the Mitfords', a force, a shape, an artistic logic: they were a writer's memories, in fact, and even if they were not literally true they had the power to convince both Nancy and her readers. Certainly the essay that she wrote about her childhood – which she said was one of the best things she had ever done – helped to convince her of how she felt about Sydney.

Although she had never been introspective (too boring for other people), and had lived her life in a way that was both intensely private and intensely social, from that time onwards the desire grew strong in Nancy to write her memoirs. It was as though she liked the idea of a literary construct that would explain her life to herself. She did not, she said, intend to revisit her childhood in the book; she intended to use it to explain her adulthood, as the 1971 letters between herself,

Jessica and Deborah make clear. Their central concern is what Nancy described, to Debo, as the 'unsatisfactory relationship I had with Muv'; so much so that it is hard not to see the planned autobiography as a kind of *J'accuse* directed at Sydney. After 1963, when the fear of that brooding presence had been removed and there could be no more sad, disapproving letters in the post, Nancy dreamed more and more intently of writing a book in which she could say exactly what she thought about her mother.

How true it would all have been is another story altogether: 'oh *I hope* I shall be honest', Nancy wrote to Jessica in 1971 about the autobiography, but where her mother was concerned there *are* doubts as to Nancy's honesty. She decided to believe that Sydney did not love her. This does not mean that what she believed was true.

Deborah instantly admits that Nancy felt this way but says: 'I don't know why it was. We had this wonderful nanny – but she didn't come until Nancy was six. And you know people now, all these psychiatrists say that a nanny and a mother must be enemies – what rubbish. We loved them both. I mean the more people you have to love the better.' Deborah's own feelings towards her mother are those of straightforward affection, but she was born sixteen years after Nancy – was the last rather than the first child – so her relationship with Sydney would undoubtedly have been very different. And even Deborah once admitted that her mother 'could come down like a ton of bricks and it was then awful'.[8]

Meanwhile Diana's feelings on the subject are intense, not least because she considers that Nancy was *not* honest about Sydney, and indeed wrote a great many downright lies about her, especially in letters. 'I can never forgive that.' Therefore her tendency is to blame Nancy for disliking Sydney rather than the other way about. 'No, I don't think they loved each other much. I adored my mother. She was so marvellous. I wouldn't say she was a great one for hugging or anything like that, but she wasn't cold, not at all. And it takes two –! Nancy was very reserved, you see . . .' To be fair, Nancy herself said something along these lines when, in a letter to Deborah in 1971, she wrote: 'I would vaguely like to try & find out if this relationship [between herself and Sydney] was one's fault or hers.' But beneath the attempt at rationality it is pretty clear that Nancy did *not* actually think it was her own fault. In Nancy's opinion, Sydney deserved all that she got from her.

Now these contradictory perceptions are not so surprising, yet they do illustrate an intriguing difficulty about the Mitfords. Sometimes, recollections of the family's past differ according to whether or not members actually *want* to agree with one another. For example Diana tends not to agree with much of what Nancy says, and regards a good deal of it as either myth-making, mischief-making or both. She would probably say that, in the writing of 'Mothering the Mitfords', Nancy's pen had been flowing pleasurably with glittering spite, that she had been relieving some frustration of her own by using her mother as material: doing so, indeed, with all the cool detachment of which Sydney herself was accused. This is a valid point of view. Nancy *was* extremely hard on her mother in her essay, to the extent that the blood does chill a little: right down to freezing point if what she had been writing was fundamentally untrue.

Yet why should it have been? Nancy may have revelled in exaggeration, she may have had a writer's facility for bending truth to her imaginative will. But there is no reason whatsoever for *inventing* the lack of love that she felt from her mother. It would be wholly pointless. And indeed, a comment like 'until Pam was born you reigned supreme' does read wintry and non-maternal, like a report from a headmistress upon a difficult pupil. Nancy might well have believed from it that the flow of motherliness towards her was not instinctively there, that from the first there had been a cool judgmental eye upon her.

And it is odd that Sydney should have given birth to this pretty, pert little thing (Nancy was no 'howling orange', she was a gorgeous-looking child, with her cloud of black hair and her mother's down-turning mouth); should have done so in the earliest days of her marriage, when all was meant to be sunlight and bliss; and yet should have created this impression of remoteness, indeed of dislike. David Mitford's joy at Nancy's arrival seems to have been boundless: 'I never dreamt of such happiness', he wrote to his mother when Sydney fell pregnant; and, after the birth – at which, most unusually for the time, he was present – 'our happiness is very great'. Sydney's own feelings are not recorded.

Nancy was not an especially easy child (she was not even easy in the producing: Sydney's labour lasted fourteen hours). Cleverness often leads to frustrations, and according to her mother she was given to uncontrollable tantrums: 'you used to get into tremendous rages, often shaming us in the street', Sydney would later tell her daughter, again in the detached and deadly tone that Nancy found so difficult. David had gone in for tantrums as a child, so possibly he understood and indulged Nancy in a way that irritated his wife. He also had a sister who tried to force Sydney to bring up her daughter in a new-fangled, give-her-anything manner, which was no doubt an added annoyance: 'She said you must never hear an angry word and you never did . . .' (more's the pity, runs the subtext). Essentially it seems that David was completely entranced by Nancy – he called her 'the pearl of the family' – and that her mother was therefore left to take a more distanced role. It is said that Sydney wanted and fully expected a son, and this might have suited her better. Possibly she felt ambivalent about the whole experience of bearing this first child, especially when those around her – not least her husband – assumed her to be delirious with joy.

She may, very simply, have been jealous of Nancy, not least because of her daughter's extreme closeness to David. The age gap between a mother and her eldest daughter is often not so great as to preclude the possibility of competitiveness. Sydney was a clever and attractive woman, and the flowering of these qualities in Nancy – her, more than the younger girls – may have given rise to tricky emotions. And Nancy would not have been someone to break through these. Diana is quite right to say that it cuts both ways. Certainly the relationship between these two women was not really like that of a mother and daughter: even at its best, it was more like that of England and France, wary and respectful enemy-friends.

It is certainly unusual for a mother to tell her daughter that she had wanted to run off with another man when the daughter was aged just two, but felt herself obliged to stay for the sake of the child. Yet according to Nancy, Sydney told her exactly that; although it must be said that both Deborah and Diana consider this to have been an invention (to what purpose, however, it is again hard to say, unless malice itself was purpose enough; contrary to Nancy's 'agenda', the story shows Sydney in a selfless light with regard to her daughter).

And it does square with another story, which sprang up amongst Sydney's contemporaries and had her walking up the aisle of St Margaret's, Westminster, weeping for a man called Jimmy Meade. He had been her suitor before David Mitford, but she had supposedly broken off the attachment on account of his womanising reputation (one cannot help but wonder whether it was the other way about). Again, proof of this is scant, but the story must have come from somewhere. Sydney had certainly had her share of suitors before her marriage (at the age of twenty-four, which was not so young in 1904), including a man who was killed in the Boer War. David Mitford may not have been the absolute choice of her heart.

Of course there is no way of knowing the feelings of this very secret woman, at the start of her life as a wife and mother. Yet there may have been unfinished business in Sydney when she married; which was still unresolved when Nancy was born, barely ten months after the wedding. And for that, in some obscure way, Sydney may have blamed her daughter, who definitively closed the door on a life half-reluctantly left. Here, perhaps, lies the source of that radiating chill.

Sydney Mitford was not really a conventional woman, although she has been viewed as such: 'full of the domestic virtues and good works, with enough dottiness to stop her being insipid', was David Pryce-Jones's judgment in his biography of her daughter Unity. 'Knowing nothing of the world at large in all its complexity, they [she and her husband] had neither the inclination nor the intellectual means to find out about it. They preferred their home, and its pursuits. They expected their children to be like themselves. Faced with originality, they were defenceless.'

Now this is true to an extent – true of most people? – but it is also reductive. And it does not take into account the fact that Sydney may have striven for an appearance of conventionality because her own upbringing had been so very bizarre for its time. Her father, Thomas Gibson Bowles ('Tap'), was illegitimate, the product of a liaison between a Liberal MP and one of his servants. Tap was taken into his father's household but educated in France, and became a man of very considerable, if eccentric, force. He founded the magazine *Vanity Fair* aged twenty-six, and later *The Lady*; he married into a military family, living with his wife Jessica in a house near the Albert Hall in which he kept chickens (Nancy later did the same in her London home, and also had a white hen in her Paris flat); he became MP for King's Lynn having fought his electoral campaign from his yacht; after his wife's death, when Sydney was aged just seven, he had three children by his children's governess, whom he made editor of *The Lady*. He retired finally aged around seventy-six – 'the capacity of man for work is almost unlimited', he had said – and died in 1921. 'I believe I was born in 1841. I am no more certain of it than I am of the birthday of Julius Caesar . . .' he wrote at the end of his life.

But no less remarkable than Tap's career was his relationship with his children, which – in externals at least – was unusually modern. Where he went, so did they. No packing off to nanny and the nursery for Tap's two daughters: dressed in sailor suits, they helped their father canvass from his yacht and sat with him at dinner tables, where he would tell other guests if he thought they were eating too much. His views on health were extreme. He had a loathing of doctors, his wife having died from an abortion performed to save her from a fifth, life-threatening pregnancy, and he disliked medicine. He also believed that the pig should not be eaten (this was on the grounds that Jews did not suffer from cancer). His daughter took these ideas directly on board. Nancy wrote in 'Mothering the Mitfords' that Sydney 'did not really believe in illness', and certainly when she was operated on, at the age of two, for an infected foot, it was her father who insisted upon the use of chloroform. Meanwhile Jessica would recall in her book *Hons and Rebels* that, at the age of twelve or so, she herself had telephoned a doctor and asked him to remove her appendix, her mother having dismissed her terrible stomach pains as a consequence of over-eating. On the question of diet, Sydney held to a sensible belief in foods such as wholegrain bread, which she baked herself, but at the same time forbade her children the meats that she and David ate: 'the occasional sucking-pig which crackled into the dining-room hardly bears contemplating, even now', wrote Nancy, and Evelyn Waugh later described (fancifully) how in childhood Deborah would stuff 'pork sausages up her knickers to consume in secret'.

It is not surprising that Sydney should have been so influenced by her father, for he dominated her life. In fact he turned her into something like a wife. From the age of fourteen, she was running his large house in Lowndes Square (and thereafter was very efficient at housekeeping; although she always hated employing men, having found it hard as a girl to impose her authority upon them). Her father must have been all things to her. Yet she, in her turn, had to vie with her younger sister for his love; and indeed Dorothy – or 'Weenie', as she was rather repulsively called – did perhaps get more than her share of it. Tap's sailing book *The Log of the Nereid* was dedicated 'To Captain Weenie (aged 3)' and is full of her irritating doings. No mention of Sydney, though – shades here of Nancy and Pamela?

And a clue, perhaps, to the difficulties Sydney had in becoming a mother. She had scarcely had one herself. What she had had instead was a relationship with her father that was unusual in its closeness and that gave her a good deal of attention, but attention of a very particular kind. It must have been satisfying to a young girl, being taken like a consort to political meetings and adult weekend parties. But at the same time she may have been dissatisfied with a father who, for all his physical proximity, had a remoteness about him, a self-centredness, and was not very much like a father to her at all.

Yet he had surely raised her expectations of life, made her feel that it would be a demanding, involved and fascinating business, that it held more than the prospects of housewifery and motherhood (although these, as it turned out, would make demands upon her that she could never have imagined). She thought of going to Girton, although nothing came of this; perhaps her father did not want to lose her. She always read a good deal – 'she loved memoirs, Queen Victoria's letters, that kind of thing', says Diana – and her own unpublished memoirs show that she wrote carefully and well. Attractive in a soulful, long-eyed way that hinted at earthy passions (the sexiness of her drooping mouth was quite something), she was a hit as a debutante. She took pleasure in sailing and met painters like Tissot during summers spent, on the yacht, at smart resorts like Deauville and Trouville. She loved ice-skating (as Unity later would) and had a passion for her Swedish instructor ('I would let him call me Sydney, I would even let him kiss me ...' she wrote in her diary for 1899). It was a free and promising life that she left when – whether dry- or wet-eyed – she walked in her white veil towards respectable penury with David Mitford.

Of course it may have seemed that the time had come for her life to take a more regular course. Her husband, although a second son, was a decent enough catch for a girl of faintly uncertain origins. And she had, or so she wrote in her memoirs, fallen in love with him ten years earlier, when she saw him leaning in front of the fireplace at his family home of Batsford Park, in Gloucestershire. He was seventeen then, an amazingly good-looking young man, tall and strong and casual, with the refined masculine features of Gary Cooper and the blue *regard* of his most beautiful daughter, Diana (and of Polly Hampton in *Love in a Cold Climate*, 'a blue flash, the bluest and most sudden thing I ever saw'). Hardly to be wondered at, that a young girl would swoon at such a vision, standing as he was in semi-possession of a baronial mansion. It must have been rather like the Queen, aged thirteen, falling for the blond and gleaming Philip: and these are the images of another person which endure, even into old age.

Yet David, too, was not all that he seemed, nor quite what his eldest daughter would later make him seem. Like his future wife, he had lived with the overwhelming presence of a father of character. Bertram Mitford, born in 1837, would later become a friend of Tap Bowles, which was how Sydney (taken everywhere as usual) came to stay at Batsford. It is not surprising that these two men should have gravitated towards each other when they entered Parliament, after the 1892 election, as they were in many ways very alike: both possessed of an almost alarming energy and restless desire to achieve. In Tap this was probably a consequence of his illegitimacy. In Bertie it may have been something similar: even if one dismisses the strong rumour that he, too, was illegitimate, he had to endure the trauma of his mother – Lady Georgina Ashburnham, a nineteenth-century Bolter – running off with a son of the Earl of Sefton when he was aged just four. The Mitford family had always been sedate landed gentry, with roots near Morpeth in Northumberland and with one reasonably well-known member, William, Nancy's great-great-great-grandfather, who had written a history of Greece. But Bertie was not like his ancestors. He and his descendants may not even have been Mitfords at all; after his death it was said that if one wanted to know who the family really was, one should look in *Burke's Peerage* under

'Sefton' rather than 'Redesdale'. This, of course, is the kind of thing that people say with more relish than cause, and it is not a rumour given universal credence. What is certain is that something in the mingling of Bertie's blood with that of Tap Bowles helped to turn the 'Mitfords' from the calm, discreet family of the past six hundred years into a wilder, more dazzling breed.

Bertie was one of those typical dynamic Victorians, but he was also more than a type. He had what Edmund Gosse would later refer to as a 'redundant vitality . . . His nature swarmed with life.' After Eton and Oxford, he became a diplomat. He immersed himself to varying degrees in foreign cultures and, while keeping his Englishness preserved, like a jar of Cooper's Oxford, he allowed his mind to be opened by his travels. He watched a samurai commit hara-kiri and was deeply moved by the ritual; was moved, too, by what he saw as the savage treatment of North American Indians. Much later he would also, and rather less endearingly, stay with the Wagner family at Bayreuth and embrace the theories of Houston Stewart Chamberlain, which set out something very like the Nazi creed. The significance of this to the future lives of Diana and Unity is, of course, pretty striking; although what really strikes one is the entranced naïvety with which Bertram Mitford absorbed Chamberlain's work. He was a man of the world, but only in the literal sense. He was on the first train to Paris after the end of the revolutionary Paris Commune of 1871, met Garibaldi in Italy, hunted buffalo (and brought a head back to Batsford), met the Mormon leader Brigham Young in Utah, and all by his middle thirties – it was quite some life, of the kind that cannot really be lived today. He subsequently wrote about it in his *Memoirs* and his *Tales of Old Japan*. This last book has never been out of print; like his granddaughter Nancy, Bertie knew how to write what people wanted to read.

When he returned home from his diplomat's life, Disraeli gave him responsibility for London's parks and monuments: plenty there to get his hungry teeth into, vast refurbishments of the Tower of London and so on. He also acquired a wife, Lady Clementine Ogilvie. This was a very good match; so much so that his mother-in-law, the Countess of Airlie, refused to acknowledge the marriage and always addressed her daughter by her maiden name. She knew all too well –

possibly, it was said, from first-hand experience – that Bertie was a womaniser, like his friend the Prince of Wales. It is almost certain that he had an affair with his sister-in-law, Lady Blanche Hozier, whose daughter (also named Clementine, later the wife of Winston Churchill) was said to resemble David Mitford.[9] Blanche's marriage to Colonel Hozier was unhappy and she solaced herself with at least nine lovers, conducting her affairs with shameless aplomb. She was given to robust pronouncements – 'I love privilege!' – that remind one of the terrible, irresistible things that Lady Montdore says in *Love in a Cold Climate* ('I love being so dry in here', she remarks from the inside of her luxurious motor car, 'and seeing all those poor people so wet'). Still, Blanche and the rest notwithstanding, the sweet-natured Clementine Mitford bore her husband six children in twelve years, of which David was the third.

The move to Batsford Park, near Moreton-in-Marsh and deep in the damp, rich, honey-coloured Cotswolds, came in 1886. Bertie inherited the large estate from a cousin named Freeman, whose name was thereafter joined to that of the Mitfords: Nancy's full name was Nancy Freeman-Mitford. Now he embarked upon the third part of his life, throwing himself with absolute intensity into the part of a country squire, becoming a magistrate, a horse breeder, a deputy Lord Lieutenant and MP for Stratford-upon-Avon. He also became a builder. He pulled down the original house at Batsford, a delightful Georgian oblong, and put in its place what now stands there: a child's dream of Rapunzel's castle which, against the sombre English sky, gives an impression of near unreality. Its colour is old gold, its shape fantastical. The main door is like a fortress, with above it an enormous Redesdale coat of arms and one vast, painted window; the other windows are small and leaded, made for the imprisoning of beautiful Gloucestershire princesses. There are gargoyles, and little turrets, and all the thrilling paraphernalia of fairytale, and so although it is conventional to lament the destruction of the symmetrical Georgian house, one cannot help but be glad that someone dared to build such a place as this. It is a work of the imagination, glowing deep ochre in the dark countryside. As such it is a magnificent one-off, testament to the vitality and – why not? – the arrogance of the man who conceived it.

Yet David Mitford cried when the old house was pulled down.

Inside his very masculine exterior he was a sensitive soul. And he must, surely, have suffered from the fact that his older brother was so very much the golden boy. Clement was loved and confident, he attended Eton where he was clever and popular; in his ability to achieve he resembled his father, although he may have been more likeable, whereas David was a rather different proposition. Handsome, strong and tough all right, but in no other way very satisfactory to a man such as Bertie Mitford.

David was the only one of the four sons to be sent to Radley, which has a reputation anyway for putting chips on the shoulders of people who had hoped to go to Eton (David's own son, Tom, *did* go there, which was perhaps David's way of righting a 'wrong'). And then he hated all the things that one is supposed to love at such places, for example team games; he had, wrote his grandson Jonathan Guinness, 'no trace of the conventional public school man's heartiness'[10], being like his daughters far too much of an individualist. His discomfort at the school must have been worsened by the fact, which nobody seems to have hidden from him, that he had been sent there in order that he should not be an embarrassment to Clement. For David, with his 'tempers', his sudden 'illnesses', was regarded as a bit of a liability. If the illnesses were psychosomatic, brought on when he felt thwarted in any way, there is no denying that the tempers were real: once, having been locked in a room by his father, he attacked him with a poker that he had been steadily heating on the fire. But were they also a product of his frustrations? It has been suggested that he may have been dyslexic, as he found reading and academic work difficult – he failed the written exam into Sandhurst – and yet spoke perfect French. Meanwhile his brother and father were highly literate, competent men, to an extent that must have made him feel excluded. And even though he himself worshipped Clement, indeed seems really to have loved him (as did all the family – he was Nancy's favourite uncle), there is a limit to how much anyone can stand being held up for comparison with a paragon.

Of course David Mitford, who was born in 1878, was a product of the Victorian upper-classes, and unlikely therefore to have been susceptible to theories about 'inferiority complexes' and other such feeble modern tosh. But he had his areas of uncertainty, all the same (as did his future wife). Being sent off as a tea-planter to what was then Ceylon was so very much the kind of thing that one did with a tricky second son. What else was there for him?

The Boer War came to his rescue, in a way. He wrote of General Brabazon, whose orderly he became, 'He is a soldier and a gentleman, and that is the most you can say for any man'. Military life gave him a sense of purpose and pride. He was decorated in the campaign, from which he returned in 1902 with only one lung. Two years after that he married Sydney, having dictated a love letter to her from his hospital bed to be sent in the event of his death. Although, when she had seen him standing like a young god up against the Batsford fireplace, all he had probably seen was an odd, sombre little creature in a sailor suit, by the time she grew up he was clearly head over heels. Her calm remoteness, which Nancy found so difficult, was just what he was looking for. He did not much care for working at his father-in-law's publication *The Lady* throughout the first ten years of his marriage – the real David was expressed through the mongoose that he took into the office and let loose on the rats in the cellar – but his letters from the time exhale the undeniable scent of true happiness.

What he liked, above anything, was to be at home with his wife, eating bread and milk in his dressing-gown. After work every Friday he would go, with his pay packet, to the market at Covent Garden and find a perfect peach for Sydney which she would eat, ceremoniously, after dinner. For a couple on barely £1,000 a year, this small gift served a sweetly symbolic purpose. It was not until twenty years or so later that David learned that Sydney hated peaches. Although she herself had never told him, there is a little paradigm for their early marriage in that story: he eager, almost unbearably so, to please; she smiling and swallowing and calmly thinking – what?

This is hardly the 'roaring, raging' Uncle Matthew of *The Pursuit of Love*. There is actually something very touching about David Mitford, with his beautiful patrician face and his huge peasant's hands, a man who had the energy of his father but not the accomplishments through which to channel them. He was a schemer and a dreamer. He had gone prospecting for gold in Ontario as a very young man and went with Sydney on what sound like very romantic little voyages, in the first years of their marriage; he got tangled up with a dubious wheeler-dealer selling papier mâché covers for wireless sets; he moved house several times, and like his father had the urge to build; these are restless activities, really. Nancy was later to say, and it is one of her most perceptive remarks, that the trouble with her father was 'he simply hadn't got enough to *do*.'[11]

She went on to tell the story of how, on her birth certificate, she had found that in the space beneath the word 'Occupation', her father had written: 'Honourable'. One would have thought that when, in 1916, he became Lord Redesdale, a landowner and a member of the House of Lords, he would have had more than enough on his plate, what with seven children and so on; but until old age and sadness quenched him this was not the case. Owning land anchored him, as his marriage had done, but it did not calm him. He fought staunchly on one lung in the First World War, although he was invalided home twice; the second time, in 1917, saw him return a thirty-nine-year-old wreck. He was never again able to ride to hounds, which must have been a terrible blow. But whereas a lesser man might have seized the opportunity to take things easy, bodily frustration had the opposite effect upon David Mitford and made him ever more wildly alive.

And this, when one thinks about it, is very much the key to the character of Uncle Matthew. He is not just an assemblage of hilarious eccentricities and sayings, although he has been seen as such; he is, as E.F. Benson wrote of a character in his Mapp and Lucia books (deeply loved by Nancy, incidentally), 'a hot coal thrown from the furnace of creation'. He is a striding mass of continually thwarted vitality. All that tooth-grinding, the obsession with punctuality ('in precisely six and three-quarter minutes the damned fella will be late'), the rising at 5 a.m. and prowling around 'clanking cups of tea, shouting at his dogs, roaring at the housemaids, cracking the stock-whips he had brought back from Canada on the lawn with a noise greater than gunfire, and all to the accompaniment of Galli-Curci on his gramophone . . .', the constant rages which rub against his knowledge that they should be suppressed – this is all unspeakably vivid stuff. But it rings true beneath the theatricality, the cardboard dimension, because it is informed by Nancy's instinctive understanding of her father: a man who was so magnificently all that he seemed, and yet more than he seemed. Even his buried vulnerability is there in Nancy's portrayal. It is delicately implied in Matthew's doglike worship of silly Lord Montdore, in his blustering hatred of leaving the domain in which he feels secure, in the security he gains from the presence of his wife. His loathing of foreigners, too ('they are all the same, and they all make me sick'), is on one level the knee-jerk jingoism of unassailable English self-confidence: somehow, Nancy implies that it is also a defence, against what is not understood. This is why, when she is writing at her best, David/Uncle Matthew is her best subject, for like any mythical creation he works on two levels: the archetypal and the particular.

In the television interview that she gave in 1966, Nancy was asked if it was true that her father, like Uncle Matthew, had read only one book – *White Fang* – which he had found so good he never bothered to try another. 'Well he read my books,' she said, her mouth twisting rather wryly. 'He liked them very much. *Madame de Pompadour* he didn't like, he was furious because he wasn't in it. But he loved the books about himself.'

Now this remark of Nancy's is reinforcing the idea of her father as a pantomime eccentric – how could he reasonably expect to feature in a book about the court of Louis XV? She was making him react to Uncle Matthew as if he were Uncle Matthew. At the same time, of course, she was saying that David delighted in the idea of his fictional self. It has been suggested that this was not in fact the case, that it was merely convenient for Nancy to think it, and that her father had been hurt rather than enthralled by her portrayal of him. The evidence for this is fairly flimsy, however. It seems to rest upon a remark made in a letter to Sydney, written in 1954, in which David said that Nancy's perception of him 'shows how savage I must have been, but without knowing it' – which could just as easily read as an apology, rather than an accusation.

Of course being written about *does* give rise to ambivalent feelings; but David's pride in what Nancy had done would surely have overridden sensitivities. How could he not have been proud, having earned such a magnificent tribute merely by being himself? Occasionally, in letters to friends, Nancy would describe him reading her novels, lost in childlike absorption: 'Uncle Matthew sat with his nose in the book & grunted out various corrections: "Never got the stock whips in Canada, a bloke from Australia gave them to me" & so on'; 'the only letters I get now are from chubb fuddlers saying that you can't fuddle chubb in Feb (already pointed out with cold fury by Uncle Matthew himself)'. It was as if the books had a complete reality for him, as if it were a wholly natural miracle that his life should appear in them in this way. For David and his daughter, fantastical Mitfords both, fact and fiction danced together in simple harmony. Why else would Nancy, post-*Pursuit of Love*, almost always refer to her father as 'Uncle Matthew', as if the two men were indeed one and the same?

To Sydney, however, her fictional self was a separate and unwanted creature. 'I wish only one thing, that you would exclude me from your books', she wrote to Nancy, admittedly just after reading the dread portrait of herself in *The Sunday Times*. But then she must have realised that, even as Aunt Sadie, she had been rendered with less love than her husband. Nancy and David had a very particular bond: as Deborah says, they were like a comic double act when they got into their stride: 'Better than anything I've ever seen on the stage. They were fantastic together, because they hit each other off.' Their sense of humour was ineffably similar. As a girl of fourteen, Nancy wrote a letter to her mother describing a performance of Gounod's *Faust* that she had attended, saying, 'Valentino . . . sang a lot of stuff after being stabbed, which is more than I could or would do': the simplicity of this joke, with its skewed clarity of the kind that most people recognise when they hear it, but do not see for themselves, is typical not just of the adult Nancy but of David also ('All the fault of that damned padre', as he says in the person of Uncle Matthew, after a performance of *Romeo and Juliet*). At the same time, and for all their mutually fascinated closeness, Nancy and David were very much father and daughter, never 'friends' in the way that parents and children often are today. It was always as if a barrier of respect was being daringly breached by Nancy: even when she created the character of Uncle Matthew, which unlike that of Aunt Sadie is definitively a portrait by a daughter.

And when three of David's other daughters – Jessica, Deborah and Pam – reminisced about him during the BBC television documentary *Nancy Mitford: A Portrait by Her Sisters*, broadcast in 1980, it was as though they, too, liked to see their father through the prism of this fictional vision. They celebrated his heightened reality. They brought back all his caprices to the glorified life that Nancy had given them: his habit of calling someone he hated a 'meaningless piece of meat'; his converse habit of taking a shine to unlikely people ('yes, he was amazing in that way', said Jessica, her eyes bright with entranced memory), who would then be expected to turn up for breakfast at eight sharp and eat brains with their new friend ('Pigs' thinkers, Davey?'). They described their father as if he were a creature of myth whom they had happened to know rather well: a figure from a Hogarth tableau who had come to life in their midst. As early as 1931, Nancy had put David Mitford into her first novel, *Highland Fling*, as the character General Murgatroyd. This was a pure pantomime version of Uncle Matthew, a package of eccentricities only, a portrait by a daughter who, at the age of twenty-five, was highly fed up with her roaring and raging father. Even so, it had its effect. As Jessica wrote in *Hons and Rebels*: 'Farve became – almost overnight – more a character of fiction than of real life, an almost legendary figure, even to us.'

Later, talking on television in 1966, Nancy said that the portrait of her parents, as Matthew and Sadie Alconleigh, was 'absolutely exact'. She must have known that this was not strictly true, as Diana now makes clear. 'Of course not!' she says. 'My mother wasn't vague, she was very practical.' Yet what a resonant – if benign – image of Sydney, of her remote yet forceful presence, is given to readers in the picture of Aunt Sadie sitting at the dinner table 'on her cloud'. 'And my father,' Diana continues, 'well he was very funny and very amusing, and wonderful value with Nancy, but he wasn't as mad as that. And the idea of him being violent – well, if he'd been a violent father, no doubt we were very annoying, he would have hit us or something – but never. I mean he had perfect manners, you know. The very worst punishment we could have would be to be sent to bed early.'

Nancy, of course, has Uncle Matthew constantly giving out 'first-class hidings' to his children; again, in the pursuit of artistic truth – the literary need to create an impression of restless, rampaging physicality – she has fiddled the facts. Or has she? Diana says that David *never* hit his children, that the essence of him lay in the charming man with 'perfect manners', who was indulgent even to the point of indulging Nancy in her portrait of him. When, in 'Mothering the Mitfords', David is once again referred to as 'violent' and handing out 'whippings', Diana would undoubtedly say that Nancy's memory had been over-run by the power of her own myth-making. 'With Nancy, it was her imagination that worked.' Nothing that she wrote could be trusted: even when – as in that essay – it purported to be fact, she was actually still using both her parents for her own clever, naughty, artistic ends.

Yet this was not absolutely the case. For example, what Nancy said about her father's propensity to physical violence might at least be partly true. In David Pryce-Jones's book *Unity Mitford: A Quest*, an interviewee recalled of Unity that 'nobody in the history of corporal punishment was ever more beaten', which apparently goes against Diana's assertion that none of the children was ever hit. And Jonathan Guinness, in *The House of Mitford*, mentions a beating given to Jessica: in other words, David would seem to have been capable of losing his temper and whacking whoever crossed his path at the wrong time in the wrong way, although this was not something that happened every day. Nancy may well have exaggerated when she wrote about her father, but she did not necessarily tell a downright lie.

And the truth, on this unimportant but tangled little question, probably lay somewhere in between the evidence given by Nancy and that given by Diana. Which is a reasonably safe formula with which to treat much of what gets said by, and on the subject of, this clever and tricky family.

So what about how an outsider saw it all? Here, from the autobiography of James Lees-Milne, *Another Self*, is an impression of how the Mitfords comported themselves *chez eux*. Lees-Milne was a close friend of Tom Mitford's at Eton and in adult life knew Nancy, Diana and Deborah, spending a good deal of time with Nancy during the war years. In his book he described a visit to the Mitford home which took place, according to his recollection, in 1926, when the family were living in their Oxfordshire house at Swinbrook.

Readers of Nancy and Jessica Mitford's books have probably concluded that their home life was a sort of nether world ruled by their parents, Lord and Lady Redesdale, in the guise of Hades . . . This was by no means my impression. On the contrary, Swinbrook House, where this large and united family then lived, was to me Elysium. Lady Redesdale . . . presided, for that is the word, over her beautiful and eccentric brood with unruffled sweetness, amusement and not a little bewilderment. Lord Redesdale was admittedly a dual personality. I cannot see that his children had much in him to complain about. Towards them he was Dr Jekyll, indulgent and even docile. Although not a cultivated man he tolerated their intellectual pursuits and allowed them to say and do whatever they liked. He submitted placidly to their ceaseless teasing, particularly Nancy's with its sharp little barb, barely concealed like the hook of an angler's fly beneath a riot of gay feathers . . .

To outsiders, and particularly his children's friends, Lord Redesdale could be Mr Hyde with a vengeance. But then he resented and hated outsiders for daring to intrude upon the family circle. He referred to one of their friends, a shy and diffident boy, as 'that hog Watson' in front of his face, threatened another with a horsewhip for putting his feet on a sofa, and glowered at those who had done nothing wrong with such vehemence that they lost their nerve, and usually smashed things, thus provoking a more justifiable expression of his distaste. I was naturally terrified of him, but respected his uncertain temper.

Nevertheless Lees-Milne goes on to recount how, over dinner, he forgets that he is in the presence of this ready-to-erupt volcano, this primed mass of patriotism, and starts spouting that England should forget about the war and make friends with Germany.

The effect was electric. The smile on Lord Redesdale's face was switched off as though by a current . . . 'You damned young puppy!' he shouted, as he thumped the surface so that the plates and glasses clashed together like cymbals. 'How dare you? You don't know what the bloody Huns are like. They are worse than all the devils in hell. And you sit there, and have the damned impudence . . .' Lady Redesdale with a pained expression on her dear face put a hand on his arm, and just said in her plaintive, drawly voice 'David'. He stopped, threw down his napkin, rose from the table and stalked out of the dining-room. For a second or two there was a chilling silence, then a chorus of breath let out of girlish lungs. 'Oh gosh! I said, 'what had I better do now?' The six sisters from Nancy, aged twenty-one,

down to Debo, aged six, looked at one another and then chanted in unison:
'We don't want to lose you,
But we think you ought to go.'

Which he does. Later, and predictably enough, he creeps back into Swinbrook only to be enveloped in the manly embrace of Lord Redesdale. 'I was dragged into his smoking room, a sanctum as remote from his children's guests as the Antipodes, plied with whisky and soda, and told I must stay with him for ever . . .'

Now this is a colourful account, of highly dubious accuracy (a letter of Nancy's dates the whole episode in 1928, shows that she too was directly involved in the quarrel with her father, and makes it all seem unpleasant and embarrassing rather than funny). All the same, Lees-Milne's recollections are wonderfully in tune with what one would *expect*. It is surprising that, after Nancy's death, he admitted in his diaries to having little admiration for her writing[12], since what he himself wrote about her family is – whether he knew it or not – deeply influenced by *The Pursuit of Love*. The Mitford myth, which his opening sentences set out as if to cut through, is simply too strong to resist.

Despite their friendship, Nancy and James Lees-Milne were not much alike, as his diaries make periodically clear ('I did not much enjoy [dinner] for Nancy's scintillations dry me up' is a fairly typical entry). Although their views of the Redesdales are superficially similar, their sympathies are subtly different. Lees-Milne regards David as a bit of a mad monster and his wife as the saintly soul of forbearance. Nancy did not see things that way at all, instead divining the essential warmth – towards her, at least – in her father, and the lack of it in her mother.

But what comes across most powerfully in this little passage of Lees-Milne's is the strength of the Mitford myth. It is there in perfect miniature, the impenetrable fascination of this family: the image of all that surging life, that blazing intimacy, that leaping drama being played out in a setting of dark panelled rooms in solid, conventional, Cotswold houses. It is an image that is English to the point of being Expressionist: enlivening and not a little theatrical and somehow wholly comfortable. In this sense it is not unlike reading a period detective story. Of course it is not the 'truth', as such, of the Mitford family; but as with *The Pursuit of Love* – which also has this infinitely reassuring quality – it is what we take most gladly from it, and what Nancy gives us freely.

And wonderfully in tune with it, once again, is the tableau conjured in Lees-Milne's story of the six girls singing together as one: childish, charming, unreachable, Mitfordian. Can they *really* all have sat there and done that? Both Nancy and Diana – in complete agreement for once – wrote in subsequent letters that they did nothing of the kind: that everyone sat appalled and furious, that this was uncomfortable reality rather than fable, that there was no possibility of transmuting the moment into a joke, a shriek, a tale. The myth must have taken a hold of the writer; so much so that it was as if Lees-Milne really did believe in the truth of what he wrote. Forty years after the event, twenty-five years after *The Pursuit of Love*, he gave his night with the Mitfords a new and more resonant life: drew the picture of twelve dancing eyes fixed upon him, of six powerfully individual girls fused into an almost terrifying vital whole, burning and laughing and sparkling within that remote country house, just as Nancy had told them to.

CHAPTER 2

'. . . such a good idea to eliminate that tiresome childhood, already *done* in the novel.' Thus wrote Nancy in a letter in 1971, when she was planning her autobiography. Her intention instead was to start the book in 1945, the year of *The Pursuit of Love*'s publication – the year in which the fictional Mitfords first appeared to the world – and to use the childhood only as it served her new and different purpose.

After all, her sister Jessica had gone over a good deal of it again, in her 1960 autobiography. In 1971 Nancy wrote to Jessica about her own book, saying, 'I shall put in a foreword that our childhood has been *done* in Hons and Rebels.' Redone, in fact, was probably what she was thinking. As with James Lees-Milne's little Swinbrook story, Jessica's book owes much of its life to *The Pursuit of Love*: to the Mitford myth that Nancy had crystallised in art. In *Hons and Rebels*, 'Muv' is very much vague Aunt Sadie, 'Farve' is blimpish Uncle Matthew, the family home at Swinbrook is the Alconleigh fortress against which the children chafe.

And, reading Jessica's book, Nancy would surely have realised that the Mitford childhood could easily become what she would have called a crasher. Little did she know that this was just the start. For the next forty years *The Pursuit of Love* was destined to have its essence extracted, diluted and polluted by biographers, journalists and scriptwriters. Stories of chubb fuddling and child-hunting were to be retold, progressively less funnily; artistic and literal truth were to become ever more lazily interchangeable. All of which Nancy would have considered unforgivably dull.

On the subject of *Hons and Rebels*, she wrote to Evelyn Waugh after its publication: 'What I feel is this. In some respects she has seen the

family, quite without knowing it herself, through the eyes of my books
– that is, if she hadn't read them hers would have been different. She is
absolutely unperceptive of . . . the characters whom I didn't describe &
who all could have been brought to life but simply were not. I haven't
said this to anyone but you as it sounds so conceited.' Conceited it may
have been, but it is spot on about Nancy's irresistible influence upon
subsequent commentators; not just Jessica.

Diana recognises with absolute clarity the effect of *The Pursuit
of Love* upon *Hons and Rebels*, a book she sees as 'very dishonest'
because it had used the art of Nancy's novel to make 'a new truth,
which it isn't really'. Indeed it has none of the deeper, sadder and
more vital ambiguities that Nancy brings to the Mitford childhood,
nor any of what Diana calls 'the fun'. Fun, when translated from
the Mitford, means something tremendously important, something
essential to the spirit, something both ephemeral and eternal. And
perhaps the greatest miracle of *The Pursuit of Love* – the simplest
secret of its success –'is that in it Nancy does make the depiction of
childhood such fun. But then Nancy amused as other people breathe.
Perhaps her greatest talent was that she was unable to make anything
boring.

Let us be honest: childhood in books is usually excruciating,
with its tales of feeling apart or different ('I endured torments in my
hand-me-downs . . .'), its variations on the *madeleine* theme ('even
now a spoonful of Ambrosia creamed rice glistening with Hartley's
strawberry jam will transport me back . . .'), its memories of scented
mothers and bullying schoolteachers and adult truths imperfectly
understood. How the reader longs to get away from it all, and hang
out with the grown-ups! Not so with Nancy Mitford. She does the
whole thing differently. We love to be with her children, roaming
the enclosure in which they have made their magical world; they are
so game, so full of life, so free from self-pity. Even those readers who
believe the privileged land of 'Hons'[1] to be an unfit subject for serious
literature still, despite themselves, find it hard to resist what Nancy
has written. Jessica herself, as a Communist who waves her red flag
across the pages of *Hons and Rebels*, must have looked sternly upon
tales of hunting foxes and, occasionally, children ('the Kentish week-
enders on their way to church were appalled by the sight of four great

hounds in full cry after two little girls'), but she used them for her own devices all the same.

The childhood of *The Pursuit of Love* is childhood writ large, alive with echoes of fairytales and Enid Blyton and the Brontës creating an enclosed world of the imagination at Haworth Parsonage. It is childhood as it is no longer lived: when houses were playgrounds and battlegrounds, when parents were monoliths of apparent certainty, when poshness was an absolute protection, when siblings were many and various and constituted the whole of existence, and when the desire to escape was a wild and delicious frustration. Of course Nancy's material was pretty special. It is less fun, for example, to describe a father who returns home from work to half an hour's reading of the Brothers Grimm than to have one not unlike a character from the book itself. It is more interesting to have a large family of outgoing, charming, emotionally volatile children than just one little misery reading books all day in a tree-house.

There is nothing introspective about the children in *The Pursuit of Love*, and it is the emphasis upon introspection which, above all, makes books about childhood such a bore: 'I felt . . .', 'She watched . . .', 'He suffered . . .'; so did we all, unless we were captain of the First XI, but thankfully we moved on to other things. Nancy must have been introspective to an extent, or she could not have become such a good writer, yet she had the sense to take this dimension out of the Radletts (Linda, for example, does not really read – except at the end of the book when, heavily pregnant and aged about thirty, she lies in the Hons' cupboard all day with books of fairy stories. Yet when Nancy was not quite six she was, according to Blor, reading as substantial a book as *Ivanhoe*, and until her last conscious day this habit never changed). The Mitford-Radlett childhood is presented instead as a series of playlets, *divertissements* with the dreary bits in between left out. Nancy gives the impression of recounting her childhood just as it was, but in fact is pulling all sorts of clever strokes to reveal its artistic truth.

Cleverest of all is the perspective that she creates. She comes at her childhood as if remembering it, beginning the book with that elegiac little passage about the 'photograph in existence of Aunt Sadie and her six children . . . I often think there is nothing quite so poignantly sad as old family groups'. Thus she tells the reader that all of this is long gone. Then she enters the past, quickly and dartingly, through a succession of intensely realised little vignettes.

'I stumbled into the hall at Alconleigh blinded by the light after a six-mile drive from Merlinford station', she writes in the person of her narrator, Fanny, and – bang – one is right there with her.

There was a tremendous scraping of chairs as I came in, and a pack of Radletts hurled themselves upon me with the intensity and almost the ferocity of a pack of hounds hurling itself upon a fox. All except Linda. She was the most pleased to see me, but determined not to show it. When the din had quieted down and I was seated before a scone and a cup of tea, she said:

'Where's Brenda?' Brenda was my white mouse.

'She got a sore back and died', I said. Aunt Sadie looked anxiously at Linda.

'Had you been riding her?' said Louisa, facetiously. Matt, who had recently come under the care of a French nursery governess, said in a high-pitched imitation of her voice: 'C'était, comme d'habitude, les voies urinaires.'

'Oh, dear', said Aunt Sadie, under her breath.

Enormous tears were pouring into Linda's plate . . .

Now this is all immediately alive, magnificently of the here-and-now. Yet somehow, over it, there always hovers a knowledge of the inescapable past and the implacable future, a sense of the churchyard that lies beyond the family home, just as the grave at Swinbrook lay waiting for Nancy. When Fanny is blinded by the light at Alconleigh, she goes on to describe what she sees there: 'It was always the same every year; I always came down by the same train, arriving at tea-time, and always found Aunt Sadie and the children round the table underneath the entrenching tool, just as they were in the photograph. It was always the same table and the same tea-things; the china with large roses on it, the tea-kettle and the silver dish for scones simmering over little flames – the human beings of course were getting imperceptibly older.' It is an *hommage* to what is unchanging which acknowledges the remorselessness of change; and it is this sweetly painful tug, within the heart of the book, which helps to make it art.

No wonder she didn't want to write about it all again. She had done that thing for which writers always pray but do not really understand, caught the truth of her story in a way that implies other truth as well; which is a definition of art, in fact; and a trick that she could not hope to pull off twice.

But what might she have written in her missing autobiography, had she been dealing in fact rather than fiction? For a start, there is one decided difference between the Radletts and the Mitfords. There is much emphasis in *The Pursuit of Love* upon Alconleigh as a home in which the family is ensconced as from time immemorial. Passages like the one above, which talk about tea-tables that seem never to have moved, are part of the rhythm of the book.

Yet the Mitfords, in truth, were far more peripatetic. As with the portrayal of her parents, Nancy has not exactly lied in her novel; but she has bent reality in order to convey a *feel*. She has turned Alconleigh into a symbol of the world that her family inhabited: parlous, unpredictable, brutal at times with its beatings and trappings of wild animals and 'cruel woods' all around, but nonetheless secure. The house gives an impression of background stability against which a character like Linda can dart and shimmer. There are elements of Alconleigh in all the country houses in which Nancy herself lived while she was growing up, but the main difference is that there were three of them rather than one.

For David Mitford was a man on the move. He had to be, really, from the time that he inherited Batsford Park in all its bizarre and ruinous glory. 'We lived', Nancy was later to say[2], 'under the shadows . . . of two hammers: that of the builder and that of the auctioneer.' Her father never had much of an income – would hardly have worked at *The Lady* had he not absolutely needed to – and then he kept on having children. By the time he succeeded his father as the second Lord Redesdale, in 1916, he already had five with two more to come. Only one of them – Tom – cost real money, in respect of public school fees (thank God for daughters and home education), but they still all had to be fed and clothed. Bertram Mitford had been a rich man, but building Batsford took a lot of his money; after tax David was left with about £17,000. He also got a lot of land, 36,000 acres, but this did not bring in fortunes, and there was simply not enough cash to maintain the exorbitant little Gloucestershire castle, with its stables the size of houses, its grounds which stretch away from the eye, its deer park, its lake, its arboretum, its magnificent sense of disregard for confined space.

Of course it was not David who was meant to inherit but his brother, Clement, who was killed in the war in 1915. After his death (which brought terrible sadness to the family, and was always remembered by eight-year-old Pamela as the first time that she saw grown-ups cry), there was a strange and awful little interlude of waiting for his widow, Helen, to deliver a baby. Had she given birth to a boy, David would not have become heir, and Nancy's life would have been rather different; but Clementine was born instead, and not long after this Bertie died, wearied at last by grief at the age of seventy-nine. The new Lord Redesdale was in France at the time, pretty weak in health himself but fighting gamely as a transport officer, dodging the bombardment of Ypres as, sometimes twice in a night, he took supplies to his battalion. It would not have been a great surprise if he too had been killed on one of his back-breaking full-speed gallops across town. But poor exhausted David was invalided home in 1917, and given a posting with rooms in Christ Church college from where he visited his family, at a little house that Sydney took in Oxford; and at Batsford Park.

They did not stay there very long. The place could not be sold until the war was over – in that sense the family dreaded peace, for they had no desire to move – but meanwhile it was mostly left under dustsheets. The Mitfords lived in the centre of the house, around and above the baronial entrance, where the sense of their presence is collected behind the stone coat of arms. It must have been a marvellous home for children of imagination, which these were *par excellence*: it is surely tremendous fun to have a ballroom with a ceiling that vaults up to the skies, and a fireplace as big as a kitchen in a *bijou* Chelsea flat. Fun too to run along corridors of panelled wood and arched stone, or up and down five staircases; to be peered at by gargoyles; to lounge on deep window seats, book in hand, with an infinity of silent space outside. As well as being a very idiosyncratic house, it was, and still is, as grand as you like – grander, certainly, than Alconleigh – and to see it is to see Nancy Mitford in all her indestructible Englishness. One imagines her, a slim and elegant girl with wiry dark hair, standing on the forecourt of the dark gold mansion, or putting gloved hands together in the little stone church of St Mary's, just outside the grounds, and one is possessed by the feeling that this would have stayed with her for life: one does not lose this. The sense, at Batsford, of being at the very heart of the country, in all its quiet rich mystery, is overwhelmingly strong. The little market town of Moreton-in-Marsh, a couple of miles away, is all the colour of ochre, all permeated by secret age-old assurance and by the assurance of Nancy's family, whose coat of arms is on the Redesdale Arms and on the hall built by her grandfather. This was where she spent her early teenage years, steeped in essence of England and in essence of herself. 'We ran across country, the beautiful bleak Cotswold uplands, starting soon after breakfast when the sun was still a red globe, hardly over the horizon, and the trees were etched in dark blue against a pale blue, mauve and pinkish sky', wrote Nancy, thirty years later, from the other world of her adult city life, and it is clear that the memory of that landscape (dark blue trees!) does not even have to be recalled: it is all still there in her.

Yet the serenity of Batsford she had only by default, and not for very long, and never properly anyway. The place was sold in 1919, and the Mitfords moved to another country house, Asthall in Oxfordshire. It must have been a wrench for Nancy: the sense of being at the centre of things, of immanence, which surely came from living at Batsford, would never quite be recaptured, and she was old enough to realise this. Asthall is terrifically attractive, a Jacobean manor built in Cotswold stone, far more homely than Batsford and with a charming asymmetry brought about, partly, by Lord Redesdale's urge to build upon it: although he cried when his father tore down his old home, he inherited the same passion for upmarket DIY. All the same, what Nancy would later teasingly call the descent from Batsford PARK to Asthall MANOR to Swinbrook HOUSE does show that the Mitfords were never quite so rooted and secure as one imagines. They were upperclass, but they were not steeped too deep in privilege for displacement. And Nancy, all her life, was aware of this.

'Dearest Nancy', her friend Evelyn Waugh was to write in 1955, in *An Open Letter* responding to her famous article on the subject of 'U and Non-U',[3]

You were at the vital age of twelve when your father succeeded to his peerage, and until less than a year before there was little likelihood of his ever succeeding. It was a great days for 'Hons' when you and your merry sisters acquired that prefix of nobility. Hitherto it had been the most shadowy of titles, never spoken, and rarely written. You brought it to light, emphasised and aspirated, and made a glory of it ... If your uncle had not been killed in action, if your posthumous cousin had been a boy, all you enchanting children would have been whisked away to a ranch in Canada or a sheep-run in New Zealand. It is fascinating to speculate what your careers would then have been. Anyway, at that impressionable age an indelible impression was made; Hons were unique and lords were rich.

Rather hard to understand Waugh's last assertion, when Nancy knew perfectly well, from her own father, that lords were not necessarily rich at all. But the point of what he writes is lethally unmissable: Nancy was intrigued by the question of what constitutes an aristocrat because she was only one herself by the skin of her pointed little teeth. 'Her tendency', wrote Anthony Powell after her death, '[was] to be a little insistent on her aristocratic side.' Nancy would always have been a lady, *cela va sans dire*, but she might have been a bit less interested in the fact had she been surer of it.

And there is a degree of truth to what Waugh wrote, if not quite in the way that he intended. So much of the joy of the Mitfords comes from the contradiction between their upper-class lineage and their bright willingness to transcend it: they are, let's face it, very much more fascinating than the majority of their kind. The conflict was so alive in them between what they were born to do and what they actually did. They used their blithe confidence as a springboard into different worlds, engaging with people and writing and ideas in a way that would seem, to a typical member of the English aristocracy, unnecessary to say the least. It might be said that the conflict was *too* alive in them; certainly in a couple of cases. But the point still holds good. Would they have had this beautiful curiosity, this glorious zest, this sometimes wayward energy, this lack of self-importance, had their background been a little more orthodox: had they been the children of Clement rather than David, had their mother been the child of a less maverick man, had they had the money to live on in Batsford's isolated grandeur? Would they ever, then, have become the Radletts?

In many ways they *were* conventional. Asthall Manor looks like a perfect example of the *Country Life* page-to-itself advertisement house, completely devoid of vulgarity but tremendously self-assured, and the little village around it is a perfect example of the same kind of thing. Outsiders, one feels, would not be welcomed. Even now, a strange car driving carefully through the tiny, winding lanes of Asthall is regarded with something like suspicion: one has a sense of unspoken codes of behaviour, of an Englishness only fully understood by those who belong to it. The Mitford family lived in this still and secret backwater for seven years. It was the house in which Nancy spent her adolescence – from age thirteen to twenty-one – and it is the house which most closely resembles Alconleigh.

If *The Pursuit of Love* gives us, pricelessly and theatrically, the sense of life played out at Alconleigh, it also gives a sense of its backdrop: the innately respectable, somewhat impoverished and – yes – conventional world of the Cotswold gentry. Again, the memories run so deep in Nancy that they hardly need to be pulled out. They imbue her book with a near Chekhovian feel for the detail so familiar it becomes almost unnoticeable. She handles a set-piece, like a coming out ball, with a wonderful grasp of its drama – the fear that there will not be enough men, the longing for the men to arrive, the disappointment with the men when they do – but there is also this deliciously subtle scenic colouring: the band, 'Clifford Essex's third string', resting beforehand 'in Mrs Craven's cottage'; the 'floating panels of taffeta' on the home-made dresses; the 'twenty oil-stoves' brought in for warmth. Warmth and the lack of it is a constant motif. Cold permeates *The Pursuit of Love* as it would surely have permeated Asthall: 'In spite of a boiler which would not have been too large for an Atlantic liner, in spite of the tons of coke which it consumed daily, the temperature of the living-room was hardly affected.' Hence the Hons' cupboard (actually a linen cupboard in Swinbrook House), where the Radlett children huddle for that wonderful sense of private cosiness.

Hence, too, the cleverness of the title *Love in a Cold Climate*, given to the novel that succeeded *The Pursuit of Love* and that also has this faded homespun backdrop, made all the funnier because contrasted with the almost appalling wealth of Lord and Lady Montdore. At the Montdore home, Hampton – geographically close to Alconleigh, spiritually on another planet – the central heating blazes 'and the temperature everywhere was that of a hot-house'. Ladylike Fanny arrives there for a flashy weekend party wearing a 'nutria coat', which is the kind of glorious touch that cannot really be invented, and with her 'Ascot dress' dyed dark red. The dinner is eight sumptuous courses of 'exaggerated food', a far cry from the shepherd's pie eaten, at Alconleigh, by the light of 'three electric bulbs hanging in a bunch from the ceiling'.

Similarly, Montdore House on Park Lane is a very different thing from the genteel London houses rented by the Radletts (just as Lady Redesdale did, for Nancy's first season), while Polly Hampton's coming out ball ('which cost £2,000, or so Lady Montdore told everybody') can hardly be compared with the twenty oil-stoves and the floating panels. Uncle Matthew and Aunt Sadie attend the ball, and bring to it their own particular flavour: Sadie chats about the 'Skilton village idiot', winner of the 'asylum 100 yards', while Matthew falls asleep 'on his feet as horses can, waiting patiently to be led back to his stable'. Of course – as Nancy would always be – they are perfectly at ease within the grandeur of the Montdore sphere, to which their birth gives them complete access. But it is not their world and nor, until fame took her into it, was it Nancy's. Nancy was brought up at Asthall to wear dresses made in the village (although, with her narrow breastless mannequin's shape, she looked extremely elegant in them), and to rub her bony shoulders in hopelessly ill-heated rooms. Like the Radletts, her family would make sudden wild attempts at household economies, as when Sydney decided to do away with napkins at meals. 'Peeress Saves Ha'Pence' ran the headline in the *Daily Sketch* (and if she thought that was embarrassing, there was much worse to come). On another occasion she asked all her children to draw up a budget of how they would spend £500 a year on running a home: 'Flowers: £490' was Nancy's first entry. It was a reasonable joke, as these flurries of panic about money never seemed to make any real difference. 'The family are in a terrible financial crisis', Nancy wrote to her brother Tom during one of the periods when the writing paper was getting thinner and the lavatory paper thicker. 'However we continue as before to eat (however humbly) drink and drive about in large Daimlers. Mitfords are like that.' All her life, however, Nancy was preoccupied with money, so the sense of growing up without much of it must have had its effect. She never, one feels, wanted to wear a nutria coat again.

Relative poverty notwithstanding, the family was happy at Asthall. The house, which overlooks a beautiful but sombre little church, was generally accepted to be haunted (a childhood friend who stayed there described the 'holy fear' of hearing an unexplained 'tick-tock of water' outside[4], and both Lord Redesdale and Diana were apparently unnerved by a 'grey lady' who wafted around the place). Yet it has, above all, a contented look. There are perhaps no more naturally joyful characters in literature than the Radletts, whose love of life is indomitable and, at times, almost unbearably touching. This surely comes straight from the Mitfords and from the years at Asthall: when problems were small and simple and busily resolvable, when 'aching' with boredom was a painfully voluptuous pleasure, and when dreams of the future gleamed as tantalisingly close as one of Lady Montdore's famous jewels. In later and unhappier years, Sydney was to say – as one does, helplessly – that none of the family's troubles would have happened if they had stayed at Asthall; she remembered their life in the house as 'all summers'.

Nancy Mitford grew up in the years between the two world wars: they took her from the age of very nearly fourteen to that of thirty-five. Now, of course, we love this interwar period. We see, in satisfying images, the febrile Art Deco world of *Vile Bodies*, Michael Arlen and cigarette holders become darker, grittier, heavy with the realities of the Depression, thick with the shadows of great and imminent events. Not a small part of the Mitford fascination is the fact that they lived so intensely through what is now such an evocative period: they are, if you like, history made personal, and – as Nancy always knew – it is the personal in history that we do indeed like. So it is strange to read this little passage from *The Pursuit of Love*, typical in its artless melancholy, in which Linda muses: 'It is rather sad . . . to belong, as we do to a lost generation. I'm sure in history the two wars will count as one war and that we shall be squashed out of it altogether, and people will forget that we ever existed . . .'

The First World War broke out when Nancy was almost ten and, in taking the life of her uncle Clement, had a profound effect upon her destiny. 'It was more than I could do to pray for peace', she wrote in her essay 'Mothering the Mitfords'. 'I prayed as hard as I could for war'. She crocheted khaki mittens while 'sitting like a *tricoteuse*, on the balcony of Grandfather Redesdale's house in Kensy High Street . . . all this crocheting was the nearest I ever got to killing an enemy, a fact which I am still regretting'. It may seem odd in so civilised a person, this fascination with warfare and lively response to conflict ('she loved trouble'[5], says her nephew, Alexander Mosley), yet it is very much part of her contradictory nature. She would have absorbed it from her father, and may have liked resembling him in this surprising way. She would also have had a sense that war was a natural part of an aristocrat's world, and that fearing it was therefore rather common. Nancy herself was rattled when living in London during the aerial bombardment of the Second World War, but she saw it as a point of honour to smile and stick it out: 'Nancy boasts that she is not the least frightened of the fly bombs', wrote James Lees-Milne in a diary entry for 1944. 'In bed at night she beckons to them, "Come on, come on" . . .'

Meanwhile, in *The Pursuit of Love*, Linda's dreary little daughter Moira is shown to be terrified of air-raids ('a child who was not thrilled by the idea of them was incomprehensible to her, and she could not imagine how she had conceived such a being'). All the Radletts have an understanding of what war means, and take it on board in their spirited way. Nancy's way, like theirs, was extremely English, yet it was also part of her feel for the old European ideals of *noblesse*. She remained enthralled by battles all her life: in her last book, *Frederick the Great*, she devoted chapters to the explication of his campaigns (Alexander Mosley: 'the only time I think I've ever understood the Seven Years War'), and towards the end of her life she wrote: 'I would like to be a pretty young General & gallop over Europe with Frederick the Great & never have another ache or pain . . .'

This is not dissimilar to the remark about longing for one more day's hunting, made on her death-bed to Deborah. Fragile and urbane in appearance though she always was, slim as a swizzle stick with a waist 'so small that one fears it may snap at any moment' (Waugh), plagued by 'low stamina' much of her life, Nancy could display a surprising robust physicality. She had a good seat on a horse – her cousin Clementine recalled seeing her on her mare, Rachel, 'looking like a Constantin Guys drawing' – and in later life impressed her nephew Jonathan Guinness by catching and holding a pony while dressed in Dior ('I was brought up in the country, you see . . .'). As a girl she hunted side-saddle with the Heythrop, as often as three times a fortnight in season. At the same time she saw the paradox within her passion for hunting:

The Radletts . . . loved foxes, they risked dreadful beatings in order to unstop their earths, they read and cried and rejoiced over Reynard the Fox, in summer they got up at four to go and see the cubs playing in the pale-green light of the woods; nevertheless, more than anything in the world they loved hunting. It was in their blood and bones and in my blood and bones, and nothing could eradicate it, though we knew it for a kind of original sin . . .

This was Nancy's upbringing, to live within a society that worships animals as it perpetrates cruelties upon them. *The Pursuit of Love* is steeped in this paradox, bright with effusions of love for baby badgers and labradors, darkly infused with the bloodstained realities of country life:

On the other side of the house . . . was the Home Farm. Here the slaughtering of poultry and pigs, the castration of lambs and the branding of cattle, took place as a matter of course, out in the open for whoever might be passing to see.

Nancy always found the cruelty hard to bear. In 1966 she wrote to Deborah about the fate of the French horses 'who used to pull the ice carts . . . condemned to death unless somebody rescues them. Their *faces* oh well, we know'. Diana later said that 'one can no more imagine

Pam or Debo without a dog than Nancy or Tom with one.'[6] In fact, although Nancy had the air of a woman whose worst nightmare would be shih-tzu hairs over her Lanvin skirt, even when she moved to London she had dogs – two silky-smart little French bulldogs named Milly and Lottie, both of whom produced litters of adored puppies.

Back in the country and the interwar years, the Mitford household ran alive with animals. Chickens were always kept by the family ('There is *nothing* I don't know about all sorts of poultry', Nancy later wrote[7]), and Sydney – whose housekeeping was efficient to the point of frugality – paid for the children's governesses out of what she made from eggs and honey. Nancy had goats at Batsford and sold their milk ('I don't want to make butter,' she said as a child, 'as it is not profitable enough'). She and Pamela also had two mice which lived in what Pam, in her irony free way, later described as a 'palace'[8], made for her by the estate carpenter; one of the mice ate the other when Nancy, who had been desperate to get her mouse into the palace, neglected to feed them. There was Brownie the pony, whom David bought one morning under Blackfriars Bridge then took back to Graham Street in a hansom cab. The pony was kept in a dark room at the house until David put him in a third-class railway carriage, along with various children and dogs, and transported them all to Sydney's cottage at High Wycombe. There were dogs of course, whippets and labradors and dachshunds, bloodhounds for child-hunting, and a terrier of Nancy's called Peter ('she adored that smelly old Border', Jessica later remembered[9]). And then came a more arcane menagerie, mostly belonging to Unity: her goat, her grass snake Enid, her salamander Sally, and her rat, Ratular – 'she usually had a rat or two', Jessica recalled to David Pryce-Jones, 'Harrods pet shop was where we constantly went buying'. For her own part, Jessica had a sheep called Miranda whom she longed to take on excursions to London ('the dear thing would love it so'). Miranda never made it to Harrods but she did make an oblique appearance in literature. As a girl in the late 1920s, Jessica would use the word 'sheepish' to describe anything nice and, to annoy Unity, 'goat-like' for anything nasty. Evelyn Waugh, at that time in love with Diana, had become not a little fascinated with the bright, mysterious ring of solidarity that drew itself around the Mitford girls; later, in letters to Nancy, he would take evident pleasure in being able to use the private nicknames that she had invented for her sisters; and in 1930 he was perhaps seeking similar entry into the magic circle when he put these two sentences into his novel *Vile Bodies*: 'He left his perfectly sheepish house in Hertford Street' and 'how goat-like, how sick-making, how too, too awful.'

The thought of all the animals that roamed and padded around the Mitford homes adds to the impression of germinating life; one imagines the smell of wet dog hair on sofas, rats scuttling beneath nursery desks, the clip-clop of hooves outside windows. Large as these houses were, there is always a sense of them bursting at the seams, spilling out children and dogs and servants and sheep. Noise would have been constant: rows, tantrums, shrieks; barks, neighs, bleats; stock-whips cracking, the twang of Nancy's ukelele (which she took up in her late teens), the ripplings from Tom's piano (the sound of Handel, Bach, Mozart and Beethoven was left out of *The Pursuit of Love*, but then music was not one of Nancy's great passions). It must have been a maelstrom. For a girl like Nancy, whose keen intelligence had shown itself early, and which now needed something to sharpen itself upon, it must also at times have been madly frustrating. Where was privacy to be found? Where conversation amongst equals? Much later she was to say: 'I feel sorry for people who have *family planning*', meaning that life without siblings was greatly impoverished; but it is interesting nonetheless that she lived alone from the age of about forty. Perhaps, when she made that remark, she too was seeing her childhood 'through the eyes of my books'? At any rate, during the time that she did have to live with a large family, she was sufficiently provoked by it to go in for what she called 'great nastiness to the others'.

This relentless teasing was, according to Nancy's nephew Alexander Mosley, a consequence of restlessness. 'It was also a highly-honed weapon to keep a lot of very competitive, bright, energetic sisters in order. She used it as a weapon, as a form of discipline, as a form of self-protection, as a form of attack. And it was quite an important part of her personality.'

Unfortunately, but perhaps unsurprisingly, the sister who suffered most from Nancy's teasing was the one least equipped to counter it: Pamela. Even though Pam lived with the effects of infantile paralysis, having endured an attack at the age of three which left her slow and weak (Sydney did, for once, call in several doctors), Nancy could not stop herself. Something about Pam's stolid shepherdess aspect seems to have brought out all that was most gleamingly mischievous in her sister, and this did not change much as the girls grew older. Nancy descended into the cheapest kind of female spite: she would, for example, find out which young men Pam fancied and then tell her that she had seen them dancing with other partners. 'I was rather fat,' Pam later recalled, which never does much for a girl's self-confidence, but according to Diana this had already been undermined by Nancy: 'She was very unkind to Pam.' There was no hint, however, in the 1980 BBC documentary that Pamela had any resentment of this. Her gentle, contented nature led her, rather, to remember Nancy as one would a meteor, a natural phenomenon requiring only to be accepted and admired, and that had left her blinking in awe and pleasure.

During the television programme a story was told of how, at the time of the 1926 General Strike, the two sisters briefly ran a café together supplying tea to the emergency services (which meant, according to Jessica, that Pam would do all the work while Nancy would 'sort of drift in – she always used to say [plaintive voice] "Oh, I don't know how to make the sandwiches"...'). One very early morning Pam was busying herself in her calm way when she was assailed by a terrible-looking tramp, who demanded a cup of tea, leered violently and darted round the counter, grabbing at her: 'Can I have a kiss?' Only when the tramp dissolved into Nancy's characteristic shrieking laugh was 'his' true identity revealed. It was a remarkably involved trick: she must have been pretty bored to go to so much trouble, although her incredible inventiveness no doubt demanded this kind of expression. And something about Pamela – irresistible butt of Nancy's most sparkling jokes, wide-eyed and gaping at the irruption into her carefully run tea-stall – seems to have demanded it also.

One account of this incident ends with Pam falling and breaking an ankle, so desperate was she to get away from the tramp. Although this would hardly have been Nancy's intention – if true – it does make the whole thing seem rather sadistic. And was it sadism that caused Nancy to force Pam and Diana to become girl guides, wholly against their wishes? Rather oddly, and at the age of nearly seventeen, Nancy started a company in which she made herself captain and her sisters patrol leaders; she was encouraged in this by her mother, who seems to have seen in it welcome signs of normality, and indeed thought it so good an idea that she would not hear of Diana backing out after a year, as she had promised. 'It was one of the great injustices of my childhood,' Diana told the BBC in 1980, amused by the memory but still, no doubt, viewing the episode as an example of what she described as 'Nancy's will to power'.[10] It may have been that Nancy drew genuine pleasure from knots and campfires; possibly the impulse to revert to childish regimentation showed a fear of imminent adulthood ('She was a very late developer,' says Deborah). But *girl guides* – what could be less Mitfordian? How could so individualistic a girl as Nancy go in for such a thing? Unless, of course, it was all an elaborate joke. 'I think the whole thing was really invented by Nancy, in order to tease me,' was the conclusion offered by Diana to the BBC.

The teasing of the younger girls, meanwhile, was more straightforward. When, for example, Nancy announced one day to Unity, Jessica and Deborah that they had revolting middle syllables to their names – nit, sick and bore – it was the simple tyranny of an older sister making a joke at the expense of those who lacked the wit to reply ('That kept her going for a week,' Debo recalled for the BBC. 'Made us all cry.'). This kind of thing was relatively free of the complications that informed Nancy's behaviour towards Pamela and Diana, with whom rivalries were far more acute. In *Hons and Rebels* Jessica wrote that Nancy was 'sharp-tongued and sarcastic', but she seemed not to bear too much of a grudge. And Deborah says, quite simply, 'I adored Nancy. She was fairly prickly, and sharp. But she certainly, certainly was not malevolent. She certainly was never malevolent with me, and I expect I was maddening – you know how children are, just really irritating and annoying. But she was always marvellous.'

Nevertheless Deborah was very much the subject of Nancy's teasing; as with Pam, if in a different way, she was a perfect butt, because it took absolutely nothing to make her cry. The poem about the 'little, houseless match' which features in *The Pursuit of Love* ('... it makes no moan ...') was frequently used upon Deborah, who could be made to well up if Nancy merely shook a matchbox in a significant way. 'Everybody cried when you were born' was another arrow that Nancy would shoot at her youngest sister. Sydney was forty when Deborah was born, and the Redesdales had seen this pregnancy as their last chance for another son; but, as Mabel the parlourmaid said, 'I knew it was a girl by the look on his lordship's face.' Thus the appearance of Deborah gave Nancy yet another toy to play with.

Is this nastiness? Or is it simply a consequence – not very nice, but inevitable – of frustrated intelligence? 'Well it was family life,' says Debo, ever the voice of sanity. 'I can't imagine anything different.' For Diana, however, Nancy unequivocally had a 'sort of strange spiteful side. She was very witty and amusing, but she was also quite spiteful.' Quite rightly, Diana emphasises that Nancy could not have been legitimately jealous of Pamela, because 'they didn't cross each other *at all*'; towards Pam, one can only say that the habit of nastiness had been instilled in Nancy at a very early age, and she saw no reason to break it. But with Diana herself – every year becoming more beautiful, clever and amusing, all the things that Nancy strove to be and that in Diana appeared so effortless – the jealousy would have been all too legitimate. This incipient goddess constituted a threat that a little girl like Deborah did not. 'Oh, I think Nancy was jealous of Diana all her life,' says Debo. What sister, close in age, would not have been? One like Pam, perhaps, but Nancy was no Pam. She was an outwardly cool but inwardly feverish person (maddeningly, Diana was cool through and through, despite her capacity for passion). And it was her needling, vibrant, competitive character that kept the Mitford maelstrom spinning so wildly. Everything, as Jessica told the BBC, 'sprang full-blown from Nancy'.

So this was family life, yes, but – as in *The Pursuit of Love* – it was writ large. The Mitford situation was such an unusually fertile breeding ground for envy, rivalry, fantasy. There was scant possibility of escape: the children were thrown utterly together. Despite sudden bursts of discipline to bring them into line, despite the sweetly regulating presence of Blor ('very *silly*, darling'), they were, in a sense, in charge of the house, living in many ways just as they wanted to, speaking their private languages, creating the world of their own that was symbolised by the Hons' cupboard. It is perhaps an exaggeration to say, as David Pryce-Jones does in his biography of Unity, that the Mitford parents 'were defenceless' in the face of their children's extreme imaginative vitality. All the same they did little to check it, which still has the power to shock.

'Oh, people are horrified by our upbringing,' says Debo, not batting an eye. Here, once again, is the Mitford paradox, that commentators are fascinated by what they feel almost obliged to condemn. However much they love reading about child-hunts among the uneducated posh, when they put the book down they return to the guise of social worker, or of Liberal Democrat spokesperson on education, and remind us that these children would have been far better off had they been *brought up like everybody else*. Pryce-Jones again:

With this poor lovable ogre of a father, and a blindly opinionated mother, Unity was bound to have a childhood out of the ordinary . . . Unity was not thwarted or narrowed deliberately. She grew up in the rhythm of the nannied class, of alternate indulgence and punishment . . .

This is harsh on the Redesdales; and a little unclear as to whether the Mitford upbringing was *sui generis* or of an upper-class type (both, in fact, are true). Yet there is certainly something in what Pryce-Jones says. The Mitfords would all, surely, have turned out as paler versions of themselves had their upbringing been a less potent mixture of restraint and freedom; had they been exposed to other influences beyond each other. This, of course, brings up the question of school, which only Unity – among the girls – attended for any length of time. Tom was sent to Eton, and fitted in easily enough. But the option was never really contemplated for his sisters. Jessica, in *Hons and Rebels*, laments this with what the rest of us, who know what schools are really like, might consider a wildly romantic passion:

The warm, bright vision of living away from home with girls my own age, learning all sorts of fascinating things, dominated my thoughts for years. But no arguments I could advance would move my mother on this point. Besides, she had heard them all before; the older children, with the exception of Pam, had all in turn begged to go.

In fact Diana has written that the thought of being sent to school made

her sick with fear (a fear that Nancy played upon, periodically
pretending to have heard her parents discussing it). Nevertheless, the
brief time that she spent at school in Paris, aged sixteen, led her later to
write: 'I learned more at the Cours Fénelon in six months than I learned
at Asthall in six years'.[11] And Nancy herself liked the idea, although
whether she would have liked the reality is another story. 'She always
wanted to go to school,' says Diana. She had had her brief time at
Francis Holland, aged five; but then there was nothing until finally, at
the age of sixteen, she spent just short of a year at a genteel establishment
called Hatherop Castle, where a handful of nice girls were educated in
French and art and music along with the principal's daughters. And
this, as Diana says, 'was a great success. She made great friends with all
the gals there. She was always very popular, always. One gal there, Mary
Milnes-Gaskell, became a bosom friend for life.'

  · It was after this interlude that Nancy acquired her passion for
being the captain of girl guides. All her life she got on very well with
women of her own age – the rivalries that snaked through her family
do not seem, on the whole, to have affected her friendships – and so
maybe there *was* an element of sincerity to the guides episode. After
Hatherop, she may have craved more non-familial female company.
Dread modern sensibilities might detect a lesbian element in this
desire, although in later life Nancy was to write *à propos* homosexuality:
'Nobody has ever been so ferociously normal as me.' Nevertheless she
was, when young, so literally innocent as to imply – in good convent
girl style – the possibility of barely comprehended erotic imaginings.
For example, a very mysterious 1948 reply to a (lost) letter from Evelyn
Waugh contains the bare word '*Masturbation*', and goes on to tell him
that she had always masturbated when she thought about Lady Jane
Grey ('so of course I thought about her continually & even executed a
fine water colour of her on the scaffold . . . I still get quite excited when
I think of Lady Jane'). Assuming that this is not a total tease, and it
does not give that impression, what can she have meant? That a young
girl's submission to death excited her? Her 'confession' to Waugh is
made quite openly, and almost naturally, with only the barest glimmer
of pride in her own daring. Prurient reaction therefore seems out of
place; all the same one cannot help but be fascinated by this hint of
what seethed within the crisp, clean folds of Nancy's mind ('Do you

think everybody's real life is quite different from what they manage to make it seem? Very likely. No dark secret, but everything different from the façade'[12]).

Hatherop did not constitute a great educational advance; it was more a chaste foretaste of debutante life, and was probably, despite Nancy's avowed longing for school, quite enough for her. Yet she did *think* that she wanted to go to school. Like her 'nastiness', this is a fairly natural consequence of being stuck at home with six younger siblings and a hungry brain. After all, being taught by governesses was hopeless in a way, as these women – about fifteen of them throughout the Mitford childhood, staying for varying periods of time – simply lacked the authority to deal with these children; this impregnable unit of rampant individualism.

Which is not to say that the perpetuated image of hapless Miss Prisms tiptoeing into a world of upper-class anarchy, tremulously demanding 'and what is the capital of Mongolia?' of a girl with a rat round her neck or a sheep under her desk, is entirely true. The uselessness of the governesses has become a part of the Mitford mythology, and is about as much fiction as fact. Here, gorgeously embroidering, is *The Pursuit of Love* on the subject:

As for governesses, they had been tried, but none had ever been able to endure for more than a few days the terror of Uncle Matthew's grinding dentures, the piercing, furious blue flash of his eyes, the stock whips cracking under their bedroom windows at dawn. Their nerves, they said, and made for the station . . .

Dutifully taking this idea on board, Jessica tells in *Hons and Rebels* of how one of the Mitford governesses, Miss Hussey, fell unconscious after finding Unity's snake, Enid, wrapped around a lavatory chain. This sounds good but is a bit of an exaggeration. In reality the serpent in question was not Enid, but a snake of Diana's and according to her it caused no such furore – Blor simply asked, in that imperturbable way of hers, that it be removed from the position it had taken up in the bathroom. Anyway Miss Hussey was not the bag of nerves into which Jessica turned her, she was a competent woman who had been trained in the perfectly acceptable PNEU system (the Parents' National

Educational Union, an organisation that conducted education by correspondence) which Sydney approved of for her daughters. Later, Miss Hussey would say of the Mitford girls: 'Some of the governesses had let them down badly.'[13] Certainly there were those who would cause shudders amongst today's violently competitive 'Eustacia is reading *Harry Potter* in Catalan' parental brigade. One woman, for example, would take Unity, Jessica and Deborah on shop-lifting trips into Oxford ('like to try a little jiggery-pokery, children?'). Another simply played Racing Demon with them all day. It was hardly the road to a fulfilling life of the mind; nonetheless Decca and Debo came out of it a good deal more intelligent than the average 'educated' person.

And Nancy's teachers were not so bad. Miss Mirams, who came to Batsford in 1917, had the sense to let her race ahead of Pam and Diana (Tom, in preparation for school, did subjects like Latin on his own, which may have annoyed his clever sister). There was also the French teacher, known as 'Zella', who according to Debo 'probably did more for Nancy than anybody else'. Mademoiselle Vanda Sereza, later Mrs Stern, was more than just a governess: 'the angelic Zella', as Nancy called her, became a good friend during the war, when both women were living in London. Nancy no doubt felt enormously grateful to Zella, whose tuition had given her an ease with the language and country that she most loved. All the same it was always to be expected that Nancy would learn to speak good French, the one female scholastic accomplishment of which Lord Redesdale unequivocally approved. His grandmother, Lady Airlie, had told Nancy at the age of four that there was 'nothing so inferior as a gentlewoman who has no French': the kind of remark that Nancy always took on board. She delights in making the characters in her novels speak French, and with a facility which nowadays would seem most unusual. Even darling simple Linda has a mastery of reflexive verbs – '*Voulez-vous vous en aller?*' – when her life is falling apart and she is sitting at the Gare du Nord, alone, penniless and on the wrong side of two husbands.

But Linda's lack of general education is palpable, nonetheless; her drifting, questing romanticism is implicitly linked to it; and Nancy blamed both her parents, in different ways, for putting her in the same position. Sydney was accused of a detachment which led to near-indifference, even discouragement. 'I had literary ambitions at a very early age', Nancy would later say[14], 'and began my career by writing a story the opening words of which, "A Youth of thirty entered the room", made my mother so shriek with laughter that I gave up writing and decided instead to express myself by art . . .' Meanwhile David had his prejudices against 'middle-class establishments' which gave girls thick calves from playing hockey. 'I have to thank my father', Nancy said, 'for having me taught, much against his better judgement, to read and write.'

Yet Sydney *did* try to engage with her daughters' education; with the three youngest, at least, whom she taught to read (*The Times* leaders at the age of six, no less). And the governess Miss Hussey contradicted the accepted opinion about David's attitude to female education – an opinion, let it be noted, started by Nancy – by saying that 'Lord Redesdale knew that the girls ought to have a better education'. In some way, then, he recognised that he was letting his bright daughters down. Again, the two Davids appear before us: the pantomime ogre who sent his son to Eton and left the girls to fend for themselves, because that was what people of his kind did; and the sensitive, intuitive man who saw in his children something special, and did not know what to do with it.

To Nancy, on her own, he certainly could respond. A letter sent to her in 1916 shows him carefully correcting her first attempt to write a letter in French: he does so with sweetness and humour, revealing a close fascination with his daughter that even today's fathers, who carry their babies in papooses in the way that David would have carried a pheasant in his poacher's pocket, could not fault. '*Il y a un nid de rouge-gorge dans un arbre*', writes Nancy, for example, underneath which David has replied: 'This is a very common occurrence – it happens most years'. His letter finishes with a funny little poem, which he must have exerted himself to compose while serving in the war in France: 'A robin in a tree has built!/ The coo coo has not changed its lilt!/ And I have no desire to quench/ My child's desire for learning French'. This is hardly Uncle Matthew, nor indeed most upper-class early-twentieth-century fathers. But the sheer number of children that David produced sent him helplessly back to type. His instinct was to indulge his daughters, despite the flashes of anger that he would display against them: he would organise the child-hunts that amused them so much, he would allow Jessica to measure his head and call him 'the old Sub-human', he would endure being stared at across the dinner-table by Unity for minutes on end, her huge pale eyes fixed upon him while she ate vast quantities of mashed potatoes – he was intrigued and delighted by these girls, however much they could enrage him, and however much Tom was his deeply adored, the special light of his life. Sydney, too, indulged her daughters, although perhaps with less delight. 'My mother was far ahead of her time, really,' says Debo. 'She never made us eat food that we didn't want, she wasn't a bit interested whether we'd been to the lavatory, she knew we'd go in the end.' Sydney was not a controlling mother, however much her strong personality may have made itself felt.

And that, with Nancy, seems to have been part of the problem: really what she wanted was *more* attention to be paid to her. From the birth of Pamela onwards, the desire to be noticed – to come first – had grown increasingly intense. Nancy was not entirely joking when, towards the end of her life, she was asked what she liked best in the world and gave this answer: 'Well, I think my absolute dream of perfection is to spend the day on the Lido with great friends in the baking sun. Then we'd be gondolaed back to Venice at sunset. And I'd be staying in much the most beautiful palazzo. Then I'd have a bath and change and when I came down to dinner I'd be *told* by everyone that I was the best dressed woman there. And – isn't it awful? – I'd be wearing the best jewels too.'[15]

No sisters, and especially no Diana, to force her to share the glory: what heaven. And what an irony that it was, in no small part, through writing about her family that Nancy would achieve the kind of fame and freedom which buys holidays on the Lido and dresses from Dior.

When, in *The Pursuit of Love*, Nancy conceived the childhood of Fanny as an alternative to the one lived by the Radlett-Mitfords, she was of course having a dig at her parents for their failure to educate her. She wrote of the Radlett children that 'they never acquired any habit of concentration, they were incapable of solid hard work', and this frustration with her own mind was something real and lasting.

But Nancy was also wondering what it would have been like to live as Fanny did: as an only child, encouraged in the art of self-discipline rather than having rules imposed from outside. The likelihood is that she would have been bored out of her mind. Much as she adores and takes comfort in Fanny, she clearly shows the Radletts to be more fascinating. And it is interesting to see that, when Fanny is quizzed by Uncle Matthew to give an example of her learning, it is Linda ('you're uneducated, thank God') who steps in with the better answer.

Yet there *is* a case, nonetheless, for asking whether the Mitford girls would have been better off had they not grown up quite so much like favoured inmates of a posh prison. With Unity, of course, this was tried. She was sent to school – presumably in an attempt to control her – and she was twice expelled ('No, darling', her mother would say, if one of her sisters used the dread word: 'Just *asked to leave*.'[16]). A contemporary at St Margaret's School, Bushey, which Unity attended between 1929 and 1930, told David Pryce-Jones of how she would 'contrive to be sent to stand outside the [headmistress's] door' – something that the other girls regarded as a shaming disgrace. 'The Mitfords seemed not to get the point, on purpose.'

This is a telling observation, and one for which Pryce-Jones considers the answer to have been, very simply, more school. 'Readers of Nancy's novels and *Hons and Rebels* may conclude that the Redesdales would have saved themselves much expense of spirit had they resorted to the safety valve of sending their children away to be educated. Boarding schools break inherited superiorities.' They also create a good many of their own. It is very easy to say, oh, if only these girls had been educated and 'socialised' and turned into fully rounded human beings – but what on earth does that mean? It is as if those who are brought up 'normally' constitute some sort of touchstone of behaviour; a misguided conclusion, since most people do odd things in their lives, but without the attendant to-the-power-of-six Mitfordian drama. And why this touching faith in the power of the English education system, when the Mitford girl who went to school ended up the oddest of the lot?

But then Unity was what she was: easier to socialise Ratular or Enid than that poor girl. Children have an essential nature, or so some of us believe. Fanny – whom Nancy shows to have been sensibly brought up – is said by Aunt Sadie to have been 'born good', as if the upbringing made no material difference in the end. Of course when one reads about the child Fascist, Unity, and the child Communist, Jessica, demanding of people what politics they supported, then shuddering with bored horror at the words 'I am a democrat', one cannot help but wonder if the passions in these girls could have been better handled. But Unity had a desperately sad adult life, and Jessica rather a fulfilling one; so who can say what difference it would have made?

Among the sisters, Jessica is certainly the one who most agreed with the modern orthodoxy about the Mitford upbringing. Diana says that they were indeed 'too many girls – I have to admit that I just couldn't wait to get away when I was eighteen', but that is not the same as wishing that she had been brought up completely differently: 'I've had a fantastic life,' she says, and one imagines that she saw her childhood as a part of that. Deborah takes a similar pragmatic view, and doubtless Pamela would have done also. Jessica, however, decided that her early life was not just peculiar but futile: what Evelyn Waugh called, in another context, 'a deformative period'.[17] Yet she used it as material, as surely as Nancy did. Her 'hatred' of where she came from supplied her with a *raison d'être*. With her vociferous espousal of Communism, her antagonism towards England, her relentless politicising, Jessica always retained a good deal of the rebellious adolescent whom she described in *Hons and Rebels*. It is quite possible that this edge would have been knocked off her had she been brought up as she professed to have wanted, which is to say 'like everyone else'.

As for Nancy – although she could not have known, as a bored teenager, that her upbringing would one day yield her such rich fruit, she may have grasped its mysterious value. Not that the frustrations should be minimised. Rivalries among the siblings *were* oppressive, sometimes unbearable. Long dark days in the dank Cotswolds *were* boring, sometimes excruciating. When Fanny and Linda ask each other the time constantly, saying 'better than that' if it is half-past rather than quarter-past the hour, there is no doubt that this is how Nancy often felt. At the same time her powerful imagination could make the world of her childhood homes into a stage set, upon which she could stride as principal boy. Her busy brain turned Mitford family life into a plaything, a construct.

In her restless quest for attention, for amusement, she could make jokes and delight herself with the thought that the others did not understand them; she could write her funny little stories without having their style deadened by orthodoxy; she could fence like a Beatrice with her father, a worthy but less nimble adversary; she could dress up as a tramp or, on another occasion, as an old lady with a vast false bosom, specs and moustaches who came to view Asthall and fell upon a horror-stricken Decca ('what a *darling* little girl!!'); she could fret and chafe and 'ache' and dream, as Linda did, of appearing like a Tolstoyan princess in a box at the opera, or of winning the love of the Prince of Wales (clever girls do this kind of thing too). And Nancy was, yes, too clever for the life she was leading. Yet the stimuli that it gave her were enduring as well as ephemeral – boredom can be a wonderfully productive thing, in the right mind – and surely greater than those to be found amongst the twittering debs of Hatherop Castle, her 'place of education'.

A quiet but highly significant figure in all of this was the one Mitford brother, Tom. According to Jessica, he was the 'only mitigating factor' in her life at Swinbrook. As a cure for the boredom that he seemed to understand, he made her read Milton and Balzac. Deborah was once asked by a census-taker what her family consisted of, and answered: 'Three Giants' (Nancy, Diana, Unity), 'three Dwarves' (Pamela, Jessica and herself) 'and one Brute'. The Brute was Tom but this spitting fury against him 'was merely', as Jessica wrote, 'the curious Honnish mirror-world expression of our devotion to him'. Of course, as the only boy, Tom was in an immensely favoured position: everyone, without exception, thought well of him and wanted his good opinion.

He was a cool character – perhaps inevitably in his outnumbered situation – and a bit of a mystery really, but he silently counterbalanced the weight of the six sisters. In him, the intellectual strain that passed lightly through the Mitfords was strengthened and solidified – his reading for choice included Kant and Schopenhauer – and if this had an effect upon Jessica then it must surely have influenced Nancy and Diana, Tom's cleverest sisters. Impossible not to imagine that these two girls were in competition for his slightly detached approbation. Even now Diana says, with some pride, that although Nancy was close to her brother – 'they were fond of each other, and she amused him very much' – the relationship was 'not like Tom and me'.

Diana and Tom were extremely near in age, with barely a year between them. They also shared a passion for music and, later, for Germany, neither of which did much for Nancy. Nevertheless she was described by a Hatherop Castle contemporary as having a 'brother-worship for Tom'[18], and Diana says that she 'looked up to him' – quite unusual with Nancy – 'because he was very clever, and very sensible'. In other words he was harder to impress than most people, and therefore worth impressing; perhaps, like all of the men whom Nancy was to worship, he gave her slightly less back than she wanted.

Tom went to Eton and so was not around for much of the time; yet his importance within the family remained. When he went away to school to develop his mind, Nancy and Diana were left behind to do the same thing, in their own way. And who is to say that they did it with less success?

'I always think once you've learned to read then you do the rest yourself, but I know that's not the fashionable view'[19], Debo was later to remark. And, indeed, Nancy and Diana read like fiends. 'There were masses of books,' says Diana, 'you see we had a wonderful library.' This was Bertram Mitford's collection. It was kept in the handsome room at Batsford with the vast, deep window seats, then later in a converted barn at Asthall which, for the children – or at least for Tom, Nancy and Diana – was a place of exquisite and happy privacy.

Both Jessica and Nancy have, in their way, propagated the image of their father as someone almost violently anti-reading, unless it was Tom who was doing it. Nancy once said that if any of the girls was seen by David with a book he would instantly dream up some errand for them to do instead. Jessica, in *Hons and Rebels*, portrays her home as a place of intellectual near-vacuity. As usual, however, the picture is not so simple: Diana says that 'my father never stopped us reading' and this is confirmed by Deborah ('my sisters and my brother could go into the barn and work and do what they liked. Not work – play. It was their pleasure'). And on the subject of *Hons and Rebels*, Diana found its image of her home so removed from fact that she felt obliged, in 1960, to write an incisive response to the *TLS* (which had recently reviewed the book): 'As children we had access, at home, to an exceptionally well-chosen library; therefore scorn of intellectual values was a matter of choice for the individual child, not of necessity.' Nancy, too, took a shot at Jessica's views during her 1966 television interview. 'She made our home life out to be barbaric really, which it really was not . . . She sees it through fifteen years in America, has told the stories before to Americans and rather embroidered them – and then through the novels which, being novels, are more of a caricature than actual fact, you know': an observation which rather implicated the speaker as well.

But at Swinbrook life was less stimulating: the family did split in half to an extent, with Asthall having been very much the home of the older children, perhaps Swinbrook that of Decca and Debo (Unity somewhat stranded between the two). And the value of the Asthall barn was immense. All the same, the love of reading was so deep in Nancy – one remembers Blor's first sight of her, aged six, 'furious little round face' buried in *Ivanhoe* – that it would surely have flourished in any circumstances. There are few people – even 'educated' ones – who would have chosen to read Macaulay during the *longueurs* of the phoney war, or a life of Talleyrand (in French, *bien entendu*) to distract them from the agonies of undiagnosed cancer, yet this was Nancy's instinct. There are few pairs of socialite sisters who would, as Nancy and Diana did, 'laugh over Carlyle' and his life of Frederick the Great; more likely they would talk coke and Blahniks instead. Which leads one to think that Debo was on to something in her praise of auto-didacticism.

For heaven's sake – Debo, Jessica, Diana and Nancy all grew up to be writers. Very possibly the influence of Nancy led the others to do something that they might otherwise have not, but still they did it extremely well, each possessing – to a greater or lesser degree – that clear tone, as of a wonderfully clever and slightly wayward child, which characterises Nancy's writing. Where would education have helped her with that? Of course she couldn't do things like punctuate ('it is not your subject', said Waugh) and her spelling was never up to much ('asparogas', 'Tchaichowsky' and 'Foust' (by Gounod) were three typical efforts). But these frailties were part of her style. Once she accepted them and allowed her own, stunningly original mind to push her prose along, rather than trying to hold it up with misplaced semi-colons and dutiful sub-clauses, she became a true writer: the writer that one hazards she would not have been had St Mary's, Wantage, got its hands on her. Indeed one is tempted to attribute a vast deal of her vitality of mind to the fact that she was *not* raised to take twelve GCSEs, nor to get into head-to-heads with swots, nor to write tutorial essays on historical totems like the Seven Years War.[20]

In a 1951 essay Evelyn Waugh wrote of Nancy that 'she received no education except in horsemanship and French. Liverish critics may sometimes detect traces of this defect in her work. But she wrote and read continually and has in the end achieved a patchy but bright culture and a way of writing so light and personal that it can almost be called a "style".' He is teasing hideously, of course, but he is also sincere; however much he may at times have deplored his own admiration for Nancy's work, he was quite capable of recognising its specialness, and applauding its extraordinary trick of standing, delicately poised, between art and artlessness. Despite himself, he might have agreed that auto-didacticism had been the making of her.

Learning was something that Nancy would do for the rest of her life. What she learned specifically during her childhood was something less tangible; but, for her, at least as important. It was the value, the absolute value, of jokes. Those stolid country houses saw the birth of the 'Mitford tease'. They were where Nancy first played upon people the prancing, probing tricks that she would practise all her life; as when at the age of fifty she drove half of England to distraction with her delicate fingering of its nerves in 'U and Non-U'. They were where she began to weave the intricate pattern of private jokes, nicknames and languages which – as if the Mitfords were a separate species, with a view of the world too fantastical for the rest to see – the sisters would use into old age: Nancy and Jessica would always address one another as Susan, Diana would be Honks, Cord or Bodley (this was from Bodley Head – as a baby Diana's head was said to be large), Pam was Woman, Deborah was Nine or Miss, Unity was Bonehead, Tom was Tuddemy (the word was thought to rhyme with adultery – a hilarious concept to the girls when applied to Tom), and Nancy herself was Naunce or Koko (from her dark and almost oriental appearance, said to resemble that of the character in *The Mikado*). Many families do this kind of thing, of course (although few writers put it into books, as Nancy did in *The Pursuit of Love*; yet few things bring characters to life so much as private jokes). With the Mitfords, however, the network became something deliberately obscure, extraordinarily exclusive: an endlessly complex game whose arcane rules were mostly invented by Nancy.

And the game was the outward expression of what became Nancy's most fervently expressed belief: that nothing in the world matters more than jokes. For her, laughter came to have an intrinsic worth. It was how she dealt with growing up, with the irruption of Pam into her paradisiacal existence (dress up as a tramp and pretend to want to rape her), with the near-unbearable gloriousness of Diana (put her in a girl guide's uniform), with the disturbing oddity of Unity ('Darling Head of Bone & Heart of Stone'[21]), with the intense irritation caused to her by the little sisters ('nit, sick and bore'), with the rivalry for the affections of her first nanny and her mother and her brother, with the tricky temperament of her father, with the whole damn lot of them in fact: everything, whether funny or not, became the subject of a joke, and that is how everything would remain. 'Oh the screams', she would write in her letters, so frequently that the phrase became its own kind of punctuation mark, 'such screams . . . are you shrieking?'

It was an article of faith for Nancy, to laugh: and how she has been misunderstood for it! In the very words 'screams' and 'shrieks', which for Nancy meant nothing more sinister than laughter, there are those who strive to hear her repressed Munchian agony. But how wrong they are, to miss the stoical, smiling bravery of what became her philosophy of life: 'I have decided', as one of her heroes Voltaire had it, 'to be happy, because it is better for my health.' In a letter to Waugh she wrote: 'In novels what I chiefly value are jokes', a typical remark, whose partial truth is made complete by the sheer strength of her belief. If something was funny, it became bearable; and nothing was unbearable, because there was nothing that could not be made funny.

And this, perhaps, is the real difference that her upbringing made to Nancy. Almost certainly, in circumstances that were more 'normal', she would not have developed this carapace, a veneer that occasionally cracked but was never stripped away. It was, as her nephew Alexander says, a defence, a weapon: a necessity, indeed, for this rampantly clever and acutely sensitive girl, this black-haired green-eyed changeling set amongst those beautiful, calm Brünnhildes ('I always felt', she would later say, 'I had come down the wrong chimney and ought to have been Anastasia').

What else was she to do, trapped as she was in that milieu and that class, except amuse and be amused? Restless and relentless in her quest for laughter, the adolescent Nancy was the spark that set that family crackling – as it still does – with vitality. 'The whole world', said Jessica, describing the Mitford childhood to the BBC, 'became a sort of tease put on by Nancy.' One imagines her, striding lightly and elegantly through enormous chilly rooms, eyes terrifyingly alert beneath their veil of languor, neat head turning this way and that as she scented out the possibility of a new joke. Nasty? Alarming? Evidence of her 'will to power'? Yes, in a way – as she herself was later to write: 'There's always surely an element of cruelty . . . I am a tease and I know it.' And might she have lived differently, written differently, had she not been? Yes, again – for at a young age she learned to deflect her feelings, and they were strong ones: loves and resentments and jealousies and frustrations, feelings for which our modern orthodoxy demands free expression (You are not being funny, Nancy, you are *in denial*).

Yet in the midst of all this, one remembers Deborah's straightforward, beautiful judgment upon her sister: 'A light – she was like a light. She was an absolute live person. Her whole life was being so alive that you couldn't imagine what she was like unless you were with her. And the funniness –!'

Surely this is the point? For all that we affect nowadays to hear sadness beneath laughter, or feel the iron thread of spite within jokes, we must never forget the pleasure that Nancy took in merriment, nor the sheer, determined, vital joy that was in her: 'the frivolity', as Rebecca West wrote after Nancy's death, 'which was her special grace'. Nor, perhaps, forget this throwaway remark from John Betjeman, who as an Oxford undergraduate came to know the family, who cast himself in the role of lovelorn admirer to 'Miss Pam' and who knew, one guesses, pretty much what was going on: 'Nancy was the warmest of them all.'[22]

CHAPTER 3

Avenue Henri-Martin is a Parisian thoroughfare typical of the *seizième* – broad, shadowy, sublimely correct – and it was described in a letter by Nancy Mitford as 'more perfect and melancholy than any place you've ever seen. I don't know why but I waited for a bus there once and when the bus came I was in tears . . .'

She continues, about Paris: 'And then one can be more cheerful there than anywhere else in the world and I have often danced all the way down the Champs-Elysées . . . I think all day La Muette, Place de la Concorde, Place de l'Etoile, Avenue Hoch, Avenue du Bois, Place des Vosges, Palais Royal, Rue de Rivoli . . .' This was written to Tom in 1927, years before Nancy went to live in the city, not long after a stay there with her mother and sisters. But these were feelings that she would never lose. Even as a girl, she seems to have intuited that fulfilment, for her, would lie outside England: that her intense Englishness would flower more brightly in a foreign setting.

She had visited Paris for the first time in 1922, aged seventeen, when she also went to Florence and Venice in the company of girls from Hatherop Castle. She fell head over heels for it all. Her excitement still vibrates, almost heartbreakingly, through the letters that she sent home: 'we had a very scrumptious "croissant" . . . How I loved the Louvre . . . I got postcards of all my favourite pictures. Mona Lisa is wonderful. Miss S. says men still fall in love with her . . . Oh! such fun . . .'[1] This was a much simpler Nancy than the one that her family had had to deal with: a straightforward adolescent, happy amongst her peers, envying them the powdered noses which Lord Redesdale forbade, shrieking at jokes which bear no trace of anything but high spirits: 'Such an amusing thing happened last night', she wrote to her mother from Florence. 'We had asparogas . . . We dared Marigold to throw her stalk over her back & she actually did it! . . . There is one old man who had an awfully nice face sitting opposite us, and he did laugh!'

Nancy fell into conversation with the old man ('he is really, quite 45') who was surprised to discover that she had read Ruskin, surely an unusual accomplishment amongst this merry band of gigglers; she was flattered by the episode but there is no real coquetry in the way she recounts it. How extraordinarily young she seems –! Innocent joy is the tone of her letters home. Yet they are full to the brim with an emotion that would develop and sustain Nancy all her life: an intense love for these new places, their sumptuous yet formal aestheticism, their worshipping at the altar of civilisation. These were the things that mattered to Nancy, as she was now powerfully realising, and beneath her girlish frivolling she drank them down in gorgeous deep draughts. 'If you knew what it is like here you would leave England for good & settle here at once', she wrote to her mother; it was something she would say, and mean, more and more.

And her mother might have agreed with her when she saw her new house: Swinbrook, or Swinebrook, as Nancy was to call it. In 1926, Sydney and her daughters returned from a hotel on the elegant Avenue Victor Hugo to the home that Lord Redesdale had built for them all. It was the first time they had seen it, and it was a hideous shock. Perhaps Sydney was partly to blame in a way, leaving her husband to get on with the house while she went back and forth from Asthall to London, and then off to France; as David Pryce-Jones put it, 'everyone who might have softened its design was away in Paris'. In 1927, when the full awfulness of Swinbrook had made itself apparent, Nancy wrote to Tom in the mocking, slightly theatrical tone that she habitually used in her letters to him:

Deep depression has the Mitford family in its clutches, the birds [her parents] never speak save to curse or groan & the rest of us are overcome with gloom. Really this house is too hideous for words & its rather pathetic attempt at aesthetic purity makes it in my opinion worse.

It is an odd-looking house, no question. Swinbrook village is a place of somnolent and secret calm, taking its name from the stream that trickles gently through its heart; a place of old stone houses, sloping fields and climbing, winding lanes against whose banks pheasants gleam like jewels. Swinbrook House, which looms aggressively on top of a hill rising out of the village, looks like some lesser Nazi's vision of a Cotswold manor house. Its eight identical window-frames seem to have been outlined with a thick dark pen, its four identical chimneys are unyieldingly square, its brickwork is rough and hard and of mysteriously bogus appearance. This was Lord Redesdale's land, and he could do with it whatever he pleased, but the horribly symmetrical house he built looks, quite frankly, like an imposition. Nobody liked it, except Deborah, who was so blissfully happy growing up in the country – riding to hounds, reading the *Sporting Life*, picking fleas off her dachshund – that even living in this odd, bare, draughty box could not depress her. Also, unlike the other children, she had not had time to get attached to Asthall.

For what Asthall had in spades, and Swinbrook had not at all, was any sense of homeliness. Of course this is something that houses acquire, but even the Mitfords would have had a hard job with Swinbrook. The downstairs floors were varnished and slippery; the eighteen bedrooms were whitewashed, their sole decoration a stripe painted round like a cornice just beneath the ceiling; this now sounds rather chic, but was hardly the thing for a country family home. Apart from anything else, it was fantastically cold. The top floor, where the children slept, was arctic: in winter they would sometimes find their sponges frozen with ice. No wonder they huddled with such delight in the linen cupboard, which gave them the delicious, elusive heat they craved. Even more importantly, perhaps, it gave them privacy. In this tiny, darkened space Jessica and Deborah ran their 'Hons' Society' and, sometimes with Unity, spoke to each other in their own languages (sounding, as *Hons and Rebels* has it, like 'a lost tribe'). Nancy would visit the cupboard only occasionally, to tell a story or some such thing; nevertheless it became an essential symbolic part of *The Pursuit of Love*. But for the Mitford children it was a strange substitute, really, for the rich life of the barn at Asthall, so idyllically separate with its quantities of books, its sounds of Handel and Bach coming from Tom's piano. At Swinbrook the books lined the walls of Lord Redesdale's Closing Room (so called because, according to Jessica, it was where 'his old eyes would close, never to open again'). The books were rarely read; while the piano stood in the 'white, tunnel-like' drawing-room, and in so public an arena was hardly ever played.

Swinbrook seems to have drained the vitality from the Mitford family; at least, from the family as an entity. So much that had given life to Asthall was now displaced or removed. Lord Redesdale was deeply hurt by the reception given to his house – he had regarded it as his gift to his family, the home for which they had all been waiting – and perhaps felt guilty when it proved so unbending to live in. His wife, who had fine taste and, as Debo puts it, 'couldn't make anything ugly', filled her new home with exquisite furniture, but even this was defeated by Swinbrook: the pieces stood there, vacantly, like Berninis in an NCP. 'Muv said of course these pictures look awful in this sort of room', Nancy wrote to Tom in 1927, 'so I said why not store them until Tom has made sufficient money to have a proper house. Which is how I think this strikes one, not somehow like a house at all.' Later she put the ugliness of Swinbrook into her description of Alconleigh, in *The Pursuit of Love* ('it was all as grim and as bare as a barracks, stuck up on the high hillside'); but Alconleigh is nevertheless a home, Asthall-like in its essence, a place in which life generates its own warmth and happiness and mysterious beauty. This, Swinbrook never did.

Everyone, except Deborah, wished themselves elsewhere. Although the family would have been breaking up anyway – Nancy, Pam and Diana were becoming marriageable, Tom was coming to the end of his education – the move to Swinbrook somehow emphasised this fragmentation. Quite simply, the house lacked the enveloping warmth to keep them all together. Later, in the early 1930s, it would become an actual embodiment of family divisions, which by that time were assuming a wider, starker significance. In a second-floor room used by Jessica and Unity, a partition was drawn up the middle. On one side, the room held a bust of Lenin and copies of the *Daily Worker*; on the other were photographs of Mussolini and Oswald Mosley, and a swastika. Jessica wrote of the room in *Hons and Rebels*: 'Sometimes we would barricade with chairs and stage pitched battles, throwing books and records until Nanny came to tell us to stop the noise.'

Nancy made much play with her yearning to escape from Swinebrook, where she was effectively trapped, penniless, from the age of twenty-four. Because she was protected by privilege, it is hard to realise just how very broke she always was – right up until the post-war success of *The Pursuit of Love*, in fact – and just how circumscribing this was for her. 'Gals like us, our allowances were tiny,' says Diana. 'My father had nothing to give us.' In fact from the time she came out Nancy had an income of £125 a year, a governess's wages, which did not go very far when one was trying to keep one's end up in society. 'If I wanted anything extra, to go to the south of France or buy clothes or anything, I had to earn it'[2], is how she later described her situation; put like that it doesn't sound very pitiable, nor did she intend it to, because in reality things were rather worse. Forget the south of France – in 1931 she was writing to a friend and saying, 'No I shall never be in London again – unless I walk. I can't possibly afford the train fare & have no clothes to wear even if I could.'[3]

'It was miserable for Nancy at home really in the end,' says Diana, 'because she was far too old. She had nothing to do, and she'd rather given up loving hunting, and all the things she used to do when she was a bit younger, and so her one idea was to get away.'

Nancy was not entirely confined to the barracks that Swinbrook resembled. If she could afford it (train fare, tips to staff, clothes that were not an embarrassment), she would stay with friends. And the Mitfords had a London house, 26 Rutland Gate (off Knightsbridge), which they bought when Asthall was sold. An impossibly tall, six-storey, off-white building, dead plain except for a large, stone balcony on the first floor, the house is nowadays empty and shabby; nor was it ever, one imagines, very elegant, although its sheer, monstrous, free-standing scale is impressive. One can see the Mitford girls, successive debutantes, standing in their bare-shouldered dresses at the balcony window, staring eagerly out on to the indigo London sky, waiting to be taken from their protected cul-de-sac on to the glamorous sweep of Knightsbridge. But the house was not often used, except during the Season. Lord Redesdale, countryman that he was, seems to have regarded it as a necessary evil (what else was he to do, with all those daughters queuing up to come out?) rather than a second home, although his wife liked being there. Much of the time it was let or simply empty: even in the pre-war days when 'poor' aristocrats could afford gigantic houses in SW7, Rutland Gate would have cost a lot to run, and Swinbrook had taken a disastrous toll upon the Mitford finances. If the family was living in London, then Swinbrook itself was let; and so the juggling act went on.

Nancy herself did not come out from Rutland Gate. She had her first dance at Asthall in 1922 ('You'll be cold,' said Nanny Blor, when she saw her ball dress) and then, the following year, Lady Redesdale rented a house in Gloucester Square from which Nancy made her debut. Quite possibly this event had been viewed, before the fact, as one that would change her life. Linda Radlett, stewing and steaming through her interminable adolescence at Alconleigh, waiting for the moment of coming out as for a transcendental experience, is not Nancy, but passages from *The Pursuit of Love* surely describe some of Nancy's feelings aged sixteen or so, her passionate boredom and despairing optimism: 'Two years seemed an absolute eternity, not worth ploughing through even with the prospect (which she never doubted, just as a religious person does not doubt the existence of heaven) of blissful love at the end of it.' Of course Linda *does* find love – or what she believes to be love – during her first season. It is what she expected to happen, what she cannot contemplate not happening, and it happens. Her marriage is a disaster, and quite clearly should not have taken place; but the book makes it equally clear that it is, nonetheless, a solution to the problem of what on earth Linda would have done with herself otherwise.

That was Nancy's problem also. She came out; her life became more interesting, despite the smiling torture of endless fork luncheons and toes crushed by burbling waltzers; yet it did not really change, because she did not move on to marriage. 'Having done the Season, or possibly two Seasons, that was it,' says Debo. 'Nothing to do.' The line in *Love in a Cold Climate* about how 'Aunt Sadie's girls' were snapped up as soon as they put their nose out of the schoolroom was true for most of Nancy's sisters[4], but not for Nancy herself. And so having no money, and no independence, she was stuck in the life that she had imagined escaping.

'You see,' says Diana, 'in one way the answer is, why didn't any of them get work? But in those days it wasn't like that.' Debo again:

'You can't imagine what it was like for girls from the age of nineteen or twenty, when they had no home of their own, they only had their parents'. Their mother did the house and so there was nothing for them to do in that line. Unless they were terribly fond of sport or something acceptable in those days, they just had twenty-four hours of nothing to do. And you couldn't go abroad with a friend, or do any of the things that people do now, you just couldn't, because there were rules and the rules were stuck to.'

Extraordinary to think that within fifteen years of Nancy's rigidly governed emergence into society – and within ten years of her being thrown out of the London house of a friend's grandmother, accused of 'holding an orgy' after a party got a bit noisy – Diana would leave her husband and two sons to set herself up as Sir Oswald Mosley's mistress; Unity would force herself into Hitler's inner circle; and Jessica would elope with Esmond Romilly, an eighteen-year-old Communist who ran off to fight in the Spanish Civil War. It all fell apart so easily in the end, even though these transgressions were, in their way, carried out within the boundaries of the society that they shook so deeply (Esmond Romilly may have been a rebel but he was a rebel educated at Wellington and a nephew of Winston Churchill[5]). It was a long way from the days when Nancy was gated because she had been 'seen' in Oxford, walking around unchaperoned with Brian Howard (a noted homosexual thus hardly a threat). Lord Redesdale's consequent verbal assault, in which he roared that had she been married her husband would have had grounds for divorce, became a similar incident in *The Pursuit of Love*. It also became high comedy – 'Linda began to say no they couldn't [divorce their wives]. She knew the laws of divorce from having read the whole of the Russell case off newspaper with which the fires in the spare bedroom were laid' – but the inflexible reality beneath it, the reality of Nancy's own life, was clear enough.

Obviously, had the Redesdales been able to, they would have come down hard on their other daughters too. They tried: the younger girls were banned from visiting Diana after she left her first husband; all sorts of tricks were pulled to prevent Decca's elopement; and, had they been able to grasp the momentousness of what Unity was doing, they would have done their best to stop her as well. But how could they, really, have prevented any of it? Of course it might be said that, had the Redesdales been less authoritarian in small ways, then their daughters might have felt less of an urge to rebel on the grand scale. In fact there was nothing unusual about the moral strictness of the Mitford upbringing; nevertheless not all nice chaperoned young things slipped the leash to go off to Fascist meetings, or shouted 'Up the Workers!' at the hunt ball. The point is that the Mitford childhood – like the Mitford parents – was a heady mixture of the conventional and the unconventional. And something in that mixture produced highly potent results, pushed into explosiveness by the extraordinary times.

For, unlike Nancy, her sisters Diana, Jessica and Unity were children of the 1930s, and that made a tremendous difference: the General Strike would not, by then, have meant merely an opportunity to dress up as a tramp. But it was more than just changing times. Nancy was not really a rebel. Probably she never would have been. Too lazy, too amused by what others took seriously, too sensible in fact; and also, perhaps, too cautious. When her own behaviour was criticised by her parents, she affected not to mind but in fact it troubled her ('I had a terrific fight with Muv about staying with Nina,' she wrote to Tom in 1927; 'I said I'd go. Do you think it was very nasty of me.'). When Diana left her husband she wrote to her, saying: 'Darling I do hope you are making a right decision. You are SO young to be getting in wrong with the world'; and to Jessica, on her elopement, 'Susan it isn't very respectable what you are doing & I see [our parents'] point of view I must say . . . Susan do come back. No Susan.' In her own way – through jokes – Nancy was subversive, but she also liked the accepted order; and understood that she needed it to bounce off. Certainly her books needed it. In her fourth novel, *Pigeon Pie*, she wrote that her heroine Sophia 'radiate[d] an atmosphere of security and of the inevitability of upper-class status quo': an oblique early example of Nancy's enchanting self-knowledge.

And her acts of rebellion were therefore small ones, although at the time they seemed like battles in the great war for emancipation. '. . . I dimly remembered,' wrote Jessica in *Hons and Rebels*, 'the hushed pall that hung over the house, meals eaten day after day in tearful silence, when Nancy at the age of twenty had her hair shingled.' ('Well anyhow no-one would look at you twice now' was the casual blow struck by Lady Redesdale; or so Nancy told Tom.) Jessica continues: 'Nancy using lipstick, Nancy playing the newly fashionable ukelele, Nancy wearing trousers, Nancy smoking a cigarette . . . she had broken ground for all of us, but only at terrific cost in violent scenes followed by silence and tears.'

Perhaps one must allow for a certain, Jessica-ish exaggeration. Yet it is perfectly possible that the Redesdales saw the end of the world as they knew it in a cigarette held between rouged lips at the dinner table, but reacted as if stupefied to the image of Unity and Diana attending the 1933 Nuremberg rally. It is also possible that Nancy's tiny bids for flapper freedom helped to open the way for her sisters. No doubt she liked the idea of herself as a pioneer in this way – when it came to it, though, she lacked the fight for anything much more than gestures. For example, rather as she had pleaded incessantly to be sent to school so, as a young woman, she yearned to be allowed to study at the Slade and, even more excitingly, to live alone in London rooms. 'I thought I'd like to be a painter,' she said on television in 1966. 'I loved doing silly little drawings. And Professor Tonks [then director of the Slade] put an end to it by saying I had no talent whatever.' At first she stayed at the Women's Union Society in London's University College, but she hankered after a bedsit and eventually someone – presumably Sydney – realised that the best thing was to let her get on with it. Accordingly in mid-1927 she moved into a boarding house in Queen's Gate, South Kensington. Within a month she was out again (and out of the Slade not much later). The story is that she had been unable to cope with the growing piles of underclothes on the floor: 'I just didn't know what to do with them,' she said in her television interview, shrieking with unapologetic laughter.

Really, of course, even Nancy (a woman who loathed and feared all housework – 'one's poor hands') would have had *some* idea. Really, she just didn't like living the 'independent' life – latchkeys and laundries, all the faint sordidness of London on no money – which nowadays girls leap at so eagerly. No doubt they would see Nancy through the eyes of the adolescent Jessica, who according to *Hons and Rebels* flew at her sister, saying, 'I think you're very weak-minded. You wouldn't catch me knuckling under because of a little thing like underclothes.'

All the same, one rather likes the plaintive honesty of Nancy's admission about her experience of bedsit land in SW7: 'I just couldn't bear it.'

She was no martyr to the cause of freedom. In many ways she was a typical debutante. With her frothy chatter, her weightless frame, her determined effervescence, she was equipped to pass herself off as a Bright Young Thing, and did so merrily enough. The 1920s were an especially amusing time to be a posh girl, if one could cope with the constant pressure to sing at top pitch: 'The young English upper-classes lived a life of total frivolity,' Nancy wrote in 1966.[6] 'The young today seem to me sobriety itself compared to what we were like then' (and this at a time when gilded youth was supposedly tuning in and dropping out to its heart's content). 'We hardly ever saw the light of day, except at dawn; there was a costume ball every night: the White Party, the Circus Party, the Boat Party, etc. . . .' If not all of these parties was as amusing as everyone hoped and pretended ('looking back upon them now, they appear like a Jerome Bosch hell', spat one ex-reveller[7]), there was a perpetual exuberance that kept everything going, as if all concerned were on a determined and constant high.

They got tremendous newspaper interest. 'Between the wars', wrote David Pryce-Jones in his biography of Unity, 'the space devoted to society news was out of all proportion to the events': the doings of the upper-classes had, for the first time, become currency in the wider world, written about in the same light-headed spirit as today's flutterings over anorexic A-listers and reality television 'stars'. No wonder the Mitford Girls were soon to find their antics dissected throughout Fleet Street; after all, it had made the papers when Lady Redesdale ditched her napkins, rather as it would nowadays if Victoria Beckham were seen coming out of Lidl.

There was a significance to all of this, however trivial it seemed, and however mocked-up a lot of the stories undoubtedly were. In a way that would not before have been possible, it scratched away at aristocratic mystique, while at the same time proving its power: the stories were underpinned, as indeed they still are, by a kind of obsequious savagery. Whether people in the 1920s read about the Marchioness of Queensberry driving herself to Rome in a two-seater sports car, or the letting of a house in St James's Square for £1,000 a week during the Season, in a spirit of envy, contempt, irony or adoration – who can say? The point is that they apparently *wanted* to read this stuff. Similarly, as Pryce-Jones wrote, 'Gossip columnists complicitly vied to appoint one or two Debutantes of the Year', and accordingly debs became much more like public property than they had been before the war. Jessica describes in *Hons and Rebels* how crowds would turn up to watch the girls, in their Daimlers and ostrich feathers, as they inched slowly down the Mall towards their presentation at Buckingham Palace. Judgments would be shouted – 'Ain't the mother an old battle-axe!' – through the car windows.

And so, as Pryce-Jones observed of this intense and sudden spotlight: 'Girls who were plain or dowdy, who for some reason failed to be noticed, had a thin time of it, and anyone of sensibility could be forgiven for disliking this particular showroom.' Beneath the formalities, it was a grimly competitive arena; judgments were being made all over the place, not just in the Mall or the *Daily Express*. The Season had a deadly serious purpose. Girls were there to get themselves a husband. They also had to prove that they could operate in the world of society, amongst the people with whom they would almost certainly be spending their lives. It was terrifying, in that it mattered so much; and to a girl like Unity Mitford the only option was to become 'a licensed eccentric', to steal writing paper from Buckingham Palace, to go to dances with Enid in her handbag and Ratular curved around her Amazonian shoulder. But Nancy, essentially, played the game. It was an arena in which girls might sink or swim, and on the whole she swam.

'I imagine she did,' says loyal Debo, 'because she was a great success. Very very pretty, very funny and all that. She made a lot of marvellous friends whom she kept.' Certainly she was popular; her letters from the time prove that she did not suffer the fate of the rejected adolescent, that she was asked to parties and balls and race meetings and weekends away, all the usual stuff which, however boring it might sometimes be, is still preferable to not being invited. If some of these letters give off a slightly shrill note of unconvincing fervour ('I am *very* drunk on one of Nina's cocktails, I really must give up this pernicious habit or my young health will be ruined & I shall run round Swinbrook having d.t.s a dreadful fate for so young a virgin'), then that is not so unexpected. Nancy was a very clever girl who was, in a sense, still playing in the nursery; later, she realised as much. But her instinct, from the time that she came out into society, was to subscribe to it. As her character Fabrice was to say in *The Pursuit of Love*: 'You should never despise social life – *de la haute société* – I mean, it can be a very satisfying one, entirely artificial of course, but absorbing. Apart from the life of the intellect and the contemplative religious life, which few people are qualified to enjoy, what else is there to distinguish man from the animals but his social life?' This is elegantly put, and perhaps more rigorously thought out than is at first apparent. Debutante dances in Pont Street (strawberry ices, chinless Etonians, puppyish bosoms in white satin frocks) would have differed from the Duc de Sauveterre's idea of *la haute société*, but the principle holds: society is a civilising concept, and as such Nancy believed in it profoundly.

She believed, too – and from the first – in friendship. 'Nancy was very much liked by her contemporaries,' says Diana. As a girl she was no doubt popular for superficial reasons – her love of chat, her relentless high spirits, her sparkling malice – and there is nothing so wrong in that; at the same time, however, she always took friendship seriously. She had very good girlfriends, such as the Countess of Seafield, a fabulously rich orphan with two huge houses in Scotland: 'Well, Nina Seafield she used to stay months with!' says Diana, which implies a gift for society, a natural ability neither to bore nor to be bored. There was also Mary Milnes-Gaskell, her friend from Hatherop; and Mary ('Middy') O'Neill, whose grandmother accused the girls of staging an orgy in her house. Middy O'Neill's grandfather had been Ambassador in Paris at the time of Nancy's stay there, and so: 'the other night I dined at the Embassy & we went on & danced at the Florida which was divine fun . . .'[8]

Her social life was always good. Yet she did not come out in the manner of Evelyn Waugh's Julia Flyte, to the sound of golden trumpets, and surely this is what in her heart she had wanted: the eagerness of her letters says as much. According to *Brideshead Revisited*, Julia was Nancy's debutante contemporary in 1923: 'Some said it was the most brilliant season since the war, that things were just getting into their stride again . . . and through those halcyon weeks Julia darted and shone, part of the sunshine between the trees, part of the candle-light in the mirror's spectrum.' Nancy's own accounts of coming out bear little resemblance to this baroque hymn. 'We really had great fun', says clear-eyed Fanny in *The Pursuit of Love*, 'although I don't think it was dancing that we enjoyed so much as being grown up and in London.' Being, however, a mysterious mixture of the realist and the romantic – of Fanny and Linda, if you like – Nancy also had her dreams of conquest: 'Pray, who is that young woman?' . . . 'That is my younger daughter Linda, your Royal Highness.' These were her innermost hopes. But it was her sister Diana, six years later, for whom they would come true. When Diana emerged into society her impact was instant and dazzling; she almost immediately became engaged to Bryan Guinness, a very rich man who utterly worshipped her: like Julia Flyte, she was what all girls surely yearn to be, the ones against whom the others measure themselves. For Nancy it was a less exalted story. Not until she wrote about her world did she truly cast a spell over it.

'To be married, soon and splendidly, was the aim of all her friends', writes Evelyn Waugh of Julia Flyte. 'If she looked further than the wedding, it was to see marriage as the beginning of individual existence.' This, too, must have been what Nancy craved, but time went on and it did not happen. And then time went on too long. There were ten years between her debut in society and her marriage, during which time she lived, as her sisters have said, in a kind of limbo: coming out and then staying out, stuck in perpetual adolescence.

Quite rightly, Debo says that it was touch and go whether a girl met a marriageable man or not, even when they were all laid out for you on a Thomas Goode plate. 'It's just luck. In those days it really was I think luck, because you met a certain number of people – a lot of people, going out to these dances and things – but you could just discard ninety per cent of them. You know, they were either so boring or unattractive or something.' In *Love in a Cold Climate* it is made clear that beyond a certain point, all too quickly reached, there was simply no one. Polly Hampton, like Nancy, shows no signs of marrying when well into her Season, and her desperate mother, Lady Montdore, is reduced to asking 'a noisy, self-opinionated young Conservative MP' to one of her parties in the hope that he will light a spark. *The Pursuit of Love*, meanwhile, is lethally succinct: 'At the dances the great bar to enjoyment was what Linda called the chaps.'

Linda, of course, finds happiness in the end with a Frenchman, and the contrast between Fabrice's irresistible confidence, and the ham-fisted Englishmen who go before him, could hardly be made clearer. 'I was forced to the conclusion', says Linda, 'that neither Tony nor Christian [her two husbands] had an inkling of what we used to call the facts of life.' She means more than just lovemaking technique: what she finds so wondrous in Fabrice is his *liking* for women, his interest in them, his fascination with them, all of which would have terrified the average Englishman in Nancy's youthful sphere (Evelyn Waugh once tried to tell her as much: 'I explained to her a lot about sexual shyness in men', he wrote in his 1930 diary, although what he said did not immediately sink in). Also Nancy observed the shenanigans – highly typical in their way – of her brother Tom, who after a homosexual phase spent his time in theatrical pursuit of women like Tilly Losch: an Austrian actress five years his senior, one of those girls whom men went after, *en masse*, in a spirit of competition amongst themselves. Nancy must have seen the silliness of this kind of male behaviour; but it would take many years and a change of country before she could acknowledge as much.

This is not to say that she didn't have suitors. She was tremendously attractive, although the charm that bloomed free and idiosyncratic in her middle age may have been a bit much for the men of her youth, who probably preferred something more pink-cheeked and bovine, or more straightforwardly sexy. Her appearance – in the fashion of the times with its evanescent slimness, its odd, slightly mournful, down-turning eyes, its air of a faintly androgynous Pierrot – was the kind more admired by women than by men. Nonetheless, men naturally took an interest (indeed her second cousin Randolph Churchill tried, as she put it, to rape her – 'it was very funny', she wrote[9]). A soldier named Archer Clive crops up in letters to Tom, although in March 1928 she wrote: 'I do nothing now but have *fearful* quarrels with Archer & then make them up again. Luckily he goes abroad in May, it becomes a little wearing' – and that, it would seem, was that. A couple of years on she was pursued by Nigel Birch (Niggy), who belonged to the group of Tom's friends that she called 'the Fat Fairs', and by Roger Fleetwood Hesketh, both of whom were rich and respectably keen. But somehow, nothing happened. Nancy remained chaste and untouched, with the persistent aspect of a rakish sixth-former.

'How is one to find the perfect man, either they seem to be half witted or half baked or absolute sinks of vice or else actively dirty like John Strachey. All *very* difficult!' Nancy wrote to Tom in 1928. John Strachey (later a Labour MP) was rather Bohemian and not to Nancy's taste; very possibly she thought the pose affected, even though she went in for plenty of posing at this time. Asked by a mutual acquaintance what she thought of Strachey, 'I said rather rashly that I preferred young men to be less clever but more cultured.' This reflects very interestingly on Nancy herself. For it is fairly certain that most of the men she met would have preferred, in their turn, that she had been rather less clever. Those penetrating jokes, those disconcerting teases: female cleverness is far more off-putting to men than they care to admit.

Yet the impression is that Nancy was *not* clever with men: not clever enough to handle them. Something in the *quality* of her cleverness – which made her too distant in one way, too excitable in another – was not to male taste. The reason why Nancy did not marry until she was twenty-nine may not just have been because the men were all so hopeless (none of them was worse than the one that she *did* marry), but because of something in her. She lacked the intuitive woman's touch. She did not have within her the instinct to gravitate towards a prospective husband; the gift for men.

This is not the sort of thing that one is supposed to say anymore, but it was clearly something that fascinated *Nancy*: her novels, and indeed her historical biographies, are full of women who *do* have this gift and are vastly admired for it, not least by their creator. Take, for instance, Albertine Marel-Desboulles in *The Blessing*, who is neither young nor beautiful but who uses her superior cleverness as a sensual tool. Diana, too, was clever ('the cleverest of us all, probably', says Debo, intriguingly); but she was also, decidedly, a clever *woman*. Nancy's cleverness had a remorseless quality to it: if she thought of something quick and funny to say, like her remark about John Strachey, then she would come right out and say it, regardless of considerations such as male ego. Later in life, when she was conducting a love affair with her own Fabrice – de Gaulle's right-hand man, Gaston Palewski – she would be unable to resist teasing him even when it was clear that, after a hard day spent dealing with the General, all he wanted was a bit of *silence sympathique* ('Poor brute,' said Sir Oswald Mosley to Diana, after hearing Nancy describe how she would laugh at her frazzled lover; secure in the knowledge that his own wife, calm and stately as a moon goddess, would never put a foot wrong in that way. Who would wish for Sir Oz's[10] approbation, one might say, but that is not the point).

It is probably significant that Nancy had such good friendships with other women; tremendously ready, on the whole, to pick up on whether another girl is a sexual threat. Nancy was not a threat: 'no B.A. at all', as Lady Montdore says of Polly. This is not to say that Nancy (or indeed Polly) had no interest in sex. That is something quite different. However, her nephew Alexander Mosley says: 'She was very feminine, yes. But was she sexy? No, she wasn't sexy.' A friend who knew her in Paris, John Julius Norwich[11], agrees. 'She was totally unflirtatious. I mean she was beautiful and exquisitely dressed, she had a wonderful figure. But I don't think there was any come-on aspect to her nature at all.' Nancy, one feels, was rather like Grace de Valhubert in *The Blessing*, who is adored by an Englishman obsessed with his inability to make a pass at her: such is her elegance, he cannot bring himself to grapple with her pristine clothes and 'grasp the waist of Grace'. The original of this Englishman was the writer and critic Cyril Connolly.[12] At a party in 1950, the year that *The Blessing* was written, he said, 'the trouble with you Nancy is one can't imagine you sitting on one's lap – have you ever sat on anybody's lap?'

'No I said, with some vehemence, nor have I ever allowed anybody to kiss me (almost true).'[13] This little incident may have given Nancy the idea for Grace's apparent *froideur*. But it *is* appearance only: Grace's husband makes passes at her all the time, but then he is French and divines her sexual nature beneath the 'buckram dresses'. And Frenchmen, for Nancy, came later.

Yet she did have one, very serious, English admirer: Sir Hugh Smiley of the Grenadier Guards, who proposed marriage to her several times in 1932, when she was twenty-seven. It seems an unlikely coupling. He was presumably dazzled by her and she, for her part, considered him as a husband for 'about five minutes'. 'Sir Hugh laid his ginger bread mansion at my feet last Monday.'[14] She accepted his proposal and then backed straight out again. 'Muv went on at me about it & said you'll die an old maid' she wrote at the time; but much later, in a letter of 1971, she made an (interestingly honest) admission to Jessica: 'I think I was telling lies if I said Muv wanted to marry me off . . . One of the reasons for my respect is that she never did urge marriage without inclination & I hardly think she knew who was rich and who was not.' Nancy was talking here about Nigel Birch and Roger Fleetwood Hesketh, either of whom – she implies – she might have married. But the closest she came, before actually doing the deed, was with Hugh Smiley.

'I'm not surprised girls do that sort of thing. Besides the old boy is really awfully nice & kind in his own way. But think of having blond & stupid children. But then one could be so *jolly well dressed* and take lovers . . . But it is better to retain one's self-respect in decent poverty isn't it?'[15]

So Nancy did not want marriage at any price: something in her – the embryonic writer? – refused to accept what most women want, or feel obliged to want. 'Proper husband, proper children,' as Debo puts it. 'I think Nancy would have loved those things, but she never had the chance.' And yet Sir Hugh *did*, surely, give her that chance? Of course he was not the perfect man for her, but she was close to being regarded, by the judgement of the time, as an old maid (the grievously hurt Hugh told her she would end up 'on the shelf'). And she was stuck in a life that increasingly frustrated her; it is fair to say that many women would have accepted the offer and made the best of it. Nancy was not like that. A mixture of immaturity and integrity prevented her from taking that particular plunge. When she later wrote in *The Pursuit of Love* about Linda's marriage to Tony Kroesig – who bears no small resemblance to Sir Hugh in his wealth, his blond denseness, his yearning to go into Parliament – it was as if she were describing what her life might have become. But Linda believes that she is in love with Tony: Nancy never did believe that about Hugh, and she was too much of a romantic to enter into a marriage without at least the illusion of love.

The fact that, a bare year after turning down this proposal, she accepted a man even less likely to bring her happiness, seems extraordinary. There was a reason for it, however; as will become clear.

But for the moment, forget boyfriends, suitors, marriage: what Nancy most preciously took from the years of her youth were enduring friendships with men who would never be lovers, yet understood her as lovers never would. 'A delicious creature, quite pyrotechnical my dear, and sometimes even profound, and would you believe it, she's hidden among the cabbages of the Cotswolds' was Brian Howard's judgment upon Nancy, given in the late 1920s to Harold Acton ('He was so scornful of feminine intellect among contemporaries that I felt it was more than a special compliment', wrote Acton in his memoir of Nancy). Nancy always got along extremely well with homosexuals, and her easiest, most satisfying relationships were probably with those male friends who were not in the running as lovers.

Brian Howard – the model for Anthony Blanche in *Brideshead Revisited* – was later described as 'one of the most amusing people in the world' and 'a genuine exponent of high camp'[16]. Camp has become debased currency, but it was once a peculiarly English, oddly subtle, gently irresistible idiom. Nancy recalled Howard saying, to a boyfriend who was spraying himself with '£100 a drop' scent in the Guerlain shop in Paris, 'Now, my dear, you're not putting out a *fire* you know!'

Other great friends were the more forceful Robert Byron (later a travel writer), another homosexual and one with whom Nancy was half in love. Byron was a genuine and energetic eccentric: 'He affected loud tweeds, a deerstalker hat, yellow gloves, horn-rimmed pince-nez, a cockney accent', wrote his friend Waugh. 'Wherever he went he created a disturbance, falling down in the street in simulated epilepsy, yelling to passers-by from the back of a motor car that he was being kidnapped . . .' John Sutro, who bankrolled the Oxford University magazine *Cherwell* and later became a film producer, was said by Nancy to be 'a marvellous correspondent because you really can say what you think to him'.[17] Oliver Messel, the set designer (later to work on a play translated by Nancy[18]), was described by her in a letter to Tom, recounting a party held in 1928 called the Pageant of Hyde Park:

'Oliver Messel was *too* wonderful as Byron, I nearly fainted away when he came limping on to the stage, this proves that I must have been Caroline Lamb in a former incarnation.' Best companion of all was Mark Ogilvie-Grant, a man of wit and sweetness, a caricaturist who illustrated covers for Nancy's early books and of whom Diana says: 'He was really like a brother to Nancy.'

And then there were the writers: Waugh of course ('I loved Evelyn really I think the best of all my friends,' Nancy said when he died[19]); Henry Yorke (whose grimly clever books were published under the name Henry Green – 'No one wrote about the poor before him,' said Waugh to Nancy, not wholly seriously); John Betjeman (whose joyful, watchful eye was the first to perceive the sisters as an entity, in his little poem 'The Mitford Girls, the Mitford Girls! I love them for their sins'); and so it went on. Tom Driberg, James Lees-Milne, Cecil Beaton ... no wonder poor old Sir Hugh of the Grenadier Guards lacked something in the conversation stakes. What made these men so fantastically attractive to Nancy was that they celebrated laughter – her favourite thing – but at the same time they gave to it an intellectual underpinning: a rigour. In many ways they were probably just as silly as any of the other young people she had ever met, what with their desire to shock and show off, their innate schoolboyishness, their faintly desperate clubbishness, their joking passion for hideous Victoriana, their sexual naïvety. But with all of this they had wonderful lively brains, which – rather as with Nancy herself – had developed way beyond everything else about them.

Mostly they were friends of Tom's, from Eton and Oxford (they all attended the university, which was near Swinbrook, and all came down with terrible degrees – indeed Betjeman left with none). Nancy later said: 'Everything changed when my brother went to Eton'[20], although it is odd that she saw Tom as the bridge between herself and her new life, when she had already begun to meet these dazzlers under her own steam. Mark Ogilvie-Grant was a cousin of Nina Seafield, and thus the means to all sorts of amusing ends: in 1928 Nancy described a fortnight at Cullen, one of Nina's homes in Scotland, as 'a perfect fortnight among highly civilised people!!' The highest praise, indeed.

'Most of the people I know are frank barbarians (Muv & Farve specially)', her letter to Tom continued. Her delicious new friendships had set up a situation that she seems almost to have relished: the pull between dank, freezing Swinbrook and joyful, coruscating London. The fact that Nancy understood both sides of the paradox equally well – the parochial and the cosmopolitan, the earthy and the worldly – was to inform her novels for many years.

For one couldn't make it up, really, the idea of a clash between Lord Redesdale and, say, Brian Howard. One thinks of *Love in a Cold Climate*, and the scene in which Uncle Matthew loses control when he sees that the glittering homosexual, Cedric Hampton, has the seams of his coat 'piped in a contrasting shade'. Nancy and Tom would turn up at their Lesser Nazi Country House with a bunch of aesthetes in tow: the Swinbrook Sewers, sloshing around in their Oxford bags (as pioneered by Harold Acton) or drooping on sofas like so many giggling Chattertons. Jessica described the scene in *Hons and Rebels*:

At week-ends they would swoop down from Oxford or London in merry hordes, to be greeted with solid disapproval by my mother and furious glares by my father. Boud [Unity], Debo and I were on the whole carefully insulated from Nancy's friends, as my mother considered them a totally bad influence. '*What* a set!' she always said when some of their more outrageous ideas were expounded by Nancy. They talked in the jargon of their day: 'Darling, too, too divine, too utterly sickmaking, how shamemaking!'

As usual with Jessica, this is teetering upon exaggeration; and, as usual, Nancy is partly responsible, because the character of Uncle Matthew, with his towering hatred of art and literature and anything remotely unmanly, has surely informed Jessica's account. In fact Robert Byron wrote a letter to his mother, possibly doctored for her consumption, that gave a (disappointingly) sober view of his Swinbrook weekend: 'The Mitford family are very amusing – especially Nancy, and I enjoy being here.' Even Brian Howard was probably saved by his ability to ride to hounds; while Mark Ogilvie-Grant became a great favourite of Lord Redesdale and was invited to eat 'brains for breakfast!' at eight o'clock sharp.

And if the aesthetes did behave like Noël Coward on a Countryside Alliance March, or – as James Lees-Milne did – put their foot in it by being insufficiently anti-German, it probably gave Lord Redesdale something to get his tired old dentures into. As for his wife, who like Aunt Sadie 'had known the world as a girl', she probably derived some amusement from these irruptions into her comfortless new home. The Redesdales didn't have to accept these people at Swinbrook, yet they visited often enough.

Anyway, how irritating it would have been to Nancy had her parents embraced the aesthetes wholeheartedly! In her first novel, *Highland Fling*, her heroine Jane has 'charming, rather cultured' parents of infinite tolerance, and it drives her mad; little is more annoying to a child than to do something shocking only to find that one's parents are not shocked at all, and Nancy was still in many ways a child. Jessica recounts how Nancy tripped home one day with a print of Stanley Spencer's *Resurrection*, which sent her father into 'one of his classic rages'. 'We rather assumed that at least a partial reason for this interest [in modern art] was to "tease the Old Sub-Human" – and tease him it did, most effectively.' If the story is true then of course Jessica's assumption is right.

Such behaviour was all part of this limbo in which Nancy was living, between the schoolroom and the marriage bed. She chafed against it; even though, when she had had her chance of escape to Queen's Gate in 1927, she couldn't stick it at all. It was part of the Mitford myth – started by Nancy, perpetuated by Jessica – to portray the girls as shrieking Rapunzels behind the walls of Swinbrook prison, yearning for the world outside to which their father barred the door. All the same: 'Leaving home – I think that's been *rather* exaggerated,' Diana later said of Nancy.[21] When Diana married in January 1929, acquiring a beautiful house in Buckingham Street to which the Swinbrook Sewers flocked, Nancy had a place where she could see her friends (now – annoyingly? – Diana's also) in total freedom. Later that year she tasted freedom again, moving to the little flat in Canonbury Square taken by Evelyn Waugh and his wife; but this cosy arrangement, which promised much fun, came to an end after a bare month, when Waugh's wife announced that she had taken a lover (a development that deeply coloured the work-in-progress *Vile Bodies*). But Nancy still had Nina Seafield and other friends; she had Rutland Gate, and the mews house behind it in which Tom was living while studying for the Bar; as prison life went, it was not so bad.

Nevertheless there was some real, not theatrical, parental exasperation at this time, which probably had concern for Nancy's future at the root of it. After all, nobody thought that she would make a career for herself as a writer. Jobs for women were not an option; what, then, was to happen to her? All she ever did, apparently, was gallivant with a bunch of shrieking urban poseurs who left her parents occasionally amused but more often bewildered. Her mother disapproved of her staying with Nina Seafield (Sydney had a genuine distrust of very rich people, no doubt seeing in their money the means to immorality; although Nina was hardly Eurotrash. According to Harold Acton she 'resembled a juvenile Queen Victoria with red hair and a hesitant stammer'). In 1931 Nancy wrote to Mark Ogilvie-Grant, saying of her parents: 'They have been simply too odious lately, & had a fearful row the other day ending up by accusing me of drinking.' This is almost comical, when one thinks that a year later Diana would be leaving Bryan Guinness to set herself up as Oswald Mosley's *maîtresse en titre*. But before 1932 it was Nancy who was deemed, relatively speaking, to be the problem.

Which is why, in *Highland Fling*, published in 1931, she created the character of General Murgatroyd: a pantomime version of Uncle Matthew, a one-dimensional Lord Redesdale, upon whom she vents her frustrations (in an act of authorial revenge, for example, the General is shown wildly beating his gundog on a shoot and then being savaged by a tiny Pekinese). At the age of twenty-five or-six she was still under her father's ultimate jurisdiction, and her parents were still treating her like a rebellious adolescent, because her adolescence was still, in a sense, going on. Yet her frustrations were not, *au fond*, with the Redesdales, but with her own life. For all its compensations and jollifications, by the end of the 1920s it was beginning to disenchant her: as her newly discovered vocation would make increasingly clear.

'I wrote a book because I wanted to earn a hundred pounds.' So Nancy would later say[22] (in fact she earned £90 from *Highland Fling*), and like many of her statements it was probably about half true. Why anyone becomes a writer is in the end a mystery. But certainly at the beginning

Nancy followed Dr Johnson, in believing that the desire to earn money was as good a reason as any: 'Oh yes, oh yes, I've always needed money! Terribly! . . . That's why I had to chuck painting, because I realised I couldn't earn any money at it.' When she said this, on television in 1966, writing had made her a rich woman. But back in the late 1920s money simply meant a sudden new shoot of independence, or a new dress, or some other kind of hand to mouth pleasure; she started to write with that uppermost in mind.

All the same it was in the blood. Bertram Mitford had written; Thomas Bowles had founded *Vanity Fair* and *The Lady*; it was not so surprising, that Nancy should think of contributing articles to magazines like *Vogue*, nor that in 1930 she should become a regular columnist (paid £5.5s.0d. a week) on *The Lady*, nor that she should try her hand – as many of her friends did – at a novel.

Much of her charm comes from the fact that she clearly had no desire, ever, to struggle with writing. Jessica described in *Hons and Rebels* how Nancy had sat writing *Highland Fling*, 'giggling helplessly by the drawing-room fire, her curiously triangular green eyes flashing with amusement, while her thin pen flew along the lines of a child's exercise book': the impression, above all, is of someone for whom this came naturally. Later – after *The Pursuit of Love* – when she discovered that this had become her job for life, she often struggled like mad and complained, during a radio broadcast in 1946, of suffering from writer's cramp. But at the start the whole point of writing was to make her life easier, not harder: agonising in noble poverty was not Nancy's scene. Nor did she ever have difficulty in getting published: 'I never had any trouble. Luckily, because I think if I had it would have put me orf completely, I don't think I'd ever have gone on.'[23]

In fact it is slightly surprising that *Highland Fling did* get published: it really isn't very good ('I blush now when I read it,' Nancy said in 1946). Because it is a comic novel of upper-class life, one might assume it to have similarities with her post-war books, but there are only the barest flashes of authentic Mitford. Jokes about the cult of Victoriana (as espoused by Robert Byron), or modern art (she describes a painter using 'prepared dung' – little did she know), or Bright Young Things staging a fake funeral for fun, are not quite her. That delicious clear voice of hers – which would later ring out with the strength and simplicity of a bell – is muffled by modishness and show-off lack of assurance. And her humour, which would become so soufflé light, is heavy going: one has the sense of a horse being flogged into desperate life.

'My book has gone to the agents whose verdict I await in a state of palpitation', Nancy wrote to Mark Ogilvie-Grant in early 1930. 'I'm afraid it won't be accepted, everyone thinks it very bad.' But Nancy, from the first, had the gift of writing the right thing at the right time, and satire on the bright young people was then all the rage. 'Have had to alter the book quite a lot as it is so like Evelyn's in little ways, *such* a bore.' In fact Nancy did not care for *Vile Bodies* ('I was frankly very much disappointed in it I must say'[24]), whose grandiose and hysterical cynicism would not have been to her taste. Nevertheless it is in a different league altogether to *Highland Fling*.

But Thornton Butterworth Ltd, Nancy's first publisher, saw something there. No doubt they liked the idea of this pretty, well-connected girl who wrote in the style *du jour*; a bit of a novelty, after all, and a good bet for publicity. 'I suppose they don't take anything that's absolutely unmarketable', Nancy wrote to Mark Ogilvie-Grant, who drew the cover for the book. And *Highland Fling* sold well for a first novel ('it sells a steady 30 a day'), not least because it was well reviewed ('specially in the *Evening News* & *Standard* which really count as I don't know who writes them'[25]). This was perhaps a by-product of privilege. Although Nancy would later be judged with the tough respect accorded to a 'real' writer, and later still would be characterised as a 'posh dizzy spinster'[26], never were her books tossed casually to the wolves in the way that happens with so many writers. She was always, to an extent, protected by who she was.

And it was her position in society that got her writing career kicked off. Not just the family connection with *The Lady*; her earliest journalism took the form of anonymous gossip sold to newspapers (as is portrayed in *Vile Bodies*). Then, from 1929, she became a sort of social commentator. For *Vogue* she anatomised the society wedding and the shooting party (for which she was paid a 'stingy' £6.6s.0d. – she always remarked upon her fee); for her column in *The Lady* she wrote about a day at a point-to-point, or an evening of Wagner at Covent Garden; and so on. It was the kind of thing that she would always do, a tease upon the upper-classes. And it was done well enough, based as it was upon close (if not especially inspired) observation. This is from 'At a Point-to-Point', published in March 1930: 'Let me here remind you that it is in no way your duty to put money on those of your acquaintances who may be riding: your pound does them no good, and is lost to you for ever. Far better to keep it to spend on flowers, books, or chocolates for them in the nursing home where they are almost certain to pass the next few weeks.' Such writing reads very cosily now, with a satirical bite as harmless as a kitten's; although it looks a little more jagged in the context of old copies of *The Lady*, among articles entitled – for instance – 'How to Knit a Chenille Beret'.

The columns give a flavour of what her life was like: conventional in the extreme and not especially congenial to her. There is a fascinating, slow-growing antipathy to the typical values and pursuits of the English upper-classes. Nancy is laughing, but she is also gritting her teeth as she describes the cold of country houses ('it is advisable to wear a little coat over your dinner dress'), or the dimness of country house guests ('It is tolerably safe to chatter away on such subjects as The Toll of the Road'). 'It is well known all over the world that the English, as a nation, take their pleasures sadly', she wrote in her article about point-to-points, meaning it about a good deal else besides. When, in *Highland Fling*, Nancy's hero says that Paris is 'the only place where he had known complete well-being', he is speaking for what Nancy herself had started, dimly, to realise.

In fact there is real disenchantment in *Highland Fling*. The dynamic of the book lies in the clash between youth and age, Bright Young Things and Blimps: the plot takes a small band of languid Londoners and sets them among a hunting, shooting and fishing house party in a Scottish castle. It is a promising idea, but the satire is all over the place. The young characters are actually less attractive than the codgers. This is probably because, deep inside herself, Nancy didn't like them much either.

She shows us, for example, the marriage of a smart, impoverished young couple – Walter and Sally Monteath – who despite Walter's careless infidelities are absolute soulmates. This could be real and interesting, but Walter is so fatally charmless that it is impossible to care. When he says, of his new baby, that he wants to call it Morris because 'we might get one free for an advertisement', it is clear that his creator is trying to be cynical. But the effect is more cynical than Nancy realises; depressingly cynical, as only young people like Walter can be, when they are both horribly confident and hopelessly at sea. Never trust the teller, trust the tale: beneath the remorseless high spirits, this book has an odd, bleak sense of dislocation. English society, declaims one of the characters, has 'no sex or brain left, only nerves and the herd instinct'. Nancy may not have known quite what she meant by this, may have thought she was being merely daring, but within the desire to shock there is a germ of confused sincerity.

Of course *Highland Fling* was received, at the time, very much as a romp: 'an excellent antidote to care or a railway journey', said the *TLS*, kindly. Nowadays, the book is fascinating in relation to Nancy's later work, for in it her real self is overlaid with attitudes: those of the iconoclastic young with whom she had little empathy. Like an elegant woman who feels obliged, in order to be modish, to dress herself in ripped jeans and Converse trainers, so Nancy writes, in *Highland Fling*, that the statues of great men should be 'put where they belong – in the Chamber of Horrors – thus serving the cause both of Art and of Morals'. As if she believed anything of the kind –! But she does not, as yet, have a clue what else she should be saying or thinking. She writes of her heroine, Jane, that 'her brain was like a mirror, reflecting the thoughts and the ideas of her more intelligent friends and the books that she read', and this was utterly true of Nancy: her book is a queasy cocktail of cut-price Waugh and bargain-basement Wodehouse, topped off with quotes from people whose remarks sounded witty at a party but on the page look downright daft.

Yet within the impenetrable maze that is *Highland Fling* are faint gleams of the writer that Nancy would become: the one who did the most daring thing of all, threw off all other influences in order to see and think entirely for herself. As the *TLS*, almost twenty years on and with deceptively simple understanding, would put it in a review of *Love in a Cold Climate*: 'She writes about things clearly as they appear to her to happen: not about things which might happen if human nature were altogether different; or things described through a fog of verbal obscurity. In doing this she does no small service to the contemporary English novel . . .'

Towards the end of *Highland Fling*, there is one of the first examples of this Mitfordian perception. It comes after Jane attends a private view of paintings by her fiancé Albert (the book's unintentionally idiotic hero). Jane has been, or so she says to herself, in a torment of anxiety lest the event be a humiliating failure for him. But when, instead, it is a raging success, she finds herself in a despairing temper: 'she, instead of being his one real friend, the guiding star of his life, would become its rather dreary background.' Now this is authentic Nancy: unexpected, caustic, utterly true, somehow benevolent in her take on human folly. Even as a girl she knew about people, and about the funny little things that bring them to literary life: she knew, for instance, that lovers do not always behave generously towards each other, that when they should delight in each other's happiness they find that they are far more worried about how it will affect *them* – that they are, in fact, deeply put out. 'I couldn't feel more jealous . . . if it were another woman', says Jane, when Albert's painting *The Absinthe Drinker* is bought by the Tate. How clever that is, and how beautifully Mitford too.

In her second novel, *Christmas Pudding*, published in 1932, the good things are more apparent still. She had begun the book very soon after finishing *Highland Fling*, which left her little time to think where she might have gone wrong or might improve; she simply got on with it, which was the best possible thing to do.

Christmas Pudding suffers from much of the same silliness as her first novel, and many of the same grievances are aired. London is portrayed as a faintly dreary place, with whose rain-grey streets, gracelessness and sexlessness, Nancy was evidently tired. But the country, which is to say the world of Swinbrook, comes across as no better: 'Nobody knows how horrible it is to live in the country always, you might just as well be in prison', she writes, a pretty straightforward *cri de coeur*. A country house dance is described as 'in no way a riot of joyous and abandoned merriment . . . the flower of Gloucestershire man and maidenhood climbed into their Morris Cowleys and drove away'. Later, this kind of thing would be rendered with clear-eyed affection, with a writerly love and without the need for scorn, but in 1931 Nancy was too close to it all for that.

And yet she gives us, in this novel, the first properly Mitfordian character: Amabelle Fortescue, an ex-prostitute of wit and style, who wears her wisdom as easily as her smart clothes, so much so that – as with her creator – it hardly seems like wisdom at all. 'The trouble is', she says, 'that people seem to expect happiness in life. I can't imagine why, but they do. They are unhappy before they marry, and they imagine to themselves that the reason of their unhappiness will be removed when they are married. When it isn't they blame the other person, which is clearly absurd. I believe that is what generally starts the trouble.' It is as if Nancy, by creating Amabelle, has found a way to bring her writing closer to its natural home. Amabelle reads like the older Nancy talking to her youthful self, and she makes it clear that Nancy's real empathy was with the sophisticated middle-aged, not the shakily arrogant young.

Nancy seems to sense, in *Christmas Pudding*, how much better her life would be if she no longer had to pretend that it was all a relentless hoot, or that she would find love among the strutting dandies of SW1. She sees, in her book, the theatrical idiocy of her young hero, Paul, and his passion for a ghastly girl whom everyone hates ('he thought himself very much in love'). She sees the hilarity of a pompous civil servant throwing himself at the feet of clever old Amabelle ('"I tell you, you have made life very sad for me, Amabelle" – "Dear Michael", said Amabelle, stifling a yawn'). She sees the bravery of Sally when Walter – back, and still unfaithful – stays out all night heaven knows where ('"He must be having a gorgeous time" – "Poor darling Sally", said Amabelle. "I must say she does behave well on these occasions".') Nancy was beginning to understand that marriage is a solution of a kind in women's lives, and yet almost never the solution that they think it will be. She was realising, too, something very important about love: that most people take it both far too lightly and far too seriously. 'It's a funny thing that people are always quite ready to admit it if they've no talent for drawing or music, whereas everyone imagines that they themselves are capable of true love, which is a talent like any other, only far more rare.'

It was as if Nancy was trying to work it all out for herself, this question that preoccupied her of how to live happily with – or without – love. It would always fascinate her: even her historical biographies are profoundly engaged with it, with the nature of Voltaire's love for Madame du Châtelet or Louis XV's for Madame de Pompadour. In *Christmas Pudding*, however, it was her own heart that she was excavating. And she was doing so with a truthfulness which she could not, yet, admit into her life. Like her essentially adolescent novel, she was still stuck in the world of her youth, even though neither of them really wanted to be there any more. But there was a very good reason for it, all the same. The reason was Hamish St Clair-Erskine; the first love of Nancy's life.

Hamish is partly to be thanked for the fact that Nancy began writing at all. She wanted money to be able to go about with him, occasionally to lend him – he was four years younger than she, a student at Oxford with wasteful habits – or, as she wrote to Mark Ogilvie-Grant in 1930, to save towards her marriage: 'Evelyn says don't save it, dress better & catch a better man. Evelyn is always so full of sound common sense.'

And Evelyn was right. Hamish was a disaster for Nancy. His effect upon her books was pervasive and entirely deleterious – without his presence in them, they would both be a hundred times better – and his effect upon her life was not much better. He was fatally immortalised as Albert (Memorial) Gates in *Highland Fling* and as Bobby Bobbin in *Christmas Pudding*; in each incarnation, he is notable for his stunning lack of likeability. Touchingly and obviously, Nancy thinks that she is giving her lucky, lucky reader a delicious taste of the person she loves. Albert, however, is a rude and humourless aesthete with orange trousers and a passion for Victoriana, while Bobby is a wretchedly precocious Etonian, mercenary and manipulative and, as he is told, 'a worldly little beast' ('Yes, aren't I? It does pay so much better'). 'I must say', Amabelle tells a silly young couple, hell-bent upon doomed marriage, 'that it would be much easier, more to your mutual advantage and eventual happiness, if you could bring yourselves to part now and lead different lives'; and one can only agree. But that kind of sense is never something that lovers want to hear. Nancy was no exception, even when it was her own self who was telling her.

The real Hamish must – surely – have had more charm than Albert and Bobby, albeit the hard, young, insouciant kind of charm that impresses at Eton and Oxford and then evaporates. He was, perhaps, what Nancy half wanted to be, someone in tune with their own youth, with all the dismissive confidence that this brings. He was also a member of a rather grand family – second son of the Earl of Rosslyn – whose Catholicism (which, in its snobbish English form, Nancy would later find very hard to take seriously) was no doubt in the full-of-itself *Brideshead* tradition. His school contemporary James Lees-Milne left an impressionistic, vital yet hollow portrait of a boy with 'the most enchanting looks although not strictly handsome, mischievous eyes, slanting eyebrows . . . slight of build, well dressed, gay as gay, always, snobbish however, and terribly conscious of his nobility'. Hamish was, continued Lees-Milne, 'shallowly sophisticated, lithe of mind [and] a smart society figure'; he 'loved being admired'.

'Gay as gay', not to put too fine a point on it, is the unconsciously significant phrase. For Hamish was homosexual, through and through. He had been present at Eton on the famous night when a handful of the smartest boys got drunk with Tallulah Bankhead then – it is implied – slept with her; but Hamish would probably not have partaken even of such a woman. Of course Nancy got on well with homosexuals, and very likely it was the gay in Hamish to which she was responding; unfortunately, and mysteriously, she seems to have thought that their love was of the heterosexual kind. Jonathan Guinness, in *The House of Mitford*, makes the very good point that Albert Gates would have worked much better as a character had he been portrayed as the homosexual that he obviously was. In depicting Hamish, Nancy had depicted a homosexual, but she had not realised it; just as she failed to realise it about her lover in real life.

But then Hamish himself seems never to have told her otherwise. He did, at one point certainly, say that 'he didn't think he would ever feel up to sleeping with a woman', but apparently in such a way as to leave the question open (Nancy went whining with this to Evelyn Waugh, who then 'explained to her a lot about sexual shyness'; which would only have encouraged her to wait and hope). Oddly enough, the basic dishonesty between Hamish and Nancy meant that their courtship dragged on far longer than many 'normal' ones would do.

From 1928 to 1933 they kept up a charade that prevented what might otherwise have been a fond and delightful friendship.

So what *was* Nancy thinking of? Her own brother had had an affair with Hamish at Eton and warned her off him; but she either didn't listen, or failed to understand what he was telling her. Yet she was surrounded by men like Brian Howard, Robert Byron, Mark Ogilvie-Grant, Tom Driberg – how could she have failed to grasp the fact that Hamish was, according to John Julius Norwich, 'as gay as a coot'? 'Nobody could have kidded themselves that Hamish was straight,' he says. 'Nancy wasn't that innocent. She was just a terrible picker.' Her sister Deborah disagrees: 'I don't think she understood – you know, those days, I don't think she knew he was queer. I doubt it very much, because otherwise why would she have said she was engaged to him? I'm sure she didn't. You've no idea of the difference – it wasn't like now. A girl brought up as she was, totally innocent. Why should girls ever know such things? She learned about homosexuals later on, no doubt. I think so. And you know the subject of sex then wasn't like it is now, the only thing that is thought of and talked of.'

And yet – Nancy was surely *not*, by that time, completely innocent. She had been brought up to be, but the circle in which she now moved would have enlightened her quickly enough. Perhaps part of the problem was that so many of the men she knew (Waugh, Tom) had homosexual inclinations yet slept with women; even so, there was a hell of a difference between a wobbling Charles Ryder and an upfront Anthony Blanche. And Nancy did apparently understand this. 'I've just been lunching with your mama', she wrote to Mark Ogilvie-Grant in 1930, '& inadvertently gave her a letter of yours to read in which a lift boy is described as a Driberg's delight. "What *is* a Driberg's delight? Dear Mark has such an amusing gift for describing people!"' More to the point, Nancy was always attracted to Robert Byron – 'I would have liked to have married [him]', she wrote to Jessica in 1971 – but knew very well that this was a non-starter. The conclusion, therefore, is that it was *Hamish* who was responsible for Nancy's absurd predicament. Robert Byron would never have allowed her to drag on in a state of pointless hope; Hamish seems to have done exactly that, advancing and retreating in a sinister little dance, for reasons that can only be guessed at. Did he like playing the role of Nancy's lover in the eyes of the world? Was he unwilling to admit, even to himself, that he was incapable of fulfilling this role? Did he fear ending an amusing relationship? Was he impelled by a kind of manipulative sadism? All of these, perhaps; Hamish was very young and uncertain beneath his aristocratic, peacock assurance. Strongest motive of all, however, was probably a willingness on his part just to let everything drift, which it therefore did for five years, in and out of a state of unofficial 'engagement' that must have later struck Nancy as quite absurd[27].

But if Hamish let things be, Nancy undoubtedly drove them along. One feels for her, reading her letters from that time: for her lack of assurance, which could not deal with the same thing in Hamish; for her almost repellent eagerness; for the naïvety that lay beneath her new-found worldliness. She would always do, she was living in a world of her imagination, but without the foundations of adult realism that would later underpin it. 'I've got a job offered to write a weekly article for £3 a week', she wrote to Mark Ogilvie-Grant in 1930, '& I keep putting off & putting off but can't start this evening as I've just spent the day in Oxford with you know who & that always stops me working. He's going to Canada in March for ever [he didn't of course], & we're both so unhappy about it specially me, isn't one's life perfect hell, that beastly old Harry [Hamish's father] has found a job for him . . . which looks as though he'll be able to support me & our 5 children jolly soon doesn't it.' One can wonder what Mark made of this; he surely only recognised his own predilections in Hamish, but whatever he said or thought would have made no difference to Nancy (Tom was the person whose opinion she most respected and she had completely ignored him). No – she was on a high-speed train, smiling brightly into the roaring wind, utterly incapable of jumping off.

Yet her early mentions of Hamish are perfectly normal. She describes to Tom, for example, a house party at Nina Seafield's in September 1928: 'Nina, Mark and Hamish are civilised, so am I & so are you.' By June 1929, the tone has changed, and another letter to Tom makes it clear that she is dangling on Hamish's pointed little hook. 'Hamish *was* funny yesterday . . . he had 5 glasses of brandy & crème de menthe (on top of sherry etc) & then began to analyse himself. He said, "The best of *me* is that I can talk Homer to Maurice[28] just as well as Noël Coward to you, in fact I am clever enough to amuse everybody."' This brief, grim taste of Hamish is pure Bobby Bobbin, but Nancy's critical faculty – usually so acute – had fled the scene.

'I do worship that child', the letter ends. An interesting aside, as it has been suggested (by Diana, for one) that Nancy's love for Hamish was essentially maternal. There is something of mummy in the way she describes how she 'curled Hamishes hair with tongs, he looked more than lovely'; or the way she discusses him with his real mother, the two of them shaking their heads over his hopeless behaviour. 'I had a perfectly heartbroken letter from Lady Rosslyn', she wrote to Mark in April 1930, '. . . saying that Hamish is going to the bad as fast as he can, can't you advise me what can be done? So in a white heat I took my pen & said "The bottom of all this is *Oxford* – Hamish at Oxford doesn't lead one day of ordinary normal life – these parties which are incessant etc etc."' Again this is slightly painful to read: its pseudo-mature tone, the self-important delusion that Hamish is a boyish riddle just waiting to be solved by his saviour. And a photograph of Nancy and Hamish together does indeed give the strange impression of a young woman with a wayward grown-up son. But the deeper impression, from the letters and events of this bizarre love affair, is that *neither* of them had made it out of the nursery. Nancy may have indulged or scolded – 'awful the way everyone treats me as Hamish's nanny isn't it'[29] – but this was simply the rôle into which she was forced: theirs was a kindergarten romance, on both sides.

And that seems to have been what she wanted. One sees this, sometimes, with highly intelligent but emotionally immature women. They deliberately hurl themselves into relationships that have no basis in truth. It is as though they prefer to love in the sphere of imagination; which would be fair enough, except that their feelings tend to move, painfully, into the sphere of reality. It is true to say, as John Julius Norwich does, that Nancy was 'a bad picker'. It is also true to say, as Diana does, that 'quite a lot of women do fall for homosexuals. And of course, if they do, it's just very sad.' But the real question, surely, is *why* Nancy would have done such a thing? She met hundreds of men. It was not love at first sight with Hamish, as her letter of September

1928 makes clear. But her feelings developed and, as is so often the case with 'love', she decided to urge them onwards. The fact that they were continually thwarted – not just by Hamish himself, but by both the Rosslyns and the Redesdales, who thought the whole affair a destructive nonsense – naturally intensified them; to such a pitch that, in February 1931, Nancy wrote to Mark Ogilvie-Grant saying: 'I tried to commit suicide by gas, it is a lovely sensation just like taking anaesthetic so I shan't be sorry any more for schoolmistresses who are found dead in that way, but just in the middle I thought that Romie[30] who I was staying with might have a miscarriage which would be disappointing for her so I got back to bed & was sick.' The absurdity of this suicide attempt ('The gas story is quite true, it makes Robert laugh so much') does not alter the fact that Nancy's unhappiness must have been real, although Amabelle Fortescue would undoubtedly have said that it was not real at all, and she would have been quite right.

But this sort of 'love' was what Nancy had chosen; and yes, one does choose, in a way. She had listened to a proposal from Sir Hugh Smiley while, at a nearby table in the Café de Paris, her little-boy lover sat watching and giggling – not wanting her himself, but not wanting her to do better elsewhere – and at the end of the evening she left to go to a nightclub with Hamish. This is not to say that Hugh would have made her happy. The point is that she chose, instead of him or someone like him, a man who could never make a husband. She called it love, of course she did. She rationalised her feelings in letters, usually to poor Mark Ogilvie-Grant (with Tom, she would not have been able to sustain the illusion): 'if anybody was ever worth a struggle it is Hamish because you know that underneath that ghastly exterior of Rosslyn charm etc he is pure gold, at least I think so, in fact I'd bank everything on it', she wrote in 1930, and was still banging on in this deluded vein in 1932: 'Hamish's character is so much improved, we travelled from Scotland in a 3rd class sleeper with 2 commercial travellers overhead & he never murmured once! He is a *sweet* angel isn't he!!!' Meanwhile the Earl of Rosslyn ('Harry') would try to send Hamish abroad, or the 'engagement' would be broken off, or it would be started up again, and in effect nothing really happened except that Nancy remained trapped: an adult whirling faster and faster on a child's merry-go-round.

It stopped, suddenly, in June 1933. Hamish realised that it had to. He did Nancy the greatest possible favour, but he did it with cruelty. It is a little surprising to learn that he fought with great bravery in Italy during the war; the manner in which he ended the relationship with Nancy was cowardly. He was young and, of course, probably panic-stricken.

He took the simplest and most dishonest way out and pretended to be engaged to another woman (this mythical fiancée was the sister of a man named Philip Dunn, who had just become engaged to Hamish's own sister, Mary). He had not intended to tell Nancy directly, but to telephone Diana and allow her to relay the message. Diana was by then living in a little house in Eaton Square – 'The Eatonry' – where she had set up as Mosley's mistress. Nancy visited often, but Hamish might have missed her had he not, unfortunately for him, rung up on the day before Diana's divorce proceedings. Feeling that their sister needed support, Nancy, Pamela and Unity had gone to stay at the house. Therefore when the telephone call came for Mrs Guinness from Mr St Clair-Erskine, it was Nancy who leapt to the receiver: to be told that Hamish was to marry Kit Dunn.

She took the story at face value. She also, heartbreakingly, tried to stay in Hamish's good books, after a scene at Diana's house in which she attacked him mercilessly (and justifiably). In her last letter to him, she wrote:

I can't sleep without saying I am so sorry & miserable that I was unkind to you just now . . .

Because I must explain to you that if you had told me you were engaged to Tanis, or Sheila Berry, I could never never have made that dreadful scene. Please believe me. I should have been unhappy for myself certainly but happy for you & as I love you better than myself I would have overcome my own feelings for your sake . . .

You see, I knew you weren't *in love* with me, but you are in love so often & for such tiny spaces of time. I thought that in your soul you loved me & that in the end we should have children & look back on life together when we are old. I thought our relationship was a valuable thing to you & that if you ever broke it you would only do so in order to replace it with another equally valuable. But that isn't so, & that is what I find intolerable.

Please understand me. Please think of me with affection always & never never blame me for what I may become without you. Don't think of me as a selfish & hysterical woman even if I appeared so tonight.

God bless you & make her be kind to you. I shall pray always for your happiness . . .

It is unlikely that Nancy really felt such noble sentiments; how could she have done? Yet the dignity of her letter is such that it may have caused Hamish to feel shame. There is wisdom – 'I knew you weren't *in love* with me' – beneath the innocence; wisdom enough to make one think that Nancy would, after this, have breathed new air, written another book, learned from her mistake, *waited*. Not so. Barely a month later, she was engaged to a man named Peter Rodd. At the age of twenty-eight, she was off the merry-go-round at last.

CHAPTER 4

'I hope', wrote Evelyn Waugh to Nancy in 1933, 'that Mr Erskine will now disappear from your novels. But listen, I won't have you writing books about Rodd because that would be too much for me to bear.' Nancy had learned her lesson. She married Peter, but unlike Hamish he was not allowed to ruin her novels with his presence. What he did to her life was another story, and one that she told in more indirect ways.

It was an odd marriage, no question. It is hard to believe that she would have gone into it, had it not been a way of shoring up the fallout from Hamish. One never knows, of course, and at the start Nancy was bright with the joys of love: 'I am going to be married to a very divine person called Peter Rodd', she wrote to Debo, before the engagement was announced in July 1933. Then, in August, to Mark Ogilvie-Grant: 'Well the happiness. Oh goodness gracious I am happy. You *must* get married darling [unlikely], everybody should this minute if they want a receipt for absolute bliss . . . And remember TRUE LOVE CAN'T BE BOUGHT. If I really thought it could I'd willingly send you £3 tomorrow.

'What I want to know is why nobody told me about Peter before.' In fact she had known him, slightly, before this effusion of love began to well in her, when she had eyes only for Hamish. Quite simply he made his move at the right time. According to Diana, Peter probably proposed just a week after the dreadful scene in Eaton Square. The story is that he had been proposing to women all evening and Nancy was the one who accepted him ('the sort of thing he was likely to do', says John Julius Norwich; 'he was probably blind drunk at the time'). Shortly afterwards he wrote her a letter implying that the proposal had been a joke. But by that time the engagement was announced and it was really too late for going back; not that either of them appeared to want to go back.

Of course Nancy didn't. Peter's proposal must have rained upon her like water on a parched throat. Her one chance of emerging from the humiliating Hamish débâcle with dignity intact was to swan off with another man, instantly and bindingly. There is nothing wrong with *me*, her engagement said to the world, I just moved on to a better prospect! 'It really was the classical thing of someone who is rejected, and then on the rebound they fall for somebody else,' says Diana. 'And it happened incredibly quickly, I mean before my very eyes.'

What else was Nancy to do but accept this bizarre proposal? She could hardly have drifted on as before; she was coming up to thirty. Nevertheless the marriage was a perversion of her true instincts, which – as so often happens – had become lost in a muddle of emotion. Nancy had turned down Sir Hugh Smiley because of her infatuation with Hamish, but she had also, deep down, been nervous of the whole idea of 'marriage' for its own sake. 'Nannies, cooks, the endless drudgery of house-keeping, the nerve-racking noise and boring repetitive conversation of small children' is how Fanny describes her (happily) married life in *The Pursuit of Love*. 'Alfred's not infrequent bouts of moodiness, his invariable complaints at meals about the pudding, the way he will always use my toothpaste and will always squeeze the tube in the middle . . .' Like Fanny, Nancy knew that there was more than this to marriage, yet something in her saw it as terrifying: the attraction of Hamish was partly that he kept the prospect in never-never land. And so the complicated irony was that because the marriage to Hamish didn't come off – was revealed to be the unreality that Nancy had subconsciously craved – she felt herself obliged to get into a marriage for real. Despite her free-spiritedness, she was in the end too conventional to shun that path altogether (and, perhaps, too closely surrounded by nubile sisters).

So the irruption of Peter on to the arid scene that was Nancy's life in June 1933 was an almighty relief; a solution, a way out, an ego-restorative; it would have been surprising had she not, as Charlotte Mosley put it, 'decided to fall in love with him'.[1] The whole story was a skewed fairytale for the depression years: the pity of it was that the man cast as prince should have been the Hon. Peter Rodd (or Prod, as Nancy called him; even lovers were lassooed by the Mitford tease). That was bad luck indeed.

Falling for Peter was, of course, far more about Hamish than about Peter himself. It was behaviour of which Amabelle Fortescue would have roundly disapproved ('People should take themselves off to Antarctica, or some other place cooling to the brain, and remind themselves that sudden new loves may act as salt, rather than balm, upon a wound' is the kind of thing that beacon of sense might have said). But Nancy was going to do whatever it took to feel better, and who can blame her? Part of her pleasure may have come from the idea that she was triumphing over Diana, in whose house she had been so ridiculed by Hamish, and who cut a scandalous figure at this time in her role as Sir Oswald Mosley's mistress. Diana was ostracised less than almost any other young woman would have been. She was simply too remarkable for other people to bear to leave her alone. But in 1933 she was in a very odd position. Mosley's wife Cynthia had died unexpectedly in May, yet this had not brought him closer to marriage with Diana; rather the reverse. It had thrown him into a turmoil of embarrassed guilt and back into the arms of his sister-in-law, Baba, with whom he had also been having an affair.[2] Really it was only Diana's formidable sense of purpose ('I was convinced of the permanency of what I had decided to do') and her Mitfordian freedom from *bourgeois* shame ('I never thought of it as risky, or as a great gamble') that allowed her to sail, beautiful brow clear, through this period of her life. And so Nancy – who four years earlier had been obliged to traipse behind Diana at her marriage to eligible Bryan – might have been forgiven for gloating a little, as she merrily made plans for her own wedding.

And Peter Rodd had qualities, albeit of the kind that showed best at early viewings. He was extremely good-looking, for a start. Everyone remembers this about him. Waugh, who was fascinated by him in an appalled sort of way (Basil Seal, the wayward chancer in *Black Mischief*, was very much based on Peter), wrote that he had 'the sulky, arrogant looks of the young Rimbaud'; and photographs show his physical glamour, the dashingly handsome face, the thick swoop of fair hair, the aspect of a chorister on his way to a brothel. Nancy, beside him, again seems to be with her grown-up son; she is at least as tall as he and looks older, although she was the same age. Presumably his appearance pleased her, or at least emphasised the fact that he was a catch (although her later passion for Gaston Palewski, whose face was like an unpeeled King Edward, showed that attraction for Nancy did not lie in good looks).

What she *did* like were good brains; and these Peter also had. He was not, like Hugh Smiley, 'blond and stupid', but blond and erudite. He went to Balliol (where he was apparently beaten up by Evelyn Waugh; why is not known), from where he was sent down for having a woman in his rooms after hours. His mind was exceptional, as it had to be then for Balliol. He could pick up a language in days, could retain facts to an encyclopaedic extent; in fact there was nothing he did not know. John Julius Norwich – who met Peter after the war – recalls, 'when I started writing my first book, which was about the Norman kingdom in Sicily, which nobody knew about at all – Prod knew everything. And where that came from . . . ? Because there were no books, certainly not in English, written about it.' Jessica Mitford – who liked Peter, not least because his politics leaned leftwards, remembered that the family used to call him 'the old Tollgater', because he knew everything about the tollgate system in England and Wales. He had given Lord Redesdale chapter and verse about tollgates in between asking for Nancy's hand. 'Talks like a ferret with his mouth sewn up', was David's judgment upon his future son-in-law, whom he nonetheless regarded as an improvement upon Hamish St Clair-Erskine.

This erudition of Peter's may have impressed Nancy, a woman always conscious of the gaps in her own learning. She may have enjoyed luxuriating in a sense of her lover's superiority (she would later, in *Madame de Pompadour*, express the view that 'in every satisfactory union it was the man who kept the upper hand'; not the sort of thing one is supposed to say, but not without its gritty little pearl of truth). But there was a downside to Peter's elite computer brain: it had no notion of when to switch itself off. 'He had', says Alexander Mosley, 'this awful habit of spilling out everything he knew.' Consequently the other thing that everyone remembers about him, besides his good looks, is that he was outstandingly boring. 'He was very handsome when he was young,' says Diana, 'but the incredible thing is that he was just such a bore. And you'd think she'd simply hate that.' Quite so: nothing, for Nancy, was worse than a crasher.

'I remember going to these nightclubs with him in Paris,' says John Julius Norwich, 'and you know when you're eighteen and someone asks you to go to a nightclub you're rather flattered, and this was a man of fifty. But then at five o'clock in the morning Prod was still telling me about the Normans in Sicily.'

In the first flush of love, however, nobody is boring. There was a converse quality to Peter, what Lord Norwich calls 'the rapscallion in him': his devil-may-care nonchalance about life, his gleaming confidence, his sexiness ('oh Prod was *extremely* heterosexual'). So perhaps he was not such a bore with Nancy: at least not at the start. In the novel that she wrote early in her marriage, *Wigs on the Green*, a character bearing a close resemblance to Peter is portrayed as enormous – if dangerous – fun: 'you are the only person I've ever met who makes me laugh all the time without stopping', says the girl who decides to marry him. One example of his humour – he was sent an invitation from von Ribbentrop to a party at the German embassy, and replied to it in Yiddish – has a distinctly Mitfordian flavour.

Above all, what Nancy probably felt was that Peter was carrying her off to a new life: an adventure and an escape. Not a life that would rob her of autonomy, put her in a different kind of trap, as Hugh Smiley's would have done, with its dinners full of guardsmen and its joke-free parties; but one that would allow her to blossom freely, as she so much longed to do. 'I think it's top-hole about you and Rodd and I foresee a very wild and vigorous life in front of you', wrote Evelyn Waugh. It was an affectionate blessing; yet in that 'wild and vigorous' there sounded a warning note, faint as the bailiff's knock when the champagne corks are being popped upstairs.

For there was a downside to the 'rapscallion' in Peter Rodd. He was, in fact, one of the world's great wastrels. 'Peter was a wild, wild man,' says Diana, echoing Waugh. It is unusual for a black sheep to manage the simultaneous feat of being a bore, but Peter was both. Nancy failed at first to see that her beloved lacked, as Debo puts it, 'the backbone that would make anybody a husband'. Had she waited before plunging in, even she might have been unable to ignore the signs, which were already grimly plentiful.

The sending down from Balliol was inauspicious, as were subsequent events. In the manner of the times, when unsatisfactory young men (like David Mitford) were foisted upon hapless foreign lands, Peter was packed off to work in a bank in Brazil. There he was eventually arrested for being destitute. He was sacked from a job in the City, then from *The Times* in Germany. Drink was the problem; but drink is always a symptom of a problem, and the real trouble with Peter was – what? His mysterious, restless self. It has been said, as with the Mitfords, that his upbringing was the cause of his troubles. Really, though, Peter simply was what he was: 'a wild, wild man'.

Which is not to say that his background didn't encourage the urge to rebel. His older brother, Francis, was a paragon of sense and success against whom Peter refused to measure himself, and to whom he had constantly to be grateful (it was Francis's position in the Foreign Office that helped to bail Peter out of overseas holes). The Rodd parents, too, embodied an impregnable righteousness that sent him off as far as possible in the opposite direction. Lord Rennell of Rodd was a diplomat who, in 1908, became the Ambassador to Rome. He was a perfect, courteous gentleman of the Lord Montdore variety (described in *Love in a Cold Climate* as 'a wonderful old man, in short, who nothing common ever did or mean. My cousin Linda and I, two irreverent little girls whose opinion makes no odds, used to think that he was a wonderful old fraud'). Meanwhile Lady Rennell, a forceful, eccentric presence whom Nancy viewed with fascination and dislike, bore a distinct similarity to Lady Montdore. Although rich, she was peculiar about money (in 1936 she gave Nancy 'a bath salt jar with no bath salts for Xmas'), and she kept Peter very short ('Oh you *always* manage to keep alive somehow', Nancy reported her saying to him). This may not have been a good idea. Certainly he would have wasted what he was given, but deprivation fired in him a sense of grievance, a desire to become as bad as his parents believed him to be. Meanwhile his father sighed – 'all the rest of the family are only joy to us' – and his mother huffed and puffed, and neither had the least idea how to deal with the renegade in their midst. 'I think he was the despair of his father and mother, and his older brother,' says Diana.

Peter, as much as Nancy, craved the idea of marriage. Lost soul that he was, he perhaps saw in her a solution; just as she did in him. Here was a pretty woman, a clever companion, who took him seriously and loudly proclaimed how wonderful it was to be in love with him, whose good humour may (wrongly) have seemed like maturity. There must have been *something* to turn that sudden impulse of his into an engagement announcement in the *Daily Telegraph*. Although it may have been something as cruelly simple as the judgment of his sister-in-law: '. . . marriage is the only thing he has not tried'.

No doubt it is significant that he did not, until the formal announcement, see fit to inform his parents that he was to marry the Hon. Miss Mitford. Whether this reluctance was about his relationship with them, or with her, or with both, who can say. The sainted Rennells were not especially overjoyed ('The whole thing has its inexplicable side', said Lord Rennell, in his Montdore idiom, 'and it worries me not a little') but this may have been because Nancy had no money: it was a fight between the two sets of parents as to which could be the most tight-fisted. But Peter, by July 1933, was suddenly galvanised by the new turn that his life had taken. In his swooping way he too decided to be in love and began to deluge Nancy with letters, including one which read: 'My darling I am glad that this all started as a joke . . . I should like to see your head lying on your pillow. This Peter who loves only you.'

The wedding was postponed twice, but finally took place at St John's, Smith Square, on 4 December 1933, when Nancy had just turned twenty-nine. It must have been a pretty affair, despite the wintry day: the details given in *The Times* paint a picture delicately suffused with Nancy's impeccable taste. 'The bride . . . wore a gown of white chiffon, trimmed with narrow frills of the same material' (this dress was a present from kind Bryan Guinness); 'her tulle veil was held in place with a wreath of gardenias' and she 'carried a bouquet of white gardenias and roses'. Peter looked remarkably good in his tails. Eleven pages, including Diana's tiny sons Jonathan and Desmond, followed in white satin.

A reception was then held at Rutland Gate (let at the time, but repossessed for the occasion): two ambassadors attended, as well as two duchesses (Marlborough and Sutherland) and a couple of aesthetes (the poet and critic Sir John Squire, the painter Clive Bell). Many of Nancy's old friends were there, including Mary Milnes-Gaskell, Nina Seafield, Mark Ogilvie-Grant and Hugh Smiley, no less, now married to Cecil Beaton's sister. Evelyn Waugh was not present: he had just begun proceedings for the annulment of his first marriage. *The Times* informed its readers that 'the honeymoon is being spent in Rome, and the bride travelled in a dark green woollen coat and skirt with a duck-egg-green jumper'. It sounded idyllic: Peter and the new Mrs Rodd were to have use of an apartment in the Palazzo Giulia, a beautiful hangover from Lord Rennell's days as ambassador. The eternal city and eternal bliss, no less.

At first, it did sound blissful. 'Why do people say they don't enjoy honeymoons?' Nancy wrote to Unity. 'I am adoring mine.' With awful immediacy, however, a strained note crept into the song of gaiety. A postcard sent to Mark Ogilvie-Grant is of course ironic: 'I am having a *really dreadful* time, dragging a badly sprained ankle round major & minor basilicas & suffering hideous indigestion from eating goats' cheese. However I manage to keep my spirits up somehow. NR. And all my shoes hurt.' But it is not the tone that one would expect from a brand new bride, wandering through one of Europe's most glorious cities, arm in arm with her best beloved. It hints – to say the least – at real and instant dissatisfaction. It conveys an image of Nancy and Peter, aimless, tired and slightly bored, she longing to get out of her shoes, he longing for a drink, connecting with neither Rome nor each other.

It later transpired – uncharacteristically, Nancy confessed it to Peter's sister, Gloria – that the couple had spent much of their honeymoon arguing. Peter was spending money like it was going out of fashion and showing few signs that this, for him, was any sort of new life at all. Thereafter Nancy never felt about Rome in the way she did the other great European cities. 'Surely no other capital city can be quite so uninhibited about its underclothes or allow them to hang like flags across the streets', she wrote in 1952, in an essay – 'Rome is Only a Village' – which reads almost like a revenge upon the place. Understandably, in the circumstances. How disillusioned she must have been there, as she approached the new year of 1934.

She struggled against such feelings, as anyone would – Nancy more than most – and when she returned to England her will to happiness asserted itself. She remembered what marriage had brought her: a life of her own at last. It wasn't total independence, as the couple relied on a small allowance from both sets of parents (slightly uncomfortable this; she and Peter were getting on in years to be living off handouts). Nonetheless a letter to Mark Ogilvie-Grant in January 1934 – 'I am awfully busy learning to be a rather wonderful old housewife' – reeks of restored good cheer.

The Rodds had moved to Strand-on-the-Green, a small stretch of intense prettiness, edged with smart little dolls' houses, that borders the Thames just beyond Kew Bridge. Nancy's home, Rose Cottage, was on the road behind the river and was actually rather plain, a dark pink square with over-large windows, a walled garden and 'a pig & two parrots over the porch'. It was far from the world of Rutland Gate and Eaton Square, and heaven knows what Lady Montdore would have thought. 'We are going to be damned poor you see', Nancy wrote to Mark. But with his help, and much enthusiasm and taste, she gave her first home an air of spare and simple chic. 'That little house was really exquisite,' Debo later recalled; 'there wasn't an ugly thing in it.' Like her mother, Nancy had a real talent for giving ease and beauty to her surroundings, even on a very short shoestring. 'She had', says Alexander Mosley, 'a great gift for *mise en scène.*'

And she enjoyed playing at being a wife. Very nice it must have been for her, and a very attractive sight she must have been for her neighbours, this slim alert figure full of smiles. Merrily she busied herself finding cheap pieces of furniture to set alongside her Sheraton desk, and walking her beloved bulldogs, Milly[3] and Lottie, along the towpath. She had a servant, of course, to spare her the agonies of picking up underclothes ('I think housework is far more tiring and frightening than hunting', says Linda in *The Pursuit of Love*, when she is married to the impoverished Christian, 'and yet after hunting we had eggs for tea and were made to rest for hours, but after housework people expect one to go on just as if nothing special had happened'). Peter was working in a bank again; things looked better, as if Rome had been a bad dream. Nancy acquired a little car but, as she wrote (a little over-enthusiastically?) to Unity, 'I go less and less to London as I *love* it here so much'. This was not a marriage as Diana's had been and Deborah's would be; as Nancy's might have been, had she accepted Hugh Smiley. It was more what we would think of as modern, the stuff of one of our more upmarket colour supplements: the skinny stylish career woman, her delicious and faintly delinquent husband, their pert little dogs, the *jolie-laide* house in W4.

But this is image only. Beneath the sunlit surface of smart living on the cheap, of bridge parties reported in the *Evening Standard* ('a gay, light-hearted affair of the cheerful kind that hasn't happened much since the days of the fabulous past', a bit effusive for a night of card-playing) – beneath all this, what was really going on? The rogue factor was Peter. What were the Rodds' feelings for one another? How did their relationship develop after that uneasy honeymoon? Nancy's mixture of volubility and reserve makes it difficult to say.

Perhaps the most striking thing is how much less she writes about Peter than she ever did about Hamish. He appears occasionally in her letters, as an acquaintance would, and is usually doing separate things from his wife: 'Peter went to a cocktail party at the Lancasters . . .'; 'Peter didn't enjoy his cruise much as they had such bad weather . . .' Lottie the bulldog gets more coverage from Nancy than her husband does: 'Lottie is away being married – oh how sweet. I long for the puppies – her husband is an angelic dog.'

This reticence in itself is enough to arouse suspicion. Had Nancy been happy with her husband, had he also been an angelic dog, she would have said so: happiness was the theme to which she would always, if possible, return in her letters. Conversely, had she been disappointed, she would have kept quiet about it. That was her nature. Therefore one assumes that all was *not* as she would have wished it. She had wanted to be in love with Peter, she had wanted to marry him, but the reality was not what she had expected. And this was not, as with Hamish, a child's infatuation: it was a grown-up situation. She probably despaired about it, behind her resolute veneer.

'She took it very seriously,' says Debo. 'Because you know brought up as we were, marriage was pretty important.' (As late as 1952, when Peter was long out of her life, Nancy praised the undergraduates of the Cambridge Union for using her married name: 'The boys are heaven . . . very polite (Mrs Rodd, no nonsense about Mitford).[4]) Debo continues: 'I mean for instance when Diana and Bryan got divorced, it was like the end of the world. So I think Nancy would have gone into it really meaning it – and I think she was a very staunch person you know, she did her best, but nobody could have coped with Peter. Not as a serious character, not for ever.'

Within a short time, Peter had left his banking job. He had done so in expectation of something that would eventually be much better, but which did not come to pass. 'What you say about Peter has rather upset me,' wrote Lord Rennell to Francis, rattled beneath his diplomat's poise; 'I was under the belief that he had a definite engagement with Hamburger and was to begin on £500 a year. It was on the strength of this assurance that I went into the question of settlements and discussed the whole matter with Lord Redesdale who was equally convinced that he had a definite undertaking from H. I am now afraid that as usual the whole story was built on a mere possibility without any substance.' The Rennells were clearly panicked by the idea that they might be tapped for more money. 'What on earth have they got to live on except the allowance he gets from us', boomed her ladyship, not quite accurately as a good deal of the Rodds' income came from Nancy: her writing, and dividends from the stocks and shares she had bought with the money from her first two books. All in all they had about £500 a year. Even in the 1930s this wasn't much, and certainly it was not ideal that Peter had lost the chance to double it. Before the announcement of her engagement, Nancy had said that the wedding would not take place if there were not enough money to live on properly ('if we can get some we shall marry and if we can't we shan't'[5]). It had not occurred to her that, once in the marriage, things would get much worse.

Her father-in-law expressed real concern, beneath his cautiousness. 'One feels a little scared about the young couple and I am wondering whether their house is healthy or whether they get enough to eat and keep warm . . . They do not tell us much, but one cannot help realising that since he gave up £600 a year on an over optimistic hope of a better job it must be rather difficult for them to get along on the remainder . . . I should like to be reassured that these repeated attacks of flu are not the result of inadequate resources.'

If the attacks of flu were Peter's, they were probably an excuse for not getting up and doing anything. But there was a sense, in Lord Rennell's words, of something not at all right within the Rodd household, as if beneath the façade lay a creeping squalor. The bailiffs were more than once at the door (Nancy deployed Mitfordian insouciance, offering cups of tea and blithe smiles, although what she felt is anyone's guess). 'Peter was so bad about money,' says Diana, 'because when Nancy made a little money he just used to borrow it from her. I don't know whether he gambled – I just don't think he ever had a proper job.' What he did was continue to drink heavily, and go on benders in nightclubs. Quite early on, he began to see other women. It is impossible to know when exactly he was first unfaithful, but certainly by 1935 – after little more than a year – he was declaring love for the married Mary Sewell (also a novelist, and the daughter of Edwin Lutyens).

However she might have tried to be realistic and French about it all, this would have been agonising to a woman as proud and romantic as Nancy. In the first two years of her marriage, whilst she was bustling with determined good cheer around Strand-on-the-Green, her husband had denied her everything that she could reasonably have expected of him: love, support, fidelity. She was forced to grow up in ways she would not have dreamed. Loyalty, and a desire not to admit that she had once again made a bad bet, demanded that she stick it out with Peter. But he was quite possibly the worst man she could have picked. All the things she wanted, like cheerfulness, stability, elegance, money, good behaviour, amusement – things which might have come her way through marriage, but which she found when she lived alone – were impossible to achieve with Peter. A different kind of woman (more managing, more experienced) might have forced him to hold down a job, turned a coolly blind eye to his debauches, kept him in some sort of line. Perhaps Mary Sewell might have done this, although being a successful mistress does not necessarily make one a successful wife. But she would probably have handled Peter better than Nancy did (certainly she got more joy out of him: she was said to remember him as a most tender lover). Nancy's smiling stoicism, desperate optimism, ineffectual sniping and essential lack of grasp upon her situation made her a hopeless wife to this hopeless man. She was far too good for him, and she was also not much good to him.

In fact it is hard to imagine Nancy living the reality of marriage. 'A girl must marry once. You can't go on being called Miss – Miss all your life, it sounds too idiotic', says a character in *Wigs on the Green*, written in 1934. It goes on: 'All the same, marriage is a great bore – chap's waistcoats lying about in one's bedroom, and so on. It gets one down in time.' Of course Nancy liked the idea of marriage, the status, the home-making side. And she believed, always, in the supreme importance of love. Yet at the same time she was not fitted for intimacy: one can scarcely picture the pristine Nancy sharing a bathroom with a man, or making love on the Aubusson, or wandering about semi-naked while Peter fastened a collar-stud. Always there is this sense of innate separateness, something both girlish and spinsterish, something hooked-and-eyed into rigid place. And Peter – like most husbands – would probably have felt easier with someone less bright and clever and unpractised, more consolingly womanly.

Quite soon, then, he was slipping out of the marriage, as he slipped out of everything: what had been a dream of something new and free had become a prison of unwanted responsibility. It was the pattern of his life, and one can't help but feel a little sorry for someone so gifted and so all at sea. Yet the humiliations and privations that he inflicted on his wife, out of sheer moral indolence, were unforgivable, and only intensified as the marriage went on. Harold Acton, whose dislike of Peter ('a superior con-man') leaps like a tiger off his fragrant pages, blames the failure of his life with Nancy on a simple inability to be faithful: 'Probably he was a natural philanderer who could not endure the marriage tie.' True though this is, philandering is a symptom of something deeper-rooted: either that a man doesn't care enough about his wife, or that he is restless about his life, or (as with Peter) both. Perhaps he would have liked to be faithful to Nancy? Perhaps she was unable to hold him? For whatever reason, the wild urge for the new and the free took a grip; and off he would go to the Savile Club for a booze-up, or to Mary Sewell's for some illicit sex, and the horrors of poverty and miserable matrimony would dissolve in a haze of pleasure. Pretty commonplace stuff, really – except that neither Peter nor Nancy were commonplace people.

In 1936 they moved back into London, possibly in an attempt at a new start. Peter was earning again, and the couple took a house in

Blomfield Road, near the canal at Maida Vale. Nowadays this is a serene oasis, in which multi-million-pound villas sit calm and unassailable around the water. Before the war it was rather raggedy, and the houses not considered particularly desirable ('It was one enormous red light district', according to John Julius Norwich. 'Brothel brothel brothel Nancy brothel brothel brothel – you know, all the way').

'Dear you should see this house,' Nancy wrote in November 1936 to Simon Elwes, the husband of her sister-in-law Gloria. 'You see everybody's houses are so pretty nowadays so I set out to try & make this as ugly as I could for a change & my goodness me I've succeeded.' Typical Mitfordian exaggeration; but with a tense, darting hilarity about it that hints at unhappiness.

Later in the letter she did more than hint. She liked Simon and his wife[6], and anyway was telling them what they already knew about the state of play *chez* Rodd. First she refers to their persistent money troubles: 'However, the boom. That's all Rodd says when I point out what a jolly new set of bailiffs we are acquiring.' Clearly Peter's job in the City was not solving all their problems (he may have stuck to it because it enabled him to meet Mary Sewell every day, both at lunch and in the evenings). Nancy knew all about this affair of Peter's, as did the Elweses: 'it's lovely being *in* London because now Rodd can go out with his girlfriend who has a spoon face & dresses at Gorringes & I can go to bed & this is fine for everybody's temper. Also I can go out with people like Raymond Mortimer and Willie [Somerset] Maugham who like the sound of their own voices punctuated by giggles, but who hate being told about the origin of toll-gates by Rodd. And all these things were more difficult at Rose Cottage.' This is written with bravery, and with the faith in jokes upheld, but it shakes with a kind of furious misery. It is as if she can't even trust herself to write Peter's name.

Nor was she always so stoical. At bridge parties attended by the Sewells, where Peter and Mary would smoulder at each other across the score-cards, Nancy's absurd trick was to stand up and faint; her husband would then carry her out of the room ('she's only trying to get attention') and return, metaphorically rubbing his hands, to his mistress. These hysterics were hardly the behaviour of the woman Nancy wanted to be. In her 1940 novel, *Pigeon Pie*, she describes her heroine, Sophia, sitting at a dinner whilst a vampish rival for her lover, Rudolph, 'droops her eyelids' at him; Sophia, cool as vichysoisse, simply waits it out. 'Women are divided into two categories', Nancy wrote in the book, 'those who can deal with the men they are in love with, and those who cannot. Sophia was one of those who can.'

By the time of *Pigeon Pie* it was really too late for Nancy to 'deal with' Peter. But Rudolph bears a certain resemblance to her tricky, sexy husband, and there was surely some retrospective wish-fulfilment in her conception of Sophia as a calm, controlling charmer. She knew full well that it was better not to faint at the bridge table. Diana would never have done such a thing. But Nancy, for all her restrained outward appearance, was a woman who felt things passionately; and although she was able to distance her emotions she always found it hard to deal with them.

So it is almost unbelievable that in 1936 – that grim and grinding year – she should have gone away to Normandy with Peter and the Sewells. The holiday was given an air of respectability by the presence of Jessica Mitford; but heaven only knows what the couples thought they were doing. It was a disaster for Nancy, who simply left Peter and Mary to it every night and went to bed ('She thinks nightclubs are boring', Decca wrote to Deborah, with a touchingly scathing innocence). A photograph from the time tells all anyone needs to know about where this marriage had got to. Nancy has a matronly arm around Peter's shoulder and a face like malt vinegar; he, meanwhile, looks unrelaxed and unrepentant, although aware that there is something to repent over. It is a stunningly miserable image, of a shrew and the man who has made her shrewish. One thinks of the breathless hope with which Nancy went into her life with Peter ('I am going to be married to a very divine person'), of the real and intense dedication that she made to her marriage, and one feels for her pointless sufferings.

She knew that husbands had mistresses. Her novels are full of that knowledge; many of her friends were living embodiments of it. But knowing about it is not the same as living through it. She could assume a kind of detachment when writing to the Elweses, but not when being taunted at the bridge table. The wisdom that she displayed about love in her books was often Nancy talking to herself, reasoning herself into adult acceptance of what was, in reality, hard and humiliating. Few philosophers are able to live by what they believe. Nancy – who, in her light and graceful way, was indeed a philosopher – became better at it than most, but not yet.

In her writing, the question that interested her was this: how to live a sensible and happy life while accepting, and embracing, the irrationalities of love. As a total romantic who nonetheless viewed the eighteenth century as the most perfect of all eras, this conundrum was bound to fascinate her; and it is the question that underpins almost all her books. Even her first two novels – plagued though they were by immaturity – are closely engaged with it. And by the time she had entered upon life with Peter Rodd, she knew far more of what she was talking about; as is clear from *Wigs on the Green*, the novel that she wrote in the first year of her marriage.

This book is known now, if it is known at all, for its timely parody of Fascism and the British Unionist Party. In 1934 Sir Oswald Mosley and his Blackshirts were moving towards the height of their influence, and Nancy saw a subject ripe for mockery. Yet despite the showiness of this theme, it is not the book's real focus. It simply takes its place within Nancy's wider view of human beings, their rather pitiful silliness, their irrepressible deviousness, their machinations, above all their touching egotism. *That* is what interests her, and is the sane and ordinary context into which she puts her political satire.

Of course it was the satire that got the book noticed, within the Mitford family at least, where – as will be seen – it caused quite a brouhaha. Outside, few people paid much heed to *Wigs on the Green*. But the book is fascinating now, to those who love Nancy's writing, because it shows such a marked development from the two novels that she wrote as a footloose girl. Here, for the first time, she appears in control of her material: she has an overview, an authorial distance. The book is no more than a pretty piece of marivaudage, apparently soufflé-light, but it is permeated by a cool and smiling cynicism that feels real rather than assumed. It also somehow feels connected to the fact of her marriage. It is perhaps surprising that Nancy began a book so soon – in the spring of 1934 – when one might have expected her to be lost in the bliss of her changed circumstances. The Rodds needed the money, so Nancy needed to write. But, although the book feels very different from what she wrote before, there is no sense that *Wigs on the Green* is suffused with the joys of love, sex, marriage and so on. Rather it is as if these things had blown the clouds away from Nancy's mind and left it assured, clean and a little distanced. Here, for example, is her heroine Poppy St Julien, considering whether she wants to hitch her divorced cart to Jasper Aspect, who bears no small resemblance to Peter Rodd: 'She was a good deal in love with Jasper, but not sure that she wanted to marry him. Certain aspects of his nature seemed far from satisfactory.' Which is an odd way for a bride of three or four months to be expressing herself.

Far from being all about Sir Ogre, as Nancy called her brother-in-law to be, *Wigs on the Green* is in fact wholly intrigued by Peter. It is dedicated to him, and much of it gives the odd impression of having been written by him, or at least by someone engrossed with the casual male viewpoint. Nancy's book is filled with bracing manly views on women; it is a very particular take on the pursuit of love. 'The great thing about women ... is that they have a passion for getting relationships cut and dried ... Oh! what maddening creatures', says Jasper. And then: 'The precious little thing likes to have a nice long cosy chat between nine and ten am, she doesn't realise that you, meanwhile, are shivering half-way up your landlady's staircase with an old woman scrubbing linoleum round your feet.' Jasper is a highly intelligent young man who chooses to be an upmarket sponger, and steals money out of women's handbags just as Peter did out of Nancy's: 'wives aren't expected to keep their husbands', says his lover Poppy, to which Jasper replies: 'I never could see why not. It seems so unfair.'

'Not at all. The least the chaps can do is to provide for us financially when you consider that women have all the trouble of pregnancy and so on.'

'Well, us boys have hang overs don't we? Comes to the same thing in the end.'

How did Nancy understand Peter so quickly and so thoroughly? Her portrayal is sympathetic, non-judgmental, attracted yet almost resigned; clear-eyed in a way that she never managed to be about Hamish. She describes Jasper's modus vivendi, living 'from one day to another, picking up by fair means or foul enough cash for the needs of the moment and being dragged out of the bankruptcy courts about once every three years by protesting relations': Lady Rennell would surely have nodded in recognition.

Nancy did not merely have a handle on her husband, but on her own situation. Why else would she have Jasper say, about a girl whom he hopes to marry, and whose engagement has just been broken off: 'In the case of Lady M. we have a powerful ally in the Rebound. Fantastic what a girl will do on the Rebound' –? That is Nancy laughing at herself, with all the unflinching charm of which she was capable. Was Peter willing to get the joke as well? Was he flattered? Or was he a little appalled by the adoring new wife who saw through him so easily?

There are other dry delights in *Wigs on the Green*, and there are some tremendous jokes. The aristocrats' asylum, 'Peersmont', which is run in the image of the House of Lords – and where a 'Toll of the Roads' bill is heard by the inmates – is worthy of Lewis Carroll. The authentic Mitford cocktail of robust sanity and sparkling delicacy – a half of Guinness topped with a crisp splash of Krug – is starting to pour forth with ease. What Nancy does not quite have yet is the assured benevolence that would later inform her writing: a realism that does not need to be cynical, a sense of the ridiculous that does not need to sneer. In *Wigs on the Green* this is starting to emerge, but there is still an edginess about her, as if she is confusing maturity with world-weariness. This, for example, is Poppy on whether she should leave her rich husband and marry Jasper: 'In a position in which many women would be weighing an old loyalty against a new passion, she found herself wondering whether it would be possible to smuggle her writing-table out of the house, should she decide to throw in her lot with Mr Aspect.' This slightly terrifying honesty, this cool understanding of female susceptibility is Nancy through and through; but there is something else – a desire to shock or even perhaps to hurt – that would later slip unregretted from her writing.

And was she trying to shock or to hurt when she used the political passions of her sisters Diana and Unity as material for her book? *They*, certainly, were far from happy about it. 'Peter says I can't put a movement like Fascism into a work of fiction *by name* and so I am calling it the Union Jack movement, the members wear Union

Jackshirts & their Lead is called Colonel Jack', Nancy wrote to Diana in November 1934 (one can imagine the reaction). By then the book was almost finished, but the letter – breezy and chock-full of niceness about Mosley – invited Diana 'to edit [it] before publication because although it is very pro-Fascism there are one or two jokes & you could tell better than I whether they would be Leaderteases'.

All very well, but by then the deed was done, and anyway it was Nancy's very breeziness that was the cause of the problem. Diana felt that a basic insult had been perpetrated upon Fascism by putting it into a comic novel. In fact an even greater insult was the dismissive way in which Nancy treats it: commentators give the impression that political satire sits plum in the middle of the book, like a dark and dangerous doberman, yet what strikes one is how unimportant it is all made to seem. This may be because some of the references to Fascism (specifically to Colonel Jack) were excised to placate Diana, but it is also a question of tone. Into Nancy's book goes Unity, reproduced to the life as Eugenia Malmains, a handsome young giantess with 'the aspect of a young Joan of Arc' and 'eyes like enormous blue headlamps'. She is pursued by Noël and Jasper, but her own sole passion is for declaiming 'Social Unionist' speeches on 'an overturned wash-tub on Chalford village green'. Meanwhile, as she rants on the sidelines, the book remains preoccupied with its good, sound, normal themes of love and money: company too frivolous, in the eyes of Nancy's sisters, for Fascism to consort with.

Because of this refusal to 'take fascism seriously', Nancy has been called politically naïve: as if the massiveness of the theme was beyond her, and she could only respond to it with mockery. Yet this is, one might say, the opposite of the truth. Nancy made fun of Fascism precisely because she *did* understand it. Beneath all the regimentation, the uniforms and the marching men, she perceived something innately silly. And she realised that taking away the trappings, planting Fascism squarely in the world of the Gloucestershire village green, where Eugenia denounces her nanny as the pacifist enemy and eats twopenny chocolate bars between orations, was the surest way to reveal this silliness. 'When you find schoolgirls like Eugenia going mad about something, you can be pretty sure that it is nonsense', says one of her characters.

And she was right: right to dismiss political extremism as the sort of behaviour that nanny would call showing off. She was right to show that, for all its exalted aims, most followers of Fascism were motivated by simple xenophobia; right to show the banality of the Nazi creed by giving this speech to Poppy: 'I'm sure Hitler must be a wonderful man. Hasn't he forbidden German women to work in offices and told them they need never worry about anything again, except arranging the flowers? How they must love him.' She was right, too, to show that Fascism was, for Unity, a glorious opportunity to validate her own oddity. Yet it is also true that Nancy's airy, ironic and civilised soul did not truly grasp the tumultuous passions that had been raised in Europe, and in her own family, by the political situation. She saw it all later, of course. But in 1934 she thought that it could be treated, like everything else, as a joke: this was not political naïvety, but it was a failure of imagination (does a Voltaire ever truly understand a Wagner?), a wrongful belief that rationality would triumph over a very certain kind of dark romance.

Most surprisingly – 'we were young & high spirited then and didn't know about Buchenwald'[7] – she and Peter had actually attended some of Mosley's meetings, including the famous Olympia rally of June 1934 ('Prod looked very pretty in a black shirt'). According to Diana, the Rodds were Blackshirts 'for sort of a year. I never say that because it hardly seems fair, because she became so anti. And so that was that. But yes, they were.' So much for Peter's pink politics –! although almost certainly they went along to the meetings in a spirit of curiosity, as if on a rather special kind of family outing. Nancy may have been influenced by the fact that Tom Mitford had become pro-Fascist: his views were always something that she wanted to respect, although she was defeated in the end by his enduring Germanophilia.

Meanwhile Diana and Unity attended the first Nuremberg rally, in late 1933, and, after this, became more and more enamoured of the Fascist viewpoint. Hard not to think that Unity was strongly influenced by her sister in this: calm, majestic Diana, whose every move was made to seem the right one by her serene self-confidence. Of course Unity eventually went much further in her association with Nazism, but it was Diana who showed up initially with a cause, and a man to espouse it. Unity, whose aspect was that of Diana's slightly strange, overgrown, malformed twin, was almost bound to be impressed by this impregnable package.

Diana had gone to Munich in 1933 partly to put distance between herself and Mosley (who was not behaving satisfactorily after the death of his wife), but also to make contacts in Germany that would later be of use to him. Her attendance at Nuremberg was a relatively reasoned act, therefore, however much she was emotionally impressed by what she saw. To Unity, however, the event was an epiphany, and from then on she never looked back. She moved to Munich, began feverishly to learn German and, by March 1935, was in a position to introduce Diana to Adolf Hitler, whom she had met the previous month (her method of procuring an introduction was simple: she sat every day at a table in his favourite restaurant, the Osteria Bavaria, and bestowed upon him her perfect Aryan gaze). Back in England, the activities of the British Unionist Party were gaining ever more attention. The Olympia rally had seen the pro- and anti-Fascist brigades ranged against each other in violent combat: it was a moment in which the obligation to take sides in 1930s politics became theatrically clear. Not that Nancy saw it that way. Once again, she refused to take it seriously; once again, she was right and wrong to do so. In *Wigs on the Green* she parodied the whole affair as a historical pageant, set in a country house garden, that Eugenia tries to turn into a Union Jackshirt rally (she writes a speech for the character of George III which begins: 'Hail! And thanks for all your good wishes, we are happy to be among our loyal Aryan subjects of Chalford and district . . .'). The pageant is disrupted by a band of pacifist aesthetes who not only take on the Fascists but also prove themselves better fighters. Chief amongst the aesthetes is a man called Mr Leader: a pointed dig at Mosley, whom Nancy always called 'The Leader' when she was not calling him something worse.

He was furious about the book and, after his marriage to Diana in 1936 (in Goebbels' drawing-room, with Hitler present), refused to have Nancy at their home in Staffordshire. Unity's reaction one can only guess at. By the time of the book's publication, in June 1935, she was far enough gone in her passion for Nazism to have written a letter to *Der Stürmer*[8] whose postscript read: 'I want everyone to know I am a Jew hater.' This made her immensely welcome in the Führer's inner circle, but it also meant that Nancy cared little for her opinion of *Wigs on the Green*. 'Darling Head of Bone & Heart of Stone', she wrote to Unity, 'Oh dear oh dear the book comes out on Tuesday . . . Oh dear I wish I had never been born into such a family of fanatics . . . *Please* don't read the book if it's going to stone you up against me.' For all its sisterly wheedling, the tone of this letter is essentially indifferent.

With Diana, as always, it was different. The only time Nancy strikes a note of anxiety in her letter to Unity is when she refers to 'Nardie' (another nickname for Diana): 'Oh dear, I am going to Oxford with Nardie tomorrow, our last day I suppose before the clouds of her displeasure burst over me.' Which they did, inevitably, causing Nancy genuine disquiet. After all, Diana was her equal within the family. She was the White Queen with the dark and mysterious soul who stood in opposition to her blacker but simpler sister, and her antagonism was something that Nancy both feared and provoked.

Yet a year earlier Nancy had written another tease on Oswald Mosley. He appeared as a character called the Little Leader in her unpublished story 'Two Old Ladies of Eaton Square'.[9] Diana had apparently not minded about this: perhaps she was unworried by jokes about the Leader arming himself with 'Ex Lax the delicious chocolate laxative' (Mussolini's men used castor oil upon their opponents), or perhaps she dismissed it as a one-off. The sisters were close in 1933, providing mutual support at a time when Hamish was dumping Nancy and Mosley was dancing between mistresses. Therefore Diana probably saw no spite in what Nancy wrote, only the usual irresistible urge to shriek.

When the tease reappeared, however, in *Wigs on the Green*, full-grown and ready for public consumption, she felt very differently. And although Nancy may have hoped that Diana would take the book in the same spirit as she had taken 'Two Old Ladies of Eaton Square' – or even that she would see it as a friendly warning – she cannot really have thought she would get away with it. Excising a few passages was a concession of sorts. But the book was always going to cause trouble within the family, and Nancy must have known it.

Her letter to Diana just before publication is sternly self-defensive, but clearly uncomfortable.

... I read it all through & found that it would be impossible to eliminate the bits that you & the Leader objected to. As you know our finances are such that I really couldn't afford to scrap the book then. I did however hold it up for about a month (thus missing the Spring list) ...

... I am very much worried at the idea of publishing a book which you may object to. It completely blights all the pleasure which one ordinarily feels in a forthcoming book.

And yet, consider. A book of this kind *can't* do your movement any harm. Honestly, if I thought it could set the Leader back by so much as half an hour I would have scrapped it, or indeed never written it in the first place ...

In which case, Diana no doubt thought, why *did* you write the damn thing?

It was a question of principle. Nancy held to her right to publish her book, and Diana held to her right to condemn it: both, in true 1930s style, saw their beliefs as more important than their relationship (although literary rather than bloody, it was a stand-off along the lines of the one envisaged by Jessica and Unity, when each imagined what they would do if ordered to shoot the other). Yet as Nancy herself always said in her books (including *Wigs on the Green*), with women it is the personal that counts, and there was a personal element to this conflict with Diana. Without even realising it, Nancy may have been perturbed by her sister's immersion in this cause and this man. She saw that they brought to Diana a fulfilment that she herself could barely comprehend. Nowadays, of course, it is a deep mystery that Diana – so civilised, so beautiful, so full of humour – should have thrown in her lot with Fascism and Mosley. But she did it at a time when things were very different, and she stuck to it (above all else, she was loyal to her husband). Mosley was a charismatic and attractive man – women fell for him constantly – and, whether one likes it or not, his sexual appeal was bound up with his political daring. Although Nancy saw through his demagogic pyrotechnics, she may still have been put out by the sparks that flew between him and her sister; no one ever looked at her the way that Mosley looked at Diana.

So it amused her to write this book, to make her delicate little digs at the great Sir Ogre, and to see his mistress riled by it. Of course – as

Jan Dalley astutely points out in her biography of Diana – the obvious butt of *Wigs on the Green* is Unity: 'the satire fell mainly on poor crazy Bobo, a soft target, not on the adult sister who might bite back'. Nancy's spite against Diana is subtler, and undeniably personal. The book is punctuated by little stabs at Diana's situation: references to the stigma of divorce (Eugenia's aunt will not let a divorcee in her house), and to 'the tainted blood of an adulteress'. Nonetheless it was the political content that caused the offence. Diana resented any mockery aimed at the man she loved, and perhaps saw that the mockery was not even done with much bravery.

Certainly *Wigs on the Green* raised, in its apparently artless way, one of the great moral questions of fiction writing: how far is it acceptable to use the stuff of one's own life as material? Where does responsibility to other people end, and to artistic truth begin? Was Nancy failing to play cricket by using Unity as her butt, by nonchalantly ridiculing what Diana took most seriously?

It is a key question with such a highly autobiographical writer – and one who did not attempt to hide the fact. Lord Redesdale probably never minded anything that Nancy wrote about him, but then (silly *Highland Fling* excepted) there was always love in the portrayals of her father. Lady Redesdale and Diana felt very differently. They sensed betrayal in some of what Nancy wrote, as if she had dealt with them casually, shown insufficient concern for their feelings. There is some truth in this. Despite appearances, Nancy was a real writer with real things that she wanted to say, whether they hurt or not. And beyond that there was a personal dimension to her motivation. Whereas, in portraying her father as Uncle Matthew, Nancy did so with a care for his vulnerability, she felt that the two women could handle whatever she wrote about them. They were the people who, as she saw it, made things more difficult for her than they need have been, by their superiority on the one hand, their coldness on the other. Without even realising it, she may have enjoyed taking them on in print as she could not in life.

But here is the oddest thing about the *Wigs on the Green* controversy: some of what Eugenia Malmains says, in her village-green hymns to Fascism, is what Nancy herself also believed.

In so far as she was a political animal, she described herself as 'a sort of vague Socialist': according to Diana, her views were the colour of 'synthetic cochineal', whilst Evelyn Waugh accused her, post-war, of moving to Paris after 'having voted socialist and so done her best to make England uninhabitable'. Those who know Nancy from her dissection of class differences in 'U and Non-U', which labelled her for once and all as a raging snob, would no doubt find her view of herself as a Labour supporter highly hilarious. And indeed it is pretty hard to imagine her as a fan of, say, Tony Benn or Anthony Crosland, although sometimes the protected aristocrat has an indulgence towards this kind of politician that the middle-classes cannot afford.

Her centre-left leanings started, however, as a simple reaction against the extreme views held not just by Unity and Diana but by Tom (also pro-Fascist) and Jessica (Communist). Being a socialist in the 1930s was, for someone like Nancy, a slightly cop-out way of saying that she wanted none of any of it: all that drama and flag-waving and what nanny would call showing off. 'I think,' says Alexander Mosley, 'she believed in the personal aspect of politics', which is to say that she did not, could not, believe in ideologies. As the decade rolled on, tank-like, she would find this becoming more and more true and it would help shape her philosophy of living, her increasingly determined belief in a creed that celebrated jokes, moderation, civilisation, common sense and – above all – the pursuit of small-scale human happiness rather than a political heaven on earth.

Yet Eugenia Malmains, for all that her blind passion for Fascism is cause for mockery, is not entirely satirised. In fact Nancy seems a little uncertain as to whether Eugenia is a nutter or a sage; and this is not because she is trying to keep Unity sweet, it is because she sees (as perhaps occasionally she did at Blackshirt meetings?) the power of some of her views. This, for example, is delivered from the overturned wash-tub:

'Respect for parents, love of the home, veneration of the marriage tie, are all at a discount in England to-day, society is rotten with vice, selfishness, and indolence. The rich have betrayed their trust, preferring the fetid atmosphere of cocktail-bars and night-clubs to the sanity of useful country life . . . The poor are no better than the rich, they also have learnt to put self before State, and satisfied with the bread and circuses which are flung to them by their politicians, they also take no steps to achieve a better spirit in this unhappy land.'

'The girl's a lunatic but she's not stupid', said Jasper . . .

What is definitively Nancy, in this speech of Eugenia's, is the inveighing against rich people who desert their responsibilities. It is a theme to which she would return in *The Pursuit of Love*. There she contrasts the old Tory creed of Lord Alconleigh (that is to say, her father) – who has an intense relationship with his land, and a benevolent communion with its workers – with the brash new Conservatism of the MP Tony Kroesig (Linda's first husband), who 'was full of large, clear-sighted ideas for bettering the condition of the capitalist classes, and made no bones of his hatred and distrust for the workers. "I hate the lower classes", he said one day . . .' This was the kind of thing that Nancy despised, and that perhaps led her to call herself a socialist.

As both Harold Acton and Jonathan Guinness make clear, in their books, she was not really anything of the kind. Her political creed, such as it was, belonged to an earlier era. *Wigs on the Green* despairs of the present day – 'Western civilisation is old and tired' – and Nancy was in sympathy; but her own hankerings were not for a brave new world, more for a seemly shifting back to the certainties of the vanished one. And this she found, with considerable joy, in the work she undertook after *Wigs on the Green*: editing the letters of the Stanley family, to whom she was related through her father[10].

Her cousin and friend Edward, Lord Stanley of Alderley, commissioned her to do the job, and she adored it. 'I thought you might like to know that my search has been almost *too* successful', she wrote in December 1937 to Robert Byron, from Alderley Park; '10000 letters all quite legible . . . Simply fascinating. I have been working 9 & 10 hours a day & am the Wonder of Cheshire, & have enjoyed every minute of it. Now the real work will begin . . .'

The letters are a delight, but the most revealing results of Nancy's editing job are the introductions that she wrote for the two volumes: *The Ladies of Alderley*, published in 1938, and *The Stanleys of Alderley*, published the following year. They contain something like her 'political' philosophy. It is articulated in a style dissimilar to anything else she ever wrote, as if she has been infused with the orotund spirit of the age. Nancy removes her elegant mask, lays aside all irony and sly restraint, and expresses herself with total and unabashed sincerity.

During the whole of the nineteenth century the English and their rulers were in perfect accord, they understood and trusted the integrity of each other's aims and methods, and consequently this country was enabled to achieve a greatness, not only material, but spiritual, which has never been equalled in the history of the world. Today [that is, in 1939] our rulers have a holy responsibility. Will they uphold or will they destroy that greatness . . .

We still put our trust in sensible men of ample means and in lords, but doubts are beginning to arise . . . These sensible men, are they by any chance afraid, afraid of losing their ample means? These lords, divorced from the land which was the reason for their being, do they fly, shuddering with strange new fears hitherto unknown in this country, into the arms of alien creeds; and worse still, do they begin to hate and fear the people? The segregation of the classes, which has resulted from the abandonment of the now impoverished land by its former owners, who prefer seeking their fortune in the City . . . has been most harmful to the aristocracy; they are losing their hitherto intimate knowledge of, and trust in, the people. The English are like a fine and nervous horse, which, ridden with good heart can surmount any obstacle, but which, when out of sympathy with its timid rider, will shy at the shadow of an ice cream cart or the distant growling of a dachshund.

This people must be ruled with generosity and dignity . . .

And if all of this reads a little as though Tom Lehrer had broken into a dead straight version of 'The Star Spangled Banner', one must nonetheless respect it as the words of the 'real' Nancy – as real as the woman who, beneath her elegant dresses and frail frame, craved a day at the forefront of a cavalry charge. It is, of course, easy to dismiss what she wrote as the maunderings of a hopeless reactionary (although Evelyn Waugh, typically, called them 'subversive'); but this is modern squeamishness, unable to consider the idea that, within Nancy's massively sweeping statements, there might be the odd sunlit mote of truth. Her image of the English people as a 'fine and nervous horse' is bold and apt; her concept of attachment to land is profound. Nancy was no reactionary; she simply had the courage of her own convictions, and was not ashamed to distinguish between different types of snob and different types of money.

These are, after all, the views that she expressed more elliptically in *The Pursuit of Love*, a book which leaves one in no doubt that Nancy loved, in her deepest soul, her vision of an older England. And they help to explain her ambivalence towards Eugenia Malmains, whose philosophy is both viscerally stirring and innately 'alien'.

Is it significant that, in the acknowledgments page of the first volume of the Stanley letters, Nancy writes: 'My husband read the manuscript and encouraged me', while in the second volume there is no such sentence? In 1938 she had at least kept up a semi-pretence of marital communion. By 1939 she was not bothering, for at that time there was not much left of the Rodd marriage.

The Mitfords were in disarray altogether, in fact; no wonder Nancy had so enjoyed losing herself in the world of the Stanleys: 'Secure in their financial situation . . . Secure in their domestic relations . . . Secure in their religious beliefs and in the knowledge of immortality . . . Above all, secure in their Whig outlook, they never questioned the fact that each individual has his allotted place in the realm and that their own allotted place was among the ruling, the leisured and the moneyed classes.' By comparison with this mid-nineteenth-century nirvana, the late 1930s must have seemed as though chaos had come again.

Diana was married to Mosley, Unity was in Germany swooning over Hitler; and Jessica had done her bit for the far left by eloping, in 1937, with her cousin Esmond Romilly. She met him in glamorous circumstances, when he was invalided home after fighting for the Loyalist Front in the Spanish Civil War. Irresistible, of course, and her nineteen-year-old heart had leaped just as Linda Radlett's does when she meets the Communist Christian Talbot, who 'talked without cease' about 'the betterment of the world through political change', and who gets away with it because he is so sexy. Like Christian, Esmond Romilly was coolly enthralled with the idea of so deliciously pretty a comrade-in-arms. Jessica, meanwhile, had become more like her Fascist sisters than she would have cared to realise: in tangled thrall to both a creed and a man.

'Linda has always felt the need of a cause', says Fanny in *The Pursuit of Love*, to the wise old sophisticate Lord Merlin, whose throwaway reply cuts straight to the heart of the matter. '"Cause," he said scornfully. "My dear Fanny, I think you are mixing up cause with effect. No, Christian is an attractive fellow . . ."' How Nancy must have annoyed her sisters, with the implication that neither Fascism nor Communism would have seemed quite so fascinating had they come in plainer wrappings than Mosley and Romilly –! But then neither man would have been so desirable without the visionary fires that burned in his eyes. Look at Unity with Hitler. At any rate man plus cause – in whatever relative quantities – equalled falling head-over-heels into another life. And Jessica, having told her mother that she was on a girlish weekend in Dieppe, flew heedless of consequences into the arms of her red-flag-waving lover.

The instant, hapless family reaction was to try and entice her home again. Because of their pinkish sympathies, Nancy and Peter were sent by the Redesdales on a mission to the south of France, where Jessica and Esmond were then holed up: 'We saw them at the end of the gangplank', Jessica later wrote in *Hons and Rebels*, 'Nancy, tall and beautiful, waving at us with her gloves, and Peter, rather square and stocky, hands in pockets in his usual "tough" attitude. They were completely surrounded by press photographers, and we descended the gangplank in a barrage of popping bulbs.'

Nancy made doomed attempts to persuade her sister that she should give up the idea of going to Spain. 'Decca, really you are a naughty little thing, worrying us all like that', was the general tone, at least according to Jessica's recollections. 'Poor Muv has been in floods ever since you left, and so has Nanny. Nanny keeps saying you didn't have any suitable clothes to fight in.' Now this, as is usual with Jessica, sounds not quite believable. Nancy surely said nothing quite so silly, although she probably said nothing very serious either. Impossible to imagine her having the will or the desire to change another person's mind for them; her style was far more languid and *laissez-faire* than that. In 1955 Nancy would comment upon Jessica's desire to visit Russia[11] with her second husband: 'The awful thing is it won't teach them (that'll teach them) because nothing ever does teach people.' That, essentially, was her view; and so, back in 1936, she simply left Jessica to it. Having made her dramatic bid for freedom, Jessica was hardly going to return like a lamb to the fold, especially as the whole episode had attracted hitherto unknown levels of Mitfordian publicity. 'You were the first one in the family to be on posters', Nancy said. 'Boud was frightfully jealous.'

Jessica married soon afterwards in Bayonne. 'Esmond was the most horrible human being I have ever met', Nancy later wrote in a letter to Evelyn Waugh, an opinion widely shared. Even Jessica admitted in *Hons and Rebels* that Esmond was 'a gifted hater', although she wrote that he had mellowed and matured by the time of his death, in the war, in 1941. She remained wholly loyal to his beliefs; again, despite political polarisation, the similarity to Diana and Unity is striking.

For the Redesdales, it must have felt as though they were sustaining one body blow after another: as parents they were two ageing punch-bags. Their confusion about the unravelling of the fabric of their family is palpable. They had no notion of how to stop any of it and, despite their Canute-like efforts to hold back the tide of rebelliousness, it grew ever more overwhelming. At first they were appalled when Diana left Bryan Guinness and set herself up as Mosley's mistress. Then they were furious when Diana took Unity to Nuremberg in 1933: 'I suppose you know without being told how absolutely horrified Muv and I were to think of you and Bobo accepting any form of hospitality from people we regard as a gang of murderous pests', wrote Lord Redesdale. 'That you should associate yourself with such people is a source of utter misery to both of us . . . What we can do, and what we intend to do, is to try and keep Bobo out of it all.' Which would be funny, when one thinks of what Unity subsequently got up to, were it not so ghastly. Within a year her parents had accepted Unity's move to Munich, as at least giving her a purpose in life. Not only that, Lady Redesdale had also become smitten by Germany; even her husband, whose hatred of the Hun had hitherto been a consuming passion, found himself quite taken with both the place and its politics. Possibly Tom's influence had led his father to this position, for he could do little wrong in Lord Redesdale's eyes.

But the gameness with which the Mitford parents tried to go along with their children was almost pathetic. Sydney had an enjoyable tea with Hitler ('I fear the whole thing was wasted on Muv, she is just the same as before', wrote Unity to Diana), David too became impressed by him, and both Redesdales attended the Nuremberg rally of 1938. This admiration was not unusual: it is well known that amongst the British upper-classes there was considerable sympathy for the Nazi regime ('von Ribbentrop had the most elegant embassy in London', Nancy was later to recall, in a tone of helpless amazement. 'Everybody went! They deny it now, of course...'[12]). Yet the feeling persists that the Redesdales were fundamentally swayed, not so much by the mighty oratory of the Führer, as by the desire to keep a weak handle on the mysterious passions of their children. They would probably have remained unmoved by Nazism had it not been thrust upon them.

What Lord Alconleigh describes in *The Pursuit of Love* as 'the Thin End of the Wedge' was being inserted into the Redesdales' lives at every possible opening. In the book, the process refers to a banished labrador being let into the house for five minutes ('Oh, I see – the thin end of the wedge. All right, this time he can stay . . .'). In reality it referred to more cataclysmic events, like Diana's and Jessica's marriages. Oswald Mosley had been viewed as the devil in a black shirt, but now he was greeted with muted relief, as at least legitimising Diana's position. Jessica's elopement had been seen as a complete catastrophe, but once again there was the mitigating factor of marriage and so, obediently, Sydney attended the Romilly wedding. The Redesdales tried, as they always had, to establish some sort of order. They refused to receive Mosley, they refused Deborah permission to visit the Romillys when they moved to London. But they surely felt that the incipient anarchy of the Mitford childhood, created by this alarmingly diverse group of autonomous and imaginative beings, had finally been let loose. At last the inmates had taken over their posh Cotswold prison: they had broken free and were running merrily amok, thumbing pretty noses at their warders. What a long road had been travelled, from the days when the heavens were seen to fall over Nancy's powdered nose and reddened lips.

It was not all revolution. Pamela behaved herself, as always. In 1936 she married the dashing Derek Jackson: gentleman rider, distinguished physicist, Fascist sympathiser ('he was marvellous,' says Diana. 'Not only brilliantly clever but enormously rich!'). Pam had been engaged before but the attachment was broken off; she then gave her ring to Unity, who gave it to Hitler. Because of her husband, Pam was ranged slightly on the right wing of the family (the name of Derek's twin brother, Vivian Jackson, was given to Eugenia Malmains' horse in *Wigs on the Green*). But it did not interest her much. She met Hitler, as did all of her family except Nancy and Jessica, and in her wonderful calm way described him as 'very ordinary, like a farmer in his old khaki suit'.[13]

Lastly there was Deborah, who grew up gorgeous and sensible and unfazed by any thought that scandal might taint her ('At it Again, the Mad, Mad Mitfords', was a fairly typical newspaper headline of the time). She came out in 1938, as storms gathered over her ostrich feathers. Before her debut in society she, too, had met Hitler, having attended the tea party at which he was present with her mother ('Muv asked if there were any laws about having good flour for bread, wasn't it killing?'). On her return she went to the races and to balls, all the usual stuff in unusual circumstances, and danced with apparent serenity through the family debris that showered about her. She also wrote a letter to Jessica whose comment on the situation was oblique, droll, perceptive and utterly Mitfordian: '. . . nothing has changed much', it read. 'Farve goes off to *The Lady* and the House of Lords, and Muv paints chairs and reads books like "Stalin, my Father", or "Mussolini, The Man", or "Hitler, my Brother's Uncle", or "I was in Spain", or "The Jews, by one who knows them".'

In August 1938, Nancy fell pregnant. She had been trying to conceive for three years or so, but this was difficult for two reasons: firstly there were physical problems that required curettage, and secondly her husband was as often as not making love to another woman. But eventually she wrote to Robert Byron, saying, 'I am in the family way isn't it nice. But only just so don't tell anybody as I don't want the Rodds to find out, they are such demons of gynaecological enthusiasm. Besides it may all come to nothing. I am awfully excited though.'

Nancy miscarried in September, despite having rested up as instructed. She had in fact told Lady Rennell about her pregnancy: 'I suppose she is furious at my improvident behaviour', she wrote, again to Byron. '(Of course it is *lunatic* really I quite see that but one must never be deterred from doing what one wants for lack of money don't you agree) . . . Actually if I thought for a minute it would be a boy I should go for a long bicycle ride here & now – 2 Peter Rodds in 1 house is unthinkable.'

As usual, Nancy's reference to her husband is taut with oddity. It is impossible to know how she felt about the miscarriage, because she made no reference to it; but it appears that she was ambivalent about the prospect of being irrevocably tied to Peter by a child. Also, despite her airy remark to Byron, she would surely have been worried sick about how the baby would be paid for. Peter was out of work again, having been scuppered by his own brother when he tried for a job at the BBC (Francis had advised that Peter was not a responsible employee. 'I have put F's name in a drawer and *I hope he dies*', wrote Nancy to Robert Byron, probably in real despair). And so, although Nancy – now thirty-four – was told that she would be able to conceive again, lack of money seemed to make it unwise; while the lack of Peter's presence in her bed made it unlikely.

These, at any rate, may have been her feelings in 1938. Yet had she conceived earlier in her marriage, unequivocal joy might have overridden them. It is impossible to say whether a baby would have made Nancy's life with Peter happier, more productive. He was unfaithful after only a year or so; had he wanted a child he would surely have tried harder for one by sleeping more often with his wife. Possibly he recognised that he was unsuited to fatherhood, incapable of living up to responsibility. Yet a baby – had it arrived before mutual exhaustion set in – might have made a difference for the better.

'There's no doubt', says Diana, 'that when she was young she would have liked children. I think it's something that people do long for really, and then she saw me, very happy' – in 1938 Diana gave birth to her third son, Alexander – 'and I think all that was perhaps rather sad.'

So Nancy set about mating her French bulldog Milly, who in 1939 had four puppies.

CHAPTER 5

Towards the end of *The Pursuit of Love*, when Linda Radlett looks back on her first marriage to Tony Kroesig, she says, 'The really important thing, if a marriage is to go well, without much love, is very very great niceness – *gentillesse* – and wonderful good manners.'

She has, in her musing and childlike way, come to understand her marriage very well.

I was never *gentille* with Tony, and often I was hardly polite to him, and, very soon after our honeymoon, I became exceedingly disagreeable. I'm ashamed now to think what I was like. And poor old Tony was so good-natured, he never snapped back, he put up with it all for years and then just ambled off to Pixie. I can't blame him. It was my fault from beginning to end.

Nancy is not describing her own marriage, nor is she blaming herself for its failure. After all Peter, unlike Tony, 'ambled off' to other women almost immediately and it was Nancy who 'put up' with things 'for years'. Nonetheless by 1945, when she was writing her novel, she had achieved a perspective on her life with Peter. She had even acquired a fondness for him, and this comes through in Linda's words. Nancy's marriage, she saw by then, had been contracted 'without much love'; and, without 'very great niceness' to make up the balance, it had been doomed to fail. Not that either Nancy or Linda would have necessarily wanted their marriages to succeed, since both women valued romantic love above all else. Perhaps Nancy realised, through Linda, that this craving of theirs for love fitted them both badly for marriage; however much they liked the idea of it.

What little steam there had ever been in the Rodd marriage had almost evaporated by the time the war approached. The miscarried baby no doubt seemed like a death blow: as if fate, through Nancy's uterus, was giving the couple a message of doom. And yet not long after this, in early 1939, Nancy and Peter performed a significant act together, perhaps for the first time in their marriage. They travelled to Perpignan, in the south of France, to help with the refugees from the Spanish Civil War. Around half a million Republicans had been pushed over the Pyrenees by the encroachment northwards of General Franco's army; France did not want them, and they had to be fed and looked after until they could be sent on elsewhere. Peter left for Perpignan early in 1939. Nancy followed in May, having meanwhile tried to bring official attention to Peter's reports on the refugees. It was not exactly an act of union on their part, but there was something comradely about it, something to imply that the couple *did* have feelings for each other, although not those that made for a successful marriage.

The Perpignan episode shows both Nancy and Peter in their most serious, perhaps most attractive light. Neither went out there because they were saints, but equally neither had to do it. For all Nancy's posing as airy-fairy joker in the midst of her politically-minded siblings, it was actually she who engaged most closely – in practical terms, at least – with the international situation of the time. Jessica preached anti-Fascism and made a lot of gestures; Diana did anything that she could to help her husband's cause; Unity made Nazism the absolute centre of her life. But Nancy rolled up her sleeves and tried to give concrete, dispassionate help to unknown people: she did what many of us think of doing, as we watch the hungry and dispossessed on television, and few of us actually do. She had grit, and a sense of duty, beneath her frivolous languor. No doubt she had personal motives for going to France: she wanted to be with her husband, doing something that she could, for once, honourably share with him, and she also enjoyed standing on the moral high ground and waving down to her 'fanatical' family. Nor could she resist a dodgy joke when she got out to Perpignan: Unity, she announced to the workers in the refugee camps, was on her way to help. Nevertheless the letters that she wrote from the camps show that she was utterly and genuinely involved with what she was doing, and that she did it with a mixture of practicality, cheerfulness and compassion.

Peter, too, was doing his best for the refugees; even though, to judge by *The Pursuit of Love*, he was also getting one hell of a kick out of it. The book's description of the Perpignan episode is pretty much taken from life. Linda arrives to find her second husband (Christian, the handsome Communist) 'in a whirl of business', working 'in an office financed by various English humanitarians with the object of improving the camps, putting refugee families in touch again, and getting as many as possible out of France.' Christian gives his wife 'an absent-minded peck on the forehead' and immediately bustles her into this office; he is, she realises, in his element, dealing with mass misery in an impersonal way, expunging his 'half-guilty feeling about not having fought in Spain'. Cleverly, without malice, Nancy hints at the self-regarding quality of Christian's selflessness, the pomposity with which he celebrates his own detachment. This surely came from her observations of her husband. 'Peter sees to everything', Nancy wrote to her mother soon after her arrival in Perpignan, 'even down to how many STs [sanitary towels] are allowed! I believe he will be here for life.'

It was a perfect job for Peter. It demanded energy and initiative, as banking had never done; it suspended him from having to deal with dreary real life; and it was never going to go on beyond his dwarfish boredom threshold (happily for him, there was no question of having to be there 'for life'). If only Peter's existence could have given him more such occasions to rise to, he might have been a better and a happier man. This, after all, was the age of political engagement, which should have been a godsend to someone so lost and feckless.

But although Peter could embrace a cause at a distance and in the short term, a lifetime's commitment was beyond him: to a woman, to a job, probably to a child. His problem was that he was too clever not to know that he was wasting his time, and too clever not to feel that most things were a waste of time. Like his wife, he had a degree of detachment; but whereas Nancy's clear-eyed view of the world brought her mostly pleasure, Peter's led to frustration. He must surely have dreamed of a Perpignan to seize him by the scruff of the neck and force him into action, even for a brief period of time. Almost certainly he felt – as Christian did – that he should have gone off like Esmond

Romilly to fight in the Spanish Civil War, since the Republican cause was indeed one that he believed in. Yet he had stayed in London instead: got drunk at the Savile Club, slept with Mary Sewell, made Nancy fruitlessly pregnant, wasted another couple of years.

One wonders how Nancy felt out there in Perpignan, seeing her husband busy and authoritative. Was she taken with this different Peter, or did she see through him to the man she knew, all too well, beneath? Both, probably. One also wonders how bothered Peter was about whether Nancy turned up or not. He was on the go all the time and they saw little of each other: 'I haven't had a single word with Peter although I've been here 2 days', Nancy wrote to her mother, not quite truly as in the next paragraph she is quoting him. There is no rancour in what Nancy says, she is simply making the point that Peter is working fantastically hard; but – like Linda – she did spend more time with his two charming young helpers than with her husband. They were '2 chaps who talk the "New Statesmans" English which is always a comfort abroad I find'. These two chaps – Donald Darling and Humphrey Hare – no doubt found her a refreshing and elegant presence; and while Peter strode about, too busy doing everything to delegate any of it, they found her work. She delivered supplies and messages and – again like Linda – assigned cabins to the Spanish families, who were sailing off to what they hoped would be safety (Linda gives all the best accommodation to the labourers – 'most democratic' – because they have the word *labrador* by their names).

So Nancy and Peter were apart, but together. They were sharing something that mattered, even though they hardly spoke to each other. It was a contradictory situation, companionable and distant, and this is echoed in *The Pursuit of Love*. When Linda goes to see Christian in Perpignan, she is hoping simultaneously to save her marriage and to be confirmed in her instinct that it is over. This was not quite the case with Nancy; she did not, as Linda does, arrive in France to learn that her husband had become deeply attached to another woman. Yet she rarely invented in her novels: she took the stuff of her life and transmuted it into something that had truth at its heart, the kind of truth that one only understands at a distance. And so, perhaps without even realising it at the time, she may well have felt something of Linda's ambivalent sadness: watching the husband she does not really love behave so admirably, knowing that their life together will almost certainly end, when peace and normality return.

What she certainly felt – and this too comes across in her book – is pain and outrage at the suffering of the refugees: 'the sight of these thousands of human beings, young and healthy, herded behind wire away from their womenfolk, with nothing on earth to do day after dismal day, was a recurring torture to Linda.' In *The House of Mitford* Jonathan Guinness makes the point that the refugees were not all as innocent as their vulnerable state made them appear to be – 'there were certainly some with crimes on their personal conscience' – and implies that Nancy, suffused as she was with rage against the kind of political system supported by half her family, was unable to grasp this ambiguity. This is probably true; although helping the guilty along with the innocent is an occupational hazard for aid workers, whether they are aware of it or not.

What Nancy minded most was the affront to the refugees' pride: 'The Red X are not much help', she wrote to her mother in late May, 'they issue shorts which Spaniards abominate, having a sense of dignity, & refuse to help with special diet for the many cases of colitis in the camps.' This letter is proof of Nancy's hands-on engagement. She describes getting off 'our ship' after a hurricane had forced a change of port – 'at 3 hours' notice special trains had to be changed etc etc the result was Peter was up for 2 *whole* nights, never went to bed at all. However he is none the worse; I was up all yesterday night as the embarkation went on until 6am & the people on the quay had to be fed & the babies given their bottles. There were 200 babies under 2 & 12 women are to have babies on board' (what did the barely fertile Nancy make of this fecundity all around her: did it pain her? did she feel relief, not to suffer appalling anxiety for another human being?). 'One poor shell-shocked man went mad and had to be given an anaesthetic & taken off, but apart from that all went smoothly and slowly.' There is a real sense, from this letter, of how hard it all was: the endless petty organisational details, the patience of the helpers, the stoicism of the refugees, Nancy's bright and exhausted smiles. As the boat sailed off, 'the pathetic little band on board' played the Spanish national anthem, and 'the poor things gave 3 Vivas for España which they will never see again. I don't think there was a single person not crying – I have never cried so much in my life.'

Nancy goes on to say there is no guarantee that the ship will elude Franco and make it to Mexico. And this, perhaps, is the real point of her letter, to show her mother (who 'seems to regard Adolf as her favourite son-in-law'[1]) the disgusting truth about the political creed that Sydney now so calmly supported. 'If you could have a look, as I have, at some of the less agreeable results of fascism in a country I think you would be less anxious for the swastika to become a flag on which the sun never sets. And, whatever may be the *good* produced by that regime, that the first result is always a horde of unhappy refugees cannot be denied.' This last remark was key: while her sisters Unity, Diana and Jessica (and, according to Nancy, her mother) were apparently prepared to accept the consequences of pursuing an ideological goal, Nancy quite simply was not. 'I would join hands with the devil himself to stop any further extension of the disease [of Fascism]', she wrote. This, of course, could lead to terrible consequences in itself: but the point is that the war against Fascism was necessary and Fascism, in Nancy's opinion, was not.

By 1939 she was digging her heels hard into the middle ground, holding to her pinko stance with a frankly humourless tenacity. The days of *Wigs on the Green* were over; at last, Nancy agreed with Diana that here was where the jokes stopped. She had been deeply shocked by Perpignan, and by the human cost of political ideology. Yet it is impossible to resist the thought that it was, in fact, *her family* who had pushed Nancy into this ferocious position as: if she was, *au fond*, in violent reaction against them, rather than against their strange beliefs.

There *were* principles involved. Yet there is also a strong sense that Nancy was guided by the personal: by the tense dealings she had had with Diana and Unity over *Wigs on the Green*, by the cool obduracy shown by Jessica when Nancy had gone to see her in France, by the lack of affection she felt from Sydney. The family's wild political allegiances had, yes, forced Nancy to take a stance against them. That was what principle could do in the 1930s. And although this was painful it was also, perhaps, rather liberating. It allowed Nancy to detach herself. It gave her a certain freedom, to stand apart and watch them all fly off so blindly to right and left. Lady Redesdale was damning herself quite wonderfully in Nancy's eyes with her dread of going to war with her friend Hitler: from this point on, Nancy seems to have felt justified in the dislike that she had for her mother. There may, too, have been satisfaction in the spectacle of Jessica's antics, since Nancy's feelings for her least Mitfordian sister were, in adulthood, very much at one remove ('I don't die for her as much as I pretend to', she later confessed). And then there was the pleasure of being able to condemn Diana, the sister for whom her feelings were decidedly *not* at one remove. Hard to think that Nancy took no secret enjoyment in watching the immaculate Diana go so spectacularly wrong.

'There isn't a pin to put between Nazis & Bolshies', she wrote to the family friend Violet Hammersley.[2] 'If one is a Jew one prefers one & if an aristocrat the other, that's all as far as I can see. *Fiends!*'

Which is proof of what her nephew Alexander says, that it was 'the personal aspect of politics' which counted with Nancy. The personal, in the end, was the only thing that made sense. It gave life its meaning and interest and happiness. Nothing else could ever be so important, no philosophy or theory or ideology, however much it dressed itself up and promised heaven on earth. Of course, to those who were plunged in the profundities of political philosophy, Nancy was a hopelessly shallow thinker. She confessed as much with this pointed little aside in *Wigs on the Green*, when Jasper Aspect says to his lover Poppy that 'Like most women, you only care about personalities, things don't interest you'. 'That's simply not true', she replies. 'I'm fearfully interested in things – I absolutely long for a sable coat.' Nancy took pleasure in this kind of 'shallowness': partly because she knew that it annoyed people, but also because she felt it to be refreshingly rooted in sanity. What she wrote about Nazis and Bolshies may sound simplistic. Yet it was, when one came down to it, pretty much the truth, even if it had been arrived at by nothing more than common sense. Just as Linda's simple soul was filled with despair when she wandered through the Perpignan camps, so Nancy felt, she *knew*, that the life she cared about was threatened by an evil, an affront to normal human happiness. She was glad to be married to a man who was on the side of the angels. So much so that her marriage – unlike Linda's – gave one last leap into a semblance of unexpected life.

She left Peter and the camps in June, and returned to Blomfield

Road. Her bulldog, Milly, had just had quads and one of the puppies, Agnes, was given to Robert Byron: 'She is very anti-appeasement,' Nancy told him.

Then Nancy spent a rather febrile summer ('I am leading a very gay life') in Blomfield Road, waiting for a war that she saw as nasty and necessary. It 'must be got over with', she was to write in her next novel, *Pigeon Pie*, 'before we can go on with our lives. Like in the night when you want to go to the loo and it is miles away down a freezing cold passage and yet you know you have to go down that passage before you can sleep again. We are starting down it now.'

Her family saw it in their own ways. Jessica viewed it, or so she wrote in *Hons and Rebels*, as the gateway to 'the new post-war social order that we were convinced was on the way'. Diana and Unity were opposed to it; Tom eventually chose to fight against Japan rather than his beloved Germany; Sydney took the side of most of her children. She saw war against Hitler as a dreadful thing: '*When* the Germans have won', she told her husband, 'you'll see, everything will be wonderful and they'll treat us very differently to those wretched beastly Poles.' David, meanwhile, had gratefully viewed Nazism as a counterbalance to Communism, and had become mildly friendly with Hitler out in Germany (especially when the Führer paid for Unity's treatment for pneumonia in 1938. David insisted on paying him back; it was an amicable man-to-man meeting). But the moment war was declared, his feelings changed dramatically. He reverted to hatred of the Hun. It seemed to him that he had been duped, or foolish, or horribly weak to have stood at Nuremberg in 1938 and been carried away by it all.

By the time war broke out David was only just over sixty, but he was old before his time. The tall, striding force of nature, whom Nancy called in *The Pursuit of Love* 'a sort of criterion of English manhood; there seemed something not quite right about any man who greatly differed from him', was now bent and frosty-headed, his brilliant blue eyes clouded with cataracts and bewilderment. His dazzling daughters had done for him. Where once he had been able to control them, command their respect, or at least their fascinated attention, now he was a cipher in most of their lives, and he took it hard. Perhaps he felt a kind of guilt, that he had not been able to give them more money, that he had built them a home (Swinbrook) which they all except Deborah fought to escape. He thought little of their men (he called them the man Mosley, the boy Romilly, and the bore Rodd; Derek Jackson he couldn't make head nor tail of). Probably he could not understand why such lively, funny creatures, such beauties as his girls were, had not made happier, easier lives for themselves – and for him.

And there was far worse to come. If the build-up to war had begun to take the Mitford family apart, war itself would finish the job. Afterwards life would go on, new happiness would be found and *rapprochements* made; but some of the damage would be irreparable. For example nothing would bring Unity back to the girl she had once been, the eccentric over-sized Boud with the rat on her shoulder and the strange zest for life, not after she had put a gun to her head on the day that war broke out, and fallen in a great ruined heap in the Englischer Garten in Munich.

She had been unable to bear the thought that Germany and England should be enemies; and she had believed that she was playing some role in preventing this. The shattering of that belief shattered Unity, as she had known it would. For several days before the outbreak of war she was alone in her Munich flat, listening obsessively to the wireless, waiting in dread for news. On 1 September, she lunched for the last time at the Osteria Bavaria, where she had first met Hitler. On the morning of 3 September she picked up a telegram from the British Consulate confirming that war had indeed been declared. Then she telephoned a friend named Rudi von St Paul who said, subsequently: 'I was frightened because three or four months beforehand . . . she had said then that unless she could stop the war, she would have to shoot herself. She had shown me the pistol . . . I was terrified for her.' The following morning Baroness von St Paul received a letter from Unity, along with her keys and a will, explaining that she had killed herself.

But Unity was not dead. She had bungled it, as was so often the case in her odd and uncoordinated life, and the bullet that should have killed her had lodged itself in her head, in so precarious a place that it was impossible to move. 'The dead-end which she had reached', wrote David Pryce-Jones in his biography, 'was cruelly embodied, as well as over-symbolised, by the bullet in her brain.'

He also wrote, quite truly, that although Unity's support of the Nazi regime would have made it difficult for her to return home when war broke out, her position was not impossible. She might have been imprisoned under the Emergency Defence Regulations, but nothing worse. 'She had done no more than make a fool of herself.'

So Unity had not shot herself out of cowardice, or fear of being unable to live with the consequences of her support for Germany. In a perverse way, her motives were nobler than that. 'She was sincere when she put the pistol to her temple.' This pitiful, uncontrollable girl had found her fulfilment in Munich, and in the belief 'that she had weighed in the balance of politics, that she had had a role, a mission'. When this was taken away from her, all she wanted was to die. And the bullet did, effectively, bring her life to an end; as, in a way, it also ended the lives of her parents.

In *The Pursuit of Love*, Nancy wrote that 'the parents of our contemporaries would console themselves, if things did not go quite as they hoped for their children, by saying: "Never mind, just think of the poor Alconleighs!"' But that was to minimise the pain. Nothing in *The Pursuit of Love* compares with what happened to Unity: the blinding, horrific sense of impotence that caused her to do what she did, and the damage that her action caused to her parents. Nancy had been staying with the Redesdales on the day that war broke out, when the hitherto vague fear for Unity took an instant and terrible grip. Incongruously, they were all stuck on an island in the Inner Hebrides named Inch Kenneth, bought – along with a stark and rather terrible-looking house – by Lord Redesdale in 1938, when Swinbrook was finally sold: it was one of those sudden, somehow attractive impulses that had driven his life. The island was beautiful, but intractably remote. Reaching it from London was, according to Nancy, 'the worst journey in the world'.[3] It required an overnight train, a long ferry ride to Mull, a drive, then a boat trip. Many years later Lady Redesdale took on the job of collecting and delivering the islanders' letters; no one else was willing to do it. Inch Kenneth was not Nancy's kind of place – she hated cold in her bones – but she was there in September, lending support to the mother from whom she had begun to feel so agreeably detached.

As war was declared, the atmosphere on the island became less forgiving than ever. Retreating to this hermitage had no doubt seemed, in the summer, a comforting idea; but on 3 September 1939 the enforced remoteness led to desperate frustration. For although there was no actual intelligence of what had happened to Unity, her family was waiting to hear something bad. Tom and Diana knew that she had threatened suicide should war break out, and everyone knew that she had become obsessive about relations between England and Germany. What had started, back in the early 1930s, as a huge tease (swastikas on the wall to annoy Decca), then had become a joyful reason for living (the bliss of being in Munich, being made to feel important), had come to this end: a twenty-five-year-old girl lying neither alive nor dead, only the bullet in her brain for company, small shadows cast on her bed from the flowers sent by Goebbels, von Ribbentrop and Hitler.

After Chamberlain's speech, Nancy prepared to make the marathon journey back to London. She quarrelled with her mother during the drive to the station, which was perhaps to be expected. 'I said something only fairly rude about Hitler & she said get out of this car & walk to the station then so after I had to be honey about Adolph.' Of course Nancy should not have tried to upset Sydney in these circumstances, although Sydney was being quite nasty as well (according to Nancy, at least). 'I said Peter had joined up so she said I expect he'll be shot soon which I thought fairly tactless of her. Altogether she is acting *very* queer.' Lady Redesdale was out of her mind, as anyone would have been with a child in what had overnight in fact become enemy territory. No doubt the thought of Hitler was torment to her, as to her husband. Had Unity not supported him, she would not be in this situation, but if everyone else were not so against him, the situation need surely not have happened. Meanwhile what to do? How to find out about her daughter? And what about Diana, who had so publicly ranged herself on the Fascist side? What about Tom, who at the age of thirty would be required for his country? The agony of any parent on 3 September was, for the Redesdales, hideously intensified, and for Nancy to blame her mother was wrong, but irresistible. True to form, she continued not to resist: 'Well the family', she wrote to Violet Hammersley. 'Muv has gone finally off her head . . . Poor thing I suppose she is quite wretched so one must make allowances . . .'

By 4 September Nancy was already plunged into war work. Wearing her flamboyant hat of righteousness, she wrote to her mother: 'I am driving an ARP [Air Raid Protection] car every night from 8-8. So far have had only one go at it & feel more or less OK (it is mostly waiting about of course).' In fact she had crashed her car within hours: 'wasn't it awful . . . driving in the dark is too devilish. All the other people of course are charming, they think I'm rather a joke, so obviously incompetent.' Peter, she continued, 'is working day & night at a 1ˢᵗ aid post in Chelsea'. Causes were now coming his way thick and fast. He may have felt that the war represented a chance for a new life, just as his marriage had done six years earlier.

Of Unity there was still no real news, only rumour. 'Bobo we hear on fairly good authority is in a concentration camp for Czech women which much as I deplore it has a sort of poetic justice', Nancy wrote to Mrs Hammersley on 15 September. Germany was treating Unity's suicide attempt as a literal state secret; nobody knew anything. The family could only try to go about its business, Sydney returning to London and pressing for news, Tom 'stationed near us [the Rodds] . . . tired but cheerful', Diana pregnant and contemplating her husband's ruin, whilst in a Munich clinic Unity lay like a swollen ghost and tried to kill herself again. She swallowed her swastika badge, which was later removed from her stomach with a probe.

In early October some news reached the family: one of Unity's friends wrote, very cagily, to say that she was ill and in hospital. A month later there was, at last, a rather uninformative official communication, stating that Unity had tried to kill herself but was getting on well. Then of course the story got out. Facts were sketchy, turned easily into melodrama. A reporter actually telephoned Sydney to ask if Unity was dead. This rumour reached Jessica, who was in America at the time and terrified by it; a variation even had Unity executed on Himmler's orders. But a letter of Nancy's, dated 25 October, mentions a report in the *Daily Express* that got the story essentially right, saying that Unity was – as Nancy put it – 'ill with attempted suicide'. By which time she had, according to her concerned hospital visitor Herr Hitler, expressed the desire to go home.

Hitler eventually paid for Unity's stay in the Munich clinic, and arranged for her to be taken to neutral Switzerland. At the very end of 1939, her mother and sister Deborah went to Berne and brought her back to England. On her return, the press was waiting for her.

Flashbulbs exploded in her collapsed and vacant face; she was offered, through her mother, £5,000 for an interview with the *Daily Express*, although she could barely remember the words 'salt' and 'sugar'. In the first week of 1940, cinemas showed a newsreel of her arrival at Folkestone, being helped by her father to stagger off a stretcher; the audiences hollered abuse at the screens. Meanwhile she had been taken to a nursing home in Oxford, near to the cottage at High Wycombe owned by her mother, which was given police protection for several months.

'It wasn't an embarrassment,' Nancy said of Unity's actions, years later, in the television interview that she gave in 1966. 'It was a terrible sadness. It was dreadful.' But what strikes one, in Nancy's letters from this strange time, is how extraordinarily detached she was; or appeared to be.

On 10 October, for example, when very little was known about Unity's condition and the family must have been worrying itself to death, Nancy was writing to Mrs Hammersley a long, detailed narrative about her cousin Edward Stanley, who had become innocently involved in a scandal at White's Club over an unpaid backgammon debt. This was followed by an equally long account of Randolph Churchill's marriage to Pamela Digby[4] ('a pretty, luscious little piece . . . it seems she was the 8th girl Randolph had proposed to since the war began'). The letter ends with a throwaway sentence about Tom Mitford, then staying in Nancy's house, whose 'leisure hours are beguiled by a belle from Watford'.

A couple of weeks later, Nancy wrote to Jessica in Washington DC. This letter is equally airy and teasing. It is full of digs about Americans, which she always loved to make ('they are so terrified of war & air raids'), and full of spite towards Lady Redesdale ('I gather the Fem is engaged upon an acrimonious correspondent with her MP about how wicked it is to attack dear little Hittle. Last war she would have found herself in jail'). In the midst of all this is a single sentence about Unity: 'Poor Bowd *do* write to her it must be lonely.'

Perhaps Nancy could not lament Unity's fate too much with Jessica, who was hardly going to sympathise with her sister's inability to live without the love of Nazi Germany (although in fact Decca's affection for Unity remained strong as ever: principle once again foundering in the face of the personal). But with Violet Hammersley, a bystander, Nancy might have shown more concern? Not so. Writing to these two enabled her *not* to show concern, to be honest instead, to make jokes, talk about other things, insist upon her own, new, sane agenda.

Yet it comes across coolly – almost shockingly so – when she writes 'I'm simply as happy as a bird', and one thinks of Sydney sitting beside the Rutland Gate telephone, David stumbling half-blind around bleak Inch Kenneth, both anguishing over the girl in her shadowy clinic bed – where were Nancy's feelings for all of this? She cared, of course she did. But there *was* a cool side to her (for which she would, no doubt, have blamed her mother). And the cool Nancy believed, or had decided to believe, that her family had brought these troubles upon themselves, what with their idiotic days out to Nuremberg, their adolescent infatuations with a moustachioed madman and his smiling henchmen. They had distanced themselves from her; now she would do the same. Now, in some fundamental way, she cut free from her family, from the clinging muddy vines of its problems. Perhaps *that* was why she was as happy as a bird?

It is almost certainly the reason why, for the first time since her engagement, she was writing about her husband with respect and something like affection. Peter had become a bit of a hero to Nancy: a man who did refugee work for the dispossessed rather than made that work necessary, who volunteered within a day of war being declared and urged war work upon his wife ('Sophia agreed with him really', Nancy wrote in *Pigeon Pie*. 'The huns must be fought').

Along with several of his friends, Prod had a commission in the Welsh Guards: 'Peter is all dressed up in his uniform looking very pretty – he goes to Essex for training on Sat: next', Nancy told Mrs Hammersley. A couple of weeks later, she wrote to her about Unity. 'I remember so well, some 5 years ago Peter wrote an immense letter to Farve begging him to remove her from a situation which *must* lead to tragedy. The family were very pooh pooh-ey & thought it all a great impertinence. Fools.' One wonders if Nancy herself had been quite so impressed by Peter's prescience back in 1934, when she was busy turning Unity into the mad but harmless Eugenia Malmains. But by

1939 her husband was flavour of the month. To Jessica she mentioned a quarrel between Peter and Giles Romilly, Esmond's brother: 'Rodd lost his temper & was most awfully rude (quite like Farve, & I have never seen it happen before, I was quite shaken up).' She deplored the falling-out with Giles but there was a hint of 'Why, Mr Rodd! You're so . . . manly!' about Nancy's description.

Of course Peter was going away, and there is nothing like that for making people feel fondly towards each other. But the fact is that their near-dead marriage had been gently rekindled by circumstances. Had no war come, had the Rodds still been living that semi-squalid, wholly dreary routine of jobs gained, jobs lost; baby conceived, baby lost; adultery; bridge; drunkenness; with nothing but litters of gorgeous, slithery puppies to lighten Nancy's days, then that would have been it. But the international situation, and Peter's impeccable response to it all, gave Nancy the chance to care for her husband again.

'It is perhaps something', he wrote to her in 1940, 'to be destined to fight in the biggest battle since the world began. I don't pretend not to be frightened, but duty and destiny are all so clearly defined that it will be easier to take a proper part.' The mere fact of his writing this implies sincere feeling for Nancy, even if only a desire to look good in her eyes. Yet a throwaway remark of Harold Acton's acts as a deadly counterbalance: in his memoir of Nancy, Acton writes that when he encountered Peter at the Savile Club, on leave during the war, 'he would ask me not to tell Nancy that he was in London'.

Commentators tend to see the Rodd marriage as irretrievably over by this time, indeed from about 1936 onwards; they say that Nancy was merely carrying on with Peter for form's sake, that she was suffering agonies over his infidelity and unreliability, that her life with him was a half-life only. This is true, in essentials; yet it does not quite square with the tone of the letters written, by both of them, in the early years of the war. It does not allow sufficiently for ambiguity. Marriage is never – except at its beginning and end, and not even always then – just one thing or another. It is often thought to be, but perhaps women like Nancy (and her sisters) knew better. The funny little revival in her marriage, born of residual affection, possibly of residual physical attraction, above all of circumstance, was not so surprising; nor did it require from her great forgiveness or painful compromises. In 1941 she wrote, inside the cover of her diary: 'Marriage is the most important thing in life & must be kept going at almost any cost . . .', And she believed this, even when her own behaviour betrayed her.

As for Peter, dodging his wife in the Savile Club: of course that was him all over, still playing the delinquent, still yearning for escape. It did not mean that he had no fondness for Nancy, more that he couldn't be bothered with anything that made steady demands upon him. Nancy probably knew this. She knew that war was transitory, that it was not life, that everything would be different when it was all over. 'War psychology', as she would write of her heroine, Sophia, in her next novel, 'so incomprehensible during peace time, already had her in its grip'. But for the time being, she was enjoying her strange state of limbo, and her even stranger state of looking up to her husband.

Given that her life had frankly stagnated in the mid-1930s, the novelty of the situation must have been very welcome. 'Well I enjoyed the war very much, I'm ashamed to say,' Nancy told her television interviewer in 1966. It energised her, and it actually made her happy again. Dreadful though it might be and had already been, it at least shook things up. Before war broke out Nancy felt that the years of her marriage had been about nothing, that all they had done was to take her down towards the end of youth. But she was only thirty-five, and in a sense was still like someone at the start of their life: 'she had', says Diana, 'the *joie de vivre* that goes with a prolonged adolescence.' It took little to make her buoyantly attractive once again, and wartime London seems to have done the trick. She relished it. 'Everyone was in a very good temper. Nice and jolly,' she said, which for her was paramount. It is surely significant that after little more than a month of war, she began a new novel (hoping, no doubt, to exorcise the memory of *Wigs on the Green*, whose publication had been made so utterly bloody by family feuds).

. She wrote *Pigeon Pie* while working at a first-aid post in Praed Street, near to her home (her stint as an all-night driver clearly hadn't lasted). The new job was atrociously boring: 'this is my 9th day and feels like 7 years', she wrote to Violet Hammersley. 'Anyway in case I didn't I must tell you about the foreheads. Well my job is writing on the foreheads of dead & dying in indelible pencil. *What* I write I haven't yet discovered . . . I think I shall write Mrs Hammersley 31 Tite Street & see what happens, it might produce interesting complications in a case of loss of memory.'

Yet it is obvious from Nancy's letters – which have a terrific zest, quite different from the taut misery of a couple of years earlier – that she was champing at the bit. And so, despite extremely unpropitious circumstances – the cold, the 'electric light all day' and what she called a brain 'like the inside of a bad walnut' – she started her book. 'I am . . . writing a funny book about spies it is very funny indeed (*I* think!)' she wrote to Jessica, in November 1939.

Not everyone would agree that *Pigeon Pie* is very funny indeed. Those people who don't really get Nancy – who view her style as amusing, but also as the precious ramblings of a superficial snob – would be deeply irritated by the book. It has in fact been called her worst novel (by Jonathan Guinness). One can see why, in a way. She wrote it in fits and starts and the plot is, at first glance, terribly silly. Yet to those people who *do* get Nancy, who can't get enough of that sparkling stream of consciousness, the book makes clear what has hitherto been hinted at: that here is a writer with the priceless gift of infinite readability.

This heroine, Lady Sophia Garfield, is the prime ingredient in Nancy's *Pigeon Pie*. She is an extremely satisfying person for a reader to live with: feminine, rather sexy, emotional yet controlled, able to handle husband and lover and competition. She copes admirably when her lover, Rudolph (attractive, irresponsible, very much Prod), shows signs of being interested in another woman, the idiotic vampish Olga. 'Sophia saw that she must look out. She knew very well that when a man is thoroughly disloyal about a woman, and at the same time begins to indulge in her company, he nearly always intends to have an affair with that woman.' So Sophia puts an end to a date with Rudolph – 'this new predilection . . . was becoming a bore' – by telling him she is dining with another man: 'Rudolph said no more. He stopped the cab . . . hailed another cab going in the opposite direction, jumped into it and disappeared.

'Sophia minded rather . . . but he must be taught a lesson.'

This is enchanting, capable without being smug; and it shows that in many ways Sophia is the woman Nancy would like to have been.

She later wrote that Sophia was based upon her pretty friend, the political hostess Lady Pamela Berry,[5] who handled her life with a light but sure touch. But of course Sophia is also Nancy. Indeed writing her may have made Nancy more like her. 'Sophia had a happy character and was amused by life': it became true of her creator, too, because for Nancy imagining did not stop on the page, it permeated reality. And there was something else, something in the *way* that she wrote Sophia, the detached and benevolent assurance of the phrases that bring her to life. With Nancy, so much was a question of idiom, of portraying a view of life in a style so decided, so complete, that style becomes substance. By writing in this way, with these delicate flicks of the pen that reveal a good deal and conceal even more, Nancy began to make for herself a persona, a perspective, a philosophy that would sustain her through life: sustain her readers also.

Sophia's charm is the book's charm: easy, gossipy, intimate, slightly restrained. This was Nancy's charm too, and for the first time what she wrote is marinated in her particular and inimitable flavour. Sophia's voice infuses the novel, as Fanny's was later to do. Moving from the third to the first person would, in *The Pursuit of Love*, complete the job, but even here it works beautifully. Nancy had learned, or intuited, that she need do nothing but write in her own way, that everything else is excess baggage; possibly the difficulties involved in getting *Pigeon Pie* on to the page forced her to keep it simple, and what luck that was. The reader is wholly comfortable with the book because Nancy too is *à son aise*. She is completely confident about what she is doing, even though she knew that she could probably do better. As she would, of course, with the book that followed *Pigeon Pie*. In *The Pursuit of Love*, her complete confidence would be completely justified; there, she would have every reason in the world to believe that she knew what she was doing. There, she found her subject at last, and it danced to perfection with her voice. But the voice – clear, clean, childlike; knowing, good-natured, apparently artless – she had found already: in *Pigeon Pie*.

The plot, however, can surely be dismissed as a spy story so ludicrous that Sapper wouldn't have given it house room. Or can it? In fact, *Pigeon Pie* holds up pretty well on that front also. 'I must tell you it's very evocative of the phoney war', Nancy wrote to Evelyn Waugh in 1951, when the novel was reissued, as passages such as this one show: 'Rather soon after the war was declared, it became obvious that nobody intended it to begin. The belligerent countries were behaving like children in a round game, picking up sides.'[6]

This is the kind of simple, sensible thing that Nancy wrote and that turns her silly spy story into light but legitimate satire. She creates an old singer, Sir Ivor King, much beloved by the English and known as 'The King of Song', who is kidnapped by the Nazis and forced to make wireless broadcasts for them ('"Good night dears", said the old König, "keep your hairs on. By the way, where *is* the Ark Royal?"'). Ridiculous, of course; but the whole point is that it is *meant* to be. It is a joke on the phoney-war mentality, when people were so primed for action that they saw nuns as Huns and carrier pigeons as enemy agents. Sophia is a part of this. She wants to be a secret agent, she wants to inhabit the world of Bulldog Drummond and save her country; but when it comes down to it 'she had not really the temperament best suited to the work. It was not in her nature, for instance, to relish being sent out on a cold and foggy evening, after she had had her bath and changed her clothes.' Nancy's joke is to put an unlikely person bang in the middle of a spy story; like Flora Poste in *Cold Comfort Farm*, Sophia shows up her surroundings just by being in them. 'You've known the whole works since Greta disappeared, haven't you?' says Heatherley, the American (double) agent with whom Sophia thinks she is in league. 'What works? Darling Heth, do tell me; it does sound such heaven . . .'

Nancy is pulling the same trick as she did in *Wigs on the Green*, when she put Fascism into the village of Chalford and yokels into Union Jack shirts. She was cutting through the mists that grow around ideas, concepts, ideologies, and picking out the personal motivations that lie within (later she would do this, to delectable effect, in her historical biographies). It is a wonderful way of telling the truth about people. Sophia wants to be a spy for noble reasons, because she wants to help England win the war; but she also wants to be a spy because Olga has been hinting at her own secret-agent activities. 'How fortunate', Sophia thinks, wishing that Heatherley were more attractive, 'she loved her work for its own sake (and that of Olga).'

This kind of satire is not really satire at all: it is just Nancy's way of looking at things, which is so clear as to seem almost skewed. As such, it is easy to see why *Pigeon Pie* has been condemned as silly to the point of irresponsibility. Again, however, this misses the point. From the time of *Pigeon Pie* onwards, Nancy was not attempting to be a satirist, she was simply relating things as she saw them. Those who criticise her writing – as naïve, trivial, frivolous, snobbish – do so as if, in their collective mind, there was some mysterious ideal of correctness against which she is refusing to measure up. They judge her in relation to something that she is not, rather than according to what she is. Yet by 1940 Nancy was pretty much *sui generis* as a writer: 'purely idiosyncratic', as Evelyn Waugh was to say[7]. Criticising *Pigeon Pie* as naïve, trivial etc. therefore seems meaningless, like criticising a poodle for failing to be a Dobermann.

Anyway the book is not wholly silly. When Sophia rescues the King of Song from his kidnappers at the end of the book, he 'looked at her, she thought, as if he never expected to see her again in life; he spoke with the abruptness and irritation of a badly frightened man'. Even at this preliminary stage of the war, Nancy knows where the necessary loyalties lie: any character who has ever been remotely keen on Germany is subjected to a delicate, merciless contempt. Of Sophia's husband – based upon her brother-in-law Francis Rodd – Nancy writes that 'the chief reason he loved the Germans was because they buttered him up so much. All those free rides in motors and aeroplanes.' Anyone who dodges war work is also made to suffer. Jessica Romilly appears in the book as a character called Mary Pencill, who 'loved Sophia but thought her incurably frivolous', and who is stuffed to the brim with principle, little of which translates into action. Mary mocks Sophia's job of writing on foreheads at the first-aid post, 'Sophia said that it was better than doing nothing like Mary, and they rang off, each in a huff.'

Nancy felt very deeply about what she saw as shirking. 'I really think it rather queer that out of 7 able-bodied Mitfords only Tom and I are attempting any sort of war work', she wrote to Mrs Hammersley in October 1939. This was a little unfair: Unity was *hors de combat*, Diana had a very young child (Alexander Mosley, born in 1938) and was pregnant with her fourth son (Max, born April 1940). Jessica had

travelled with Esmond to America, where he would join up with the
Canadian Air Force and she would conceive his child (Constancia,
born in February 1941) Pamela, whose husband Derek Jackson was
in the RAF, was running a farm; and Deborah, of whom Nancy wrote
in 1939 that she was 'having a wild time with young cannon fodder at
the Ritz etc.', later worked in a YMCA canteen (although she did admit
that marriage, to Lord Andrew Cavendish in 1941, was a preferable
kind of 'work of national importance'). But these anti-family remarks
of Nancy's were in keeping with her detachment from them all at this
time; as was her dig at Jessica in *Pigeon Pie*. The book, incidentally, was
not liked by Nanny Blor, who may have intuited its coolness towards
the girls she loved.

Pigeon Pie sets forth what Nancy considered the correct form of
behaviour: insouciant courage, and unrelenting patriotism. Germans
are ghastly ('they have always been the same since the days of the
Roman Empire'), Americans are almost worse ('Luke hates jokes and
hates the war . . . so isn't he lucky to be going to America where they
have neither?'). Meanwhile there is an instinctive faith in Englishness:
'Mind you, of course, we're bound to win really, in the end', says one of
Sophia's light-hearted Cabinet minister friends: 'we always do.'

It is a joke, but Nancy means it. In its way her philosophy had,
by this time, become as simple as that of her sisters. It gave her life
a straightforward and satisfying meaning, not least because of the
respect it enabled her to feel for her husband. She would never have
written Rudolph as such a sexy character – a devil, but deep down
on the side of righteousness – had relations with Peter not revived
themselves. This was what war could do. It simplified, and it brought
to life as it destroyed. For Nancy, more than most people, this would
be very precisely the case.

There is a strange, semi-poetic passage early in *Pigeon Pie*, in which
Sophia delves beneath the polished surface of her life, and remembers
buried days of hunting. 'Riding home from the last meet of a season,
late in the afternoon of a spring day, there would be primroses and
violets under the hedges, far far away the sound of a horn, and later
an owl. The world is not a bad place, it is a pity to have to die. But of
course, it is only a good place for a very few people.'

It is the kind of memory – so surprising in so urban a woman –
that would inform *The Pursuit of Love*: infuse it, indeed. Here it is
uncharacteristic, and one wonders what was in Nancy's mind when
she wrote it. It is as though she was impelled in some unconscious
way by thoughts of the life now gone, when the Mitford family had
seemed an indestructible entity beneath the Cotswold sky. Perhaps
she was thinking not just of herself but of Unity, whose memories of
that former life were now scattered about her brain like refugees, or
lost in the hole she believed the doctors to have made in her head. At
the start of 1940, Unity made her halting way back to Oxfordshire
and to the world of the Mitford past. 'She is like a child in many ways',
Nancy wrote to Mrs Hammersley. 'She is very happy to be back, keeps
on saying "I thought you all hated me but I don't remember why". She
said to me You are not one of those who would be cruel to somebody
are you? So I said I was very much against that.'

Nancy's detachment failed her when, for the first time, she saw
great galumphing Boud lying in her nursing home bed, incontinent,
with yellow teeth and matted hair and eyes whose blue glare had been
switched to dim: for Unity, the world was not a good place, it was
sad and still, filled only with pity, and would never be much more
again. Nancy had to leave the room to weep for the wreckage of her
sister. Then she stayed for a while with her mother at Old Mill Cottage
in High Wycombe, helping out while she tried to finish *Pigeon Pie*
('Darling I hasten to write a word . . . such a scribble . . .' she wrote to
Violet Hammersley: every second was clearly precious). But Nancy
could not have left Lady Redesdale after a mere flying visit. This was
a duty too, as much as war work.

Unity was not just an outcast, who had blistered her family name
by its searing contact with Nazism (even now, seventy years on, it is
what people say first: 'Oh the Mitfords, wasn't one of them in love
with Hitler?'). She was not just destructive, she was destroyed; and the
mother whose life she had effectively ended had now to tend the ruin
of her daughter. Unity needed continual nursing. There was the bed
linen to be changed daily, the feeding as of an elderly stroke patient,
the endless attempts to understand and to convey meaning, and all
for a twenty-five-year-old girl who, a few months earlier, had had the
massive life force of a six-month-old St Bernard. Those who condemn

Unity as a wicked fool who got all that she deserved forget that she was not the only casualty. Her parents had to live with the consequences of her pointless action, and it is hard to imagine anything much harder to bear.

It brought their marriage to an end. Grief is conventionally thought to bring people closer together; in fact, at its strongest, when both parties are feeling with equal intensity, it separates them. And so it was with the Redesdales, who anyway were not the kind of people to share their emotions. David could not bear to be with his daughter. More sensitive than Sydney, he also became more useless; he had always shuddered at clumsiness or messiness in children ('spilling food on the good table-cloth' he would say – this may partly explain Nancy's own fastidiousness) and now, in a grown girl, he had to watch the dribblings of a new-born baby. Beyond this, however, was the sense that Hitler was to blame for it all. David must have torn himself apart over his own brief infatuation with that gimcrack regime, but he at least was over it. Sydney – perhaps for similar reasons of self-justification – still professed admiration for Germany, which was ridiculous but understandable. But it was too much for her husband. 'Things are terrible', Nancy wrote to Mrs Hammersley from High Wycombe in February. 'Muv & Farve absolutely at loggerheads . . .'

One feels for both of them, to an appalling degree. It was not David's fault that he could not cope with it, that he took refuge in Inch Kenneth or Rutland Gate: his solitary misery must have been acute. It was from Sydney, however, that the day-in, day-out bravery was required. There was not much else she could have done, of course; it was one of those situations that can only be endured (Blor helped out for a while, but she had her own family). Nonetheless Sydney's stoicism and competence were admirable. Even Nancy said as much, in a letter to Decca: 'Muv has been too wonderful with her [Unity] and has absolutely given up her whole life.' Conversely, David 'hardly goes near her, and has never been there to relieve Muv and give her a chance to have a little holiday'. David had been told, quite early on, that Unity would never recover, while Sydney was given a 'kindlier' prognosis. 'I think, for her sake, one should cling to the former don't you?' wrote Nancy. But the harsher version was the true one, as so often is the case. Unity did regain strength and mobility, and would embark on little excursions from the cottage that Sydney took next door to the pub in Swinbrook (near the hated old Mitford home), taking a bus into Oxford, sometimes simply wandering off like a vagrant. She had become a shambolic figure: bursting hugely out of her clothes, seething with frustrations that she barely understood. Her pleasures were the goats that Sydney kept (making cheese 'off the ration' from their milk), and the collages that she made on tables in the cottage sitting room. '...if I so much as put my knitting on one of them she hies up and shrieks BLOODY FOOL in my ear which becomes rather irksome'[8], wrote Deborah, who lived in Swinbrook before her marriage to Lord Andrew Cavendish. Unity had taken an irrational hatred to Deborah: 'She is completely different to what she was and I think the worst thing...is that she's completely lost her sense of humour and never laughs.' The worst thing, indeed, for a Mitford.

But Nancy, who despite frequent visits to Swinbrook was less grindingly exposed to Unity, decided to view things differently. In March 1940, she wrote to Jessica that 'Bowd is so wonderfully much better...now she is her old self again. Of course very ill still, but the same person, not a *quite* different one.' Perhaps Nancy was trying to console both Jessica and herself. At any rate she achieved what she wanted, which was to absorb the sadness of her sister's situation and nurture the small flame of her own happiness.

If she had hopes for *Pigeon Pie*, however, these would come to nothing. That clever little creature was stillborn in May 1940: the phoney war had got too real for readers to laugh at the kidnapping of the King of Song. 'It should be just what people are in the mood for, if we are quick', said her new publisher, Hamish Hamilton. They were not quick enough. Holland and Belgium fell as Nancy's novel emerged with its pretty hands over its eyes. 'Poor, sweet, charming Sophia!' wrote the *Spectator*. 'She is, alas! An unimportant casualty', concluded the review, not unkindly.

So *Pigeon Pie* bit the dust just as *Wigs on the Green* had done. One has to wonder how Nancy felt at this time about her writing career, and whether it seemed like a career at all. One suspects not. She had written four novels, a considerable achievement for someone doing it, as it were, on the side; the books were always reviewed, usually politely and never savagely; she had improved immeasurably as a writer, as she must have been aware, yet there had been no real change in her status since she came up with *Highland Fling* back in 1931.

Almost certainly she would not have sought such a thing. She just wrote her books, as and when, for satisfaction and for money, with pride but apparently without expectation. It is an attitude hardly conceivable nowadays, when so many authors plot their careers like graphs on a business plan. Which is not to say that Nancy did not care about the fate of *Wigs on the Green* and *Pigeon Pie*: they were a great deal better than her first two novels, they deserved better, and they were both scuppered by circumstance. Apart from anything else, she needed them to sell because she was, as always, desperately poor. (When *Pigeon Pie* was reissued in 1952, it sold more than 10,000 copies: 'What madness', wrote Nancy to Evelyn Waugh. 'Rather sad when you think what it would have meant to me when it first appeared and I was penniless.') Probably no one would have been more amazed than Nancy had she been told, in May 1940, that the publication of her next book would transform her life: that *The Pursuit of Love* would sell, and succeed, with the unstoppable force of the Germans then marching upon Europe, and that a writing 'career' would suddenly, and triumphantly, be hers.

When *Pigeon Pie* made its abortive appearance, however, Nancy had much of her mind on other things. She was, for instance, pregnant again: further evidence of the revival of her marriage, as she did not conceive with ease. When Peter was home – in between training in Cambridge and commanding his company in Colchester – he must have been mostly in his wife's bed, playing Rudolph to Nancy's Sophia.

In May, he was sent to France. This can't have been easy for Nancy, although her letters are hardly seized up with anxiety about him; this, in its turn, implies that what she felt for Peter was very much bound up with the war, and with the decent way in which he was answering its moral questions. She writes with pride about the fact that Simon Elwes (married to Nancy's sister-in-law) had joined the Welsh Guards 'so will be vastly junior to Pete which is nice'. Peter was proud of his wife, too. Nancy wrote to Mark Ogilvie-Grant that she had hoped to send him a copy of *Pigeon Pie* (the character of Sir Ivor is a teasing take on Mark), 'but when I got home I found that Rodd had bagged

all my comp: copies to give to his brother officers'. Which no doubt
pleased her.

Nancy's letters make no reference to the second miscarriage that
she suffered in June 1940, and so one can only imagine how she
felt about it. She may have tried to dismiss it. At the same time she
probably saw it as a death to hope. Her sisters had lost babies too:
Jessica's first daughter, Julia, died at five months from measles; Debo's
first child was stillborn in 1941; Pamela suffered two miscarriages;
only Diana seemed unstoppably fecund. But these women were all
younger than Nancy. Their chances of having children were therefore
better (although Pam, in fact, never carried a baby to term), and this
may have filled her with some of the old, bitter, sisterly envy.

Her reaction to the loss was to leave Blomfield Road, firstly to
stay with Mrs Hammersley on the Isle of Wight, then with Peter's
aunt, Violet Stuart-Wortley, in Hampshire. Aunt Vi was a marvellous
woman who thought the world of Nancy ('my word, how lucky Peter
was to find a wife like that', she had said when the Rodds first married).
And in a letter to Deborah in 1971, Nancy wrote that she had had a
'love for old ladies: Aunt Vi, Mrs H', because of the 'unsatisfactory
relationship I had with Muv'.

For it should surely have been her mother to whom Nancy turned?
Of course she may have thought that Sydney had her hands full with
Unity, which was certainly true. But when Deborah had her stillborn
baby, Unity was moved out of the Swinbrook cottage for a while so
that her sister could stay there. Nancy, it is clear, felt more comfortable
elsewhere; she would not have relied on her mother to give the right
sort of sympathy, nor on herself to elicit it. She may even have felt
embarrassed, unwilling to demand comfort. And so she went instead
to help Aunt Vi with a consignment of evacuees (a hard thing to
do, for someone who had just lost a child). She planned to take 'a
job on the land. True I am very soft at present but I could get fit no
doubt & it would be nice to feel one was growing things.' She was a
countrywoman at heart, after all, and working the land might have
seemed a fitting way to bury her various griefs.

But this idea of an idyll did not last: perhaps Nancy was bored,
perhaps the introspection of the life was not really bearable. At any
rate, as if magnetised, as if wanting to endure all that war could throw

at her, back she went to the iron furnace of Blomfield Road and to the full force of 'Hitty's' bombs. The Blitz began on 7 September 1940, kindling in Nancy a perverse vitality. Proximity to Paddington Station put her in the firing line and, on 9 September, she wrote to Mrs Hammersley in a state of stoical hysteria: 'Darling the nights! Nobody who hasn't been in it can have the smallest idea of the horror one is going through. I never don't feel sick, can't eat anything & although dropping with tiredness can't sleep either. No doubt one will get used to it soon – last night I shall never forget as long as I live. I emerged this morning confident that, apart from 12 Blomfield, not one stone in the neighbourhood could possibly be left upon another. Actually, search as I might, I could see no damage of any kind! However there has been a good deal actually & very near, in streets behind the house . . . Ten hours is *too* long, you know of concentrated noise & terror, in a house alone. Thank heaven for Milly who is a rock.' The maid, Gladys, had spent the night 'in a trench' in Hyde Park, and things became easier when she was there. As Nancy wrote, she was 'really a heroine. She arrived back at 6 this morning all smiles & was ready with my breakfast punctually at 8.' It was the kind of behaviour that Nancy admired above any other, and although she said of herself 'it is terrible to be such a coward' this was not in fact true. Nancy always had courage: it was one of her defining characteristics, and it showed itself most in the good humour that she strove to retain. Bravery was not bravery, unless it wore a mask of cheerfulness – so she thought, and she was probably right.

Her letters from September 1940 convey the chaos of the Blitz, the way in which tragedy was subsumed into a petty, relentless inconvenience. She told Mrs Hammersley an exhausting, terrible saga that began when Peter turned up at Blomfield Road 'with the two babies (5 & 3) of one of his soldiers. They and their mother had had their house in Brixton collapse on them & the mother had a ghastly miscarriage & was dying. The poor man couldn't even be given 4 hrs leave to arrange things . . .' In the night 'a Molotoff bread basket descended on the next door house which caught fire'. Nancy sent for the fire brigade and fled with the two children to Hampstead, where her old French governess Zella was living; then returned to Blomfield Road, 'shot at on the way by the Home Guard because the taxi didn't stop. Had a *fearful* pasting here all the rest of the night – 5 large houses in the next street just vanished into thin air.' Eventually Nancy sent the children, Gladys, Milly, 'my fur coat & all my linen' to the Buckinghamshire home of her friend Lady Diana Worthington. 'They were such darling children & so good.'

Gladys had not wanted to leave Nancy, even though 'this part (Mai Vale) has got it worse than almost anywhere (except the East End of course).' But as Nancy wrote to Mrs Hammersley: 'I think every living thing that can be got out of this hell should be – NOBODY can have the slightest idea of what it is like until they've experienced it. Asfor the screaming bombs they simply make your flesh creep but the whole thing is so fearful that they are actually only a slight added horror . . . Oh dear there are the sirens again what a horrid life.' Her nerves, understandably, were in shreds; despite her gallant nature Nancy was not a robust person; her insubstantial body shrank very easily to skin and bone, and she had not long since had a miscarriage. Yet she wrote on 12 September that she was 'trying to get some work in the East End': one can only admire.

She felt that she should stick the war out, as people like Gladys and Peter were doing, and she seems to have been almost high on this belief. She was fanatical about observing measures like four inches of water in the bath, no water heater and walking everywhere to save resources. Later she took up fire-watching, which would have meant hardly any sleep at all, and after dealing competently with an incendiary that landed in Hill Street in 1944 was asked to lecture on the subject. (Then she was asked to stop: 'Well you see it's your voice. It irritates people so much, they said they'd like to put you on the fire.'⁹)

In 1942 she refused to attend a ball thrown by Debo, because she thought dancing inappropriate while Tom Mitford (in Libya) and Peter (in Ethopia) were fighting overseas. James Lees-Milne, in his diaries, mused upon this new stern conventionality of Nancy's: 'she so often shocks me', he wrote in March 1942, 'accustomed as I still am to think of her running contrary to conventions in her old girlish, mocking manner.' He saw in this a mixture of sincerity and perversity, and he probably had a point. He quoted Nancy as saying that it was the duty of the upper-classes 'to remain in England after the war, whatever the temptations to get out', which is quite funny when one knows that the first thing Nancy did, after peace was declared, was to leave for Paris.

Yet she meant what she was saying at the time, she lived by what she said; and this intense emphasis upon duty may well have derived – like so much else – from her relationship with her family. When she wrote in 1942 that Deborah had become 'simply horrid . . . a very *exigeante* [demanding] little creature & dreadfully spoilt', this was not what she really thought. Nor, in different circumstances, would she have been so much against attending a ball in wartime. She was simply, obdurately against her family. In the first half of the war, what sustained her rather comfortless life – alongside the occasional attentions of Peter and the more faithful ones of Milly – was the sense that she was the sole Mitford (except Tom) to be behaving as a person should.

And so, possessed by righteousness, Nancy performed one of the most extraordinary acts of her life.

In May 1940, when the war got serious, Sir Oswald Mosley was arrested under Defence Regulation 18B, a severe emergency power that allowed the Government to detain without trial. Rightly or wrongly, Mosley was regarded as a threat to national security. He had certainly opposed war with Germany; nevertheless he had, since its outbreak, urged members of the British Unionist party to fight for their country and 'do nothing . . . to help any other power'. Nor had he had dealings of any significant kind with Hitler. The notion that he believed he might rule a conquered Britain, as a puppet of the Germans, was utterly ludicrous.

But for an avowed supporter of fascism to be free, when Britain faced a powerfully real threat of invasion by the Nazis, was regarded as an insult, an affront to a national morale that needed clear and simple enmities to feed upon. And so Mosley was banged up in Brixton, along with a few hundred other internees, in a part of the prison that had been on the point of demolition and was running alive with bedbugs. 'I am thankful that Sir Oswald Quisling has been jugged aren't you', wrote Nancy to Mark Ogilvie-Grant. She too required straightforward gestures. Nor had she ever liked Mosley. But, she continued, 'I think it quite useless if Lady Q is still at large.' If Mosley had to be jailed then Diana should be too. If she, Nancy, was suffering the privations of war whilst supporting its rightful prosecution, then Diana, who supported the regime that was the cause of the war, should surely suffer too.

A month later, Nancy received a request from the Home Office to give information about Diana (whose putative imprisonment had been urged by her former father-in-law, Lord Moyne). She went to be interviewed by Gladwyn Jebb[10], then working for the Under-Secretary of State. She was obliged to do so. She could hardly refuse to help a wartime Government on the grounds of family loyalty. What *would* anyone do in such a situation? Realistically, one would probably go along, feeling rather grim and torn by the necessity, and say as little as was consistent with honesty.

Nancy did far more than that. On the subject of Diana's visits to Germany: 'I advised him [Jebb] to examine her passport to see how often she went.' She had gone quite often, in fact. Her reason was that she was trying to win a concession for her husband to start a wireless station, not as a propaganda vehicle but purely as a money-making exercise, a sort of Teutonic Radio Luxembourg. This was impossible to do in Britain, where the BBC had a monopoly of the wavelengths, and Diana's connections in the Nazi high command made Germany the obvious country. So she talked to Hitler about it, hoping that he would override Goebbels (who wanted all the wavelengths for himself); and her success seemed assured around the time that war broke out.

Nancy did not know that Diana had a motive for spending long evenings chatting with Hitler, beyond her admitted pleasure in his company. As Jan Dalley put it in her biography of Diana, 'some of the stigma of her flirtation with the Nazis might have been mitigated (in Nancy's eyes, for instance) by the fact that she was doing business, as it were, for the family firm.' But the radio station 'alibi' looked dodgy, all the same. MI5 knew about Diana's visits to Hitler, knew the reason for them, and – Dalley again – 'found it hard to believe that there were no direct propaganda intentions'. The alibi, in fact, only helped to convince the British Government of Diana's 'guilt'. No doubt Nancy felt much the same way.

She did not *want* to get Diana off the hook; she wanted to think the worst of her. Why else would she have said to Gladwyn Jebb, when there was no actual need for her to do so: 'I regard her as an extremely dangerous person' –? It is scarcely believable. This was Nancy's sister, a woman with a small son and a baby whom she was breast-feeding, whose husband was in prison, who was burning in the fires of public vilification. She was almost certainly going to be jailed anyway; that was the climate of the times, and of course the decision would have been way beyond Nancy's control. But would one not, in such circumstances, do all that was reasonably possible to help a sister: say yes, she has been to Germany, yes, she has been an advocate of Fascism, but she would never actually oppose Britain in the war? That was the truth, after all. Whether it would have been believed, or would have made any difference to Diana's fate, is another story. But Nancy did not even try to say those things. She made it worse, not better; she played her part in making sure that, on 29 June, Diana would be taken away from an eleven-week-old baby to Holloway, imprisoned without trial under Defence Regulation 18B, locked in a dirty cell with a mattress on a wet floor and a window covered by rotting sandbags, left with aching breasts and a plate of gristle to eat.

'Not very sisterly behaviour', Nancy wrote to Violet Hammersley, 'but in such times I think it one's duty?' The question mark perhaps betrayed a small tingle of disturbing guilt. Perhaps she knew that she had carried out the threat, made to her mother a year earlier, to 'join hands with the devil himself to stop any further extension of the disease [of Fascism]'. Yet she may have felt no guilt at all. Her letter to Mrs Hammersley begins with a lament for the Spanish refugees whom she and Peter had helped in 1939, and who had found homes in the now conquered France: 'all our poor refugees . . . no doubt will be handed over for Franco to shoot them.' Around 25,000 of them would die at the hands of the Germans, and this must have been hard for Nancy to contemplate. Writing about it was the best possible way to justify her meeting with Gladwyn Jebb, both to Mrs Hammersley and to herself. Diana's behaviour had made her own behaviour necessary; it was as simple as that.

Nevertheless it took some doing. Not everyone could have done it. Nor could they have done what Nancy subsequently did, which was to treat Diana in the most sympathetic possible way: write gossipy and cheering letters ('I saw your little Alexander the other day he *is* a darling how I wish they were living with me'); have Diana's elder sons, Jonathan and Desmond Guinness, to stay before they visited their mother in Holloway ('Fancy favourite aunt how blissful'); and accept money from her sister with which to buy a Christmas present ('I have bought some much needed facial condiments . . . actually managed to find a Guerlain lipstick'). Perhaps, again, Nancy saw no hypocrisy in this. She had done her duty for her country; now she was doing it for her sister, while at the same time writing to Mrs Hammersley: 'I would die of the lights out at 5.30 rule wouldn't you? I suppose she sits & thinks of Adolf.'

One can hardly blame Diana for subsequently describing Nancy as someone impelled by spite, not to be believed, 'the most disloyal person I ever knew'.[11] 'Disloyal' was a significant word to choose, for loyalty towards her husband was perhaps the real agent of Diana's downfall in 1940. But Nancy had played her part in it too. Diana knew nothing of this part until years after the war had ended. She must have remembered those kindnesses of Nancy's, offered when she was in her cell, and shuddered.

The Mosleys were detained for more than three years. They were released – in the face of public opinion – at the end of 1943, then placed under house arrest. During her time in prison, it was really only Diana's remarkable nature that saw her through unbowed. She became friends with the other women in F Block (when Churchill asked that Diana be allowed a bath a day, rather than once a week, she refused it as an unfair privilege). And she simply did not accept the concept of shame. She knew that her imprisonment was an illegality, a gimcrack construction made to satisfy public opinion. She suffered terribly, nonetheless. When Nancy wrote that 'Zella who went to see her says she has never looked more blooming'[12], this can only have been from a twisted kind of wishful thinking. Diana had entered prison a young woman of thirty in the prime of health; three years of living on parcels of Stilton, of unclean lavatories and semi-underground cells, wore her down, and in 1943 – by which time she and Mosley were living together, in a prison block for couples – she suffered an apparently incurable attack of diarrhoea. Another ex-BUF internee named Major de Laessoe gave her an opium pill, 'which he said always did the trick. I passed into a deep coma for four or five days. One would have felt so awful for the poor major if one had died.'[13]

Worse than the physical suffering was the torment of being separated from her sons, who were taken to live with Pam. All the BUF women with young children were released from jail in 1940, except Diana. She did not see her new baby for ten months after her arrest. She had to endure a night in her cell, waiting for news, while Jonathan was taken to hospital for an emergency appendectomy. At the end of visits to the prison, two-year-old Alexander 'often had to be forcibly dragged away from Diana, his tears soaking her clothes'[14]. It is hard to accept that she deserved this kind of agony; she was punished for being married to the wrong person, for being high-profile and charismatic. A hearing of her case, in October 1940, concluded that she was 'an attractive and forceful personality' who 'could be extremely dangerous if she were at large'. She had admitted, at this hearing, that she supported her husband in his Fascist beliefs: '. . . he told me a great deal about it . . . I thought that is the thing for me'. She admitted that Hitler had attended her wedding to Mosley: 'Because he is a friend of mine.' She did not attempt to hide her desire for a Fascist state in Britain, nor that she had opposed war with Germany; but, she said, 'I absolutely differentiate between my government and my country.' She had known, of course, that whatever she said before the Advisory Committee would make no odds. The Mosleys would stay in prison because that was what people wanted. Nancy, apparently, wanted it more than anyone.

Was it purely a question of principle, that led her to denounce her sister? Was it principle, indeed, that led Lord Moyne to urge Diana's imprisonment in the first place? Can it ever be said, in fact, that there is such a thing as 'pure' principle? Does the personal not obtrude, whether one is aware of it or not? Nancy probably *thought* that she was acting according to principle alone. No doubt she believed, as she marched into the Home Office bearing her metaphorical sword of truth, that she was merely a vessel filled to the brim with disinterested duty.

But she – had she been writing about herself – would have seen through this slightly terrifying image to the motivations within. She would have picked out the gleaming thread that led back to *Wigs on the Green*, and the cold falling-out with Diana over the whole question of political belief. She would have followed the thread back further, tracing the rivalry that she had felt since childhood with her beautiful, clever, moon-goddess sister. Then she might have moved onwards and sideways, and seen the mysterious fulfilment that Diana had achieved with her second marriage. She might, too, have conjured an image of Diana sitting, calm and satisfied and exquisite, with four sons around her. And she would have imagined her own self, whose adult life had so far been a raggedy clutching at happiness, and discerned the sad, small, spiteful compulsion that lurked within her grand gesture. Mistrust principle, she might have written, about herself and indeed about her family. It is rarely what it seems to be; and when it is sincere it is worst of all.

From 1941 onwards, Nancy herself would steer well clear of it. Like Sophia with her spying, it really was not her thing. Now she would detach herself differently, by finding a new and happy life, which would begin after the saddest event of all.

CHAPTER 6

In November 1941, when Nancy was staying in Oxford with her friends Roy and Billa Harrod[1], she was seized with appalling pains in her stomach. Typically, she made light of it; foolishly, she walked off with her suitcase and made her own way back to London. Then she went to the University College Hospital in Bloomsbury.

It was, she was told, an ectopic pregnancy. The condition was serious, and it would be necessary to operate. All she could do was make a desperate plea to the surgeon, before she went under the anaesthetic, to try to preserve her fertility. But she awoke to learn that her fallopian tubes had been damaged beyond repair and removed. At the age of thirty-seven, Nancy was now definitively barren.

She must have feared as much, but that is not the same as having one's fears confirmed, hearing the final judgment pronounced, realising that one's life, now, will be different from that of most women. It must have been a cold and terrible awakening for her, coming round in that hospital bed with her stitched and cavernous abdomen, preparing to face this particular fact. 'I have had a horrible time, so depressing', she wrote to Diana in Holloway. It was the closest she came to a confession of anguish. 'I can't say I suffered great agony but quite enough discomfort . . .'

Her loneliness was intense. No doubt she wished that Diana had not been put in prison, that she could have had her there to laugh with, to be told how lucky it was that 'one was lovely *One*'[2]. She tried for jokes, in the letter, and certainly she achieved irony: 'Muv was wonderful . . . When my symptoms were explained to her she said "ovaries – I thought one had 700 like caviar". Then I said how I couldn't bear the idea of a great scar on my tum to which she replied "But

darling who's ever going to see it?"' Nancy also had a conversation
with Sydney in which she first learned that she might, as a child,
have been infected with syphilis. Her doctor had asked if she had
ever had contact with the disease, a question that she in turn put to
her mother. Sydney apparently then admitted to having employed a
syphilitic nurserymaid and, from that point onwards, Nancy chose
to believe that her mother had caused her infertility. She could not
have *really* believed it: she had absolutely no symptoms of syphilitic
infection, and her doctor should probably never have put the idea
into her head in the first place. Nor should her mother have confessed
about the nurserymaid, when a modicum of imagination would have
said that this could only intensify Nancy's anguish. Of course Sydney
may never have said anything of the kind, although it is unlikely that
Nancy completely invented it. But she certainly seized upon it, and in
a very characteristic way: as usual with Sydney, she *wanted* to believe
in her guilt. She wanted to be able to attribute her own pain to the
actions of her mother.

Small wonder that she had run to Mrs Hammersley and Aunt Vi
after her miscarriage the year before. Leave aside the story about the
syphilitic nurserymaid: the remark about the ovaries, which Nancy
cannot possibly have invented, is confirmation enough of her mother's
innate detachment. Meanwhile Deborah, who had given birth to a
stillborn baby around the time of Nancy's hysterectomy, was being
looked after by Sydney at the Swinbrook cottage. This contrasting
treatment surely caused Nancy more pain, and she mustered a strange
sort of sympathy for her sister in the letter to Diana. 'Poor Debo it
must be wretched the worst thing in the world I should think – except
losing a manuscript which I always think must be *the* worst.'

And that, from then on, would be Nancy's view. She would not
have a baby; but she would have her writing still, and writing would
become a real and solid life to her. It is customary, nowadays, to
pretend that women can write books with an equal level of intensity
as men while at the same time raising children, but in truth this is
not usual: for whatever reason, the finest female artists have tended
to be childless. Selfishness *is* required. And when Nancy was able to
give her selfishness free rein, she became an artist: not a Jane Austen,
nor an Emily Brontë, but someone who found her deepest fulfilment

through her work, who realised through it her own vision of life. She did not 'write like a man', or any such nonsense. She remained intensely feminine, intensely herself – 'a survival of the time before feminism', as Evelyn Waugh wrote, semi-seriously, 'when it was thought feminine to be capricious'[3] – and she kept up the illusion that her books were produced with semi-detached casualness. But this was, indeed, an illusion, and an extremely clever one. Nancy's books took all the sustained effort that any proper, lasting work demands: for all their apparent ease of manner, their integrity was an unfathomable distance away from chick-lit.

The ballerina Alicia Markova was once asked if she regretted not having had a family, and she was fearless enough to say that her art would have suffered: 'Concentration, you see.' Nancy was not a writer whose work overwhelmed the whole of her life, that was not the nature of her absorption in it; but there is no doubt that the books she produced after her hysterectomy were better, surer, more fully formed, than those that she wrote when she had thought of herself – whether seriously or not – as a wife and potential mother. In fact they were in a different league altogether. This could be coincidence, or simply maturity. But there is probably more to it than that. Nancy was in many ways there already with *Pigeon Pie*, yet the book has a slightly amateurish quality. It really *is* semi-detached. Even then she was trying to get pregnant, playing house with Peter as he came back and forth, seeing marriage still as her natural destiny. 'The worst of it is I can't work when he's here', she wrote in 1949. 'I'm sure it's very silly but I can't. He has no respect for work & wanders in & out chatting.' Which implies that she could not dedicate herself to writing until she was fully free, living the kind of life that was, in those days, almost always lived by a man.

'*Faute de mieux*,' says Debo, who is in no doubt that had Nancy had her 'proper husband, proper children' she would have happily consigned writing to the level of a well-executed hobby. 'She had success as a writer – I think that's a second thing, myself. Being a total female, you see. And I think Nancy would have been but she never had the chance – and I don't think, I may be absolutely wrong, but I don't think anything makes up for women having husbands, lovers and children, and whatever it is that women want. I really don't.

I mean Diana's life – it was very sad in lots of ways, all those years in prison, but on the other hand it was much more what the papers now call fulfilled. Whatever that may mean, but I think I know what it means.

'Nancy adored children. She pretended not to much, but my children adored her – all children adored her, from me onwards.' Of Nancy's hysterectomy, she says: 'It was a terrible thing.'

It is true, and striking, that Nancy's writings are full of references to the loveliness of other people's children. Even the letter to Diana about the hysterectomy speaks of Roy and Billa Harrod's son Henry in the sweetest possible terms: 'They have an ideal child called Hen – I think the prettiest, most amusing little boy I ever saw.' This reads courageously. What also required courage was the knowledge, for Nancy, that she must face a life surrounded by other children, those of Diana and Deborah[4] probably being the hardest to bear.

And yet: although Diana accepts that Nancy wanted children when she was young – 'I think it's something that people do long for really' – she also believes that she adjusted more easily than most to their absence. 'I think probably they'd have been a great pest to her later on.' What Nancy really liked was to have charming young men like the Mosley boys or Debo's son Stoker[5] to visit: they were amusing and fun, they roared at her jokes and she, in turn, was what Alexander Mosley calls 'a wonderful aunt'. She also liked being godmother to Evelyn Waugh's daughter Harriet, upon whom she bestowed many carefully chosen presents: 'it's such fun getting things for a little girl, nearly all my relations of that age are boys except Emma [Debo's daughter] who has too many adorers & doesn't even glance at a present if you give her one.' 'You are the most wonderful godmother,' wrote Waugh, 'something out of a pantomime.'

But this demanded relatively little; and the question is whether in her heart she would have wanted to give more. Later, Harriet Waugh implied not: 'She had minimal interest in children and so on my brief glimpses of her I thought her chilly and unlikeable.'[6] This is a little surprising in the light of all the presents,[7] over which Nancy took so much trouble and pleasure. But it is interesting as it shows her to have been much keener on children when they were at a safe distance. 'She'd have been a lousy mother,' says John Julius Norwich robustly.

'Nancy was *not* maternal. I don't think she would have minded the hysterectomy all that much. I mean certainly not as much as other women would have minded. I really don't think so. How old was she when she had it? Getting a bit long in the tooth for having children, and particularly in those days.' (As Nancy would later write of Emilie du Châtelet, heroine of her historical biography *Voltaire in Love*: 'Her pregnancy, at her age, made her a figure of fun and she knew it.')

This is very much the anti-sentimentalist viewpoint, and it is offered by someone who knew Nancy socially, rather than intimately: to Lord Norwich, Nancy valued friends and wit and the adult pleasures of civilisation; the untidy world of the nursery would have been a drag and a bore. To Deborah, on the other hand, this was all a front. What Nancy really wanted was what women have always wanted, the mysterious, miraculous rewards of child-bearing.

As for Nancy herself – once her ability to have a baby had been taken from her, the last thing she would have wanted was pity. Nor would she have entertained for a second the notion that her life was ruined ('I am not quite so wonderfully well as I was', she wrote to James Lees-Milne, a couple of days after her operation, 'running a little temperature'). She would have considered that a commonplace idea, contrary to her creed. In a letter to Evelyn Waugh in 1946, she took an honest stance. 'There is a young woman who lives next door here (Blomfield Road) with 3 & I pity her from morning to night (and she pities me, so all is well really). I mind less and less not having any except I do think when they are puppies, from 1 to 4 they are rather heaven. 4–20 is unbearable.' But this was not the whole truth, of course. In 1949 she wrote to Waugh: 'I deplore not having any children.'

Her novels tell the same story. There are openly unwanted babies, like Linda's Moira in *The Pursuit of Love* and Polly's stillborn in *Love in a Cold Climate* (which 'took one look, according to the Radletts, at its father, and quickly died again'). These children are not expected to bring happiness, and Moira – that 'besotted little coward', as Linda unashamedly thinks of her – does not. But then there are the children who bring obvious and irreplaceable pleasure, who cause worry and heartache but are simply in the joyful nature of things: the Radletts themselves, Grace du Valhubert's son Sigismond in *The Blessing*, Fanny's three boys in *Don't Tell Alfred* ('I am always pleased when my children turn up. The sight of them rejoices me, I rush forward, I smile and I embrace').

Nancy was immensely sane about the whole thing, really. With some grace, she stood poised between an ineffable regret for what she had lost, and a relieved realism about what she had gained. She resisted bitterness, although she could never quite relax about the subject. Typical of her remarks was this coolly gallant one to Deborah, in 1964: 'I always think what a mercy not to have children but now I see Sto I'm not so sure . . . Perhaps I will leave him *everything*.' And to Evelyn Waugh, a little raggedly: 'Don't . . . tease me about not having children, it was God's idea, not mine.'

But who, at the time of her hysterectomy, would Nancy have wanted to have a baby with? Not her husband, that was for sure. The fragile dream of a child to kick the Rodd marriage into lasting life was over. Indeed an interesting question would have been posed to Nancy, had the ectopic pregnancy not saved her from having to answer it: how *on earth* would she have explained to everyone that she was carrying a baby who was not her husband's?

Peter disappeared into the war in 1941 and did not properly return until March 1944. The child could hardly have been his. Nor would she have wanted it to be. Although Nancy had quite liked the idea of Peter's baby when she conceived it in 1940, a year on the glamour of his wartime heroism had pretty well worn off. He was Prod again, unsatisfactory and unfaithful, self-important and self-centred (another one of those in the house? no thank you). He was also away much of the time in Addis Ababa, and not very interested in receiving visits from Nancy. In fact the marriage, as had been inevitable once the flurry of war died down, was reverting to the way it had been before Perpignan. The only difference was that the war – and other things – had made Peter even cockier than before.

In a letter to Mrs Hammersley from August 1940, Nancy had told of how some casual new friends were 'most kind but trying to induce me to leave my (I must say wretch of a) husband . . . As it is only a question of £.s.d. & the said hubby having a hole apparently in his pocket like a bottomless pit, I shall struggle on in matrimony despite them. How people do long to break up ménages I have often remarked on this in life . . .' So she would not then have taken such a step. She believed in marriage. As she wrote in her appointments diary for 1941: 'Marriage is the most important thing in life & must be kept going at almost any cost'. She was starting to see, however, that the 'cost' was getting just a little too high.

For some time Peter had been having an affair with Adelaide Lubbock, Nancy's cousin, whose son, Eric, had been a page at the Rodds' wedding. In the early years of the war, the 'sweet-voiced' Mrs Lubbock was 'in charge of another ARP post in distant Chelsea'[8], and Peter would hare off to see her when on leave in London.

A 1950 letter to Evelyn Waugh suggests that this affair of Peter's had been going on since as early as 1938: 'he said that for the last 12 years he has considered himself as married to Adelaide', Nancy wrote. If this is accurate, and there is no reason to think otherwise, it would mean that Peter had been sleeping with Mrs Lubbock at the time that he and Nancy were in Perpignan, and when Nancy became pregnant by him in 1940. Peter would have been quite capable of enjoying a little revival in his marriage while pleasuring a new mistress. It is also possible that Nancy knew about the affair all along, and was sufficiently insouciant not to worry about it. Adelaide was a relation and a friend; Nancy may have simply thought good luck to her. But this does not quite square with the impression one gets from her letters: those that she wrote between 1939 and the end of 1940 are, as has been shown, pretty much pro-Peter, and although they do refer to his mistress it is in the most innocent of terms ('Golly[9] and Adelaide Lubbock are sending their children away by the next boat', Nancy wrote in June 1940). It would appear from this that she did *not* know about the affair, or at least that it was not serious.

Yet a letter to Mrs Hammersley, written at the end of 1940, is almost openly despairing, so much so as to suggest that Nancy recently found out what was going on. It reeks of the fear of a sexually unwanted woman: 'My hair is going quite grey – I don't think you'll know me, my skirts fall off and my clothes hang on me. I feel older than the hills – not a bit young any more isn't it horrid and my own life has honestly ceased to interest me which must be a bad sign.' Not long afterwards, writing with painful sincerity in her 1941 diary, Nancy is clearly struggling to grasp the reality of her marriage. She may in the past have acknowledged what Peter was like – she did so in *Wigs on the Green*, when she portrayed him as the feckless charmer Jasper Aspect – but the tone in the diary was new: sadly and sternly rigorous. She wrote that 'the most critical moment in a marriage is the falling off of physical love, which is bound to occur sooner or later & only an experienced woman can know how to cope with this. If not properly dealt with the marriage is bound to go on the rocks.' This was true of the Rodds, and had been for a long time. But Nancy had not wanted to admit it, had not known *how* to admit it. She would express it better, at a greater distance, in the passage in *The Pursuit of Love* where Linda muses upon her life with Tony Kroesig. Here, she was only just starting to understand what it all really meant: that the marriage was over and that she had nothing else to go to. It is amazing how stoically cheerful she remained, how seldom she lapsed into despair.

She and Peter had been living together, on and off as usual, at Rutland Gate. Nancy moved there in October 1940 when the nightly bombardment around Blomfield Road became too much. The Mitford family home was filled with Polish Jews evacuated from the East End. Nancy was genuinely fond of them ('my sweet refugees') while enjoying the annoyance that she imagined they caused to her mother: 'You can't imagine how beastly Muv is being – she now regards me as a Jewess & is so horrid both to & about me. Also says if she had all the money in the world she would not ever live in the house again after the Jews have had it.' Exaggerated? Probably. Sydney *was* irritated by the dirty state of her house – unreasonably, as there was just one maid – but a letter to Jessica refers to the evacuees in quite sympathetic terms. Nancy's dislike of her mother knew no bounds at this time, however; and a houseful of Jews *chez l'amie de Hitler* presented an opportunity for an irritable tease.

The evacuees kept Nancy extremely busy, and sometimes in surprising ways. 'Oh dear a little creature here aged 16 is in the family way . . . shall I be obliged to wield a knitting needle & go down to fame as Mrs Rodd the abortionist? (I might join Diana which would be rather nice).'[10] Meanwhile the bombs continued to threaten an end to such sad little personal agonies. 'These ton bombs are Hitty's new joke & quite a good one the effect is of an earthquake & besides you hear them screaming down for ages . . . Ha ha ha *such* a little comedian.'

But Nancy had become as stoical about Hitler as about her husband (Osbert Lancaster[11] was later to say that her troubles with Peter had trained her to put up with the bombs). James Lees-Milne recorded in his diary for 1944: 'Nancy boasts that she is not the least frightened of the fly bombs.' Certainly that was what she wanted people to think: 'do pray I shan't be hit, I feel you have a pull', she wrote to Violet Hammersley in characteristic tone.

Once again, as she saw it, her family was letting the side down. There was her mother, whose temper had indeed become worn by the constant to-and-fro between what Nancy no doubt saw as the Fascist outposts of Unity in Swinbrook and Diana in Holloway. Then, in December 1940: 'Farve has turned up roaring like a bull because everything is not just as he always has it.' This uneasy trio was on each other's nerves even in that vast house, as they all were by sorrow and feuds and simple lack of food and sleep. Again, too, Nancy was flat broke. Peter sent money only irregularly from Ethiopia, her allowance from her father had been cut at the start of the war, and handouts from Lady Rennell stopped on the death of her father-in-law (who had probably been the one conscientiously urging the payments). According to Nancy, the money was now being used 'to build a ball room in memory of my pa in law. I keep saying how I wish she were religious, a nice marble X would cost far less.' Penniless and bombarded, she nonetheless continued to draw a rigorous comfort from her endurance of it all. She was in there with the Londoners, smiling and sticking it out ('if somebody does take cover you can be sure they are up from the country').

And a couple of fairly casual sentences, in a letter of March 1941 to Mrs Hammersley, held the promise of her reward; although she did not know it as she wrote them.

A friend of mine at the War Office (M.I.) begs me (this is a secret) to worm my way into the Free Frog Officers' Club in any capacity & try to find out something about them. They are all here under assumed names, all splashing mysteriously large sums of money about & our people can't find out anything about them & are getting very worried. I'm afraid it's no good for me as I have never moved in Frog society & wouldn't know who was who anyway. I feel it is *your* duty! . . . It is known they are riddled with spies eg Dakar [details of which planned operation had been leaked to the Vichy administration]. Isn't it tricky. Seriously I don't see what I could do & it would bore me to death to work in an officers' club anyway.

In fact this unnamed War Office friend was one of the most powerful agents of fate in Nancy's life. Presumably he had asked her to do her Trojan *cheval* act because she spoke unusually good French, if 'of the *est-ce-que* variety'.[12] Also she was asked because she was a pretty and elegant woman (Mrs Hammersley, who looked like a sixty-three-year-old Cassandra, swathed as she always was in a dark entanglement of shawls and veils, would not have done so well). But the friend could not, for one moment, have imagined what extraordinary riches would flow – towards Nancy, rather than him – from his plea.

It is amazing how reluctant she sounds, in her letter to Mrs H: hob-nobbing with French officers was surely preferable to scavenging for a 'proper' dinner for her father, or listening to the sullen fears of a pregnant teenager, or watching her mother run her fingers over Rutland Gate for dust. Back in September 1940, however, Nancy had shown herself rather exasperated with 'the Frogs' for whom she was helping to run a canteen at White City. It was the height of the Blitz, everyone was trying to keep their heads up, and meanwhile – she wrote to Mrs Hammersley – they 'really are behaving like spoilt children, complaining they are kept awake at night & one today started a long *histoire* about how he hadn't been taken to the theatre at all . . .' At this point, Nancy's feelings about the French were fairly typically English. With her unbending attitude towards the war, she would not have been impressed with the way France had caved in and let the Nazis goose-step all over Paris. The White City Frogs were temporary internees from Dunkirk, and Nancy had neither admiration nor longing for them. She treated them like so many '*kittens*, I never stop laughing all day . . . English soldiers or brave de Gaulle ones can never replace these nice lily-livered jokers.'

She did not really think this. What Nancy desired above all was to be able to look up to a man. His morals in the bedroom might be suspect, but outside it they must be honourable. Peter managed, just about, to fit the bill on this score. But what Nancy *then* craved –

as had become clear in her novels – was that this impeccable moral courage be the source not of self-regard, but of self-mockery: that a man should be able to laugh as he went into battle, shriek in the face of both *la gloire* and *la mort*. If he could not do that, he became the kind of crasher that Peter was now hopelessly revealing himself to be. Not just in his conversation ('he talked incessantly in his boring manner without appearing to listen to one word we said', wrote James Lees-Milne after an evening with him at the Ritz in 1944; 'the sad truth is that one should believe only a quarter of what Peter says'); but in the endless, sordid, humiliating grind of his behaviour, which – as Nancy now saw with deadly clarity – was unleavened by charm or grace.

She did not really think, yet, that joking men could be lovers: that a lover could be *fun*. As a girl she had had her jokes with Hamish while her potential husband, Sir Hugh Smiley, sat across a dinner table, a monolith of gravity. Peter, too, was always pompous when behaving well. He had been able to make Nancy laugh, but it was not to him she turned when she wanted to 'scream'; his nature lacked that innate sense of the ridiculous. No – the greatest fun was to be had with those who were *hors de combat* sexually, like the cowardly Frogs, or men such as Robert Byron and Mark Ogilvie-Grant. And so, like Louis XV before he met La Pompadour, she 'had never known that particularly delightful relationship of sex mixed up with laughter'. Nor, it seemed, could an English soldier supply it. But 'brave de Gaulle ones' could; and would.

Having obeyed instructions and infiltrated the world of the Free French Officers, Nancy wrote to Jessica in July 1941: 'I live in a slight world of frogs now, always the nicest & funniest. You can't imagine how wonderful they have been, the free ones I mean.' What bliss these men must have seemed to her, water in the desert with their manners, their flattery, their straightforward male appreciation of a woman in all her late-blooming glory. How different from Englishmen; how very, very different from Peter. The Free French were elegantly ranged on the side of righteousness, they opposed Pétain and Vichy and everything that Nancy abhorred. But they saw no loss of face in fun and frivolity: rather they saw necessity.

Perhaps Nancy exaggerated this joking aspect of the Free Frogs;

she so wanted it to be true, and so deserved a break from Peter, who is to blame her if she turned this band of Gallic sophisticates into a sexy male chorus of shrieking Mitfords? But there was more to it than that. What she recognised was that here, for the first time in her life, were men who knew how to deal with women. The jokes, indeed, were part of that ('you've only got to make it laugh', as Alfie says, 'and you're home and dry'). These were not hung-up public school boys who regarded the female breast as a dummy to suck, or a mistress as something to show off to the (forty-year-old) chaps in Pop. These, Nancy felt, were the kind of men who would handle her naïvety while relishing her worldliness. They might make her happy as individual lovers but, even more importantly, they would do so as a *race*.

The Pursuit of Love is, of course, profoundly engaged with this difference between Englishmen and Frenchmen. Nancy had presumably been longing to say it, and she did not hold back. Here is Linda, lunching at the Ritz with her lover, Fabrice, who is on brief leave from his own work as a Free Frog:

They talked of this and that, mostly jokes. Fabrice told her scandalous stories about some of the other lunchers known to him of old, with a wealth of unlikely detail. He spoke only once about France, only to say that the struggle must be carried on, everything would be all right in the end. Linda thought how different it would have been with Tony or Christian. Tony would have held forth about his own experiences and made boring arrangements for his own future, Christian would have launched a monologue on world conditions subsequent to the fall of France ... Both would have spoken to her exactly, in every respect, as if she had been some chap in their club. Fabrice talked to her, at her, and for only her, it was absolutely personal talk, scattered with jokes and allusions private to them both.

This was the renaissance of the 'personal' in Nancy's life, after too long of aridity and sorrow and schism. In the summer of 1941 she began a love affair with one of her Frenchmen: Roy André Desplats-Pilter, a rich and cultivated man of her own age, *nom de guerre* André Roy.

It is ironic that after so much infidelity on the part of Peter, it was Nancy's love affair that brought her marriage to an effective end. For all the acceptance with which she wrote about adultery, it was not really her style: she was innately pure of heart, and what she liked was to lose herself in the love of one person then 'never look to right or left'.[13] She did not sleep with André Roy out of a *desire* to end her marriage, nor a desire to even the score (although she would have been entitled). But she would have regarded an affair – on her part, that is – as *proof* that her marriage was at an end. Otherwise she would not have been able to do it.

She was not in love with André Roy. Perhaps because of this, their affair is the only one that she conducted in an 'adult' manner: she didn't attribute to it emotions that were inappropriate, she actually took it for what it was, which is rarer than one might think in the vertiginous world of love. What it was, undoubtedly, was the most glorious respite from the wearisome world of Peter Rodd. Roy makes the occasional, rather circumspect appearance in her letters (perhaps it amused her to tell and yet not tell about him): 'I found a delicious piece of Hôtel Montalembert notepaper', she wrote to Jessica in July, 'but didn't dare write on it . . . so I wrote to a glamorous Free Frog I know instead & I expect he'll think it a poor-taste joke.' And then to Mrs Hammersley: 'Actually this Sunday I am making an effort for the Entente & taking the glamorous Capitaine Roy to West Wycombe[14] for the day. Praiseworthy?'

Whether Nancy regretted her affair when it led to the ectopic pregnancy; whether she shuddered to think that she might have given birth to André Roy's child, with all the shame that would have implied – who knows? She does not seem to have thought like that: it was not her way. The love affair had given her new life in a dark time, that was how she saw it then, and how she continued to see it. Roy visited her in hospital, where he found her reading *Mémoires d'Outre-Tombe* ('*Châteaubriand – assommant*,'* he remarked). He may have been shaken to see her there, shocked by so disproportionate an outcome to their light and pleasurable liaison. Nancy had almost died, after all ('my mother-in-law was told by the surgeon that I shld be in danger for 3 days . . . I long to know if they bothered to look under R in the deaths column'[15]). And Roy himself had only four years to live; he died of tuberculosis at the end of the war.

* 'Châteaubriand sends one to sleep'

When Nancy recovered – which took several months, spent at West Wycombe – the couple almost certainly resumed their affair, if more casually than before. They may have just been friends, but that is unlikely; the Frenchmen in Nancy's novels like chatting to women but they also like making love to them, and there is no reason to believe that André Roy was any different. What is certain is that there was no rancour between them, no sense that things had been hideously soured, could never be the same again and indeed required relationship counselling: this amiable couple simply picked up the shattered pieces, and tried to be happy again. In 1942 Roy attended a party thrown by Nancy at Blomfield Road, at which Unity was present. She had arrived with 'a ghastly old dress full of moth-holes', so Nancy 'crammed' her into one of her own, leaving the back undone and putting a coat on top. But when she refused to make up her face, it was Roy who – trying to please? or perhaps he was just naturally, practically kind – did it for her. 'So in the end she looked awfully pretty.'[16]

Meanwhile another good thing had come into Nancy's life. Her war work had been irreproachable, but remorseless. After her operation she may have felt the need for something less noble, and it turned up in March 1942, just as she was getting her strength back. She was given a job as assistant at the bookshop in Mayfair's Curzon Street which her friend Heywood Hill founded in 1936; a blue plaque marks the years of Nancy's time there.

Heywood Hill is probably the most delightful bookshop in London, and it must have been almost as balming to Nancy as *le Capitaine Roy*. Entering the shop is an almost tentative business, rather like walking into the library of a slightly untidy, entirely civilised old person, the corners of whose home and mind are stuffed with fascinating things. This ambience cannot be replicated or faked or interior designed, although some do try. Heywood Hill obviously never *tried* to achieve its particular flavour, which was born of its private and highly personal ownership, and has accreted over years of calm and concentrated care.

'Oh it was lovely,' says Diana Mosley. 'It's still rather nice, isn't it?' During the war, when Nancy worked there, it was even more than that. Its ground-floor room didn't just *look* like a private club, it very nearly was one, with a membership that included Evelyn

Waugh, James Lees-Milne (at whose suggestion Nancy had taken the job), Osbert and Sacheverell Sitwell[17], Cecil Beaton, Cyril Connolly ('Smartyboots')[18], Raymond Mortimer and Gerald Berners[19], in fact Nancy's most amusing friends, all of whom came regularly to see her for a life-enhancing infusion of chat. Trumper's was next door; the men could have a haircut then step straight into Heywood Hill where, as Lees-Milne recounts in his 1942 diary, 'the horrid, pungent Brilliantine which they put on my hair nearly asphyxiated everybody. Nancy said that if there had been a window that opened, she would open it.' Then, amid the scented heads and the rhythmic rustling of pages, the gossip would begin: of the parties in Emerald Cunard's suite at the Dorchester, where she lived throughout the war, or at Sybil Colefax's[20] 'canteen' in Belgrave Square; of how 'Osbert S. [is] on top of the world as he has been left £10,000 . . . Sachie whom I saw rather sour "Ten pounds would have been so welcome."'[21]; of how – according to Nancy – 'the tart in Curzon Street, when asked how the war was treating her, replied that for a reserved occupation, £700 a week tax free, plus emoluments from the Government for reporting the indiscretions of soldier clients, was so satisfactory that she only wished she could open a second front.'[22] As Harold Acton put it: 'the very books seemed to join in the laughter during their exchange of gossip.'

It was frivolous, but it was also necessary, as the bombs continued to fall, as Tom Mitford fought in Libya, Mark Ogilvie-Grant languished in a POW camp in Italy, Hamish St Clair-Erskine was taken prisoner after Tobruk and Robert Byron lay drowned in the sea, having been torpedoed on his way to Egypt. The world of Heywood Hill served a purpose for those left behind, or on fleeting return visits. It became a bright totem of civilisation, a small unifying force, an ITMA for the literary aristocracy.

'Cecil Beaton came into the shop "such an oasis" & roared with laughter for an hour', Nancy wrote to Diana, who from her Holloway cell perhaps found reports of this jollity a little hard to take. 'The shop is really very gay now, full of people all day, & I am installed *in* the gas fire so manage to keep fairly warm.' Diana did benefit from Nancy's job in that she was sent parcels of books (Nancy also sent them to Jonathan Guinness at Eton, including a medical manual which was 'pure porn, *illustrated*'[23]). Evelyn Waugh also received the parcels when, at the end of the war, he served in Croatia ('A lovely parcel of books from you. Connolly's "Grave"[24] . . . I think Connolly has lived too much with communist young ladies. He *must* spend more time in White's').

'Went to Nancy's bookshop', Waugh wrote in his 1943 diary, 'where I was told that it is now a daily occurrence for enormous majors in the Foot Guards to come in and ask for the works of sixteenth-century Spanish mystics.' Of course it wasn't *Nancy*'s shop, as such. But it is significant that this is how Waugh thought of it: although Nancy was an employee of Heywood Hill she had, through him, acquired her own Mayfair *salon*. The money was nice – £3.10s. a week made quite a difference, although later she would think it a pittance[25] – but nicer still was being at the very heart of what Waugh called 'a centre for all that was left of fashionable and intellectual London'. For the first time, Nancy was almost wholly surrounded by people who saw the best in her: who were, she realised with increasing pleasure, unable to resist her mixture of sharpness and cosiness, of high polish and good sense. The job at Heywood Hill, coming on top of the time with the Free Frogs, was truly allowing one to be lovely *One*.

As was usual with Nancy, she gave the appearance of playing at her role of shop assistant with dilettante amateurism. In fact, as was also usual, she was rather efficient. The people she scared away were outnumbered by the ones she attracted. Of course entering the shop would have been like going into a small country pub filled with inter-related locals: all very well if you liked that sort of thing, but chilly or even irritating if you did not. It is easy to imagine the intimidatory nature of so much self-assurance gathered together in one room. One woman refused to put up with the club atmosphere: 'A little less darling and a little more attention please', she rapped out to Nancy, who was cooing into the telephone at the time.

Harold Acton wrote an evocative picture of Nancy at the time she began to work at Heywood Hill, when euphoria pushed aside the creep of tiredness. He conveys her crisp, bright zest, her febrile *chic*, her resolute energy.

Nearly always she walked to and from the shop, many miles from her

dwelling in Blomfield Road regardless of blackouts, air raids and encounters
with drunken soldiers ['leave me alone I'm forty' she squawked at one who
made a grab for her waist].

She walked briskly, for the sake of the exercise *faute de mieux*, even after
a tiring day's work or a night's rest broken by air raids. Taxis were sporadic
luxuries, and Lady Anne Hill remembers waiting with her for hours in
pouring rain while at least sixteen packed buses rumbled tantalisingly
down Park Lane. During weekdays they would lunch at a neighbouring
canteen or at a British Restaurant.[26]

In his affectionate, old-maidish way Acton goes on to describe Nancy's
physical presence, which had of course been enhanced by the best *soin
de beauté* of all: flattery.

Hers was a peculiarly English type of beauty and it did not belong entirely
to this age. Her clear smooth skin and clear quizzical eyes under a high
forehead with chestnut hair like a wavy turban above it would have been
portrayed to perfection by Sir Joshua Reynolds [in fact her hair was nearly
black as a girl – had she been dyeing it? More likely Acton simply got it
wrong]. She appeared much younger than her age and her humour had the
gaiety of girlhood.

James Lees-Milne, a more caustic observer, created a very different
impression of Nancy at this time. In a bizarre little vignette he
described, in his 1943 diary, seeing her run towards the shop 'to get
warm. She made a strange spectacle, very thin and upright, her arms
folded over her chest, and her long legs jerking to left and right of her
like a marionette's. I really believe she finds it easier to run than to
walk.' The image is evocative but not kind: Lees-Milne is frequently
hard on her in his diaries (Heywood Hill's wife Anne, he wrote, was
'worth a million more than the glittering women, like Nancy'). But
his view of her, as some sort of mechanised ostrich, was peculiarly
his own. Acton may have been biased also, but he restores some sort
of balance with his eulogy to Nancy's 'natural good taste, not only in
the clothes she wore. In those days she could not afford to indulge her
love of elegance yet in the neat black velvet jacket and black wool skirt
she usually wore in the shop she looked better dressed than many a

more prosperous friend'. He cannot then resist a dig at his blond bête noire, the dreaded Prod: 'her husband contributed nothing to her few amenities, if he ever wasted a thought on them.'

But by that time – 1943 – Nancy would scarcely have noticed if Peter had given her a cheque for £1,000 to spend at Dior. Nor would she have cared if she never saw glamorous André Roy again. She had met the man of her life, Gaston Palewski: the *ne plus ultra* of Free Frogs, the original Fabrice de Sauveterre, and the person who more than any other opened her to the pursuit of happiness.

Nancy was clever enough not to make the French lovers in her novels – all of whom contain the essence of Palewski – look like him. Even she knew that this would be pushing it. True, Fabrice is described as 'short, stocky, very dark', and 'not even good-looking', but he nonetheless lacked Gaston's pitted skin, his receding hair, his almost Hitlerian little moustache. And Charles-Edouard de Valhubert in *The Blessing* is given the physical appearance – 'tall, dark, and elegant' – of a text-book French lover, or indeed of André Roy.

'Oh Gaston – he was *very* ugly...!' says Diana. But Nancy's passion for him had nothing to do with the pleasure she had once taken in Peter's boyish handsomeness. It went beyond that, far beyond normal notions of desirability into something deeper, more stirring and more demanding.

Linda was feeling, what she had never so far felt for any man, an overwhelming physical attraction. It made her quite giddy, it terrified her. She could see that Fabrice was perfectly certain of the outcome, so was she perfectly certain, and that was what frightened her ...

She is unable to account for this attraction:

... he was exactly like dozens of other dark men in Homburgs that can be seen in the streets of any French town. But there was something about the way he looked at her which seemed to be depriving her of all balance.

That *was* Palewski, all right. Although not a handsome man he had sexual confidence, and to a degree that Nancy had never known.

When Gaston set out to seduce it made Prod and his little affairs look like showing-off to Mummy: here was a professional in action, and he made his move on Nancy not long after they met in September 1942, at the Allies Club off Park Lane. This first encounter came about because he had met Peter out in Ethiopia and could give Nancy news of him; the opening of *The Blessing* has Grace and Charles-Edouard meeting in exactly the same, ironical way. Charles-Edouard says – of Grace's fiancé – that there is 'Good news – that is to say there is no news.' Palewski probably said something much the same to Nancy, then moved on to more interesting subjects.

One wonders what he had expected her to be like, having met Peter in Addis Ababa, and imagines that he was surprised by this clever, nervy Francophile, so different from what Fabrice calls 'these Veronicas and Sheilas and Brendas'. Palewski, meanwhile, was more than Nancy had expected. Even James Lees-Milne called him 'a cultivated man', and his standards were exigent. Indeed Palewski was, according to Harold Nicolson[27], 'one of the most conversational men I know, being able to converse with equal facility on Wedgwood dinner services and who was Albertine'. He was versed in both English and French culture, perhaps not deeply so, but to the highly civilised extent with which Nancy felt most at home. He himself was at home in London society; he was living in a Belgravia house belonging to an acquaintance of Nancy's – Anne Rosse, sister of the designer Oliver Messel – and he knew the Axis powers of Cunard and Colefax (James Lees-Milne recorded, in his 1943 diary, meeting de Gaulle's 'rather spotty' *chef de cabinet* at one of Sybil Colefax's luncheon parties). So Nancy's world was one that he understood, although he saw it through the enlivening gaze of a foreigner. Nothing could have delighted her more than this little tug between the familiar and the exotic.

Above all, though, Palewski was funny: in Nancy's idiom, filtered through Frenchness. '*Comme amateur de porcelaine . . .*'* was the start of his reply to a pompous dinner guest asking his opinion of the atom bomb (this remark made its way into Charles-Edouard's mouth; it really was too good to waste). His friend Alistair Forbes wrote that there 'never was a more devout believer than Gaston in that maxim of

* 'As a lover of fine china . . .'

Chamfort's which says that the most wasted of all days is the one that has to pass without laughter'.[28] None, perhaps, except Nancy? She had found in Palewski what she had never expected, a potential lover with whom she could develop her great gift of turning the stuff of life into jokes, stories, 'wonderful confections embellished with the aromatic and exotic fruits of her own sugary imagination'.[29]

At the same time he was someone whom she could admire. He was a man of substance: *un homme politique* of conviction as well as charm. Most importantly he was on the side of righteousness, a colonel in the Free French forces (Nancy would always call him 'Colonel' or 'Col'). Originally from Poland, his family had been assimilated into France by the time of his birth in 1901; and indeed no one could have been more French than he ('Charles-Edouard was the forty kings of France rolled into one'). He was educated to the hilt, including a year at Oxford. But the defining moment of his life came when he met Charles de Gaulle in 1934. From that instant he became his most faithful admirer, and remained so for all time. He accepted absolutely the belief – then derided in France – that a terrible German threat lay behind the supposedly impenetrable Maginot Line; and, when war broke out, he rejected pacifism. In June 1940 he wrote to de Gaulle saying that he was entirely at his disposal. On his arrival in London, at the Free French headquarters in Carlton Gardens, Palewski was appointed de Gaulle's principal political adviser: effectively, the General's right-hand man. More diplomatic than his boss, he was immensely useful in keeping the Allies sweet. In 1941 he was put in charge of Free French affairs in East Africa, and when he met Nancy had recently returned from Ethiopia; hence Peter. What a refreshing solace she must have seemed to this tired and jolly sophisticate, when they met for their drinks in the garden of the Allies Club.

Nancy asked Gaston to dine with her a few days later at Blomfield Road; he accepted with pleasure; and that, as one might say, was that. In the London autumn, as the trees sighed their leaves into the Maida Vale canal, they began their affair. 'Being made love to by Fabrice was an intoxication, quite different from anything she had hitherto experienced', Nancy writes of Linda.

Now the fact that Nancy wrote this doesn't absolutely mean that it was true of herself. She was a highly autobiographical writer, but she did not always deal in literal fact. And indeed, some commentators think that Linda's sexual awakening with Fabrice was not Nancy's. They believe that she loved her Colonel with a passion that was not so much physical as a craving for romantic chat, the 'banter'.[30] In fact they view her as uncomfortable with sex; partly no doubt because of the starched and pressed appearance that she always maintained, and partly because she was not particularly fanciable: too clever, too quick, too distant. But giving off an aura of sex is not at all the same thing as enjoying it; quite the opposite, sometimes. Despite her school-prefect-cum-spinster aspect, her air of perpetual virginity, there is no reason to think that Nancy felt anything other than that 'lovemaking is delightful', as she said in an interview many years later.[31]

Yet in *The House of Mitford* (by Jonathan Guinness with Catherine Guinness) it is pretty well asserted that Nancy had 'a very lukewarm attitude towards the joys of sex'. Why? Firstly because she put up with Hamish St Clair-Erskine for so long (although that can be explained in more ambivalent ways); and secondly because of the way she writes about the relationship between Louis XV and his mistress in *Madame de Pompadour*. This book, according to *The House of Mitford*, is full of 'unconscious self-revelations' about Nancy's view of sex. 'She plays down Pompadour's physical role ... she underlines the fact that too much sex made Pompadour ill.' But there is no reason to think that this was also true of Nancy. It was simply a fact that the Bourbon kings were like sexual maniacs and that one of their mistresses was, as Nancy puts it, 'physically a cold woman'. Why assume that she wrote everything from her own perceptions, that everything with Nancy was a form of autobiography? She was, yes, a highly personal writer; but she was also someone with an imagination, and indeed one of her greatest gifts is her ability to 'personalise' the experience of other people.

Yet when she equates Pompadour's 'sex appeal' with her 'charm', this leads *The House of Mitford* to conclude: 'So to Nancy, sex appeal is just charm under another name; its base is not anything so crude as physical desire.' Not so: she is simply writing about one particular woman, about Pompadour's particular type of attraction. If that is Nancy's last word on the subject, then where does this leave Linda's physical weakening before the measured, knowing stare of Fabrice de Sauveterre? Linda understands 'physical desire' through and through; so too does Polly Hampton, who longs to 'roll and roll' with Boy Dougdale; there really is no reason why the Marquise de Pompadour should be taken as the benchmark for Nancy's attitudes towards sex. Nor why it should be said, as a downright statement of fact, that 'Nancy never came to terms with sensuality'. True, she was not a woman who enjoyed a great many love affairs; she valued friendship and conversation in a love affair; she was a romantic realist rather than a realistic sensualist; and she was not an epicurean in any area of her life, although this may imply that she was a *connoisseur* rather than a *gourmande*.

Certainly she saw through the *faux*-daring of those who tried to make sex too important, too serious. In 1971 she wrote to Heywood Hill, saying, 'I tried Nicky Mosley's book.[32] How can people read such stuff? I love the way he sort of stands back, breathes deeply, & inserts some dirty thought, too obviously in order to be with it . . .' But this hardly implies an inability to come to terms with sensuality, more an intense boredom with a modern obsession. As she wrote in *Pompadour*: 'in those pre-Freudian days the act of love was not yet regarded with an almost mystical awe'; and there, yes, one *does* sense a brisk authorial voice.

Essentially, the impression given by her mature writings is that she had an adult acceptance of the place of sex. Within their well-dressed exterior, her post-war books have a comfortable understanding of physical passion, in all its wonder and absurdity. She does not, as she would say, go droning on about it; that was not her way. Her take on the physical is more like that of, say, Muriel Spark, whose novels, although highly eroticised, always let clues and implications pulse delicately beneath their smooth texture. Nancy's own books are stuffed full of sex: how could they not be, when they are so intimately concerned with the pursuit of love and *la ronde* of society? The Bolter, Cedric Hampton, Charles-Edouard de Valhubert: all are driven by their sexuality, although none of this is made explicit. None of it needs to be. Nancy didn't pry into the ways of the world, she simply knew what they were. And beneath her pristine veneer she was almost shockingly unshockable. In *Don't Tell Alfred*, one of Fanny's young sons turns up at the Embassy (Fanny is now English Ambassadress in Paris) and starts telling her about his low-life exploits as a Spanish tour operator: 'some of the girls do sleep with customs officers', he says, trying to *épater* his hopeless old mother. To which Fanny replies, in the authentic voice of Nancy: 'But how do they have time? I always seem to be in too much of a hurry to sleep with people at customs.'

Meanwhile, back with Nancy and Palewski: her sexual awakening is clearly accepted as fact by those who were closest to her. Diana alludes delicately to it: 'She probably first knew happiness with him, on a certain level . . .' and Debo refers to the 'extraordinary experience' of the early months with Palewski. These are women who feel no need to explain what is in the nature of things; it is obvious what they are saying. On the other hand Alistair Forbes, in his *Spectator* review of Nancy's letters, just comes right out with it: '. . . to a beguiled and consenting party like Nancy his [Palewski's] pleasure-giving skills in the sack made her conclude that although she had at the time adored her honeymoon [not quite true in fact] with her Wagnerianly pretty but pretty rum husband, Peter Rodd had quite simply been ignorant of the facts of love-making life.' Again of course, this relies on the evidence of *The Pursuit of Love*, which is not to say that Nancy *didn't* experience bliss in the arms of Gaston Palewski. It is simply to underline that so much, with Nancy, is inferred from her novels.

And Fabrice is, undoubtedly, an idealisation: a Palewski who is not a third-generation immigrant with terrible skin, but a rich duke with impeccable antecedents, and a magnificent spare flat in the 16ème into which he installs Linda. He is also the greatest lover since Don Giovanni. Everyone wants to go to bed with Fabrice: when news of his imminent arrival reaches Lady Montdore's house party, at the start of *Love in a Cold Climate*, 'the women . . . turned their heads like dogs who think they hear someone unwrapping a piece of chocolate.' This was not quite the case with 'Monsieur Piebald Palewski', as Diana Cooper called him in a letter to Evelyn Waugh.[33] His status as a love-maker was rather the obverse of Fabrice de Sauveterre's: *he* wanted to go to bed with *everyone*.

He had to conceal this behaviour from the puritanical de Gaulle, whose 'female llama surprised in her bath'[34] aspect would have turned to stone had he been forced to confront the *faiblesse* of his aide. 'I once saw Gaston', says John Julius Norwich,

at the British Embassy in Paris [where Lord Norwich's father Duff Cooper was ambassador after the war], at some big dinner party, sitting on a sofa with Daphne Weymouth as she then was[35], who was lovely and funny and sexy, though not I think interested in the Colonel. But after dinner he was sitting next to her, and he was bouncing up and down with excitement going 'j'ai envie de toi, j'ai envie de toi', over and over . . .

Another time at the Embassy – he was sitting next to Virginia Charteris at dinner, and he went over like a ripe ninepin at this jolly fresh-faced English rose, you know. And he invited her to lunch the next day. And she was rather pleased, and said oh, Gaston Palewski's invited me out to lunch, and we said: watch it. Just watch it, that's all. This man's a terror. And she said oh, come on, don't be silly, I'm a married woman, I can look after myself. So off she goes at 1 o'clock to his flat, and at twenty past one she's back. And we said: what happened? And she said well, it's the most extraordinary thing that ever happened. I go up to his flat, I ring the bell, expecting a sort of man in a white coat to say come in and offer me a glass of sherry – what I get is the Colonel, stark naked and in a considerable state of excitement.

All in a day's work for such an *homme à femmes*. As was the apocryphal reply given by one clever lady, to whom he offered a lift home after a party in his official car: 'No thank you Gaston, I'm very tired, I had better walk.' But this? 'I once actually asked somebody', says Lord Norwich, 'what it was like going to bed with the Colonel. And she said it was rather like being run over by an express train.'

This really is not Fabrice, that civilised yet earthy connoisseur of the female response. Was Nancy such an innocent as to think that it was? And was Palewski such a figure of fun, such a Casanova in cap and bells?

Who knows? But one must say this: the set around people like Nancy and Palewski was above all a gossipy one, which loved little better than urban myths like the Naked Colonel and the Lady. Too many people say that Palewski was a rampant womaniser for it not to be true, but it was also a totem of tittle-tattle amongst the mid-century social *gratin*: any story that confirmed it would have been embraced with open arms ('my dear, did you *hear* what that terrible Colonel did the other day in Mollie Madrigal's *entresol* . . . ?'). And Nancy's version of the Daphne Weymouth story is quite different from John Julius Norwich's: 'Daphne was here – oh what a bitch she is', she wrote to Diana from Paris in 1946. 'She made a terrific pass at the Col & her tactics were absolutely all in, for getting me out of the way. However the Col roared with laughter & (I believe) resisted.' Which may not have been true either; but should not be dismissed just because it doesn't fit the myth. As for the story that Palewski was a frantic rather than an accomplished lover – here, too, the lady beneath the express train would have known the funniness of what she was saying, and probably did not resist the desire to exaggerate.

Alistair Forbes wrote that Palewski was one of those men who – as Voltaire said of himself – could 'talk away their face' with a woman within half an hour. Evelyn Waugh's son Auberon wrote that his own young daughter had met Palewski when he was in his eighties, and 'fell for him completely'. So too did many women in French society. Diana, on the other hand, says: 'I was fond of him, and he was fun. But he wasn't charming, really, because he was very clumsy, you know, making passes at people who weren't the least bit interested in him . . . He was awfully nice. But I don't think being in love with him – one *couldn't* have been.' Diana, however, had her own sexually confident man in Oswald Mosley and so, unlike Nancy, she would not have been susceptible. Palewski must have had *something*, even if not everybody saw it. Perhaps Nancy, with her implicit insistence upon the cultured, joking, chit-chatting side of a love affair, brought out the best in him; which, sadly for her, left the worst for a great many other women.

And this, above all, one must also say: whether Nancy was truly transported to ecstasy by Palewski is not, in the end, the issue. The point is what she wrote about it all, the effect it had upon her mind, her soul, her sensibility, rather than upon her body. Something in the quality of her lovemaking with Gaston made her want to describe Linda's with Fabrice as transfiguring, poetic, the greatest imaginable happiness. *That* is the important thing. After Fabrice has joined the Free French, and Linda is forced to return to London and wait for him there, he visits her unexpectedly one morning, and 'all was light and warmth'. The couple fall into bed for hours; then Linda says to him:

> 'Oh Fabrice, I feel – well, I suppose religious people sometimes feel like this.'
> She put her head on his shoulder, and they sat for a long time in silence.

Nancy had believed in love for as long as she could remember, she had looked for it in the wrong places, she had resisted it with her French *capitaine* ('But what of Roy?' wrote a bewildered Mrs Hammersley); and now, with this urbane and not unkindly man, she fell completely. It was as if a dam had burst. The feelings flowed over Palewski in unstoppable gushes. Again, he was not a suitable recipient: like Peter, he was utterly incapable of fidelity. But in a way this did not matter. He had so much of what Nancy wanted: *unlike* Peter, who had always somehow been able to diminish her natural capacity for happiness, Gaston opened it up to the skies with his laughter, his lightness of touch, his belief in civilised values. He made her feel that life was a joyful business, and he did this even though he would also, in time, make her very unhappy.

In some mysterious way, this cutting loose with Palewski may have been connected to Nancy's hysterectomy: she could take a man for pure pleasure, her ties had been cut as surely as her poor fallopian tubes. By becoming free from one part of the female destiny – children – she also became free to fulfil another part of it: love.

That is not to say that she felt no guilt about the ending of her marriage, nor that Peter was sanguine about her behaviour. He came back from Italy in Easter 1944 'looking bronzed, tough and well', and marched into Heywood Hill in a barely contained rage. James Lees-Milne, who saw the Rodds that night at the Ritz, noticed how it seemed that Peter 'might lash out at poor Nancy at a moment's notice'. In August he described seeing them for dinner at Claridge's, where he was again stuck in the midst of a terrible, to him incomprehensible, atmosphere such as only marital rows can create. 'If Peter had not been present it would have been more enjoyable ... He puts Nancy on edge, and makes her pathetically anxious not to displease him. Now why should a husband put a wife under such an obligation?' Why, indeed? Because he knew that he was not the only unfaithful party in the Rodd marriage. (André Roy he had probably not been aware of; he need not have known the reason for Nancy's hysterectomy, as he was not then in contact with his wife: 'I never hear from Peter or he from me it is too depressing like the grave', she had written to Diana from her hospital bed.) He also knew that he could, with sadistic ease, induce guilt in as innately moral a woman as Nancy. She would have disliked the idea of confrontation – hence her conciliatory conduct – even though Peter could hardly have won any argument on the subject of unfaithfulness. But what she really wanted, from the time she began her affair with Gaston, was a quiet life. How far she thought beyond that is difficult to say: the war put the whole situation into limbo.

She had had eight, one imagines perfect, months with the Colonel in London, lunches at the Connaught Hotel and evenings at Blomfield Road – and oh, the romance of him turning up there late at night, whistling Kurt Weill songs at the window – during which time the future would have been another country: a fact, but not one that needed consideration. For most women, however, such present-tense living cannot last. As Jasper Aspect says in *Wigs on the Green* (written in what would have then seemed another life), they 'have a passion for getting relationships cut and dried'. When Palewski went off to Algeria with de Gaulle in May 1943, no doubt with regret but without undue pain, Nancy was left to fret and agonise. This was war, of course. Partings were inevitable. But the masochistic love of sacrifice, which had sustained her through the Blitz, was a different business now that her loss was so directly personal. And it was bound up with Palewski's own nature, which was frustratingly elusive. When he left, he would leave completely, even if he later returned to her. Absence, with him, would make the body grow randier; Nancy probably realised this in the clear-sighted part of herself, while the romantic part desperately hoped otherwise. She must have suffered when left to sleep alone again in bombed-out Blomfield Road, listening to the falling V1s or, on a quiet night, to the scuffling of the chickens in her garden.

She wrote many letters to Palewski, so many indeed that he referred to being showered in a *'charmante avalanche grise'* (her Harrods envelopes were grey); this must have hurt, all the more for being said so pleasantly. *'J'avais employé le mot "avalanche" pour des raisons de style mais non pour me plaindre de l'abondance de vos lettres'**, he wrote in retraction; yet they both knew that his remark had been an acknowledgment of the truth. It *was* Nancy who was making the running, who wrote about visiting him in Algiers, who wrote, full stop – while Palewski was simply receiving it all, saying *'Venez donc'* when he knew that she couldn't, encouraging her to *'Écrivez, écrivez'* even though he could not always be bothered to reply to the letters. Now she needed the advice of one of her heroines: Amabelle Fortescue from *Christmas Pudding*, who would have told her to invest in her affair with Palewski no more or less than it deserved; or Sophia Garfield from *Pigeon Pie*, who would have delicately eased into her own hands the reins that controlled the relationship. *They* could do it, and Nancy could tell them how, but she was unable, all her life, to do it for herself.

'I feel rather anxious about you darling', wrote Mrs Hammersley. 'I must tell you that I never would have thought your heart would prevail over your reason ... Perhaps it's a good thing P[alewski] will be absent for a bit. I don't mean to be harsh but, at one remove, you will be able better to take stock of the future and of your own feelings. It's important in life to keep balanced.'

Mrs H would not have written this had Nancy not given her good cause. Not since the days of Hamish St Clair-Erskine was Nancy talking about a lover as she did about Gaston, telling her friends so much about the affair (and its shortcomings). She was a strange mixture, in this respect, of reserve and candour. As John Julius Norwich says, she would come right out to people with 'oh darling, the *Colonel*, I worship the ground he walks on'. But even here there was an element of concealment, as if the very blatancy with which she shared her feelings was a way of masking them.

Yet this contradiction implied another: between the adult nature of her love affair with Palewski, and the very girlish manner in which she conducted it. In one way hers was a very grown-up passion. This was a real man, after all, a figure of standing and experience,

---

* 'I used the word "avalanche" for reasons of style, not to complain about the number of letters you send.'

not an overgrown boy: he required handling as such, and up to a point Nancy was capable of doing this; she kept Gaston amused and contented in her company. But in another way she treated him as a sort of teen idol, a very public crush. Like a teenager in the delirious throes of a first affair, she loved to show off about him. This is from a letter written to Palewski in June 1944: 'Osbert Lancaster said at luncheon on Fri: that Aly F[orbes] told him you were so frightened in that raid on Thurs: that you kept ringing him up[36] – I said furiously that is a total lie I was with Palewski *all night.* Sybil Colefax: *all night?* N.R. Well, you know what I mean.' It is purest adolescence, and who knows what Palewski made of it ('*ma chère amie!* Do these people *need* this information?').

It really *is* the kind of behaviour she went in for during the Hamish phase. And one has to wonder if maybe, just maybe, this was how she liked it. However keen she was on Gaston, she surely knew enough not to run after him – a man who loved *la chasse* as he did – and proclaim her love at every opportunity: she was practically forty, she must have learned that much by then. Yet that is how she behaved. And by so doing she handed Palewski the power to make her extremely miserable, which actually need not have happened. Love, as she knew very well, was something that should be handled by the head as well as felt in the heart.

Palewski's greatest hold over Nancy was his eternal elusiveness; had he been doing the pursuing then he might have become less of a fascinator, might instead have shown himself in a light that revealed his Flying Scotsman lovemaking and his acne-scarred skin. But this he never did, because he never got close enough for long enough. John Julius Norwich says, quite rightly, that the Naked Colonel and the Lady story is, 'as Nancy would have said, a hoot, but not so funny if you were Nancy, because I don't think he ever did that sort of thing to her'. Yet the irony is that had he done so, had he pursued her in the blatant way that he did other women, she would almost certainly not have wanted him quite so much. No doubt he knew this. Nancy made Palewski more desirable by her unfulfilled desire, and this probably sustained him through the trials of his other amatory adventures. Her regard meant something to him; he had no desire to lose it; it suited him very well to keep *her* trying to keep *him*. Indeed, the complete imbalance in the relationship – Nancy saying 'I love you', Gaston saying 'That's awfully kind of you' – was what maintained it for so long: far longer, on both sides, than any of their other liaisons. As she herself would later say, perhaps thinking just a little of her own situation, the man should have the upper hand in a love affair; although she may not have meant this to *quite* such an extent.

But she was not, as has been said, a pitiable figure. So she liked a man better than he liked her: big deal. Yet this idea about Nancy has taken a grip so firm it is almost impossible to loosen: that her passion for Palewski overwhelmed her life, that he became as necessary to her as oxygen, while she, to him, was nothing more than an aristocratic bit on the side, a nuisance; and that therefore she was pathetic, unloved, dissatisfied, what you will. The BBC *Omnibus* programme took exactly this line, as did an essay in *The Sunday Times* which referred to Nancy spending 'nearly 30 years as [Palewski]'s tragic, ridiculous hanger-on' and writing, post-*Pursuit of Love*, 'novels whose cleverness was overshadowed by an empty gaiety and brittle chill'.

But this, surely, is a very conventional take upon a highly unusual woman. It applies to her an orthodoxy that contains a dash of sixth-former feminism and a dollop of Women's Institute traditionalism: it says that she should not have been hurling herself in so unsisterly a manner at this man, while at the same time it laments the fact that she did not manage to snare him. 'She referred to herself, with bright sadness, as La Palewska'.[37] Poor Nancy! – a failure, then, on all female fronts. And all the time refusing to admit her terrible sadness, keeping up the glittering mask, behind which lay her broken heart, her empty pelvis, her anguished mind.

For a start, the 'La Palewska' remark was initially made about her by another person: in 1946 her enemy-friend Violet Trefusis[38] had said that Palewski had become so English he should be called Colonel Mitford, whilst Nancy was now so foreign that she should be called La Palewska. So to attribute tragic implications to this name is misleading, and typical of the way Nancy's love for Palewski has been treated, which ignores so much of what she was actually like. In her own mind, her life was a *joyful* one, even if she never waltzed down the Champs-Élysées in white Dior with the man of her dreams. Why must she be assumed to be lying, or suppressing her true feelings? And why, in an age which professes to believe absolutely in the idea of female autonomy, should this bright-spirited woman, whose inner resources were so many, be condemned as a pitiable Mariana because she had neither a successful marriage nor a child? She had, as Diana says, 'great compensations'. Not least of which was her own temperament: what Alistair Forbes called 'her wonderful capacity for happiness'.

In June 1944 Palewski returned to London, and to her. It was only for a couple of weeks, during which time they dined together (although not as a couple) at Alvilde Chaplin's[39] along with James Lees-Milne, Emerald Cunard and Harold Acton: an intensely civilised evening, at which Lady Cunard made the unconsciously apposite remark, 'What is the use of a handsome husband? They soon become less handsome, and in the end they are nothing but an incubus.' How Nancy would have agreed; and how happy she must have been contemplating her lover as he chatted knowledgeably about French literature to Harold Acton, or about de Gaulle's anti-Americanism to James Lees-Milne.

But then Palewski went home to France, with his General, for the imminent liberation; and this time it would be for good. All Nancy now had to look forward to was the occasional visit to Paris. According to the Cassandra commentators she should have been contemplating suicide, and yet she wrote to Mrs Hammersley in fine mood, saying, 'Yes I do feel gloomy without the Col but I don't believe it will be another year before I see him again & I must say it cheered me up – all the jokes you know & they are in *such* spirits . . . The Colonel knew all my letters by heart (flattering?).' Hardly the voice of a Lydia Languish; of course some of it was probably front, but the front was successful.

And even while Palewski had been away in Algiers, all had not been unrelieved gloom. Diana and her husband were released from prison at the end of November 1943, which relieved Nancy from any deep-buried guilt ('the first thing she did was ask, could she come to stay?' says Diana). Work at Heywood Hill continued to give pleasure: 'I am still entirely running the bookshop & like it', Nancy wrote to Jessica in March 1944, 'though I get rather tired and discouraged sometimes'. (Anne Hill had left the shop to have a baby; Nancy had acquired an assistant, Mollie Friese-Greene, with whom she got along very well, although she now believed herself to be seriously underpaid.)

Despite long hours (firewatching as well as bookshop-management), little food ('I found a chicken chez Jackson . . . on presenting this much heralded fowl to Gladys she immediately discovered it to be *crawling with maggots!* . . . we all cried a great deal'), and no decent clothes ('the most utter horrors [dresses] you ever saw for £23, cheap & dreadful looking, what is one to do?'), Nancy maintained her urbane social life among the usual suspects. A party at Cecil Beaton's; a dinner at Boulestin; a lunch at Emerald Cunard's; it doesn't sound too bad for life during wartime. She also had the glorious retreat of Gerald Berners' supremely beautiful house at Faringdon in Oxfordshire, where she would spend weekends and find 'a double relief from discomfort and from boredom', as she wrote in 1948.[40] 'I can remember, during the tedious or frightening but always sleepless nights of fire-watching in wartime London, that the place I longed to be most intensely was the red bedroom at Faringdon, with its cracking fire, its Bessabarian carpet of bunchy flowers and above all its four-post bed.' As her marriage moved off into the middle distance, and her love affair hovered tactfully in the wings, so Nancy's friends began to assume the structural importance that they would have for the rest of her life. Lord Berners was a good friend to everyone whom he cared about – he visited Diana in Holloway with aristocratic disdain for censure – and Nancy valued him as much for his kindness as for the aesthetic refreshment that she found in his home (although the sight of Lord Berners' dyed pigeons fluttering 'like a cloud of confetti', or the touch of Sèvres and Dresden, would have been welcome compared with the chickens that wandered through her Blomfield Road garden[41], and the clink of British Restaurant cutlery).

Nancy was not at all unhappy at Faringdon House. Despite the absence of Palewski, she found intense pleasure in these weekends. Then there was the day in April 1944, described by James Lees-Milne in his diary, when Nancy (and the beloved, stalwart bulldog Milly) drove with him to the National Trust property of Polesden Lacey: 'we ate sandwiches on the south verandah. Nancy even sunbathed in the afternoon. When I had finished my work we wandered in the fields, picking cowslips (nearly over already). N. at her sweetest and happiest. A heavenly day.' So where, one wonders, is this woman in torment?

It was Palewski who had released in her the 'wonderful capacity for happiness'; even in his absence this was there, waiting for whatever might fill it. It is simply, demonstrably, wrong to say that only his presence could do so.

She wanted to be with him, she wanted the hope of seeing him, she wanted – in June 1944 – to feel that she would visit him in Paris. But *did* she want, more than anything in the world, to be 'La Palewska'? Would her capacity for happiness have been filled to bursting point had the Colonel proposed marriage and whisked her off to his apartment in the Rue Bonaparte, for a life of nightly bliss and daily blind-eye turning? 'I suppose she'd have very much welcomed it,' says Diana; 'whether it would have been a success is another matter. I think he would still have hurt her, probably.' Almost certainly; and anyway one wonders if, in the end, marriage to Palewski was what she truly craved. She would have liked to be asked, of course, but that is not the same thing.

Nancy longed for love but what she wanted was love of the all-consuming kind, which she undoubtedly felt for Gaston Palewski: '. . . she was filled with a strange, wild, unfamiliar happiness, and knew that this was love', she would later write of Linda, and the strength of emotion is unmistakable. But Linda's affair with Fabrice is cut short; it never has to deal with reality; and this was Nancy's ideal of love. One comes back to the early days, to her infatuation with Hamish St Clair-Erskine, and to the unchanging blend of romanticism and separateness that was her nature. She was not a person who could integrate love into life. In some mysterious way, of which she was probably not conscious, she preferred the state of yearning, of dramatising her situation to her friends, of non-attainment. She greatly valued the idea of marriage: she liked its sanity, its structure, the way in which it put a woman's life into some sort of order. At the same time, and over and over again, she put herself into positions that made the idea unfeasible.

Why *did* she have to fall every time for impossible men? She was, as many people say, 'a bad picker'. And this was, as Debo says, 'bad luck'. But was it not, also, something to do with Nancy herself? She preferred Hamish to Hugh Smiley, Peter to (for example) Nigel Birch, Gaston Palewski to André Roy: to choose wrongly twice may be considered a misfortune, but three times looks like carelessness. What about the Free Frenchman Marc, Prince de Beauvau-Craon, who pursued her during Palewski's absence in Algiers, and who wrote to her: 'Nancy darling . . . do you think of me a little bit, if so how much?' (The answer, despite some nice dinners at the Savoy, was no: Marc was years too young for her [42], but his real crime was probably to be so hideously smitten.)

This was an attractive woman, who could have found a man with whom to share a happy life. She could also have made a far better fist of being happy with Palewski – who obviously liked her enough to return to her from Algiers – had she not let her emotions rush her off into the rapids of impotent jealousy (which, as her beloved Proust would have reminded her, is the fuel that feeds Nancy's kind of love). This is the kind of truth that she knew all too well and put into her novels. Yet something in her resisted it in reality. Which makes one feel that this was how she wanted it: to live in a state of being poised, eternally, at the edges of celestial fulfilment.

For when she wrote about Linda and Fabrice, and the affair that exists in an enclosed world (a visit from two English friends almost shatters the crystal bubble of Linda's contentment), she was describing her own image of perfection. 'Sun, silence, and happiness.' Of course Linda and Fabrice are mutually in love: therein lay the great, the chasm-like difference between them and their real-life counterparts. But the point remains, that what gave Nancy most pleasure of all was an *ideal* of love, such as she makes Linda and Fabrice embody. She was, after all, an artist; she had the power to create; it is of immense importance, this transcendent dimension that she had in her life. She created Fabrice out of love for Palewski, but also because by the time the war ended she had become a real writer, with a writer's independent spirit. And when Palewski let her down, she still had the power to make Fabrice say to Linda: 'I came to tell you that I love you.' It was poignant, this rewriting of her affair; it was born of a sometimes desperate longing; but it brought its own purer, truer, untouchable satisfaction.

CHAPTER 7

And who knows? Maybe the *grande passion* of Nancy's life was for France, rather than for the man who embodied it. Maybe *that* was why she loved him so much: because in Gaston Palewski she saw another world, and through him she glimpsed the possibility of escape to a place that would allow her to flourish as never before. Nancy was as English as tea and walnut cake at Gunter's, but it was only in France that this Englishness would truly bloom. More than almost anyone, she was an example of the freedom that moving to a foreign country can bring: the freedom to be her best possible self.

As a girl she had fallen for Paris – she had stood at the top of the Avenue Henri-Martin and felt tears gather at its sheer sweeping perfection – and now, through her dealings with the Free French officers (not just Palewski), she had come to feel that this was the place in which she would be happiest. 'Oh to live in Paris, I'd give anything', she wrote to her mother in September 1944. Just as when she married Peter, back in 1933, she was in real need of a new life. Her old one held almost nothing for her.

In Paris, Nancy believed, she would find all that she craved: the right things taken seriously, the right things laughed at, an enlivening tension between *politesse* and pleasure, above all an appreciation of *One*. And then there was what she would leave behind: the schoolboyish men, the dowdy women ('English girls in navy blue with white touches'), the bombed streets like mouths with missing teeth, the wretched husband and the family feuds. It was a dream, of course, as was so much for Nancy. Post-war Paris was poor, hungry, humiliated, still blazing with feral memories of muffled screams in the Gestapo headquarters on the Avenue Foch, of collaborators shot without trial, of women wandering even the smartest streets with shaven heads, of a prostitute who had served Germans kicked to death in the 18ᵉᵐᵉ. Nancy must have known all this; yet her image of the place was too strong for the reality, she believed those dusk- and champagne-coloured streets to hold the secret of all joy: and so strong was her belief that it did, indeed, prove true.

But was it because the streets also held Gaston Palewski? This is the conventional wisdom: 'Because of the Colonel she went to live in France', wrote James Lees-Milne after Nancy's death, in a manner that brooked no dissent. She wanted to go haring off to Paris not because she yearned for the view from the Pont-Neuf, but because she wanted to be near the Colonel. Which she did. But would she have hankered to be near him quite so much had he lived in Antwerp or Belfast? Palewski and Paris were intertwined, inseparable. As London grew ever drearier, so he brought a vision of this wonderful other world – this Paris, not of the Occupation, but of Louis XV and Madame de Pompadour – into her drawing-room at Blomfield Road. She had heard the sound of Voltaire in his voice, traced the outlines of Fragonards on the dank walls behind his head. And it was this – at least as much as Palewski himself – that she had fallen for. Her lover was, indeed, the forty kings of France rolled into one; had he been Ethelred the Unready and George V, Nancy's passion for him would not – however powerful his various charms – have sustained itself. No, she was in love with a country as well as with a man; each love intensified the other, impelled by her imagination. And her affair with France would be the most successful of her life.

She thought of visiting Paris from the moment Palewski left for France in June 1944 – would have leaped on the first boat train had she dared – but then the idea began to grow that she might do more than visit. This idea was born of an urge to see her lover, yet it was also something more. 'I am angling like mad for a job in Paris', she wrote to her mother in September, 'but all rather nebulous, tho' I think it may come off . . . I got a lot of books from there last week by a wangle, the only bookseller who has. They are like water in a drought & I sold £20 worth the first day!'

The plan – commercially sensible, but pursued with an ulterior motive – was to establish a Parisian connection for Heywood Hill ('selling Cobbett's *Rural Rides* to the French', as Evelyn Waugh put it). Meanwhile the final months of the war had still to be got through, irksome and drab, during which the shop became a bit of a bore to Nancy. '*I do not like* hard regular work,' she wrote to Diana in March 1945. 'However many people it seems *do* which is lucky.' Not Heywood or Anne Hill, however; at least not according to Nancy. 'Neither Hill has been near [the shop] since the bombs began & they say they won't come back to London until an *armistice* has been *signed*.'[1] This annoyed her, as did the affront to her status when, at the end of 1944, Heywood Hill hired 'an old Jew called Jutro to be my boss [in fact this mysterious character never joined the firm[2]]. I am biding my time,' Nancy wrote to Evelyn Waugh. 'If I can keep him like Caliban in the cellar & get him to do my work when I feel like a brisk walk round the Park, well & good. But if he is going to join in the cocktail party atmosphere I so carefully foster, I shall leave & write a book.'

And here, in fact, lay the reason for her frustration with her job. She did not want to be selling other people's work. She wanted to be doing the work herself. Her mind was elsewhere as the war came to an end; she was fed up with what now seemed like the banalities of daily work; but it was not so much that she ached to get to Palewski as that she was desperate to get started on a book. 'Oh how I long to', she continued in her letter to Waugh, 'but £ s d rears its ugly head – I write so slowly & my books always come out at moments of crisis & flop.' This time, however, she may have known that she was, as Diana puts it, 'on to something'. Although the urge to get to Paris was slow-burning in Nancy, what was positively flaming was the desire to write ('my fingers itch for a pen'[3]).

According to most commentators, Nancy's love for the Colonel was all-consuming by this time: she was, at the end of the war, a desperate woman separated hopelessly from her man, smiling twitchily at the customers of Heywood Hill as she plotted her escape to Paris. Yet this image does not quite square with the evidence. Until she got the book out of her system she was at least as concerned with *The Pursuit of Love* as with pursuing love; and more concerned that Heywood Hill should give her three months' writing leave (which he did), than that they should discuss his offer of a partnership. This was made in October 1944, and it would obviously have advanced her Paris plan no end. Yet she reacted with odd spikiness: 'could we wait until the end of the war & then think? . . . I don't think I do much want to play at bookshops all the rest of my life, though I may have to. Also I believe we might find it difficult to work together, both having been bosses.' Hardly the words of someone willing to try any route to get to her lover. Only when *The Pursuit of Love* was written – in June 1945 – did she return, with full attention, to the idea of buying and selling books in Paris.

Nancy's friends were producing books, and this may have increased her almost panicky desire to get going with her own. Cyril Connolly sent Nancy *The Unquiet Grave* in November 1944 ('I see it is going to be a *great great* pleasure to one', she wrote, perhaps not wholly sincerely), and the following month she received a handsome copy of *Brideshead Revisited*: 'a great English classic in my humble opinion', she wrote to Evelyn Waugh (he loved this phrase). Seeking further to flatter, she went on to tell him about her own book, of which she had done 10,000 words before her leave had even been granted: 'also in the 1st person. (Only now has it occurred to me everybody will say what a copy cat – never mind that won't hurt you only me.) It's about my family, a very different cup of tea, not grand & far madder. Did I begin it before reading "B.head" or after – I can't remember.'

The implication here is that Nancy's *The Pursuit of Love* was trailing in Waugh's wake: a little girl book prancing after its stately big brother. This is typical Mitford – 'oh you are *so* clever, so unlike idiotic *One*' – although Nancy probably did feel the lack of gravitas within her own book when compared with her friend's. She acknowledged, with honest grace, what she saw as Waugh's straight-forward superiority: 'your well known knack of one tap on the nail & in it goes, whereas the rest of us hammer & pound for hours'. Yet there is the sense that, this time around at least, she preferred what she herself was doing.

Nancy seems to have seen an essential silliness in *Brideshead Revisited*. She knew the book was beyond her own capabilities; she was, as she called herself to Waugh, 'an *uneducated woman*'; but as such she had a clear-sightedness that the average Oxonian male could only dream of (she later referred in a letter to a young graduate who had 'a double 1st at Oxford, and also a spark of intelligence': the two did not necessarily go together). She could never have written a book whose subject, according to its author, was God. She could never have composed the series of poems on the theme of fated aristocracy that comprise so much of *Brideshead* ('He was entrancing, with that epicene beauty which in extreme youth sings aloud for love and withers at the first cold wind'). But then, she would not have wanted to. She could not compete with such splendours, yet beside all that overwrought baroque architecture *The Pursuit of Love* is as alive as a new-born puppy; and, as such, more moving as a hymn to loss. It is quite hard to care about the destruction of the Flyte family in *Brideshead Revisited*, so deeply besotted are they with their own doom. But when sadness, which has lain patiently in wait throughout the whole of Nancy's book, moves finally centre stage, one's heart breaks for those joyful Radletts, as when a glorious steeplechaser takes its last buoyant leap towards death.

Of course she raved about *Brideshead* – 'so true to life being in love with a whole family', she wrote to Waugh, which is indeed the book's great fascination – but then, in her delicate way, she cut to the heart of its faults. 'I think Charles [the ponderous narrator] might have had a little bit more glamour – I can't explain why but he seemed to me a tiny bit dim & that is the *only* criticism I have to make because I am literally dazzled with admiration.'[4] But a few weeks later she returned to this only criticism, and brought with it another:

I quite see how the person who tells is dim but then would Julia *and* her brother *and* her sister all be in love with him if he was? Well love is like that & one never can tell. What I can't understand is about God. Now I believe in God & I talk to him a very great deal & often tell him jokes but the God I believe in simply *hates* fools more than anything & he also likes people to be happy & people who love each other to live together – so long as nobody else's life is upset (& then he's not sure). Now I see that I am absolutely un religious . . .

This dig would be made again, in *The Pursuit of Love*, in a way that shows the difference between the books. Linda is asking Fabrice about his Catholicism, and how it permits him to keep her as his mistress.

'But then aren't you living in mortal sin? So what about when you confess?'

'*On ne précise pas*', said Fabrice carelessly, 'and, in any case, these little sins of the body are quite unimportant' . . .

'In England', she said, 'people are always renouncing each other on account of being Roman Catholics. It's sometimes very sad for them. A lot of English books are about this, you know.'

'*Les Anglais sont des insensés, je l'ai toujours dit* . . .'

Waugh might have laughed at that, but it would have confirmed his belief that Nancy was beyond the theological pale (as would certain lines in *Pigeon Pie*, a book he did not rate: 'For a short time, many years ago, he had been married to a woman so pious and so lavish with Sir Ivor's money that she had posthumously been made a Papal Duchess'). Nancy never had much time for Catholicism. As with *Brideshead Revisited*, she saw in it both splendour and silliness. She also thought – acutely – that Waugh was 'an amateur and not a professional Catholic'.[5]

Fabrice could absorb sin into his religion: he was like the Marquise who, after receiving the last sacraments, took up her knitting again saying, '*ce n'est pas là une raison pour perdre son temps*'.[6] Waugh could not do these things; he remained a goggling convert all his life, bedazzled by the Brideshead set, and incidentally disapproving of the married Nancy's love affair with Gaston Palewski, although apart from one serious scolding in 1949 he kept quiet about it.[7]

Waugh did not expect Nancy fully to understand *Brideshead*: 'I know it will shock you in parts on account of its piety.' Yet he was keen to know that she had enjoyed the book: 'A letter from Nancy proclaiming *Brideshead Revisited* a classic', he took the trouble to note in his 1945 diary.

'Of course I value your opinion above all others about most things. But well no not about religion,' Waugh wrote to her in 1950. Nancy's opinions were simultaneously of great value to him and of no value at all: a healthy state of affairs. But what of the other way around? Did Nancy care what Waugh thought? 'Well,' says Diana Mosley, 'no doubt she would have had him in mind, thinking to herself, you know, what would he say? Because he was a very strong character, really.' Indeed, he has been called her literary mentor. His influence is highly visible in a book like *Highland Fling*, which bears a certain – distant – resemblance to *Vile Bodies*, although this may have been coincidence: young people tend to write in a similar style, which at that time was nervy and semi-hysterical, as if puffing at top speed through a cigarette holder (although even then Waugh had a far deeper moral dimension).

Nancy's subsequent books, however, bore little resemblance, other than the sharing of a certain set of social assumptions. Still, from *The Pursuit of Love* onwards, he offered opinions on her work; it had, as he thought, become worthy of comment, and as mutual respect grew so friendship metamorphosed into something more solid and important. Instead of seeing each other at Heywood Hill, or at parties where Nancy would be brightly sober and Evelyn problematically drunk, they wrote to each other – a correspondence of unrelenting hilarity and ruthlessness – and this was how they got along best. Books were obviously one of the subjects that most engaged them. They were not Flaubert and Turgenev – if they exchanged views about the ethics or mechanics of writing then they did so only obliquely; but they always made and sought comments upon each other's work.

Christopher Sykes, who wrote a biography of Waugh, said that he was 'responsible for some of the more felicitous details' in *The Pursuit of Love* (this has a faint air of 'how could a middle-class Stratford actor write those plays?'). Waugh did suggest the simple but ambivalent title (Nancy had intended to call it 'My Cousin Linda' – 'I'm very bad at titles . . . I'm always in favour of calling books what they *are*'). He also gave her the idea that Alconleigh, home to the Radletts, should be dominated by images of death[8]: 'Not death of maidens, not death romantically associated with urns and weeping willows, cypresses and valedictory odes, but the death of warriors and of animals, stark and real.' This is clever, but it is also a symbolic underlining of what is already implicit in the text: in the intensely realistic descriptions of country life ('it was not unusual to be awoken by the screams of a rabbit running in horrified circles round a stoat, by the strange and

awful cry of the dog-fox, or to see from one's bedroom window a live
hen being carried away in the mouth of a vixen'); and indeed in the
elegiac, *à la recherche* quality that suffuses the whole book.

Waugh also made a fairly detailed critique to Nancy of the passage
set in the refugee camp at Perpignan, based upon her experience with
Peter back in 1939.

The contrast of Linda with her manorial soup and port benefactions and
her communist husband with his zeal to re-equip the militant workers for
the class struggle in Mexico could be excellent. It would give point to her
bewilderment that the Spanish gentry did nothing to help. You could make
a dramatic climax in the sailing of the evacuation ship with the communists
taking off the distressed families in order to pack it with international
thugs . . .

This, Nancy completely ignored. It was advice that was inappropriate
to her, and she knew it. (She may – if she thought about it that way –
have also disliked the implication that she herself had been foolishly
playing Lady Bountiful when she had tried to help the Spanish
refugees.) The Perpignan episode, where Linda dimly then clearly
realises that her husband is the wrong man for her, and where she both
dimly and clearly understands the plight of the refugees, is dislocated,
but that is the point. It is not by any means the strongest part of the
book, being something of a hiatus before Linda meets Fabrice, but this
too is in a sense intentional. Making neat political points would have
been an irrelevance; even if Nancy had been capable of it, which
Waugh probably knew she was not.

In September 1945 he wrote to say:

I am sorry you have not been able to rewrite the unsatisfactory section of
your book [Perpignan] in time for the first edition. Start rewriting it *now*
for the Penguins. It is the difference (one of 1000 differences) between a
real writer & a journalist that she cares to go on improving after the reviews
are out & her friends have read it & there is nothing whatever to be gained
by the extra work.

This is partly written out of a belief that Nancy should be kept up to the mark: 'that was just his sadistic side!' as Diana says. But it is also genuine, indeed kindly meant, written out of respect for what she *had* achieved, for what he saw as her worthiness to join the clan of 'real' writers.

She gave his advice even less consideration than he had given to her criticisms of *Brideshead*. High on the praise of Hamish Hamilton ('the word brilliant has been used'[9]), she wrote to Waugh perfunctorily: 'I can't begin again on Linda so I am a journalist. Besides I meant Xian [Christian] to be like that even if Communism isn't . . .' In other words: awfully nice of you but I know best. She also takes a small revenge: 'Hamilton advertises Linda as one long scream. I knew it. But Fabrice [that is, Palewski] says he thinks in many ways it's more serious than your book but perhaps that's just sucking up.'

So much for being a literary mentor. Waugh's opinions were treated by Nancy rather as hers were by him, as something hugely important that would almost always be ignored. She had immense confidence in *The Pursuit of Love* and saw the dissection of the Perpignan episode for what it was: pointless. In 1948, however, she sent the manuscript of *Love in a Cold Climate* to Waugh, and received even more detailed criticism:

Six months hard I am afraid without remission for good conduct. The manuscript was a delight to read, full of fun & wit & fantasy . . . But it isn't a book at all yet. No more 40 hour week. Blood, sweat & tears. That is to say if you want to produce a work of art. There is a work of art there, lurking in a hole, occasionally visible by the tip of its whiskers.

This time, Nancy was less unassailably sure about the book, and had sent it to Waugh despite the fact that Hamish Hamilton was begging for it. Her apparent motive had been for Waugh to tell her what corrections she should make. What she had *really* wanted no doubt was for him to tell her that none were necessary: the book was absolutely perfect. 'I agree with nearly all you say', she begins in reply to his criticisms. Then her tone becomes pathetic and defensive: 'I have rewritten the *whole thing* once already you know. What I wonder is whether I can (am capable of) doing better. You speak of Henry James but he was a *man* of intellect . . .' and so on. Finally, in contradiction of her first remark: 'What you say about the minor characters I don't agree with. Your complaint is that they are not photographs of existing people, but one must be allowed to invent people if one is a novelist . . .

'Oh dear. You see I'm afraid that what you really criticise are my own inherent limitations . . .'

If Nancy thought that Waugh was an amateur rather than a professional Catholic, then he surely thought that she was an amateur rather than a professional writer; this was at the root of his criticisms, that she did not push herself the extra yard. 'I will have a go at Cedric's talk[10] & do some revising on the lines that you suggest', she wrote, but what he had actually said was that the whole book needed rewriting, and this she had no intention of doing. Once again, she had pronounced herself in thrall to his judgment, and almost completely ignored it. For a literary mentor, Waugh had scant influence over his pupil. 'I long to read your novel & criticize tho what's the good you never take my advice', he wrote to Nancy in 1950 with regard to *The Blessing*, to which she replied, clearly in fond mood: 'When you say I never take your advice it's because you've only ever read them in proof when one can't alter – if you could endure the hell of manuscript I promise to be obedient.' Yet when she sent *The Blessing* the same thing happened all over again ('The Captain doesn't ring true to me'; 'I *don't know* why you have this idea of the Captain . . . Truly I think you are wrong'). For all their delight in each other's jokes, and all their seeming similarity in wit and wickedness, they were very different animals as writers.

Their mutual respect was intense, however, and became more so. Waugh would later modify his opinion of Nancy as a writer: around the time of *The Blessing*'s publication he seems to have accepted the fact that Nancy's faults and virtues were indissolubly linked, and that criticising the one might impact upon the other. As for Nancy, even though she apparently ignored much of Waugh's advice this does not mean that he did not affect her writing. Diana Mosley is surely right to think that Nancy would have had him in her mind, wanted his approval, measured herself against his standards. She was in continual contact with the most highly regarded writer of her generation; this kept her on her toes. Her authorial horizons were sharpened by exposure to Waugh's magnificently decisive style, broadened by the seriousness with which he took his work. Yet Nancy had her own calling, and this was something that, at the time of *The Pursuit of Love*, Waugh only semi-understood. Indeed there was always an element of tolerance in his admiration for Nancy: in his 1962 review of her collected essays, *The Water Beetle*, he put her into the category of an author who 'can write but cannot think'. Up to a point, he was taken in by the apparently dilettante quality of her style (if Cyril Connolly thought that the problem with *Brideshead* was that Waugh went 'too much to White's', then Waugh probably thought the problem with *The Pursuit of Love* was that Nancy went too much to bed with the Colonel). Certainly with this book he felt that she had allowed her facility to make her lazy. He could not quite accept that *The Pursuit of Love* was, as Diana says, 'in its way just about perfect. I can't find a criticism. Evelyn couldn't have done it.' Which was as completely true as saying that Nancy could not have done *Brideshead Revisited*.

After reading the book Waugh wrote in his diary: 'Nancy has written a novel full of exquisite detail of Mitford family life, but planless and flat and hasty in patches.' Also true, to an extent: parts of the book are not so much writing as simply talking on to the page, parts are not so much structured as simply saying what happened next. But this, again, was irrelevant. The occasional drift from artful candour into real artlessness, from intentional vernacular into downright cliché, was all part of Nancy's charm, which by then was so impregnable that trying to pick holes in it was a total waste of time. It smiled dazzlingly at its critics and sailed merrily on. Of course *Brideshead Revisited* contains Waugh's famous attack upon charm, 'the great English blight', which 'spots and kills anything it touches. It kills love; it kills art.' This superb *aperçu* is relevant to Waugh's view of Nancy's writing (and perhaps of the whole Mitford family, so light and airy, so dark and remorseless). Clearly he felt that the Mitford charm was enabling her, and tempting her, to sidestep her responsibilities as an artist. Yet charm does not have to be a merely shallow thing; Nancy's was also profound, not least because she understood it. She seemed to be engaged with the surfaces: she wanted them to be as brightly polished as possible. But there was far, far more to her than that. *The Pursuit of Love* is above all else a sincere book, suffused to its considerable depths with feeling: bright with hope, shadowed with sadness, sometimes cold and stony with realism. It is also – as are the three novels that would follow – steeped in a homespun, benevolent understanding of human nature, which shows as clear and clean beneath the sparkle as dolphins moving steadily under a sunlit sea.

And which came, or so it is said, from Nancy's overpowering love for Gaston Palewski. This is what opened her virginal heart, put the cleverest-girl-in-the-school writer of *Pigeon Pie* in touch with her deepest emotions, and transformed her into the creator of a moving little masterpiece.

Yet love is notoriously a distraction from work, and Palewski's absence at the time of writing would have been as much of a help to Nancy as his presence beforehand. She could think about him, turn him into whatever she wanted in her head, and without the worry of having to deal with him. Even a book as easily written as *The Pursuit of Love* – it took about three months, from January to March 1945 – required her steely and selfish attention. Although it has the air of an outpouring, and although it was dedicated to Gaston Palewski, it is more than simply a two-hundred-page love poem: to say that it was 'inspired by love', or that Nancy's ability to write it was somehow induced by being 'put in touch with her feelings' is simplistic. Like any other real novel with a life of its own, *The Pursuit of Love* was the mysterious possession of its creator: nothing, perhaps, is more solipsistic than the act of producing a book as good as this one, whatever the effect may have been upon the writer of love, hate, sadness, or any other strong emotion.

Perhaps Harold Acton comes closer to the truth when, in his lady-like but acute way, he writes that 'the Free French had fired her imagination with a growing love of France. I suspect that she was already looking forward to pastures new when she embarked on her semi-autobiographical novel, *The Pursuit of Love.*' In other words it was the thought of freedom, of an imminent new life (connected of course to Palewski), that had pushed Nancy forwards, and enabled her to write about her family and childhood with such ease and perspective. The fact that she had grown away from that English life of hers allowed her to see it with perfect clarity, each memory as taut and separate as the vibrating strings of a guitar: the dark blue trees on a Cotswold morning; the image of Uncle Matthew standing behind Linda to tie her hunting stock in a looking-glass, 'both the very picture of concentration'; the debutante dance with the floating panels of taffeta on the ballgowns and the twenty oil-stoves for warmth – out it all came in a rich and elegiac flow, rhythmic and symphonic and true. It could not have been written until then; Nancy was not ready to do it; but the whole of her life had brought her to the place of writing this book, it was not to be explained as a mere liberation by love.

What Palewski *had* done was liberate her into feeling that she could tell the straightforward story of her life. Great play is made, in the affair between Linda and Fabrice, of the joy that he takes in hearing stories of her family. '"*Et* Jassy – *et* Matt – *alors, racontez.*"

'And she recounted, for hours.'

Now this is not invented, it is a representation straight from Nancy's relationship with Palewski. She, like Linda, could enchant her lover with tales of her past, with the way in which she talked about Farve and Muv, Decca and Debo, this whole other world which seemed to him a magical fable, complete and separate, set in the heart of England. 'Nancy was a wonderful *raconteuse*', says John Julius Norwich, 'and I'm sure her telling the Colonel about her family was a hoot.' As Palewski said to her: '*La famille Mitford fait ma joie*'; and by saying it he may have given Nancy her clue, her confidence, her simplifying sense that a book could be a story. At first, she had cast about for both a voice and a plot; by the time of *Pigeon Pie* she had found the voice, but still felt the need for a plot; but the key to *The Pursuit of Love* is that in it she required no devices at all. Like the Radletts, she simply 'told'. She used all that she knew, and wrote it in the way that she knew.

Her childhood, her parents, the extraordinary life force generated by her family; the search for love, the failure to find it, its sudden discovery; here – of course! – was her book. Fascinatingly, she had been pondering what she called 'my autobiography' since 1942, when on solitary evenings at Blomfield Road she had found some solace – or perhaps the promise of something more – in writing about her early life. This was the germ of *The Pursuit of Love*; but Nancy was not yet there with it, almost certainly because she had not yet grasped that

literal and artistic truth could dance felicitously together. By the end
of 1944 she knew what to do. It has been suggested that the final push
came from reading *Brideshead Revisited*: that from Waugh's novel she
had the idea of writing about her family as a complete entity; or
perhaps the idea of the first-person narrator, which certainly worked
wonderfully. This is possible, although as much as anything *Brideshead*
probably showed her how *not* to write her own book. Keep it simple,
keep it *One*, she may have realised. No: it is of course speculation, but
it is nice – as well as convincing – to think that the last, satisfying click
came from her lover's sparkling delight in her tales. And what a
revelation it would have been, to realise that the seeds of a work of art
lay within '*racontez, racontez*', that she held it all in her hands and
need only set the bird free.

Now she knew that she could write from the inside out, rather than
the outside in; and she was, at last, completely relaxed. No wonder her
fingers had itched for a pen. No wonder her voice now bloomed, in all
its casualness, its clarity, in the immediacy with which characters were
placed before the reader's eyes, in the robust concreteness of language.
It was pure mature Nancy to describe a Renoir beauty as a 'fat tomato-
coloured bathing woman', or trees as 'black skeletons against a sky of
moleskin': phrases so sure and rooted, so surprising and so *right*, that
they stay anchored in the mind.

Gaston Palewski was not exactly, as he has been called, Nancy's
'muse'; no one can turn another person into a better writer than they
are capable of being. But 'telling' to him proved a surefire way of
making other people want to listen. Nancy did not write *The Pursuit
of Love for* him, nor did she write it *because* of him. There is little
doubt, however, that she wrote it with the thought, ever present in her
mind, of holding his attention. If it could amuse the Colonel, then it
would do for all the others.

So in March 1945 the book was almost finished; peace loomed and
Paris called; but before happiness could begin, there was still one more
tragedy left to come. The war, which had done such desperate damage
to the Mitford family from the very day of its outbreak – had left Unity
with a bullet in her head, put Diana in jail, made Jessica a widow at
twenty-five, destroyed the health of Lord Redesdale, the serenity of his

Nancy in the 1920s

Opposite above: Batsford Park, the house built by Nancy's grandfather

Opposite below: Asthall Manor, where life was 'all summers', with its view overlooking the graveyard of St Nicholas Church

Right: Nancy's parents, Lord and Lady Redesdale

Below: Unity Mitford, aged eight, with her younger sister Jessica, at Asthall

Swinbrook House, built by Lord Redesdale and named 'Swinebrook' by Nancy

The Mitford town house at Rutland Gate: Lord Redesdale installed a lift for negotiating its six storeys

Nancy aged twenty-seven, when her career as a novelist was just beginning

The Mitford girls

Right: Diana, 'born beautiful, always beautiful', Nancy said of her sister

Above: Unity, wearing her Nazi swastika

Below: Deborah, on the day of her wedding to Lord Andrew Cavendish

Left: Pamela, described by Betjeman as 'the most rural of them all'

Right: Jessica, the rebellious Hon

Right: Nancy's marriage to Peter Rodd

Below: Unity (*left*) and Diana in 1935, with her two sons from her first marriage, Desmond and Jonathan Guinness

Lord and Lady Redesdale sit with Unity (again wearing her swastika) at an aAnglo-German Fellowship meeting held in 1938. Dr Fitz-Randolph of the German Embassy is on Unity's left

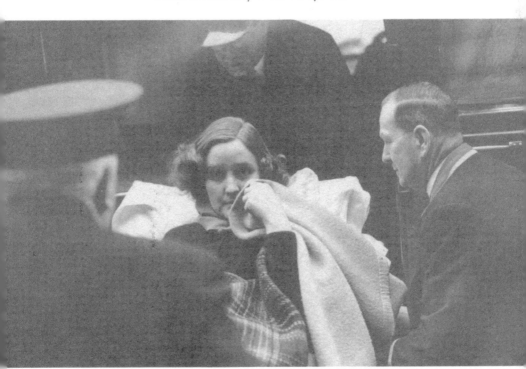

Unity returns to England in 1940 after her attempted suicide

Gaston Palewski, the real life Fabrice du Sauveterre

Nancy in the happy years of the 1950s, in the *salon* of her beloved
flat at Rue Monsieur

Opposite above: Lady Pamela Berry, a good friend of Nancy's during the 1950s, seen here at a 1955 party to celebrate London fashion (a barely existent concept, in Nancy's view, although Norman Hartnell – pictured to the left of Pam Berry – would not have agreed with her)

Opposite below: Evelyn Waugh in 1955, Nancy's favourite correspondent: 'I loved Evelyn I really think the best of all my friends...'

Left: Duff and Diana Cooper: their tenure at the British Embassy in Paris helped to provide Nancy with a glorious social life during her early years in France

Left: Cyril Connolly, 'Boots': butt of some of the best jokes in the letters of Nancy and Evelyn Waugh

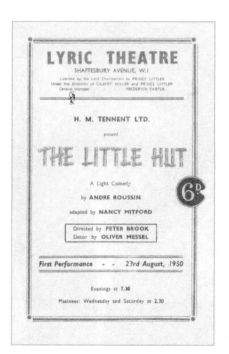

Programme for *The Little Hut*, 'Nancy Mitford's naughty thing', the risqué boulevard comedy that she translated from the French and that ran for three years in the West End

An original programme for the play, signed by Nancy

A rehearsal still from *The Little Hut*: Nancy's friend Robert Morley plays the husband, with Joan Tetzel as the wife

Ava Gardner as the wife in the film version of *The Little Hut*. Her grass skirt was by Dior, Nancy's favourite designer

Left: Nancy at Rue Monsieur in the late 1950s, when she had become a writer of dedication and substance

Below: A book signing from around the same time

Left: Nancy at her house in Versailles. Her love of clothes stayed with her until the end of her life: will you be dignified or ridiculous?, she was asked when the mini-skirt came into fashion. Oh, ridiculous, of course, was her reply

Left: Nancy in her sixties

Below: The last letter written by Nancy to her friend Theodore Besterman, who had given her invaluable help in the writing of *Voltaire in Love*. By this time she had become very ill, although she would live for almost three more years

11 Holland Villas Road
W14

22 Oct 70

My dear Theodore
        The trouble is I'm either
in severe pain or dopey
& therefore not much pleasure
to anybody. If the treatment
I'm having does good & I
become more human I'll
telephone if I may – I would
love to see you
        Love from Nancy

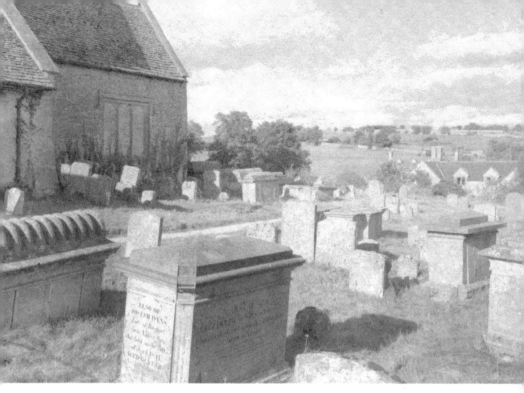

The little churchyard of St Mary, Swinbrook,
where Nancy is buried next to Unity

The interior of St Mary's, where in 1973
Nancy's funeral was attended
by the ageing *beau monde*

Nancy's grave

Nancy in 1970

wife and the marriage of both – waited, cruelly, until hostilities were almost over before throwing its last grenade. Tom died in Burma on 30 March 1945, aged thirty-six. He sustained several machine-gun wounds at the hands of the Japanese and, like Unity, had a bullet lodged inside him; Tom's was in his spine. He knew this, and knew also that although he had been paralysed, he was not expected to die. In fact pneumonia killed him. Nancy heard the news while staying in the enchanted fairyland of Lord Berners' house, where she had gone to finish *The Pursuit of Love*. Gerald Berners took the call and went upstairs to tell Nancy that her brother was dead; smiling more brightly than ever, she came down with the other guests to sit among the jewel-coloured birds at dinner.

She broke a little, however, in the letter she wrote to Jessica a couple of weeks later. 'I thought you would like a line to say Muv & Farve are being simply wonderful & much much better than we had feared at first. But it is almost unbearable oh *Tud* if you knew how sweet & nice & gay he has been of late & on his last leave.'

Nancy had adored Tom. No doubt she now remembered him as 'the fattest boy' upon whom she had tested teases, or as the clever young man whose friends had brought the outside world to her during the Rapunzel years at Swinbrook. And she and Tom had grown into a new closeness during the war, when he had stayed at Blomfield Road and, perhaps, provided silent solidarity with Nancy in the fury she then felt against her family, and the suffering she was enduring with her husband. Her brother mattered to her, merely through his cool and judicious presence. She had for him the respect, the sense of equality, that she had for Diana; but without the jealousy. Always she wanted to think well of him – something she resisted easily with the rest of her family – and for him to think well of her. Of course Tom was a lover of Germany, a friend of Oswald Mosley and an intellectual supporter of Fascism, although he resisted anti-Semitism; his sympathies were violently inimical to Nancy yet she took little notice, apparently convincing herself that that these were *not* his real feelings, that he simply affected them when he was *chez* Mosley. 'Tud was a fearful old twister', she wrote to Jessica in 1968, '& probably was a fascist when he was with Diana. When with me he used to mock to any extent & he hated Sir Os no doubt about that.' Yet it is documented fact that Tom had been a paid-up member of the British Union of Fascists, and had thrown a Fascist salute at one of Mosley's pro-peace meetings in 1939, so at least part of what Nancy wrote is untrue (as she surely knew?). And according to Diana – whose view would naturally be on the opposite side – Tom and Mosley adored each other. 'My brother completely agreed with my husband about politics and the war and so on.' Tom had requested that he be sent to Burma because, according to his old Eton friend James Lees-Milne (whose first love Tom was): 'He does not wish to go to Germany killing German civilians whom he likes. He prefers to kill Japanese whom he does not like.' Yet Nancy forgave the beliefs that she could not share, just as she had denounced them in Diana and reproached them in her mother: principle proving itself, once more, to be an uneasy master of the emotions.

It could be said that Tom's love of Germany helped bring about his premature death, just as it would Unity's. ('I do envy Tom', said Unity when she was told the news, 'having such fascinating arguments with Dr Johnson now.') But his fate was not as desperate as Unity's; his life had been short, but it had been properly lived. His death might have been expected to bring about a reconciliation within the Mitford family, as a tragedy that they all felt similarly deeply. Yet in terms of healing the schisms it had mixed results. Diana had not spoken to her father for years – not since her beyond-the-pale conduct with Mosley – when she turned up at Rutland Gate Mews in April 1945, where the family (including Nanny Blor, even including Peter Rodd) had gathered after Tom's death. The Mosleys were still under house arrest but Diana had left her home near Newbury, and set off for London with her husband and two policemen (no one else could afford two footmen now but you, Lord Berners had remarked). According to Nancy, whose account was recorded in James Lees-Milne's diary, there was a sharp intake of breath when her sister entered the room; but 'she sailed in unabashed, and at once, like the old Diana, held the stage and became the centre of them all. To their amazement Lord Redesdale greeted her affectionately.' When she left, David insisted on escorting her to the car. 'Finally she had to explain, "Farve, the man Mosley is waiting in the motor for me."' At which, 'Lord Redesdale laughed and let her go.' Certain *rapprochements* could never, it was understood, be made.

And the most serious of these unbridgeable chasms was between Tom's parents: this churning renewal of grief would ensure that they stayed apart for the rest of their lives. What had happened to these two was too massive for assimilation. Of course they were not the kind of people to know how to do this, to want to share their feelings, but it would probably have made no difference anyway. David, especially, found no comfort from his wife, nor indeed much from his daughters. It was a great change from the days when he had thought of Sydney as his rock, his saviour, and had found such fiery pleasure in the family that had made him its hero, its top-of-the-bill act.

Indeed despite Nancy's reassurance, given to a distraught Jessica in America, that their parents were 'being simply wonderful', this final blow half-killed the Redesdales. Sydney wrote an appallingly touching letter to Jessica which told of how the news had reached her, first through a telegram saying that Tom had been wounded: 'As the days passed we grew hopeful, and the shock was so bad when it came that I nearly went mad.' She made the interminable journey from Inch Kenneth to her husband in London: 'he is sadly down, and you can imagine what it is to us both, and in fact I know all of you, to lose Tom. He was certainly the best of sons and brothers and I think we all relied so much on him.' His presence had never dominated that family, but he had been its touchstone of sanity: the person who cut through feuds and jealousies, the almost invisible yet essential element with which everybody – from Esmond Romilly through to Oswald Mosley – could mix.

For David, the loss of Tom completed the job started by Unity, and made him an old man: 'he was not well preserved', wrote Nancy in her last novel, *Don't Tell Alfred*, in which Uncle Matthew appears as a diminished figure, although less poignantly than his real-life counterpart.

He had gone through life with one lung, the other having been shot away in the Boer War . . . After that he had hunted, shot and played lawn tennis as though he had been perfectly fit. I can often remember, as a child, seeing him fight to get his breath – it must have been a strain on the heart. He had known sorrow, too, which always ages people . . .

In August 1945 David visited Nancy at Heywood Hill, where he was seen by James Lees-Milne.

Nancy said, 'You know Farve', and there, leaning on a stick was a bent figure with a shrunken, twisted face, wearing round, thick spectacles, looking like a piano-tuner. Last time I saw him he was upstanding and one of the best-looking men of his generation . . .

Nancy was kind to her parents at this time: her letters to her mother have a gentleness, a sweet searching for anything that would provide comfort. 'You will be glad to hear that Mark is back', she wrote in April 1945, about the return of Mark Ogilvie-Grant from his POW camp. 'He says in prison they dreamed of nothing but food & *his* dream was – do you remember that layer-cake with jam you used to have? Well that! Isn't it too funny . . .' Even Nancy's reluctant heart was going out to Sydney, living on Inch Kenneth with Unity while her husband remained in London. Nancy stayed for a time with David, and tried to console her mother about his unwillingness to be with her. 'I'm sending you a present from Farve, on Monday', she wrote in May 1945. 'You must unpack it carefully.' Then: 'Farve is really all right, rather weak of course, but up all night making tea wh is a good sign!' However, Nancy was feeling the strain when she returned to Heywood Hill in June.

What *do* you think I did? I decided not to come here Sat: morning as I was really tired, & forgot to lock the door on Friday, so the shop was full of wandering people trying to buy books from each other . . . By the mercy of Providence Heywood was passing through London & happened to look in. HE WASN'T BEST PLEASED. And I don't blame him. The fact is I'm too tired but it's no excuse for such dottiness.

Another fact was that she had had it with being Heywood's chief shop assistant – in 1942 she would *always* have bothered to open on a Saturday morning – and her time there had become like a sentence being served out. Nancy saw herself cutting loose from the ties of England, family and its clinging sorrows. Over the horizon she saw something new and wonderful. The life she was leading seemed less real than the one she was dreaming of: Paris, sunlight, success; and sadness left behind along with bombed-out streets, whalemeat steaks and wooden suspender belts.

Her buoyancy was returning; it could not help itself. The loss of Tom was terrible, the separate griefs of her parents tugged at her heart, she had her wretched husband to deal with (now trying to find a constituency as a Labour candidate in the 1945 election. 'I fear it will be no good though, married to a Mitford' – it wasn't). And she knew that Gaston Palewski was hardly desperate for her arrival in Paris, despite his occasional crooning of 'venez, venez'. But she could not control her longing for her own future; and the most wonderful thing of all was that reality, like a miraculous racehorse, was beginning to catch up with her illusions.

On 8 June she wrote to her mother that Hamish Hamilton, her publishers, liked *The Pursuit of Love* so much that they were giving her 'a £250 advance which I call enormous'. What a magnificent moment for Nancy. Her last two novels had died, but this one, she knew, was different, and here was her vindication. *The Pursuit of Love* was due to appear in December, and for six months, Nancy lived with a warm fire of hope inside her.

There were other hopes too, threatening almost unbearable joy. When her book was written she had returned to the question of setting up her *de facto* branch of Heywood Hill in Paris. Her father, who through the solipsistic haze of his misery may have been proud of Nancy's wartime stoicism, and of course now had no son to inherit from him, suddenly extended to his daughter a gift of £3,000. With this – as she wrote to her mother – she could buy a partnership in the shop. Heywood liked the idea of the French connection, and encouraged Nancy to proceed. It took a lot of organising at this difficult time – travelling abroad required an exit permit, there were rigorous currency restrictions in place – but Nancy pushed the red tape through her fingers with energy and excitement, eyes fixed upon France.

She felt now that life held the possibility of true happiness, and that the only sin – *pace* Evelyn Waugh – would be not to seize it. 'Is one's failure in life always absolutely one's own fault – I believe it is', she wrote to the Colonel in 1944, a stern creed to which she at least partly subscribed; but she also believed in its obverse, that one could bring about one's *success* in life. As Voltaire wrote, one could decide to be happy. Nancy was forty, she had just written the best book she knew how to write, she had had it with war and sorrow and exhaustion, she was weary of grasping at the ephemeral shadows of pleasure. She wanted to be happy day in and day out, to turn her philosophy of joy and jokes into reality, as she sensed now that she could. And this meant not just the Colonel; but France.

Nancy travelled to Paris at the beginning of September and arrived in the middle of an auspicious heatwave. Later she would always say that when she came to England by boat the skies grew grey but that on the way back, halfway across the Channel, a brilliant sun would emerge.

She wrote to her mother on 3 September, from a little hotel in the 6ème called the Jacob et d'Angleterre ('Do you think the name of this pub the funniest thing you ever heard?'), ecstatically close to Palewski's apartment in the Rue Bonaparte. Although smart today, in 1945 it was, according to Nancy,

the kind of hotel that O Wilde died in – *aucun confort*, no bathroom, or loo except dans le couloir, dry bread & water for breakfast etc. You see utter parsimony has set in, I'm rigid with terror lest I shall run out of money & be forced home . . .

So I eat in workmen's restaurants mostly little bits of cat I think, & feel alternately very hungry & very sick. Like this I can live on £1 a day for everything – rather wonderful. I suppose when the weather gets cold I shall die, like a geranium.[11]

Then in mid-September Nancy found a flat, closer than ever to her prey, in the Rue Bonaparte itself. She was at Number 20, while Palewski lived at the top of the road at Number 1: '*Ici vecut* Gaston Palewski' reads the plaque outside the stone building, inside which a spiral staircase takes one along a marble landing, past a Greek statue in a shadowy alcove, to his door. In that dark, cool, entirely French interior one can feel Nancy's nervous excitement as she tapped her way up the 'grand escalier', feel the Colonel's bounding energy as he raced down for an evening with his 'pretty ladies'.

What he thought, when Nancy turned up on this doorstep, one can only guess. No doubt he welcomed her with a lot of *'ma chère amie'* and a night of Parisian passion, but he must have been wary. He had become a prominent figure in French political life. In de Gaulle's provisional, post-liberation government he was again *chef du cabinet*, no mean task as France was in disarray. The country was not even recognised as a sovereign power; the Communist threat was real and potent; there were areas still ruled, Wars-of-the-Roses style, by bands of armed men who sensed the tremulous nature of central authority. In Paris, many government positions were filled by officials who had supported the puppet regime of Pétain against de Gaulle's Free French: the foreign ministry at the Quai d'Orsay was said to be *'peuplé de Vichy'*.

So there were few that de Gaulle could truly trust, but Palewski was first among them. He was the buffer between the General and the rest of the world, a tricky job that inevitably brought him enemies. People went to him for favours and blamed him when these were not granted. And he was seen as more horribly regal than de Gaulle himself: the letters GPRF (Gouvernement Provisoire de la République Francaise) were said to stand for 'Gaston Palewski Régent de France'. Jealous colleagues called him *'l'empereur'* or *'la lavande'* (such was the strength of his lavender eau de cologne). Palewski played the role of whipping boy, and absorbed the attacks that would otherwise have undermined de Gaulle. He was as able to do this as any man can reasonably be, with his urbanity and his tolerance of human frailty. His own little weaknesses, which he always feared would offend the absurdly puritanical de Gaulle, were part of what made him so useful; they gave him a worldly, forgiving understanding of how to deal with people (not something the General ever got the hang of: Diana Cooper, then the British Ambassadress, said that conversation with de Gaulle 'flowed like glue'[12]).

But Palewski could always tell Nancy that their affair must be kept ultra-discreet because – in sitcom parlance – the boss wouldn't like it. *'Vous connaissez notre froide respectabilité'*, he wrote to her, meaning: don't think you can come swanning in and out of the Rue Bonaparte as my *maîtresse en titre*. Nancy was, of course, a married woman. This may have become an irrelevance, as far as she was concerned; but it made a difference in the wider world, where social codes were adhered to very rigidly. '*A cette époque on se demandait comment recevoir les gens qui n'étaient pas mariés, c'était toute une affaire*', wrote a correspondent in *Le Figaro*[13] whose parents had known Nancy and Palewski after the war. John Julius Norwich confirms that

there was never any question of inviting Nancy and Gaston together to the Embassy. It was very rare, you see, in those days in Paris. You didn't invite people together if they weren't married. There was the wife and there was the mistress, but the wife got invited out. Of course my mother would have been enchanted to have them both at the same table, there was nobody less prudish than my mum, but I think that at dinner, although they would have probably come together and left together, they would have come as two dear friends, and, you know, one had given the other a lift.

Therefore Palewski could legitimately say that Nancy's marital status was relevant to *him*; or at least to de Gaulle. There was enough truth in it to convince ('gone are those cheerful days when Fr politicians expected to die in the arms of their mistresses', Nancy said in 1947), but the real truth was that it helped Palewski to keep Nancy at arm's length.

'I think', says Diana, 'he was always sort of half-hoping she'd go back. Well, you know, saying things like it would spoil his career if she got divorced – I don't know. I don't think it was easy for her, at all.' Meanwhile John Julius Norwich puts himself in the Colonel's position and shudders: 'I mean I can't imagine anything more terrible, trying to have a mild fling with someone and then they up sticks and come and move as close as possible to me. You know, terrifying.'

But this image ('*L'Attirance Fatale*') is perhaps exaggerated; Palewski knew that he could handle Nancy. He also knew that she was too dignified to do anything that would compromise him: 'Nancy never behaved badly in her life,' says Lord Norwich (meaning socially). And Palewski was very fond of his sparkling, smitten Mitford girl. As Nancy's nephew, Alexander Mosley, says, 'the amount of effort he put into that relationship shows how fond he was of her': a man like Palewski would simply not have bothered to spend time with Nancy, had he not wanted to. Why should he? He owed her nothing. No: he took great pleasure in talking to her, pleasure no doubt also in her bed. Although she has been viewed as a slightly embarrassing figure in his life, a semi-desperate woman who had come tagging across the Channel, this is in fact unfair to both of them. Which is not to deny that he treated her in a cavalier manner. 'I've got a heavy political day LET ME SEE – can you come at 2 minutes to 6?' was how she teasingly characterised it.

It is true to say, as John Julius Norwich does, that 'the Colonel could deal with the situation largely because Nancy was prepared to accept any terms. She was always available. If somebody else had plonked him at 8 o'clock, he could ring up Nancy and take her out to dinner. If she had another engagement, which she probably did, she would cancel it. She would sit for a week beside the telephone.' So Palewski could live his life away from Nancy to the full, and have the enjoyment of her company when he had an hour to spare. She asked nothing from him, very unusual in a woman; a sign of her touching naïvety, and of her fear that, should she dare to make demands, the Colonel would walk away. 'Frenchwomen generally keep their lovers if they want to because they know that there is one infallible method of doing so', says Fabrice to Fanny in *Love in a Cold Climate*. 'It's very simple. You must give way to them in every respect . . . these English *femmes du monde* . . . are proud and distant, out when the telephone bell rings, not free to dine unless you ask them a week before – in short, *elles cherchent à se faire valoir*, and it never never succeeds.' What heresy this sounds –! One wonders what a clever handler of men like Sophia Garfield, in *Pigeon Pie*, would have thought of it. There is some truth in what Nancy wrote, more than most women would like to believe; but what she was *really* doing was dutifully setting out the philosophy of love according to Gaston Palewski ('no Frenchman would put up with it for a day', says Fabrice, of the not-tonight-darling-I'm-washing-my-hair brigade). Giving in to her lover in every respect was what Nancy was prepared to do. No doubt it consoled her to take this personal acquiescence, and sell it as a piece of universal advice.

So things were not perfect when Nancy arrived in Paris, but in her heart she had probably not expected them to be. When Linda doubts the constancy of Fabrice, she turns up at his flat to confront him and then, as she sits waiting, decides upon a different course: 'Better go, better ignore the whole affair. Her only hope was to keep things on the present footing, to keep the happiness which she was enjoying day by day, hour by hour.' This was Nancy's own conclusion; again, perhaps, it gave her solace to bring it out into the open in this way. And perhaps doing so made it easier for her to cope with. If Linda could live by this philosophy, so too could her creator.

But the misery and frustration that Palewski caused her were only part of the story. 'I am so completely happy here', she wrote to her mother from her flat in the Rue Bonaparte; and there is no reason to doubt her word. Paris had struck a match to light up her soul. One is reminded of another female writer upon whom Paris had this same emotional effect: Jean Rhys, who moved to the city in the 1920s with her new husband and became a fringe member of the Hemingway-Gertrude Stein literary set. In her autobiography she wrote that, had she never left London and gone to live in Paris, 'there would have been no aliveness. I can't imagine what my life would have been: useless and boring.' This is Nancy speaking, with the social guard dropped and the nerves exposed. So too is this, from Rhys's novel *Good Morning, Midnight*: 'It was a lovely autumn in Paris. I've never been so happy in my life. I'm alive, eating ravioli, drinking wine. I've escaped. A door has opened and let me out into the sun. What more do I want? Anything might happen.'

The man who took Jean Rhys to Paris was a feckless con-man; the man who made Nancy want to live in Paris was a hopeless philanderer; but in neither case did this change the fact of the real, solid happiness that they brought to these women. As Rhys put it in her novel *Quartet*, looking out on to Paris from the balcony of a hotel at night, 'One realised all sorts of things. The value of an illusion, for instance, and that the shadow can be more important than the substance.' Again, this is the hidden voice of Nancy Mitford; even though she would never have expressed such a thought, such a feeling, never have turned her sunlit happiness to reveal its dark indigo underside.

Her idiom was always social, as was her milieu, and her instinct was to play delightedly upon the surfaces of her new life, shot through as they were with shafts of joy. She kept herself busy, engaged with her beloved city through activity rather than reverie. That was her style. She pursued her job for Heywood Hill – 'I'm doing business in rather a desultory way', she wrote to her mother, although as usual she was actually quite assiduous, and complained: 'Nobody in London takes the slightest interest in my activities, Dearest [Heywood] doesn't answer my letters and Mollie [Friese-Greene] just says it makes more work for her – I see her point vividly but it is all rather discouraging I must say. What I've done in fact is to establish a branch of HH here which will take any amount of books from us at 30% more than we pay for them which must be quite a cop.' Impressive stuff, although one doubts she would have worked so hard at selling Cobbett to the Norwegians.

She was also 'writing articles for French papers like mad & getting £10 for 500 words (thank heaven for paper shortage) which you must say not bad', she told Evelyn Waugh. Randolph Churchill, then writing a column about Paris for a group of American newspapers, had asked her to send him 'gossip' that he could use (under his own name) for £2 a time. 'No shame, no effort', said Waugh; so Nancy gossiped away. She told Churchill, for example, that Gaston Palewski was nicknamed 'Régent de France' and under 'venomous' attack in the lead-up to the French elections. If it gave her a small kick to do this, she would have regretted the impulse when Churchill went on to write 'an absolutely hateful article about Fabrice in a French communist paper – how I wish none of my friends could hold a pen'. Palewski, with some dignity, asked Nancy to tell Randolph Churchill *'qu'il n'est pas d'usage en France d'écrire sur les gens avec lesquels on est en relations d'amitié ou de camaraderie'*. In England, unfortunately, traducing one's friends was, and remains, a favourite hobby among journalists. Although Nancy felt she had escaped this kind of thing in France, it is a dismal fact of life that no one ever quite does.

Such nasty, schoolboyish behaviour only served to underline the superiority of France. 'Oh my passion for the French', she wrote to her mother, 'I see all through rose-coloured spectacles . . . !' In this letter, written in September 1945, she tells a little story of finding a 'char' for Rue Bonaparte, and is quite delirious about the whole event: 'The angelic concierge (how helpful the French are) got into the Métro at rush hour for me, went all the way to Montmartre & returned with the prettiest femme de ménage you ever saw, all like magic. Imagine a London porter, all grumbles & groans & certainly no lovely girl at the end of it!' Of course, not everybody finds the French so wonderfully obliging. But they and Nancy got along together. They shared an elegant bustling spirit, a love of brightly correct formality, a set of standards applied to daily life: food, clothes, social interchanges. And this sense that she had of belonging, of being so welcome a part of society, put her in a marvellous mood. '*I like* the human race, & I long to be liked back, & here I am liked back', she wrote to Evelyn Waugh. Everything was suffused with light and fun; she was like someone who had had two strong martinis on an empty stomach at the bar of the Hôtel Crillon. But Nancy was drunk only on happiness.

'She saw everything *en rose,* she really did,' says Diana. 'I think, at the end of the war, everybody wanted to go to Paris! England had become so terribly dreary, so dirty, so everything. But Paris was not all that one would wish either, there wasn't really enough to eat, although Nancy would always pretend it was wonderful. She wasn't at all truthful. And there's a marvellous comparison, when she was staying with Alvilde Chaplin [later Lees-Milne] as she was then, and they both wrote to England on the same day for some reason, and Nancy said "so marvellous here, you can go to one farm and get a chicken, another and get a leg of mutton", and Alvilde said we walked about ten kilometres and in the end managed to get a few turnips.

'It was extraordinary. She just didn't see the snags.' Because it is, when one thinks about it, quite brave of Nancy to have upped sticks and taken herself off to Paris. She had no idea of where she would stay, or for how long. She certainly had no reason to believe that she would find a flat ('she was lent it by two awfully nice lesbians', says Diana), and it is indeed hard to imagine her inside this plain grey and black house at 20 Rue Bonaparte: 'an ice box, never a ray of sun'. It looks like student digs, where all one wants is a bed, a gas ring and the boy one fancies up the road. It brings home the adolescent nature of this venture. Nancy was not a girl who could start a new life abroad with the knowledge that, if everything went wrong, there was plenty of time to start again. She was a grown woman, launching herself into a barely known world, with nothing but a few francs and hope to sustain her.

Of course there was nothing much to keep her in England; but that, too, might have seemed sad rather than enlivening. At forty most people expect to have a family, or at least things that they do not want to leave. But Nancy cut loose completely, backed by a kind of impulsive certainty, and loved the fact that she could do so. She stayed closely in touch with her family. And she had good connections in Paris – not just Palewski, but Duff and Diana Cooper, who had just taken over the British Embassy – which meant that she was, as always, protected by the mysterious safety nets of privilege. Yet it is remarkable that a person of her age and apparent conformity should have taken this step: should, at the end of the war, have found herself living alone in a dark *appartement*, as excited as the girl who had longed to dance down the Champs-Élysées in 1926. This was the adventure of her life.

So she did not mind that until she found a flat of her own, at the end of 1947, she had to move back and forth between England and France, in and out of hotels and apartments. She stayed at the Hôtel Pont Royal, the Hôtel de Bourgogne, the Hôtel Madison, and a flat on the Quai Malaquais; as well as the Rue Bonaparte. These all fell within the protection zone of the posh; they were in the 6ème or 7ème, the latter being, as John Julius Norwich says, 'the grandest for the old French aristocracy. All the *gratin*, as they were called, would have always lived in the 7ème. À *la rigueur* you might just ooze over into the 6ème. There was the other sort of grand who lived in the 16ème, because the houses were larger, but it's not where anyone with any pretensions to artistic sensibility would have dreamt of living.' The artistic connection was apparent almost everywhere that Nancy lived. Her first hotel was in the Rue Jacob, where Jean Cocteau held soirées after the liberation; the Pont Royal was a '*hôtel littéraire*', today hung about with photographs of Dylan Thomas and Françoise Sagan; the Hôtel Madison was on the Boulevard St Germain, opposite the cafés where Sartre and de Beauvoir conducted their highly public love affair, the Quai Malaquais flat had been the home of George Sand. And the flat in the Rue Bonaparte was owned by Betty Chetwynd (one of Diana's 'lesbians'), who wrote on modern French literature in the *TLS*; in an obituary written by Nancy, Miss Chetwynd's flat was described as 'an Anglo-French centre which will be sadly missed'. So it was all of a piece, atmospherically. Nancy had probably received her education in where

to go from Palewski and co.; as a girl she had stayed in the 16ᵉᵐᵉ, a safe
if more glamorous Mayfair, but mixing with the Free Frogs she would
have picked up that she should gravitate across the river. (Accordingly
she gives Fabrice an *appartement* in – surprise surprise – Rue
Bonaparte, and Charles-Edouard de Valhubert an enormous *hôtel
particulier* in the Faubourg St Germain). But for all the smartness of
her milieu, the impression remains of a very young person, trawling
around from hotel to flat to hotel, excited as a backpacker by the whole
affair: considerations such as how do I move my possessions? how do
I get my mail? were the bourgeois worries of a middle-aged person. Yet
Nancy *was* a middle-aged person, living the peripatetic life of a gap-
year student, with dinners at the Hôtel de Charost thrown in.

But for her – and this is one of her most defining, reassuring traits
– middle age was the prime of life. 'You are *lucky* to be middle-aged,'
her nephew Jonathan Guinness told her in 1947. 'I agree.' Nancy
disdained any notion of being over the hill. She was aware of physical
ageing, of course, and wore 'frownies' (a Heath Robinson version of
Botox, put on the forehead at night to smooth out wrinkles), but the
little vanity she had would have neither lessened nor increased as she
grew older. She was too confident for that. She had no truck whatever
with the idea that a young girl was any more desirable than an elegant
grown woman. ('I don't happen to be attracted by children,' says
Charles-Edouard de Valhubert, whose eternal *tendresse* is for the
clever, fortyish seductress Albertine, 'one whom people never get out
of their systems.')

No: middle age was when a person was at their most interesting
and desirable; the perfect time, in fact, to embark upon new adventures.
Nancy, like Jean Brodie, reached her peak in her forties ('Never have I
seen her look prettier: a rose in full bloom', wrote loyal Harold Acton).
Her aristocrat's assurance fell into glamorous, individualistic place.
And this flowering allowed her to express what she had always,
intuitively, believed: that youth was all very nice but adulthood was
when life really began. There is a sense, in her first two novels, of
unease with the young; although she was one with them, like Sophia
Garfield 'she was never a romper', nor could she ever quite get along
with the silliness that takes itself so seriously. The qualities that Nancy
valued in people – charm, wit, elegance, cheerfulness, confidence,

learning – were more likely to be found in an adult than in an adolescent. This was especially true in France. Indeed the two novels set in Paris – *The Blessing* and *Don't Tell Alfred* – return repeatedly to this theme. In *The Blessing*, Nancy's terrible (caricature) creation, 'a large Teddy-bear of an American' named Hector Dexter, delivers a long speech in praise of the young to his dinner-party neighbour, the fabulously ripe and sexy septuagenarian Madame Rocher des Innouïs. "'Now I am over forty [he says] but many and many's the time, in French houses, when I have been the youngest person present, and I've never yet, at any parties, seen really young folks, college boys and girls and teen-agers. How do your French teen-agers amuse themselves, Madame Innouïs?"

"'They are young, surely that is enough," she said indignantly. "Surely they don't need to amuse themselves as well.'"

This was Nancy's view entirely: she liked young people on the whole, and was kindly – in her rigorous way – towards those who came to visit her in Paris. ('Did I tell you about my Beauty of 18 who is staying here?' she wrote to Waugh in 1949, describing Venetia, the daughter of her friends Pauline and Basil Murray. 'You never saw such a heavenly girl . . . She has been a magnet for other little creatures who run in & out of the flat all day using my telephone & trying on my clothes – I have very much enjoyed the whole thing.') But she had little indulgence for the young if they lacked adult attributes, good manners and good sense. Bring on the old people, she thought. 'The Elwes boys[14] not at all in the Jonathan [Guinness] – John Julius class', she wrote to Diana in 1948, 'deadly – or perhaps . . . young for their age. They certainly don't see the point of ONE.' Nancy thought that boys of this kind could only improve when they grew out of thinking that youth was an excuse for gracelessness; a very different attitude from that of today, when maturity is in balding thrall to the idiocies of the young. Fanny's sons, in *Don't Tell Alfred*, are portrayed as lost causes ('showing off') in their desire to make a quick buck, or swoon at pop concerts, or worship Eastern mysticism: 'lettered-beachcombers', they are called, the type of person that nowadays would be admired rather than dismissed, but Nancy knew better. She is highly prescient in her portrayal of youth culture in *Don't Tell Alfred*. She sees American values taking over; she gives us perhaps the first 'mockney', an Etonian who earns £9 a week packing razors then becomes publicity agent to his pop-star idol; the *raison d'être* of her book is to show how superior are the old European ways, as practised by people like herself and her friends. 'A Paris dinner party, both from a material point of view and as regards conversation, is certainly the most civilised gathering that our age can produce', says Fanny. The reader sees no reason to disagree, nor to think that an evening spent among flowers in Sèvres vases, couture dresses and sparkling chat about everything from sex to Stendhal, is anything other than preferable to a night on the tiles with a bunch of twenty-year-old twits. 'Paris isn't much good for teenagers', Fanny's sons tell her: there could be no higher accolade.

It was France, really, that had made being forty a new beginning. Had she stayed in London, Nancy might have felt as fleshless and grey as the city itself. 'Paris had cured me of my middle-aged blight exactly as I had hoped it would', says Fanny; 'if I was sometimes worried there I never felt depressed, bored and useless.' As her creator had come to believe, Fanny feels that the longer life goes on, the better it becomes.

Almost from the time that Nancy arrived at the Hôtel Jacob et d'Angleterre, her voice settled into a slightly different tone – different even from *The Pursuit of Love*. It acquired a note of smiling affirmation, an amused acceptance of all that life had to offer; even when it offered sadness. It grew up. What she wrote after *The Pursuit of Love* never quite recaptured its strange, semi-conscious poetry, for this was the book that saw Nancy poised between her past and her future, between memories of an England that had the distance of another life, and dreams of a France that *would* be another life. It was a book full of imaginative loves: for the father that poor Lord Redesdale had once been, for the world that had been created by herself and her sisters, for the man that she wanted Gaston Palewski to be. Afterwards, her writing settled to reality. It no longer contained wrenching, poignant longings for a vanished childhood, in which Unity and Tom were as unstoppably alive as the bloodhounds that hunted them across 'the beautiful bleak Cotswold uplands'; nor for an unattainable future, in which love was as strong and real as the sunlight on the trees in the Bois de Boulogne.

Reality would become enough for Nancy, would contain its own enchantments and delights. This sufficiency underpins her next novel,

Love in a Cold Climate, which has no poetry pulsing beneath its prosaic surface, but which brings so much of the fascination, the sheer gift that life itself has to offer. Nancy's letters, too, have this quality: they tell little stories like the one about the 'char', and her pleasure in them is so great, her phrasing and observation so natural, that the reader becomes the same contented person as she was herself. This is one of her defining talents, this ability to communicate to us what the *TLS* would call 'the kind of aerial high spirits which persuade us, for a delectable instant, that we too can be wonderfully amusing if the fancy takes us'.

And it came, once again, from France. For what she found in Paris was a means whereby her philosophy of life could become a day-to-day actuality: there are not many philosophers who learn to live by what they preach, but Nancy was one of them. Of course she still had her powerful imagination, her sadnesses and dreams. These were often as strong as ever. Yet her will to happiness had triumphed: a remarkable feat, calling upon reserves of stoicism and grit and faith, but it happened. As Alistair Forbes put it, 'she had wisely discovered [happiness] to be made up, like a coral reef, of small joys upon small joys', a discovery that sustained her for the rest of her life, throughout all the sorrow that it could throw at her.

In 1945, what Nancy dreaded more than anything was the moment of returning to London. 'Darling', she wrote to Violet Hammersley in October, 'my life has resolved itself into a mule-like struggle not to leave this spot (Paris I mean).' The spot had become home. She had not thought of this brief interlude as a visit, but as real life. She kept putting off her departure, lingering until the very last of the autumnal heat had slipped away, before writing to Diana at the end of October: '*Positively* – you won't believe it I know – I am coming back on Tues.' Her letter continued: 'Do you realize it is exactly 20 years since we were in the Av: V.Hugo? . . . Apart from love or anything I must come & live here, & if one makes up one's mind things generally happen don't you think.'

In fact Nancy did not dare to think that she might *not* live in Paris. The idea that the dullness of Blomfield Road, and daily work at Heywood Hill, would comprise her existence was too dreadful to contemplate. And she may have realised something else, connected to the writing that she now took seriously.

It was Evelyn Waugh who identified a magnificent irony in the fact that she had helped – as he saw it – to speed the decline of the elite, while plotting to live in a society that recreated an ideal of pre-revolutionary Paris. And he was right: it was a peculiar paradox. Nancy had voted for the symbolic ending of an England that she loved, the one she described in her introductions to the Stanley letters, and her homage to land-owning in *The Pursuit of Love*. She had done so for obscure reasons: because she had acquired the 'pinko' habit in reaction to her family, because she had a rogue streak of radicalism in her nature, and, perhaps, because she saw change as inevitable. She knew, in fact, that 'her kind' were on the way out. Her two post-war 'English' novels are both set in the period leading up to the war; this allowed her to depict a society that was disappearing by the time the books were published. The magnificent Park Lane home of the Montdores, described in all its splendour in *Love in a Cold Climate*, has become, in *Don't Tell Alfred*, 'a huge hotel . . . the colour of old teeth', while London itself is portrayed as a city pointlessly depredated in the name of progress: 'Every time I visit it', says the narrator Fanny, 'I am saddened by seeing changes for the worse: the growing inelegance; the loss of character; the disappearance of landmarks and their replacement by flat and faceless glass houses.' *Don't Tell Alfred* addresses the encroachment of this new world, which Nancy could warn against but not inhabit ('oh bother – what are jeans?' she once asked).

Her last novel is, *au fond*, 'French', as is its predecessor *The Blessing*. Both belong to a supremely aristocratic world, that of the British Embassy in the Rue du Faubourg St-Honoré (the 'large, beautiful, honey-coloured' Hôtel de Charost), and of the Valhubert family in St Germain (built 'between courtyard and garden' expressly to receive Marie Antoinette). And the fact is that Nancy could not have got away with this sort of thing had she continued to write 'English' books. Even *The Pursuit of Love* got her into trouble with left-wing intellectuals: 'the Bloomsbury Home Guard are gunning for me', she wrote to Evelyn Waugh, while Cyril Connolly and co. 'think my book utterly indecent on acc/ of not being about cabmen's shelters & Hons Cupboard makes them vomit.' In her 1966 television interview she was asked why she always wrote about the upper-classes. Quite rightly, she replied that 'writers write about the people they know, really, I think. I suppose it's rather natural . . . Jane Austen wouldn't have written about Siberian peasants. She couldn't do it.' And so Nancy, having mined the seam of interwar English aristocracy, made an extremely clever switch to France: to Madame de Pompadour, Louis XIV and the Marquis de Valhubert, all of whom live in the same, untouchable land of wealth and privilege.

In a semi-teasing letter of 1946, Waugh wrote to Nancy that 'Your literary future is insoluble I think. You see even the most bookish and authoritative minds . . . decay in exile . . . You are so topical and on the spot & so radically English that you must feed on a fresh English diet. As an English observer thinking foreigners absurd you might be able to write about them. As a cosmopolitan you are lost.' As it turned out, this prediction was both correct and utterly wrong. Nancy *did* remain radically English, yet she found a fresh French diet. She filtered France through her Englishness, in fact, and in a way that readers simply adored. 'Do you admit that when I came to live here you said I would never write a book that was any good?' she sang out to him in 1951. 'And that, on the contrary, I have improved?'

Privilege, as she knew, was her authorial milieu. It was what her readers expected from her. But what she wrote was also what she lived: by turning to France she found, through her imagination, the values that she sensed would be lost to her in England. 'I feel a hostility from people in England I hardly know, because they think I sound frightfully superior', she later said. With the typical survival instinct of the aristocrat, she intuited that the way for *One* to thrive was in another country. As Evelyn Waugh grew ever more embittered and frightened by the changes in England after the war ('There has been a revolution here. Your sans culottes have triumphed'), so Nancy remained untouched by them. Instead she used them for her own mischievous ends: as with the essay on class, containing the infamous distinction between U and Non-U, which she might not have dared to write had she been living in England. She was liberated indeed.

So what would have happened to her, had Paris not provided this glorious escape route? 'Yes, one does wonder,' says her sister Deborah.

'I don't know. She'd have probably found somebody else besides Peter, I just don't know, who can tell. One thing I'm quite sure of. If she'd had, at that time, what I suppose is still described as a normal life, a husband and children, she would not have written as she did.'

It is therefore fitting that Nancy's writing – product of solitude, independence, sadness, what you will – supplied the means to her own kind of fulfilment. Not the 'normal' kind, the wife and mother kind; that was closed to her. Yet by having nothing to hold her, she could become successful, rich, able to live as she pleased: in Paris, close to her lover, surrounded by courtesy and appreciation. Her second set of dreams could come true. And it would all be made possible by the fact that she had 'written as she did': by the publication of *The Pursuit of Love*, in December 1945.

CHAPTER 8

Within three weeks, *The Pursuit of Love* made Nancy more money than the rest of her books put together: £798. Within six months it made £7,000. Within a year it sold 200,000 copies. The novel was an instant sensation: it absolutely hit the spot, and the remarkable thing was that this happened pretty much by word of mouth. Although publicised to an extent, the book's popularity spread from person to person, like pollen. An equivalent success today would be on chat shows, in supermarkets, a continual source of newspaper articles ('Are Frenchmen *Really* Better Lovers?' 'Should Child-Hunting be Banned?' 'Are You a Bolter?'). It would be overhyped like the silliest piece of female fiction ('The Hon. Bridget Jones's Diary'). Linda would be portrayed as what she always threatens to become but never does: a generic man-hunter, a symbol of every woman's longing for love, fulfilment and the Duke of Rightshire.

But would *The Pursuit of Love* succeed so wildly, were it to be published today? What would certainly be relished is its extraordinary gift of immediacy, the direct and intimate voice, the hotline to the anxious banalities of the female psyche ('I have often noticed that when women look at themselves in every reflection . . . it is hardly ever, as is generally supposed, through vanity, but much more often from a fear that all is not as it should be'). Then there is its faith in the redemptive power of love, its romantic realism, qualities that still underpin 'women's' books despite the rise of neo-feminism. In other ways, however, Nancy's novel is completely different to any contemporary counterparts. Its cultural landscape is literary rather than journalistic, Evelyn Waugh rather than *Cosmopolitan*. Despite the modern technique of '*racontez, racontez*', the book is a conceived and constructed thing, rather than two hundred pages of jolly spiel: 'LINDA: V bd day today. Tony (bliss, swoon) rang but Farve (boo, hiss) picked up, ultra-disaster. Binged on jugged hare, 3 hlpgs stewed prunes (450 cals?). Gloucs. the absolute End.'

The Pursuit of Love is still adored for its autobiographical content and its 'unwriterly' style: in that sense, it is modern. What would probably go against the book, were it to be published today, is that it is set so shamelessly, so non-judgmentally, among the aristocracy. Nancy could bring the most socially remote member of the upper-classes to instant life, but there is a convention nowadays that posh people cannot be quite real. In fact Nancy was increasingly accused of uppishness during her own lifetime ('I don't like snobs,' said a member of an Audience Research Report after her starchy appearance on BBC television in 1957[1]). The world, as she knew, had grown inimical to her kind. Her compelling charm began to be seen as something false, fake, a music hall turn almost ('The U Girl from Kew'). But she was lucky; she made it under the wire, a fugitive aristo embraced by the populist fold. A few years later and she might have been consigned to the oblivion of an unvisited stately home with its roof caving in. Nowadays she might not even get published at all; although antipathy to the upper classes continues to go hand in hand with a reluctant fascination.

Back in 1946 however, Nancy's sweet, posh Radletts were devoured by readers with a near-frenzy. After the war, people were desperate for books, given near-luxury status by paper shortages; and none was more in demand than The Pursuit of Love. As with Brideshead Revisited – which also had tremendous success – readers wanted to forget the boredom and privations of war, and to lose themselves in tales of suffering upon goose-feather mattresses. Britain was in a state of depression at this time – 'It shouldn't have been,' says Debo, 'because the war had been won and so on, but it just was' – and its tired old soul yearned to wallow in semi-illicit pleasures like escapism and nostalgia. Moreover Nancy made people laugh. She energised them with the pure aliveness of her tale. What must readers have felt, encountering for the first time that firecracker Uncle Matthew? What breathless joy he must have brought, and what reassurance with his indestructible patriotism, his unassailable sense of his place in life.

Of course, as with *Brideshead*, there was more to Nancy's success than this. What *The Pursuit of Love* proves is that for a book to catch fire it must operate on two levels: give both instant and enduring pleasure. It must be fit for love at first sight and for fifty years of marriage. Obviously the novel had jokes and romance, it was a perfectly mixed cocktail of otherness and accessibility, and its fable-like aspect entranced a world that had changed for ever. All this explains why it is readable. But it is, for many people, *infinitely* readable, and this is because of its less evident qualities: its subterranean poetry, in fact. There is the slow, elegiac sadness that keeps watchful pace with the book's springing vitality. There is its rigorous treatment of the apparently simple theme of love: is it the most important thing in life? Does its pursuit preclude day-to-day happiness? Is it an eternal value, or a series of exquisite illusions? And then there is the instinctive perfection with which the passage of time is marked: again and again comes the changing of the seasons, but as the book moves inexorably towards its end these seem to happen ever more quickly until, in the final pages, there is a last, poignant shift into spring, which arrives 'with a brilliance of colouring, a richness of life' and brings with it tragedy. These are the qualities that give Nancy's book its subconscious life; and they are drunk, as great draughts of sustenance, along with the champagne bubbles.

Not that everyone perceived these profundities at the time; the truth of books is rarely immediately apparent. Evelyn Waugh wrote a rather sneaky letter to Diana Cooper saying 'Nancy Mitford has written half a brilliant novel about her childhood; the adult half is no good but do read the beginning' (he probably knew this to be a commonplace judgment, but Diana and Nancy were his two chief female correspondents, and he could not resist the occasional self-important bitch about one to the other). The *TLS*, too, said that the 'real attraction' of the book 'lies in the amusing and maliciously observed picture of family life at Alconleigh'. The intellectual brigade was almost bound to denounce it: 'they are all the more annoyed because they think it's quite well written', Nancy wrote to Waugh. Meanwhile it was being positively eaten up by the *Tatler* set: 'kind people are giving luncheon parties to discuss the book & the Windsors have given it to everyone for Xmas. Rather low brow circles I fear but still!'

A different type of person, however, adored the book completely, and understood what lay beneath. The *Spectator*, for example, wrote in its review, '(rather gratuitously I thought) this is not great literature or great wit but is otherwise all right'[2], but its conclusion was generous and accurate: 'it has more truth, more sincerity and more laughter than a year's output of novels in the bogus significant style.' John Betjeman fell completely for the book, and wrote to Nancy that she had 'produced something that really is a monument to our friends . . . Clever, clever Nancy. I am proud to know you.' No doubt the novel confirmed Betjeman in his opinion that 'Nancy was the warmest of them all.' 'Praise from you is praise indeed,' she replied to him; 'you say all the things I would have liked somebody (whose judgment I respected) most to say . . . How nice and clever we all are.'

Nancy's letter to Betjeman continued that her father was 'delighted' with *Pursuit*, 'but cried at the end & said he had read a sad book once before called *Tess of the d'Urbervilles* [not just *White Fang*, then?] & had hoped never to read another.' To Lord Redesdale it must have been a bewildering little miracle, to see his own old self conjured to such life by his daughter; although Lady Redesdale seems to have taken little pleasure in what Nancy had achieved. 'This family again', she wrote to Jessica, in an oh-dear-God sort of way, after reading a couple of chapters. 'It's about all of you as children, the heroine appears to be Debo, and you appear in it of course, and Farve and I . . .' Perhaps Sydney feared the publicity that the book would bring; she had had a bellyful with Unity, Diana and indeed Jessica. But nor was she overjoyed with her portrayal as Aunt Sadie, feeling as she did a small chill within it; although this vague, funny and benign figure left out much of what Nancy saw as her mother's steel.

As for the sisters: the 1980 television documentary showed Pamela, Deborah and Jessica to be as intensely fond of *The Pursuit of Love* as if it, too, were a member of their family, which in a sense it was. Diana, notably, took a slightly more distanced view – 'now I'm afraid that's poetic licence', she said firmly, when asked about Nancy's depiction of the Mitford child-hunts. But for the others it was as if, by osmosis, the real and fictionalised versions of their shared past had become one semi-mythic truth. This is very Mitford, to collude in the magical joke of their own immortality; and certainly they seemed to be enjoying it.

Nonetheless, back in 1945, it must have been a surprise, to say the least, when Nancy was revealed to have taken what was intensely private and laid it all out for public consumption. Within the joy that *The Pursuit of Love* would surely have given – of recognition, if of nothing else – there may have been more ambivalent emotions. Again, this is the great moral question that is asked of autobiographical novels, whether they can ever be wholly acceptable to the people who form the raw stuff of them. *The Pursuit of Love* was not *Wigs on the Green*, there was nothing overt that could hurt or offend; but this was a history belonging to seven other (living) people that Nancy had made her own. The fact of her having done so may have aroused a vague disquiet, that Nancy should profit so from her extravagant use of them all.

And specific things must have irritated. When Lord Merlin (a character based upon Gerald Berners, who no doubt loved this fantastical portrait) says that Linda has run off with Christian Talbot not so much because of his noble ideals, but because he is 'an attractive fellow', this would almost certainly have annoyed Jessica and Diana: the shot is aimed at both of them. Jessica is a further target, when her elopement with Esmond Romilly is ludicrously parodied: Jassy Radlett, 'pretty as a peach', runs off to Hollywood to marry a 'second-rate film actor' named Carey Goon (this refinement may have been suggested by the minor scandal in which Winston Churchill's daughter, Sarah, eloped with the actor Vic Oliver). In fact the whole notion of Communism is made to look futile in *The Pursuit of Love* ('Left-wing people are always sad because they mind so dreadfully about their causes', says Linda, 'and the causes are always going so badly . . . One does feel so much on their side, but it's no good, people like Sir Leicester [Kroesig] always come out on top, so what can one do?'). This sort of thing would have incensed Jessica; perhaps justifiably. There is a sense that Nancy found her loyalties relatively easy to attack, after the unyielding struggle with Diana over Fascism.

But the most interesting question is whether the sisters were *jealous* of Nancy after she achieved success on the back of their collective past. *The Pursuit of Love* seems to have incited them all, except phlegmatic

Pamela, to write their own version of its events: Jessica's *Hons and Rebels*, Diana's *A Life of Contrasts*, Deborah's *Counting My Chickens*. It is possible that these books, all of which stand alone as unusually good, would have been written anyway. Yet one suspects that they were born of Nancy's example, that she set her sisters on this particular path. She was always an *agitatrix*. Benevolent though her novel was, it surely stirred things up within the Mitfords, and jostled the rivalries that lay never too far from the surface.

Nancy's life changed for ever after *The Pursuit of Love*. 'When it came out', she would later say, 'I sat under a shower of gold.'[3] It would take her into the world of fame, protect her against want and obscurity, give her a voice to which people would always now listen. It would make her, as Diana says, 'a star: it's so lovely to have a great success, and she really did. Of course you might feel it's rather awful not to have a success by the time you're forty. But it was marvellous, and completely self-made. And she *was* a star, although she never considered herself one.' In fact, Nancy was quite shy about her success. Among her friends she took pleasure in it, in print she allowed it to give her power, to say things that an unknown writer might not dare, but she did not flaunt it. One cannot imagine her using her name to get a table at Prunier's. In 1956 she described a nightmare Air France flight made easy for her when a 'fan . . . penetrated the disguise of Mme Rodd', but a different type of person would never have worn the disguise in the first place. Nancy said of herself that she was 'timid', and in some ways this was true. She was nervous, for example, of appearing on television ('I've always said no on account of the terror,' she wrote to the producer of the 1957 BBC programme. 'The trouble is that when I am frightened I become *very* affected').

As her fame grew, from 1946 onwards, she took an ambivalent attitude to her own publicity. Personally she did not care for it; she was, wrote Harold Acton, 'a very private person in spite of the publicity she had given to her family in *The Pursuit of Love*.' At the same time she was not remotely snooty about being marketed; as long as she herself could remain withdrawn, she was more than happy to go along with it. Despite her fears she did the television interviews, because she knew the difference that they made to sales ('I sold half as many again last week', she wrote to Violet Hammersley, after a broadcast to plug *Don't Tell Alfred*. 'But can you tell me why anyone watches?'). She did newspaper interviews, although not of the probing kind, and she was on hand to give opinions to journalists (although she 'cried off' when the BBC telephoned in 1971, asking for her thoughts on Edward Heath's French accent: 'I longed to say it's his *English* accent which is so fearful'[24]). In 1971 she also – and this is extraordinary, so much so that one wonders if she quite knew what she was doing – gave her sanction to an idea, proposed by the then head of BBC Comedy, for a series of half-hour programmes based upon the Mitford family. An unintentionally comedic internal BBC memo says that the series was envisaged as 'having the same sort of interest as *The Forsyte Saga*', although the proposed writer was a veteran of the 1970s sitcom ('This could be done before he does another series of *My Wife Next Door*'). The series went a long way in the planning. It stalled, chiefly because of the difficulty in getting the rights to *The Pursuit of Love* from the film company to which they were sold in 1946, but the idea only really died with Nancy herself in 1973. Although the BBC was still keen to continue, it would seem (from internal memos) that Deborah, Nancy's literary executrix, and Anthony Jones, from her literary agency A.D. Peters, were not.

Populism was not a dirty word to Nancy. Having created her remarkably defined image, she was willing to nurture it: she knew that people liked her well-bred provocativeness, that they loved the myth of the Mitfords, that they lapped up all the 'snobbish' detail of her writing, and she saw no reason not to give them what they wanted. There is a depressing chasm nowadays between novels that are 'literary' (602 copies sold) and those that are 'readable' (903,117,531 copies sold, excluding the TV tie-in paperback); but this did not exist for Nancy. She had the essential integrity that would prevent her from doing anything solely for sales: 'she is not at all a hack; nobody can make her write unless she wants to', as the *TLS* put it, and she herself later said: 'I do not write consciously with the idea of making money.' Nonetheless she was sensible enough to court success, rather than to see it as evidence of compromise.

As for the sudden unstoppable stream of wealth that flowed from *The Pursuit of Love*, flooding the parched poverty that she had known all her adult life – it was magical, and it made all the difference in the world to her. She was absolutely sincere when, in 1966, she shrieked 'I've always needed money!' at the television interviewer who clearly thought that anyone who spoke the way she did was up to her neck in share certificates. Not so: in London she really *had* lived on an upmarket bread line, across which her husband constantly threatened to push her. Of course she was protected by who she was: she received handouts from her in-laws and her father, and she owned a few posh accessories, like her Sheraton desk, the Chinese screens brought back from diplomatic travels by her grandfather Bertram, the fur coat that she sent to the country during the Blitz. Of course she was never *truly* poor, but she did have very little: 'she was', as Debo says, 'pushed for money until she wrote *The Pursuit of Love*. She never had money to buy things. She was pushed, she really was.' What she needed, she had to earn, and she did so industriously. The neo-feminists should be proud of her.

Except – they might say – from 1945 onwards the reason she wanted money was so that she could *get close to the Colonel*. Once the royalties started flooding in, she could be off to Paris, basking in his sexy, spotty presence. Which makes some of the letters she wrote in early 1946 rather baffling, since they are full of affection towards none other than our old friend Peter Rodd. 'Peter is back', Nancy wrote to Evelyn Waugh in January, from Blomfield Road, 'which is bliss except that I hardly see him . . . What a clever man he is (Prod I mean) & so *good*. The late Colonel.' This surprising letter ends on a wifely note: 'I hear Prod stirring like a hibernating animal in the spring so must go & see to his breakfast.' To which Waugh replies: 'This Prod-worship is not healthy. Clever perhaps – good no.'

This letter of Nancy's does not fit the perceived pattern of her life; but there it is, along with the reply to Waugh which returns to the same theme: 'If *ever* there was a saintly character it is Prod & I bet you'll see him nestling away in heaven from a distance long before you get there yourself.' She was even planning to return with her husband to their shared past at Perpignan: 'Prod is off to Spain he hopes for the revolution', she wrote, although in fact he went to try and make a film (a typical shot in the dark; nowadays he would probably have an unsuccessful television documentary company, PRODuctions).

So was Nancy playing with the idea of returning to Peter, rather than ploughing on with Palewski? Or is this sudden affection for her husband better explained in a letter to Gaston Palewski, also January 1946: 'In March Peter is going to Spain then *please* come & stay with me – he wouldn't mind. I said to him, about my will, would it hurt your feelings if I left some money to the Colonel? Peter said hasn't he got any money? NR: No. PR: Then I think it is a good idea, he ought to have some.' In other words Peter had apparently become a complaisant husband, for which Nancy was lovingly grateful.

Actually it suited him to have Nancy trailing after another man, as he must have realised after the jealous fury of 1944 had subsided. In 1950 he made the remark to Nancy about having 'for the last 12 years . . . considered himself as married to Adelaide [Lubbock]', so what difference did it make to him if Nancy adored the Colonel? This may all seem rather strange today: the contemporary view of marriage has become more conventional as love lives have grown more noisily recherché. But the fact is that Peter got along fine with Palewski, Nancy frequently spent time with Mrs Lubbock and nobody really batted an eyelid. One wonders, of course, what went on beneath the surface. For example Nancy may have exaggerated Peter's complaisance in the letter to her lover, in order to prove how absolutely free she was. And Peter's *real* reason for behaving in such 'saintly' fashion may have been that he was after some money. Now that Nancy was awash with the stuff, he could anticipate being provided for. She did not let him down but then she, in her turn, saw this as the best way of keeping him quiet. 'I long to live here [Paris]', she wrote to Evelyn Waugh in June 1946, 'but what would Prod live on? Isn't one's life complicated. But I can't stay here for ever & keep Blomfield at full blast & Prod installed with unrestricted use of telephone. Even Linda can't pay for that. I wish I could see my way ahead – of course there is the path of duty – but so thorny.'

Did she give the nod to 'duty' to look good in Waugh's eyes, or did she really feel guilt about her desire to leave her husband? And what did she mean by the phrase 'the late Colonel'? Peter had been made a temporary colonel during the war, so this was her obvious meaning: but there was more to it than that. Nancy was clearly linking her 'two Colonels' in her head. Perhaps she was suggesting that Peter was someone she had once loved as she now did Palewski. But she was surely fooling herself if she was trying to see Peter in this way, for at the same time she was writing this to her lover:

Your darling voice & your darling handwriting within an hour of each other is almost *too* much happiness. And I suppose the next best thing to having one's sentiments returned is to have them *appréciés* . . . What will happen to me on Sunday mornings when I have to stop writing to you? Oh darling Colonel . . . Darling Colonel come to London. I am very rich. I can lend you masses of money a thousand pounds if you like . . . I can't settle to anything or sleep.

Poor Nancy, who despite success was suffering dreadfully from her sudden transportation. 'I long for the darling Frogs', she wrote to Waugh in February, but her tone implies that they are almost illusory, that the dim world of Blomfield Road – 'too difficult & depressing' – was the reality of her life. At the start of 1946 she seems, for a brief grey moment, to have seen her future as struggling on until death with Peter Rodd, leaving Gaston Palewski to skip down the Rue Bonaparte with his pretty ladies. 'You are in a mist for me now', she wrote to him, '& don't seem real. Come out of it Colonel . . .'

Yet it was Nancy who came out of the mist: she resisted – and thank heaven for it – the gloomy temptation to remain in England. Paris, after all, *had* been real to her, as real as the sunlight hitting the fountains in the Tuileries gardens. How could she deny it? What was all this miraculous money for, if not to facilitate the pursuit of happiness?

It was, in a way, more of a landmark decision to return to Paris in 1946 than it had been to go there the year before. The 1945 visit had been passed off, to other people at least, as a semi-holiday with a bit of work thrown in, but Nancy had now left Heywood Hill, she had no alibi about setting up bookshops and so forth, and if she went to Paris in 1946 then it meant something serious. It meant she was going purely and simply because she wanted to. She was acknowledging that this was where the future lay; it would be a turning point to affect the rest of her life.

For she *could* have stayed in England, where things would almost certainly have improved. She would have had money, continued to write, been surrounded by friends and family, had the odd love affair: nevertheless she knew that to stay would be a cowardly act. In France, the situation with the Colonel had changed a little, to Nancy's advantage. General de Gaulle had been voted out of office, Palewski had more time on his hands and Nancy had the luxury of being able to comfort him for his loss of power, while possibly relishing the fact that she was now the one with status and money ('Dear Col I shall ring you up in a week or 2, lucky I'm so rich isn't it?'). Peter was safely wasting his time in Spain. What was there to lose? In April 1946, Nancy went back to Paris. She never lived for any length of time in England again.

She moved into the upmarket Hôtel de Bourgogne (Waugh: 'a nest of Gaullists') opposite the Assemblée Nationale, and immediately threw a smart lunch party – 'lovely snails, chicken & port salut (don't cry)'[5] – for Palewski and five others. It cost £9 which then was nothing to her. She had made £1,400 from *The Pursuit of Love* by February, £3,500 for the book's film rights (the film was never made), £1,200 for serial rights, an upfront sum of £100 in April for the French edition and royalties from 20,000 copies sold in America; but this was just the start, the sales figures continued to blaze merrily and then there was, of course, the spin-off effect that ensured best-seller status to almost everything thereafter. 'By the author of *The Pursuit of Love*' would become a guarantee of success. In 1963, when *The Water Beetle* was about to be published by Penguin, a spiky little internal memo said that the book had no 'obvious intrinsic value', but publication could be justified because of 'the loyalty of the Mitford fans'; they never let Nancy down. 'But will the general public be amused by this?' Palewski would say to her, slightly cattily, jealous perhaps of her bright talent, after she had read him some new piece of her work. 'The funny thing is,' she wrote with good-humoured humility to Mrs Hammersley, 'they always are.'

Not that she ever stopped worrying about money. It is an odd human tic that rich people tend to panic more about losing everything than do the poor – especially when these rich people have *been* poor – and in May she was already writing to Diana: 'Darling I shall have to come back – I'm simply eating up money here' (although this was probably more to do with worries about currency restrictions). She didn't go back, but in late 1946 she wrote to Evelyn Waugh that 'the thousands on which I foresee I shall have, in the end, to pay 19/6 in the pound (because this thing about being abroad is most tricky unless you lived there before the war) are flying out of the window in a truly hateful way. And oh oh I missed the big prize in the lottery (8,000,000 fr:[6]) by one figure last week, you must say almost unbearable.' Waugh was not remotely sympathetic. Instead he made this droll reference to the payment for Nancy's film rights: 'If you were not a socialist I should advise you to have it paid in two instalments on Apr. 6th 1947 and 1948 so that it does not all go to the State, but of course, that is what you like.'

Although Nancy indulged in terrors about providing for her old age ('I shall want a little fire & perhaps a pair of steel-rimmed spectacles & a molar or 2 do admit'), she lived well in Paris. When Palewski arrived at her Hôtel de Bourgogne lunch party and saw a bottle of champagne waiting to be opened, he said: '*Vive la littérature!*' The couture houses of Madame Grès, Piguet and, later, Christian Dior might have said the same thing. Not least of the pleasures of living in Paris was the proximity to good clothes. Nancy was never insanely extravagant – her personality was too disciplined – but her financial fears went for nothing in the face of the latest collections. She was not a vain woman, but clothes she could not resist, and they hung to perfection on her fleshless but feminine figure (very post-war, very Barbara Goalen: *Vogue*s of the late forties are full of women who look just like Nancy in their tiny-waisted, full-skirted suits, their audacious little hats, their long, wrinkled gloves). The secret of happiness lay for her, in no small part, in treating the trivial as something vitally important. She loved the whole ritual of fittings, the snipping and pinning and frowning, the exigent standards. 'They left the luncheon together, they must have been in bed all afternoon', says a character in *The Blessing*, to which the reply is: 'I don't think so. She had a fitting at Dior.' Nancy loved this kind of chat, which held for her the essence of Paris; as did a piece of gossip that she heard about the *vendeuse* from Balmain, who turned up at a flat with dresses for her client to try, only to realise, after a few tweaks, 'that the pretty little bosoms (were) *not quite real*', and that it was the client's husband who was gratifying a passion for haute couture ('The end of it is he has ordered several dresses including a shell pink ball-dress . . . Do admit –!'[7]).

From the moment that Paris enters her novels – two-thirds of the way through *The Pursuit of Love* – the books become full of *hommages* to the uplifting power of clothes. Linda is given a wad of francs by Fabrice with which to kit herself out properly (not something Palewski would ever have done for Nancy); before entering a *maison de couture* she slopes off to the Galeries Lafayette and – a memorable, feminine touch – buys a dress off the peg, so 'appallingly dowdy' do her own things seem to her. Indeed Nancy makes great play with the contrast between English and French clothes; this was an even more fertile furrow to plough than the contrast in male lovemaking technique. Fanny is irretrievably unsmart, with her 'nutria coat' and her unspeakable 'green velvet and silver' evening dress, worn to the grand dinner at Hampton which opens *Love in a Cold Climate*. Later she wears a Schiaparelli jacket, sent by her mother, around the house 'instead of a cardigan', and is utterly horrified to discover it would have cost £25 ('There's only a yard of stuff in it, worth a pound, if that'). Nancy enjoys this sensible attitude, but it is far from being her own. She was much more like the *mondaines* Frenchwomen in *The Blessing*, clever Albertine and silly Juliette, who, despite the difference in the capacity of their brains, are united by their love of clothes. 'For days I had been seeing myself at that ball wearing my new dress, and when I found it couldn't be ready in time . . . I didn't want to spoil the mental picture by going in another dress. Don't you understand?' says Albertine to Juliette, who replies: 'I can't think of any occasion – a tea party, even – without seeing an exact picture of how I shall look at it, down to shoes and stockings.' This has the detailed air of sincerity; one assumes that Nancy felt the same way, at least by the time she had become assimilated into Parisian life.

She may have encouraged this trait in herself, because she exaggerated any part of her nature that she thought of as typically French. But it became her own. In a 1951 essay ('Chic – English, French and American'), she joyfully reiterated the hopelessness of the English with regard to clothes. 'Ladylike is the most that can be said', she writes, telling a story (apocryphal?) of how 'two English duchesses were turned away from Christian Dior. They were considered too dowdy to be admitted. In England, if you are a duchess you don't need to be well dressed – it would be thought eccentric. I cannot imagine why they ever had the idea of going to Dior, where they would certainly not have ordered anything.' (Interesting how Nancy manages to eulogise the French while giving her highest undercover praise to the grandeur of the English aristocracy; she was equally fascinated by elegance, and by the confidence that could afford to disdain it.)

But Nancy, who despite her own undeniable *chic* always looked completely English ('there's a skeleton in the Musée de l'Homme in Paris called "Englishwoman". I always look at it and think, that's me'), ordered from couture houses with the businesslike fervour of a true *Parisienne*. In the summer of 1946 she acquired a thrilling new wardrobe from Grès, where she was told she had a figure 'in one hundred' (no wonder she loved the French; whoever says such a thing in an English shop?). The centrepiece garment was a wonderful balldress, black velvet with a black transparent chiffon waistband. 'My dress a sensation that's all', Nancy wrote to her sister Diana, after an evening that included dinner, a surprise meeting with Palewski, an hour at the British Embassy and 'a "gala" at a picture gallery'. All very nice; and especially enjoyable when one is wearing 'much much the prettiest' dress of any woman present. 'Daphne [Weymouth] who is here says at Diana [Cooper]'s levee this morning D. said "now we will talk about Nancy's waist". Daphne says did my waist burn?' Nancy would soon triumph again in the New Look of Christian Dior, that gorgeous snub to the utility suits of the war years. 'You pad your hips & squeeze your waist & skirts are to the ankle it is bliss. So then you feel romantic like Mme Greffulhe & people shout ordures at you from vans because for some reason it creates class feeling in a way no sables could.' It was no doubt an image of Nancy thus dressed that Evelyn Waugh had in mind when he wrote, in 1951, a portrait of her for the 'Book of the Month Club News' (to coincide with the publication of *The Blessing)*: 'She greets you in a Dior dress, her waist so small that one fears it might snap at any moment. This is the only waspish thing about her; all else is sweetness, happiness and inexpressible levity.'

Waugh also described Nancy's *mise en scène*, which her appearance fitted as neatly as one of her twenty-two-inch *ceintures*.

You cross the Seine and penetrate the very heart of the fashionable quarter of Paris, the Faubourg St Germain. You go into a quiet side street, so exclusively aristocratic that few taxi-drivers know its name, and ring at a great, white, shabby door which in due time opens, revealing a courtyard surrounded on three sides by low buildings of the period of the restored Bourbon monarchy. Straight in front, on the ground floor, with its glass doors opening into a garden behind, lie the apartments of Miss Mitford.

These were not behind the black and grey façade of the Rue Bonaparte, or the tatty oversized grandeur of the Quai Malaquais; after more than two years of travelling back and forth around the Left Bank, Nancy had found a flat of her own to rent, at 7 Rue Monsieur in the 7ème. She moved there in December 1947. Although she would not sign her own lease on the flat for more than five years, she was – as perhaps she realised – home at last.

As Evelyn Waugh wrote, Rue Monsieur is indeed quiet. It slots unobtrusively into the dignified, subdued part of the Left Bank where people are too assured to need to proclaim themselves. The street is withdrawn, self-possessed. It was completed in 1778, named for the homosexual brother of Louis XIV (always known as 'Monsieur') of whom Nancy would later write, and it contained several *hôtels particuliers*, including one for Princesse Louise-Adelaide de Bourbon Condé, who lived there for the eleven years before everything changed for ever. Nancy would have loved these details, and dreamed them back into life with all the force of her imagination. She would also have loved what she called 'Mr Street' for its irreproachable facelessness: living there, she was doing what she knew to be the correct thing, and she was also, more obscurely, finding a kind of anonymity, a retreat in which to lead her silent writer's life: the street's remote quality is somehow her own.

The flat itself, as Waugh described, faces outwards on to a courtyard with the slightly shabby aspect, that look of dusty geraniums and ancient *poubelles*, peeling cream walls and shuffling concierges, which gives even the smartest Parisian addresses an oddly homespun air: as if one might be in any small town in France. Number 7 Rue Monsieur is probably little changed from the days when Nancy lived there.

Her flat must have been full of light with its tall windows and big rooms: hall, drawing-room, dining-room in which guests would sleep, bedroom, bathroom, maid's room above. She did not move her own furniture in properly until 1951, from which time photographs show her large, square, grey drawing-room to have been impeccable – the Sheraton desk, the Chinese screens, a Dresden china clock – and brought to life by the billowing diaphanous curtains and the slightly wild space beyond. There was also the wood stove that turned the room into what Waugh called 'your furnace-salon': Nancy always needed heat in her homes.[8] 'By no means austere, it revealed someone with consummate taste and a dislike of clutter', Lady Cynthia Gladwyn said of Rue Monsieur, in the little memoir written after Nancy's death. She compared the way in which Nancy 'pared down her writing . . . so as to get that light touch' with the clean, clear way she furnished her flat, 'retaining only objects of intrinsic merit'. A painting by another friend, Mogens Tvede[9], shows her seated at her desk in front of what she would have called her chimneypiece[10]; she is dressed in the New Look, wrists elegantly crossed, leaning slightly forward, 'frail but tense, alert like a bird folding her wings carefully about her'.[11] It is a wonderful little work. 'It looked exactly like her,' says Diana Mosley. 'Very clever, the way she sat, very characteristic.' The apartment gives an impression of harmony, maturity, confidence; its inhabitant gives, very slightly, the impression of assuming these qualities. It is a nuance only, perhaps deriving from the fact that Nancy never looks wholly relaxed in representations. Perhaps she never *was* relaxed: that ticking, fizzing brain, that writer's outlook.

Harold Acton, however, conjures a memory of someone absolutely at ease in her surroundings: 'Her individual taste was most evident in the arrangement of this luminous residence. One cannot imagine it without her, so intensely did it reflect her personality. I remember it as a serene emanation of the *entente cordiale*, French in its sophisticated simplicity yet English in a certain cosiness and feeling for privacy.' (How lucky that this most polite of men did not read the Audience

Research Report after Nancy's television interview in 1957, filmed at Rue Monsieur, which viewers criticised as 'so poky, and the décor and furniture so drab, that the establishment was hardly worth looking at (one or two compared it unfavourably with the stately homes of England)').

Nancy loved Rue Monsieur dearly. It is, her nephew Jonathan Guinness wrote, 'the place where we remember her best'. To her mother she wrote: 'I've never liked any house I've lived in as much as this one.' Its calm setting – enlivened by the Mitfordian presence of a white hen, 'such a comic we couldn't bring ourselves to kill her' – enabled her to be the person she wanted to be. She even had the blessing of a 'saintly' maid, Marie Renard, who 'literally never thinks of herself at all' and whose loyalty was as complete as her good sense (when Nancy asked Marie if she wanted to watch the television programme filmed in their home, she replied, 'But as I see Madame every day –?').

For almost ten years after moving into her beautiful flat, Nancy was as happy as she could possibly be. One imagines a merry whirl of full skirts, pealing telephones, embossed invitations flopping through the door, jokes and shrieks and smiles. And it is lovely to think of; inspirational, in its way, as an example of how life can whip itself into a confection of happiness, if one only has the will to let it.

So to Evelyn Waugh she described her first full year in Rue Monsieur as 'Heavenly 1948'. Was it? 'What an odd idea of heaven', he replied. 'Of course in my country we cannot enjoy the elegant clothes & meals & masquerades which fill your days.' True, Nancy's social life was intensely glamorous. There was a stream of soirées to fill the gap – a large one – created when the Coopers left the British Embassy, around the time of her arrival at Rue Monsieur. This meant no more of Diana's eccentric parties, which teetered at the edge of unacceptability (terrible riff-raff at the Hôtel de Charost these days, the French Ambassadress in London reported) but which were never, ever boring. Nancy was a frequent guest, singing for her supper with all the sparkle of which she was capable, enlivened by the equally omnipresent Gaston Palewski. Diana used him as her 'pilot fish', a guide to whom she might invite to her dinners (collaborators were rife, and questions like whether one should attend concerts by Maurice Chevalier[12] burned continually;

Palewski's judgment was sound, although the odd undesirable did slip through).

The world created by Diana was extremely eclectic for an embassy. Jean Cocteau ('world renowned for I don't know what', as Diana put it) made it through, and attended a successful dinner with Noël Coward and Clement Attlee; so too did the poet Paul Eluard, the comedienne Beatrice Lillie, Laurence Olivier (a failure at acting games) and Ernest Bevin, who had a crush on Diana that some said had kept Duff Cooper his job ('go the 'ole 'og Luff', Bevin counselled Mme. l'Ambassadrice, when she asked his opinion of what she should wear at dinner). Bevin was fun, so Diana liked him. Ernest Hemingway, on the other hand, she thought 'the greatest bore to end bores we've ever struck', while the Duke and Duchess of Windsor were dismissed as 'two little poor old things . . . common of course' (This slightly unwanted pair also aroused Nancy's scorn: 'he a *balloon*, she like the skeleton of some tiny bird, hopping in her hobble skirt . . . both look ravaged with misery'[13]).

So the three years of the Coopers' tenure was magnificently congenial to Nancy. It was also a source of gossip, not least about the love triangle being played out between the Coopers themselves and poetess Louise de Vilmorin, who was sleeping with Duff and an object of fascination to Diana. Louise was one of those people who mythologise themselves within their own social circle; not uncommon. Nor is it rare for other people to go along with the myth. 'All the ladies fell at her feet to be hobbled over', wrote Waugh, having observed this 'egocentric maniac' at a London party. Despite enjoying her company Nancy also saw through her: she cast her in the role of Albertine, the witch-like mistress in *The Blessing*, who has Louise's sensual power mixed with Nancy's sense of humour.

Unlike Diana Cooper, she was not taken in; Nancy was more intelligent than Diana. She was fond of her, she admired her verve and her statuesque beauty, but she thought her slightly silly, particularly in her antipathy towards the French. Nancy was also exasperated by Diana's sudden withdrawals into sadness ('*Le désespoir de Diana*'), this being exactly the kind of thing that she herself tried to resist. 'I have long regarded your euphoria as a pathological condition as morbid as Honks's[14] melancholy', wrote Evelyn Waugh in 1952. 'You each choose minor exterior conditions to explain your states – oddly enough the same one – France.'

But Nancy did not want Diana to leave the Embassy. The Coopers' departure (to a beautiful house at Chantilly) was generally viewed as a social catastrophe, and their farewell at the Gare du Nord was thus described by Philip Ziegler in his *Diana Cooper*: 'Diana was in tears, Duff was in tears, Gaston Palewski was in tears; it was a richly lachrymose occasion.' Their replacements, the far more correct Harveys, were described by Nancy as 'utter ghastly drear'; she wrote to Diana Mosley that they 'cut me on the double grounds of being mixed up with Gaullists & an habituée of Diana's embassy'. With time, however, her opinion changed into affection: 'I've greatly taken to the Harveys,' she wrote in 1950; 'he understands the French backwards, sees the whole thing crystal clear & loves what he sees. Just like me!' And they provided her with the plot for her last novel, *Don't Tell Alfred*. Fanny's husband is appointed British Ambassador to Paris, and Fanny's early days as Ambassadress are haunted by the beautiful Lady Leone, 'her brilliant predecessor', who sets up an alternative court in the Embassy entresol. Diana did not do this to Lady Maud Harvey, but it was unusual for the Coopers to continue to live nearby. Her dazzling presence did hover Rebecca-like for some months after her last leave.

Meanwhile the parties went on. Like Grace du Valhubert attending her first big Paris dinner after the war, Nancy was entranced by the scene:

The door opened upon a kaleidoscope of glitter. The women, nearly all beauties, were in huge crinolines, from which rose naked shoulders and almost naked bosoms, sparkling with jewels. They moved on warm waves of scent, their faces were gaily painted with no attempt at simulating nature, their hair looked cleaner and glossier than any hair she had ever seen . . . That the atmosphere was of untrammelled sex did not surprise her, except in so far as that sex, outside a bedroom, could be so untrammelled.

This may have been viewed, in Diana Mosley's phrase, *en rose*. Surely not everyone was so stunning, although they were probably better turned out than their London counterparts (goose-pimpled *poitrines* and Coty lipsticks). And in the French circles through which Nancy moved there was a surprising amount of confidence and money. The conversation, clothes, food and hospitality were of a standard both to admire and to keep one up to the mark. 'There has been a wild spate of entertaining, parties costing between 6 & 12 million francs, dinners off gold plates, fountains of champagne, clothes such as you never saw – all great fun', Nancy wrote to Violet Hammersley in July 1948. '*How* rich the French are. I never can get over it – living in their huge houses with huge gardens in the very centre of the town, with between 20 & 30 servants – now I'm getting to know more French people, not the cosmopolitan ones, I am *staggered* by the luxe in which they exist.'

If this reads like a eulogy to the *richissime*, it should be said that compared with other commentators Nancy retained a certain amused distance, however much she enjoyed her sallies into this gilded world. The society figure Chips Channon[15], for example, described in his diaries a day spent in Paris with quasi-religious awe:

Today was a day of fantastic elegance. Arturo Lopez gave a luncheon party for me at . . . his small Versailles, with every object in it beyond price; it is, I suppose, the most elegant 'set-up' in the world . . . I was between the Duchesse de Fesanzac and Nancy Mitford . . . Then, in the evening, Alexis de Redé – the Eugène de Rastignac of modern Paris – offered me a banquet . . . Alexis lives in eighteenth century splendour in a huge apartment in the Hôtel Lambert in the Cité.

My dear! This really is as the world of the Duchesse de Guermantes, unchanged in any detail since Proust created it; in a way Nancy saw it as such but she could, at the same time, take a less spellbound view. 'Yes the Barons Redé and Redesdale have but little in common', she wrote to her mother in 1950. 'He lives but for luxury, beauty & social life . . . Not bad, though I prefer his patron, a fat jolly Chilean called Lopez.' (One can almost hear Channon's gasp at such *lèse majesté*.)

In fact she found the real French aristocracy quite sticky. Later she referred to 'one of those quince-like old Frenchwomen who seem determined not to see, let alone speak to ONE'.[16] And she wrote this to her friend Eddy Sackville-West[17]: 'I've just been to a luncheon party so pompous, so full of Bourbon Parmes & d'Arenbergs, that the placement took 3 weeks to work out & resulted in nearly all the men sitting together. Isn't it *typical!*' She preferred a less self-conscious world, although she undoubtedly liked to know that the *gratin* existed. And she would never, as Diana Cooper did when Ambassadress, have ignored the formalities of *placement*: at one dinner Princess Dolly Radziwill (Nancy's friend, wife of the artist Mogens Tvede) lit a cigarette during the fish to show that she thought herself ill-placed. Diana thought this madness ('as the French undo their napkins, they take a look round two tables of twenty in hopes of seeing something wrong'[18]); Nancy saw it differently. She had learned to do so from the French, but she herself enjoyed these questions of etiquette, and would not have wanted – or dared – to defy them. One can call this snobbishness, which in a way it was; but as much as anything it came from Nancy's almost mystical delight in the frameworks that kept life in elegant check.

Much of the time, however, she mixed in less rigorous society: in June of 'heavenly' 1948, she breezed off to a 'very brilliant & great fun' party thrown by Daisy Fellowes[19], also attended by the Coopers (not the Harveys), Princess Radziwill and the Aga Khan ('It was the day of his third Derby so he must have been in a specially good mood', she wrote to Diana Mosley). 'The Colonel says the Aga does the most dreadful things to the Begum – I said "Oh & she looks *so* dignified". He shrieked . . .'

What a lovely life it sounds. As Fabrice says in *The Pursuit of Love*, 'social life – *de la haute société* – I mean, it can be a very satisfying one, entirely artificial of course, but absorbing'. Nancy also believed this, had done so even when making the best of it among the 'oh I say!' hunting chat of debutante dances. Now she was living out her dreams of being 'in the world', and it brought her the kind of sustained *joie de vivre* that most people have grown too tired for by the age of thirty-five.

Both Nancy and Paris knew the importance of frivolity; both were prepared to work at it. It was not always an easy task. In *The Blessing*, Grace du Valhubert is described as all at sea in the exhausting world of Paris society but loving, nonetheless, the demands that it made upon her. Nancy was never all at sea – she was far cleverer and funnier than Grace – although she understood that Paris was 'quite frankly,

a terrible effort'. But this she loved; *ça valait bien la peine*. She loved
the standards set by her social life, and the collective faith in these
standards that lay beneath the 'hours of smiling politeness'. Here was
her philosophy of life writ large: the will to happiness brought to a
peak of emphasis by the bright silks of the Dior dresses, the sparkle of
the jewels, the gleam of the Boulle and the colours of the Sèvres, the
finest examples of civilised living that man could produce.

It was all so different from England; thinking this became a near
mania with Nancy, but she had a point. Grace compares the French
with the English, who 'don't expect that the last ounce of energy will
be expended upon them in the natural order of things, and are, indeed,
pleased and flattered at the slightest attempt to entertain them'; again,
one knows what she means. Nancy and Grace were making a serious
point about France. Even today, it understands that life is easier to bear
when it is underpinned by civilised ritual.

And who wouldn't rather have been at Daisy Fellowes' soirée than
out with Peter Rodd? 'The night of Daisy's party Prod & Ed [Stanley]
went out & returned at 1 pm the following day', Nancy wrote to Diana
Mosley. 'Of course I thought they must be in prison – it is always
my nightmare that we shall have our identity cards taken away –
but it was just that they were on such a bat that they thought it was
only breakfast time. Really at their age!!!' So public schoolboyish; so
horribly reminiscent of Blomfield Road. But in 1948 Nancy *was*, in a
sense, back at Blomfield Road. Peter was living at Rue Monsieur and
there was little she could do to get rid of him. The pull of England
and the past was threatening to drag the bright whirl of her life into a
muddy vortex.

In May of heavenly 1948 Nancy wrote to Diana in something like
concealed despair: 'Peter is back for good I gather, it is a tiny bit of
a worry because he has nothing to do from morning to night & is
already hankering for London. So I say then what about a divorce so
that we could each live where we like & he says the treasury would
never let me live here . . . for some reason he is absolutely determined
not to have a divorce.' (The reason, almost certainly, was that Nancy
was far more likely to give him money if he was always liable to turn
up.) So much for the complaisant husband. He did not exactly object

(could hardly do so) to Nancy's relationship with Gaston Palewski, but it annoyed him all the same, and he must have known that his presence hampered it considerably. 'I never never see the Colonel which is too depressing', she wrote to Diana in June. Meanwhile Palewski was using the situation for his own careful ends, fluttering about the scandal of having a married mistress. When Nancy did manage to visit him 'it is like some dreadful spy film & I end by being shut up in a cupboard or hiding on the escalier de service & being found by the concierge – so undignified I nearly die of it.' So unsuitable to Nancy, with her proud ideals of love.

Whether Peter was being deliberately vengeful, by plonking himself down upon Nancy's white muslin bed, it is hard to say. Of course there was no reason why he should make it easy for her to pursue a love affair, although he certainly did not want her himself. But he was at a pitifully loose end once more, and above all desperate for money. The return to peacetime finished Peter off; war had given him a sense of purpose and dignity, he had acquitted himself with honour at Dunkirk, in Ethiopia and Italy; but now he was Prod again, *déraciné* and dissolute, a man whose wasted life lay bare to the elements like one of the bombed-out houses in Blomfield Road. In his middle forties he presented a terrible contrast to his self-respecting wife, who with her upright carriage, nimble step and chic slenderness still had the aspect of a girl. Peter's health was poor, he had a duodenal ulcer (not surprisingly), 'he's awfully unwell & awfully blind & halt & so on', and the patina of handsomeness had been wiped clean from his face. 'He has locomotor ataxia and a waistcoat made of an old rug. How you have brought him down. He was such a bright pretty boy', wrote Evelyn Waugh, having seen him at White's. And this happened almost overnight, or so it seemed; it was as if Nancy's sudden success had felled him, and left nothing but the urge to debauch (brothels with Duff Cooper, dear God) and the desire to cling on to his wife.

Illogically, but perhaps understandably, Nancy had a sense of guilt about him and a strange residual fondness. This had been clear in 1946, when she called him 'the late Colonel', and a couple of years later it was implicit. Her letters veer between accepting his presence as rightful ('there must be many many worse husbands in the world') and longing for him to go ('he is off to Timbuctoo. I hope it really exists &

is not a mere figure of speech'). He practised a form of blackmail on her: 'He sits all day editing his poems & waiting for the end & making me cry with the récit of my sins towards him', she wrote to Waugh in December 1949. Then, a couple of months later, to Diana, when Peter was back in London:

Prod is making my life hell. Our money can be transferred only through his bank, & we get it in Nov: so I had carefully budgeted till then – darling he hasn't sent me any though I've given him £600. What I suppose is that it's gone down the drain of his overdraft . . . it is dreadful being in the power of such an enfant terrible & I am in his power financially in spite of the money having been earned by me . . . What a wail . . .

It was, but with good reason. She dealt with Peter as kindly as anyone could; one does feel pity for him, the beautiful Balliol boy unable to cope with his own potential, but there is a cunning in the way that he played upon Nancy – her dislike of scandal, her fear of poverty, her sadness about the failure of her marriage, her terror that Palewski would run a mile from the whole situation – that makes him, ultimately, despicable.

So heavenly 1948 was tainted with his hovering, droning, pathetic presence, and Nancy's love affair had to step tactfully aside to accommodate him. This panicked her, beneath the smiling veneer. She was unsure of Palewski – to say the least – and spending evenings with her husband, straining to hear his mumbled tirades ('my hankies are *wet all day*'[20]) when she yearned to be *racontez*-ing to her lover, must have been close to unendurable.

There had been a rift with Palewski in 1947 when *The Pursuit of Love* was published in France, and the dedication picked up on by the French press: 'Hitler's mistress's sister dedicates daring book to M. Palewski', ran a newspaper headline. This had turned the ever-cautious Colonel's blood to ice; had he been in love with Nancy he would have laughed it off (he had, after all, wanted the dedication), but in his state of always trying to dance slightly away from her he reacted coldly: 'he is in a great do about it & really I think I shall have to go away from here for a bit', Nancy wrote to Diana. 'He says the General will be furious.' So what? would be a reasonable reaction; but as part of her desire to love all that was most French in France, and to ingratiate herself with Palewski, Nancy had conceived a girlish admiration for the charmless de Gaulle.[21] Accordingly, she went along with Palewski's fear of his disapproval rather than treating it with contempt. Palewski had wanted it both ways. He liked the kudos of having a ragingly successful book dedicated to him, but disliked the adverse publicity that went with it; and, knowing Nancy as he did, he realised that he could make *her* feel guilty rather than admitting that he himself had been naïve. ('Bad women never take the blame for anything', as a character says in Anita Brookner's *Hôtel du Lac*; and, with the Colonel, Nancy was always as good as gold.)

Like an excluded schoolgirl she accepted her exile, and went to stay with the Mosleys in London. From there she wrote placatory letters to Palewski: 'One thing about having come over here, I've got the most lovely birthday present for you so do be excited.' She also stayed with her mother, then with her old friend Mark Ogilvie-Grant in his house on Kew Green, where she worked on the script of the Ealing comedy *Kind Hearts and Coronets*. (None of her dialogue survived: 'So I was invited to Ealing the other day to write a monologue for a film', wrote Evelyn Waugh in October 1947. 'It is the film you wrote. They have scrapped everything written up till now & wouldn't show me your contribution.')

The dedication crisis had blown over by the time Nancy returned to Paris, but it made Palewski wary (what else might she do?) and she knew this. So the last thing she needed in 1948 was to have a husband come between the two of them: the least welcome gooseberry of all time. And one evening in July the situation reached a painful non-resolution, when Nancy was dining with Peter and his Elwes nephews (whom she did not like). There in the restaurant, seated at another table, was 'the Col with a girl called Margot de Gramont, a nice fat sad girl who was a Resistance heroine & who has been for ages in love with the Colonel. Well I could hardly bear that . . .'[22]

Something about this grim configuration – Nancy stuck with her uneasy little party, trapped by duty in a situation that brought pleasure to no one; Palewski leaning into his adoring dinner companion, just as on another night he might have done to Nancy herself – brought her feelings about the Colonel to a screaming pitch. She knew what he was like. She must have steeled herself continually for this sort of thing. But the frustration she had been forced to endure; the sense that her husband's stubborn presence had given Palewski carte blanche to do as he liked with another woman ('*you* are married after all'); the panic that nothing would ever be made right again; all of this caused Nancy to react with unusual despair. This time, the façade came down. She was like Grace du Valhubert in *The Blessing*, who is sitting innocently in a nightclub with her ex-fiancé when she sees her husband with another woman. 'Grace was particularly struck, stricken to the heart indeed, by Charles-Edouard's look, a happy, tender, and amused expression . . .' This is the evening of 1948 brought back to life – painfully? cathartically? – but with one essential difference: Grace was married to her errant man, and Nancy knew that she would never marry hers.

After dinner, she went with her companions to look at the statues lit up at the Louvre and there, within that exquisite scene, were the plump, prosaic figures of the Colonel and Mademoiselle de Gramont. Following that remorseless thought process which passes, in these situations, for logic, Nancy decided that Palewski had just proposed marriage. She further decided that she would go home and take 'Prod's so called poison pills'. Then – no doubt after a desperate struggle for dignity – she telephoned Palewski who 'though woken up, was absolutely angelic'. Naturally: the power of benevolence was entirely his. 'I kept saying but you looked so *happy* "no no I'm not happy I'm very unhappy". So dreadful to prefer the loved one to be unhappy.'

The next morning, after what surely was a night of torment – at what had happened, at the way she had handled it – she telephoned him again. 'Oh Colonel, I'm so ashamed of myself,' she said, to which he replied: 'The rights of passion have been proclaimed by the French Revolution', a phrase that made its way into *The Blessing*. It was a kindly – if patronising – thing to say, typical of the man, but it was also distancing: the words of someone who knows that they are profoundly loved, who respects the person in return, who feels a fondness and even a pity for their emotions, but who gently refuses to return them.

'The fact is I *couldn't* live through it if he married', Nancy wrote to Diana. 'I know he really longs to be.' Actually there is no evidence that Gaston ever stopped himself from doing anything that he wanted: self-restraint was not a notable characteristic of his. Nor was it likely, as Nancy told herself, that *she* had the power to prevent him from marrying. The probability is that in 1948 he liked his life as it was: pursuing his twin careers of *homme politique* and *homme aux femmes*. 'He says I take a novelist's view of marriage, that if he marries it will only be to have children & will make no difference at all.' That in itself can't have been easy to hear; it was a fairly blunt way of telling her that she was not in the running. Yet she seems to have taken comfort from it, as a sign that marriage would not, for him, mean overwhelming love for one person. His feelings for her would still be the same, even if he sidestepped them to rear a crop of spotty little *garçons aux fillettes* by some fecund Frenchwoman.

But these were crumbs of comfort scattered upon Nancy's famished soul. The best she could hope for was that nothing would materially change; and at the end of her letter to Diana she seems reassured on this. She pulls herself together enough to make the requisite joke, in this case about the Tour de France (with which – being as ever more French than the French – she was utterly obsessed): 'Bobet, the favourite & a *hero* to the public . . . succumbed to terrible furoncles (ONE can guess where) . . .' And *One* is amazed by her stoicism, her bravery, her determination always to turn her face to the sun.

So was 1948 heavenly, or was it not? Can it possibly have been? For it was also the year in which Nancy's sister Unity died of meningitis, aged thirty-four; a further agony for Lady Redesdale, although perhaps relief of a kind, despite the fact that Unity's health had of late improved (so much so that her mother worried about the possibility of her daughter outliving her). But the bullet in her brain had always been liable to cause infection and inflammation. Almost as if she were aware of this, Unity had, towards the end of her life, amused herself in planning her own funeral. As Nancy's would twenty-five years later, it took place in the little church at Swinbrook. The two sisters are buried side by side.

Before this, Unity had been transported from Inch Kenneth to the Scottish mainland. Owing to high winds, a doctor had been unable to reach her when she first became ill (one has to wonder at the decision to live on this island, when the churning series of disasters that befell the Mitfords emphasised its remoteness so cruelly), and by the time Unity got to Oban her temperature was flaming and her right temple bulging. 'I am coming,' she had suddenly said, from her bed at Inch Kenneth. Her mother had known what this meant. Within a few days her daughter was dead; she died on 28 May, the day that Nancy specifies for Linda Radlett's death in *The Pursuit of Love*. When Linda dies, 'a light went out, a great deal of joy that never could be replaced'. With poor Unity the light had begun to flicker when she put the bullet into her head – or earlier, when she first became the willing captive of Nazi Germany – but in a skewed way what Nancy wrote of Linda was true too of her sister: Unity, as a great galumphing girl, had been alight with joy, with vitality, with strong affections. So strong, perhaps, that they could not help but be misplaced. When Nancy said that Eugenia Malmains, Unity's fictional representation, was the nicest character in *Wigs on the Green*, this had also been true; she was the most sincere, in an odd way the most vulnerable. And that had been Boud, a girl who once said to her mother: 'No one ever had such a happy life as I did up to the war.'

The Redesdales attended the funeral together, but reconciliation would now never happen: Sydney returned to Inch Kenneth, and David to what had become his home, Redesdale Cottage in Northumberland, where he lived with his housekeeper (according to Jessica's second husband, Bob Treuhaft[23], David had 'done that old-fashioned thing and run off with the parlourmaid', but this was almost certainly wrong: until his dying day Lord Redesdale remained as unworldly as one of his own labradors). What did happen, as a consequence of Unity's funeral, was a *rapprochement* between David and Oswald Mosley, greatly welcome to Diana. Time *was* healing, in a way: the physical separations – Nancy in France, Jessica now permanently in America, Pamela in Ireland, Diana also in France from 1951 (in a marvellous house, Le Temple de La Gloire, at Orsay near Paris) – may have helped to defuse the enmities. 'Mitfords are very family-oriented,' says Diana's son Alexander Mosley. Losing touch with each other would never have been a possibility, even for Jessica, the Mitford who had checked in her family baggage at the Kremlin. But after the war it was perhaps better done at a distance; between the sisters, at least. For Lord and Lady Redesdale the loneliness must have been intense, the separations putting a near unbearable distance between themselves and the life they once had. Not long before she died Unity had asked her father whom he would most like to see walk through the door: 'Decca,' he instantly said.

Nancy felt the terrible sadness of Unity's life and death. 'I was so fond of her as you know', she wrote to Eddy Sackville-West, '& it seems such a dreadful waste of the charming beautiful & odd creature that she used to be.' Yet in January 1949 she wrote to Evelyn Waugh the phrase that annoyed him so much, as she had surely known it would: 'I am having a lovely life – only sad that heavenly 1948 is over – except for Bobo's death which I *minded* one of the happiest years I ever had.'

Despite it all – the wet hankies, 'the *horror* of love', the reminders of the sad grey past – that is what she thought; and although one can dismiss it as an act, a delusion, to do so would be contrary to the spirit of Nancy. As she wrote in her next letter to Waugh, 'you must know as well as I do that happiness doesn't depend on exterior or political events.' This is almost completely true. Nancy wanted to be happy, and if she shrieked about a cyclist's boils after laying her wretched heart on the executioner's block that was not a sign of repression, but of courage. More than that; it was her instinct, her nature. For what was the point of sorrow, when every day was 'one step nearer to THE END'? And when, in the opinion of Alexander Mosley, she had, 'I think as much as anybody I have known, a successful, fulfilled life'?

Which came, in the end, from writing; and perhaps the most heavenly thing about 1948 was the creation of *Love in a Cold Climate*. It did not come easily, partly because she was distracted by life; partly because she was now without question a 'professional' writer. What she did after *The Pursuit of Love* mattered, it would be awaited and scrutinised; this was a long way from cranking out a fey little *divertissement* in between writing names on people's foreheads at an ARP post. This novel required invention, it required construction, a tricky synthesis of the intimate voice of '*racontez, racontez*' and a plot about people whom she did not already know inside out. The Radletts were there again, as a delicious sideshow, so too were Fabrice and

Davey, and the extremely satisfying figure of Fanny was still acting as
narrator; but now Nancy tackled new worlds, familiar to her but not
a part of her own life: London high society, Oxford don society, Paris
homosexual society.

She pulled it off magnificently. Some commentators think *Love
in a Cold Climate* even better than *The Pursuit of Love* (it is, says
Philip Hensher[24], 'her masterpiece'). Certainly it is more of a 'novel';
not a flowing stream that directs itself, one does not know quite
how, into the sublime reaches of art. It is a structure, albeit one built
in the Mitfordian manner, that of a brilliant child playing with toy
bricks. And it is rooted in the real world, not that of illusion and
poetry. It has no romance about it; it is stunningly cynical, although
it has the quality of benevolence that marks Nancy's mature writing.
Its understanding of human nature is knowing and non-judgmental.
It is a comedy of manners, written to the highest possible level. And
it contains a character worthy of the best of the genre, at least as good
as anything in Congreve or Austen or Wilde: Lady Montdore, 'the
old she-wolf', who stands facing Uncle Matthew in perfect enmity,
his absolute female equal.

The key to Lady Montdore, as with Lord Alconleigh, is that neither
is purely a pantomime character: they stride through their novels like
fairytale monsters, terrorising those about them, loathing each other;
but it is Nancy's great gift to make them utterly real, to bring them
before us as people as well as semi-mythic creations. 'Miss Mitford's
people possess an authenticity not always achieved by novelists whose
characters are largely drawn from families of the peerage', said the
TLS; this was entirely true, and although a simple point it was well
worth saying.

For all the glee with which Nancy kindles Lady Montdore into
extremely large life, there is a subtlety about the characterisation. Like
her male counterpart, she has – and this is the surprise element – areas
of vulnerability. Just as Uncle Matthew's rampant xenophobia hides a
small, silent fear of the unknown, so Sonia Montdore's desire to control
hides a fear of the unpredictable. She would never have dreamed in a
million years that her daughter Polly, with whom she is obsessed, and
whose looks are such that they should have led to a brilliant marriage,
would go through her debutante years without a single proper suitor

('So beautiful and no B.A. at all'). The terror of Polly's failure – which is, of course, her mother's – is real, and the consequent panic makes her furious: 'Can't you try to be a little jollier, nicer with them, no man cares to make love to a dummy, you know.' Hilarious stuff, but within it lies bewilderment, giving substance to the jokes: "'Ever since she was born, you know, I've worried and fussed over that child, and thought of the awful things that might happen to her ... but the one thing that never even crossed my mind was that she might end up an old maid."

'There was a rising note of aggrieved hysteria in her voice ...'

Lady Montdore is not as sure as herself as she appears to be. In a sense, she is a monolith of certainty, as when she describes having 'all this' (her husband's quite stupendous wealth): 'Remember that love cannot last, it never does, but if you marry all this it's for your life. One day, don't forget, you'll be middle-aged and think what that must be like for a woman who can't have, say, a pair of diamond earrings.' Her physical demeanour is staggeringly assured: 'Lady Montdore sat well back on the sofa, both her feet on the ground. She seemed planted there, immoveable and solid, not actually fat, but solid through and through.' Her pronouncements admit of no dissent: 'No point in cluttering up the ballrooms with girls who look like that, it's simply not fair on anybody'; 'Whoever invented love should be shot.' But when Polly is removed from her life, as she is in the middle of the book, her mother reveals herself to be a slightly lost figure. She drops in constantly on the newly married Fanny – 'never bothered to ring but just stumped upstairs' – and is always rude ('yes, just a cup please. How weak you have it – no, no, this will do quite well'), but it is obvious that she is in desperate need of company. 'She was horribly lonely, you could see that.' And when Cedric Hampton, the glittering homosexual who is heir to 'all this', descends upon her from Paris and swoops her into a new life of leg lifts and skin brushing, she is almost touchingly grateful. Cedric's own motivations are dubious, as Nancy makes clear in wonderfully implicit fashion; but Lady Montdore, at the age of sixty, submits to the uncontrollable and falls in delirious love, watching for Cedric constantly with 'one spaniel-eye': it is the final touch that brings her character to indestructible life.

This stunning, endlessly funny creation probably had her origins in Nancy's mother-in-law, Lady Rennell (although she also owes something to the writer Violet Trefusis, who once scooped up Nancy's serving of fish at lunch in the same way that Lady Montdore does to Fanny). In 1946 Nancy wrote to Evelyn Waugh: 'The other shot in *my* locker is my book called *The Ambassadress*, which can be written when my ma in law has kicked the bucket' (in fact she did not bother to wait; Lady Rennell died in 1951). But the novel evolved considerably from that point. In September 1947 Nancy wrote to Waugh again, having conceived the central, impeccably signposted plot twist: that Lady Montdore's daughter, Polly, should be besotted with her mother's own lover, Boy Dougdale. (Waugh thought him an unconvincing character; perhaps he is someone that only a woman could truly understand? Such is his creepiness that one can hardly bear to read of him 'rubbing our knees with his'; his femininity – making tapestries, painting, chatting – and cosy snobbishness are perfectly rendered; and the ghastly essence of his sexual appeal is conveyed by saying that he 'was physically repulsive . . . to those women who did not find him irresistible.')

Nancy struggled on with the book – it really *was* a struggle in the beginning – writing in the first person of Fanny, then trying third person, then returning to Fanny (first person, Waugh counselled, 'suits you perfectly'). 'Oh my novel has STUCK', she wails in December 1947; then, two weeks later, 'My book has begun to *go*, isn't it wonderful when they do that. Of course it's simply a question of working whatever one may tell oneself.'

That, always, was Nancy's philosophy. Much as she loved her social life at this time (despite fatigue from her 'low stamina'), she would willingly ignore invitations and write 2,000 words a day: by hand, into long red books, quite a different thing from tip-tapping on a PC (she claimed to love the feeling of pen on paper). In the end, however, what with the to and fro of Peter, and the constant noise of the telephone ('Counted the telephone calls this morning, 10 before 11. What am I to do . . .'), Nancy decided to up sticks and accept Diana Cooper's invitation to finish *Love in a Cold Climate* at Chantilly. 'I write my book all day in the stables & at meal times there are large & cheerful parties so you see it is ideal.' In fact things still went stickily – John Julius Norwich (Diana's son) remembers Nancy's plaintive despair, 'no good darling, just won't *come*' – but she 'pegged away' and by

September 1948 was finally finished. 'I see I'm going to miss the book now it's done – I've never taken so long before – one year & 22 days. Oh I do hope it's good', she wrote to Evelyn Waugh. But surely she knew, really?

Waugh read the manuscript and gave his lecture upon the need for 'Blood, sweat & tears', which provoked a small flurry of panic and revising. Then she consigned Waugh's opinion to the sub-fusc cupboard where it belonged. 'Well I suppose you will hate me now for the rest of our lives', he had written at the end of his criticism, but of course she did not: she was far too good-natured, she valued her friendships too highly to cast them aside in pique and, as she put it, 'my skin is thick'. She also saw, crucially, that their talents were of a very different kind. When she wrote to Waugh 'I do feel quite sure that I am incapable of writing the book you want me to', that was the simple truth. As she would say a year later, 'you are cher maître to me but even so one must write as one can'. It was something that he, too, came to recognise.

Nancy's second classic novel was published in July 1949. The reviews were extremely good, and perceived the substance beneath the dazzling surface: 'So far out of the ordinary you may never hear the last of it', sang the *Daily Express*; 'It has feelings as well as fun; moments of sensibility as well as explosions of farce', said the *Evening Standard;* and Peter Quennell[25] in the *Daily Mail* wrote, 'To her sense of fun the novelist adds a mature wit, not untouched now and then by a dawning sense of tragedy.' Hamish Hamilton must have been rubbing his hands at the thought of all those sales; he was not disappointed. 'My book is a great best seller so are you impressed?' Nancy wrote to Mark Ogilvie-Grant. 'Even in America where the reviews are positively insulting, it is on the best seller list . . . Anyhow I shall never write about normal love again as I see there is a far larger and more enthusiastic public for the *other sort.*' In fact her portrayal of homosexuality – Cedric's and, later, Boy's – was a bit too much for some. 'Boy Dougdale's bad habits are made to change somewhat arbitrarily to worse ones', wrote the *TLS*, concluding manfully: 'such things are not impossible'. But there is no doubt that Nancy's acceptance, her refusal to make any comment upon what were then illegal proclivities, were attitudes ahead of their time (indeed Harold Acton suggests that Nancy's 'witty tolerance' helped to remove homosexuality's 'social stigma'; also not impossible.) America couldn't take it at all, however: 'you can have pederasts in books so long as they are fearfully gloomy & end by committing suicide', wrote Nancy. 'A cheerful one who goes from strength to strength like Cedric horrifies them . . .'

In England, too – where the novel was so successful that Nancy reported Queen Elizabeth acting it out in a charade ('she kissed the King & shivered & everybody guessed at once!!') – there was a faint, if delicious, sense of shock: that the book should end with so many people having got what they wanted, without having necessarily deserved it; that the climax should resolve itself according to a sunny, foreign philosophy, which proclaimed above all the morality of happiness. It was not the modern creed of 'the self' – Nancy didn't believe in that at all – but it was alien to the world of ration books and austerity. 'The climax is extremely bad', wrote Evelyn Waugh. Perhaps his sense of sin caused him to shudder at that cloudless *déroulement*. Even now, one is pulled up by the way the book refuses to judge, the way its characters are allowed to thrive: in its calm, cosy fashion it is something of an eye-opener, almost subversive in its remoteness from the usual value systems. Nancy's characters are not good or evil, they are not selfish or selfless, they are simply *there*, dancing their hopeful way towards happiness, finding it and losing it and, if they are lucky, finding it again.

' "So here we all are, my darling, having our lovely cake and eating it too," ' says Cedric at the end of the book: ' "*One's* great aim in life." ' How the readers of 1949 devoured it; the assorted triumphs of Cedric and Lady Montdore, of Polly and Boy, were tastier morsels any day than tales of duty rewarded or fecklessness punished, and in Nancy's hands they seemed just as real. Thereafter her readers would expect the piquancy of provocation as well as the comfort of nostalgia, they waited ecstatically to see what ladylike surprise she would give them next, and she did not let them down. Throughout the 1950s she carried on hitting the spot, becoming ever more successful in the process. Having the best cake from Fauchon and, on a good day – which she believed almost every day to be – eating it too.

CHAPTER 9

The early years of the 1950s were wonderfully busy ones for Nancy. She was harvesting her success with gleeful assiduity. At the end of 1949 she took up journalism again, and with all her new assurance, having been asked by Ian Fleming – 'handsome Mr Fleming' – to write a column for *The Sunday Times*, which she did regularly for four years. These columns began as letters from Paris, 'causeries' as the newspaper called them, but they took on other subjects when the editor-in-chief, Lord Kemsley, saw the effect that Nancy could have upon sales with her jokes and teases. Accordingly she took out her elegant quiver and shot various bows: Rome, she wrote, was 'a village' whose life was 'centred round the vicarage', Athens was 'probably the ugliest capital in Europe' and Marie Antoinette 'one of the most irritating characters in history'. All of which gave her readers plenty to be going on with.

To Evelyn Waugh she had given her usual line that she was doing the columns for money – of which half, she said, went in tax – but this was not quite true as she twice turned down offers to write them more often. (In 1954, Lord Kemsley asked her 'to write only for him and once a week. He said "you'd find your column much easier to write". I said "perhaps, but it would be impossible to read".'[1]) Despite the fact that regular journalism can become a tyranny, 'waking up in the night in a panic about what to say', Nancy enjoyed this new arena: firstly because it gave her the chance to write whatever she liked about France, and then, when her remit was broadened, because it encouraged her to make those characteristic pronouncements that were one part truth to one part naughtiness (as when, in *Madame de Pompadour*, she wrote that a love affair can only succeed if the man has the upper hand; without the kernel of truth in that statement, the naughtiness would not work).

Her columns were an instant success. Waugh was waylaid by a woman who gushed over them: 'I do admire her writing so,' she said to him. 'So do I,' he replied, 'I have just been rereading all her books.' '*Books!* D'you mean to say she writes *books* too?' Waugh was also an admirer, and wrote of her first piece, a series of general reflections upon Paris: 'I thought your *Sunday Times* article excellent – positive, funny, enterprising – all that *The Sunday Times* isn't. Also an entirely new & personal sort of journalism. If you can keep it up you will become what is called a "pioneer".' It was, he later told her, 'your *métier*'.

Which was true up to a point: her post-war journalism was certainly extremely readable, and unlike most of what then appeared in newspapers. It was, in fact, very modern. Now it is the norm to read journalists chatting away about their lives and opinions; sixty years ago this was not the case, and the directness with which Nancy spoke to her readers was innovative. 'My furniture has arrived,' she told her *Sunday Times* audience in early 1952, 'emerging from seven years of storage and its long journey in a surprisingly good state.' If one were to read that in a newspaper column today – as one is more than likely to do ('The husband is baying for my blood as I ask him to assemble Archie's activity centre') – one's eyes would roll with boredom. But at the time it felt fresh. It also flattered readers – Nancy being so famous and all – in its implication of intimacy.

Talking to readers was what she did of course. Her two great novels had precisely this directness, transmuted into art; doing the same thing in journalism was, therefore, a diminished variation on her stylistic theme, stripping away the invention and the imagination of the books, leaving the quality of the voice but without its *coloratura*. This was all very fine, but it was far from being Nancy's '*métier*'. She herself did not think so, at least not by 1954: 'Journalism isn't my talent', she wrote to her agent A.D. Peters. She did not need its discipline to make her writing clear and readable. Indeed in her articles she became regularised, predictable, a bit too grown-up: although she describes Paris, one has no sense of it being ragingly good fun, more a dutiful and rather middle-aged procession of art exhibitions and plays. Nancy lost something of her idiosyncratic spark; her natural momentum was slowed. She always said that she worked extremely hard at her journalism ('careful work', she called it), probably because she knew that simplicity of style tends to be equated with ease of production. But the fact is that she wrote better when she thought less and intuited more: as in her glorious letters, which give her fantastical side free rein. The letter to her sister Diana about the Tour de France – 'Bobet . . . succumbed to terrible furoncles (ONE can guess where)' – is infinitely more Mitfordian than the version of similar events in the *Sunday Times* in July 1950, which ended: 'But the English take no interest in the Tour. "A bicycle race", they say, "how deadly". So I expect I had better shut up.' This really was not essence of Nancy; it had her clarity, her amused slant on events, but what was missing was the energy in her prose: that disdain for rules of punctuation and construction, that rush as a simile flies like a bird into her head, the intake of delighted breath before she makes a good joke, the childlike confidence with which she lays down unexpected words.

But it is easy to see why Nancy's columns were so popular. They were produced by someone whose every word was now eagerly devoured: a felicitous state of affairs for a writer. They also brought off some very clever tricks. The 'letters from Paris' were a more sophisticated version of *A Year in Provence*, bringing France to the English in just the way that they most like it: telling them about *la mode* and *l'Académie*, encouraging the knowledge that they already had, gracefully juggling expectation with novelty. Nancy knew that her readers were fascinated by the French, that they felt France to be the only country that could compete with England, that they were intrigued by a nation which could retain so much self-assurance in the face of its recent past. At the same time, they wanted the essence of France conveyed in a way that was essentially English, and no one could do that better than Nancy. She was a filter, an ambassadress, 'in' Paris but not quite 'of' it; she told her readers its little secrets but she did so as *one of them*. 'The prices', she writes of Parisian clothes, 'are more horrifying than ever. I was with an English friend when she saw an embroidered jacket. "Darling I must have it. I don't mind what it costs . . ." So we asked for the price. £360. Collapse of my friend.

'I spoke of this to a Frenchwoman who knows about the business of *haute couture* . . .' Oh, it was a clever trick that she pulled, and Evelyn Waugh acknowledged as much when he praised the use of French in the articles: 'What the English like are phrases of which they can easily understand the literal meaning, if possible with words that look like English words, and have quaintness and drollness. That is what you give them . . .' 'What you say', she replied, 'is just what I'd figured out. My fan mail very funny . . . Must I answer them? I *can't*.' Later she said that she received letters from people who, regarding her as their intermediary between France and England, the patron saint of *La Manche*, asked her such questions as 'will my electric iron work in a French hotel?'

And what a storm these columns of Nancy's would go down still, today, among the second-home-in-the-Dordogne brigade: all those little snippets about the auctions at the Hôtel Drouot ('a small unsigned Louis XV cabinet, with two legs and its marble top missing, was sold for £800 . . . sale room wags said it would have fetched much less had it been complete'), the lack of indexes in French books ('My St Simon in sixteen volumes and Mme de Sévigné in eight . . . have not got an index between them . . . Oh! the irritation!'), the new diktats of Christian Dior ('Skirts are two inches shorter, a very nice little change, and I for one am in favour of it'). How good the readers felt about themselves, knowing that they were *au courant*, that none other than Nancy Mitford had filled them in on what the critics said about Cocteau's last play (it was so bad that they said nothing, 'writing about the difficulties of parking a motor on a first night'), or what Picasso said when asked who are the new painters ('*Moi*'); how they all chatted about it at their Sunday lunch parties, or – according to Evelyn Waugh – at White's club, 'where men of influence & discrimination congregate and all were full of praise of your "Sunday Times" article – Birch, Birkenhead, Churchill, Hartington, Head etc.' It all goes to show that when a writer is 'known' to be good, everything that they write is worthy of praise, even though – dare one say it – they sometimes wrote things that were far better before they 'became' good.

But it was a pleasant furrow for Nancy to plough, taking France to the English in this way; it was not too taxing, and she had the field pretty much to herself. So she did other things in the same vein. She translated what she would later call her favourite book, Madame Lafayette's *La Princesse de Clèves*, a delicate, serious, intelligent romance set in the court of Henri IV, and steeped in an idiosyncratic, clear-sighted sensibility comparable with, though different from, Nancy's. Her translation, which she felt overly obliged to make faithful to the original, was published in 1950 (in America, under the title *Love in a Cold Climate*) by Euphorion Books, a house recently set up by the Mosleys.

'Prod says it's the most awful translationese he's ever read', she wrote to Waugh in January. Really, these people who do nothing themselves and pronounce upon those who do – but unfortunately Peter had a point, as was made clear when Nancy came to revise the translation by Penguin in 1962. Her corrected proofs show an agonising number of changes. An example of a cut sentence – 'He knew himself that his brother was incapable of it, but feared it might be said that he had done it' – does not inspire admiration, and Penguin were in fact very rude about it. 'In 190 pages of text I have noted more than twenty verbal ineptitudes', snapped an internal memo, and the editor Betty Radice later wrote of the book: 'I hope very much that it need not be reprinted, so that we can have *la Princesse* properly translated in its proper place'. This seems extraordinary, considering that Nancy's reprinted Penguins – *Pigeon Pie, The Pursuit of Love, Love in a Cold Climate* and *The Blessing* – were selling in their thousands.

It is both heartening and depressing that a writer as rampantly successful as Nancy could be treated with the same kind of disdain as some pitiful first novelist selling tens of copies. For example, as a very particular kind of stylist, she had problems with editors. Her nephew Alexander says that 'she was always fighting them': their itching desire to replace her racy commas with sedate semi-colons, to take out sullying phrases such as 'he did not go droning on about things' (in *Madame de Pompadour*), to kill her prose stone-dead. Of her biography of Frederick the Great, Nancy wrote to her friend Sir Hugh Jackson [2]: 'The publishers took it upon them to change many colloquialisms as I know they do in America and Russia ... "They had a good gossip" became "they reminisced" and so on ... No wonder American books read so dull and flat.' In fact Nancy always retained a kind of humility about her writing, a legacy of her sense that she was 'an *uneducated woman*'. Her letter to Sir Hugh continues: 'Raymond Mortimer, a master of English, had been over the typescript and removed many horrors as I'm the first to admit – I naturally accepted all his changes but then the high school girls at Rainbird's[3] took over. Oh no. Luckily I bring them in money and they don't really want to kill the goose.' So it was that Penguin published Nancy's translation of *La Princesse de Clèves*, despite the po-faced contempt in which it was held. Nancy herself had known that the 1950 version required work, and clearly believed that she was capable of improving it: 'I think & hope I write better English than when I translated La Psse: some 10 years ago', she wrote to Penguin in 1959. 'I think the actual translation is quite correct.'

But therein lay the problem: correct translating was not Nancy's thing. As with her conscientious letters from Paris, it dimmed her vitality. Far more suitable was her next venture, in which she took an amusing, slightly louche play, André Roussin's *La Petite Hutte*, and adapted it for the British stage. Translating again, in a sense, but this time with a much freer hand. Roussin spoke not a word of English, 'so I've got away with all my own jokes & dialogue & just kept his situations which are heaven', she wrote merrily to Evelyn Waugh at the start of 1950. Once again, Nancy could perform her filtering job of pouring the essence of France into an English vessel: Dom Perignon into a teapot from Goode's.

She was a terrific admirer of Roussin: 'a great love' with a smilingly cynical eye on the world. As in *Love in a Cold Climate*, whose plot concerns a man who has an adulterous affair with an older woman, marries her daughter, then falls for her male cousin, *The Little Hut* also handled strong, sexual realism with a light and knowing acceptance. Four people are shipwrecked on a desert island – a married couple, the wife's lover and the ship's cook – and the men take it in turns to spend a night with the woman. Nothing could have been better suited to Nancy's sure but delicate touch: no one was better than she at grasping a situation of this sophisticated kind, and treating it with a different kind of sophistication, one that softened any overly cruel lines with that gift of hers, that ability to portray everything that happens as natural, that absence of judgment which, paradoxically, does not preclude a sense of morality. Nancy herself loved French worldliness. She roared at Roussin's works (such as *Le Mari, La Femme et La Mort*, about the attempts of a pretty young wife to murder her rich old husband), and the terrible behaviour of people like the Duc de Richelieu – anti-hero of *Madame de Pompadour* – did not bother her in the slightest ('his 4 wives & all his mistresses & all his men friends simply loved him, he must have been rather nice!'). Nonetheless her instinct was to keep in place the sexless safety net of English humour. Between stints in bed, her wife in *The Little Hut* laments the absence of *Tatler* on the desert island. It was the same trick again. Audiences were allowed their pleasurable shocks, but they were also wonderfully at their ease: safe in the hands of Miss Mitford, from whom the unexpected was always deliciously expected. Most people loved *The Little Hut*'s naughtiness ('the name of Dr Kinsey is introduced & they laugh for 5 minutes'[4]), although there were, no doubt to Nancy's gratification, those who found the whole thing deliriously obscene. 'I have received a rain of anonymous letters', she told Diana Cooper, '"go back to the Paris brothels where you belong, always an ENGLISHMAN" etc etc. "Who are you anyway?" one began. So hard to answer really!'

The play – rather surprisingly directed by RSC *wunderkind* Peter Brook – toured Britain in 1950 before opening at the Lyric Theatre in August. It was kindly reviewed by *The Times*: 'there are moments when the champagne does not work, but not many of them' and its glittering success anticipated. Nancy was told by a friend that Hamish Hamilton was 'afraid you'll make so much over this play that you'll never write another novel'. She wrote to her mother that 'everybody to do with it in London is borrowing money on its success which is thought to be certain'. She herself was less sure, although in fact the play ran for 1,261 performances and was attended by the same people over and over again (among them Nancy's distant cousin Bertrand Russell. 'I have always wondered who it is that goes regularly & now we know. Old philosophers'). It was not until September 1953 that she wrote to Evelyn Waugh: 'oh *The Hut* is shut, & that lovely steady hot water bottle of £300 a month has been taken out of my bed. I feel very chilly.' In fact Nancy's books were raining money on her head; one is hardly inclined to go along with the familiar refrain of 'do be sorry for me'.

She toured with the play before its first night ('sounds so indecent at my age'), an experience she found amusing and dreadful in equal parts. She adored Peter Brook – 'one of the cleverest people I have ever met' – and he adored her in return. But she was appalled by the carryings-on of her cast: 'I never knew such people,' she told Waugh. 'Any good line is "*my* good line" or "*my* laugh" & the rest are "that's a very flat line of *yours* darling" (to me).' Indeed she retained a horror of actors – 'unbridled by one ray of intelligence' – although she took to Robert Morley (the husband in *The Little Hut*), a robust bon vivant and 'the only actor I've ever met who was a human being'. The morning after the play's opening in Edinburgh, Nancy telephoned to Morley to invite him for a celebratory dinner at their hotel the next evening: come at 8 o'clock, she said. Morley was obliged to explain to her that he would not be free until eleven. 'Do you do the play twice every night?' she asked, her head two centuries away at the Versailles theatricals run by Madame de Pompadour.

Meanwhile the touring provided material for a *Sunday Times* column, 'Britain Revisited', in which she described the sensation of being 'a foreign tourist' in her own country. 'My impression is that the hotels are good, that the art galleries are full of treasures . . . and that the food, though not good, is not as bad as people suppose. The railways are truly terrible, however, and so is the climate.'

This reads quite anodyne, certainly by today's journalistic standards; but Nancy's non-Parisian columns *did* get a strong reaction, and therein lay another trick. When she wrote about Rome or Athens, when she went to Ireland and described people living in 'horrid little wooden or wattle huts . . . What was good enough for President Kennedy's ancestors is good enough for the Irish', she was, of course, trying to provoke, knowing that her readers would lap it up and get a massive kick out of hating her. And so they did: 'Rome is Only a Village' was ritually burned by an Italian countess in the presence of her friends; 'The Other Island' was greeted with a letter starting 'Hell would be a more suitable place for you than Ireland'; 'Wicked Thoughts in Greece' elicited a distraught letter from the American director of the reconstruction of the Athenian Stoa, which Nancy had described as 'said to be "of Attalos" but really of Mr Homer A. Thompson'.

So all of this was taken desperately seriously, which to Nancy made it all the funnier. She herself rarely took offence. 'The fact is, with me, my love of shrieking is greater than my amour propre', she wrote to Evelyn Waugh in 1955. She called Cyril Connolly's review of *Madame de Pompadour* 'a masterpiece', even though it contained criticisms: 'I literally screamed with laughter, in the street where I bought the paper.'

Not that she could always assume so sanguine a pose; who can? She was upset by A.J.P. Taylor's assertion (often held up as a tremendous aperçu, really just a low blow) that she had, in *Pompadour*, merely transferred the Radlett family to the court of Versailles. But she took it, all the same. After Taylor's review appeared, she wrote to the *Manchester Guardian* to correct a quotation from her book; her letter was gracious in the extreme, however, and expounded the philosophy to which she tried to adhere. 'Please don't answer, or bother Mr Taylor again', she wrote, ending with this postscript: 'I suppose what I really minded was getting such a beating from the M. Guardian which is the only English paper I ever see. However such beatings are always deserved and should be taken without complaint.' No doubt she expected the same stoicism from Mr Homer A. Thompson and co.

Shrieking of a different kind would follow, however, when in 1955 she wrote 'A Queen of France' about Marie Antoinette, of whom she said: 'She certainly deserved a traitor's death.' The brevity of the attack, just a few dismissive lines, was in inverse proportion to the brouhaha it caused. 'She got a bit more than she bargained for,' says Alexander Mosley. 'Some people actually refused to see her after it was published – there's a very stuffy side to the French aristocracy.' Nancy had caused genuine offence in 'the Faubourg', to which she reacted with a slightly shaky defiance. 'I really don't know what all the fuss is about as I am on *their side* for cutting off the head of an Austrian spy. Why do we dance on the 14th July then?' she wrote to Evelyn Waugh (who sensed a tease to taunt the teaser: 'Some of my informants say you may be readmitted to the fringes of Society. Others that you will have to change your name & go to Dakar').

Nancy must have known that 'A Queen of France' would offend some of the French people whom she professed to love (just as she knew, back in 1935, that *Wigs on the Green* would offend her sister

Diana); yet she had not let that stop her. She simply could not resist. In 1953 she had written to Evelyn Waugh, then in the eye of a social storm generated by Randolph Churchill (who had shown Duff Cooper a letter from Waugh that read 'Cooper I have never tolerated except for his enchanting wife'), saying: 'Whatever one may think of your letter, & I think you went too far really, it was quite indefensible to show it. In France that is the *one* rule, never make trouble.' Yet that is exactly what Nancy did with her piece about Marie Antoinette. It was not trouble-making of a personalised kind, but it was not, perhaps, absolutely good manners. It was, however, good journalism: and it showed that Nancy, for all her apparent reliance upon *la haute société*, was prepared to put writing – and teasing – ahead of such considerations.

She loved to tease; she admitted as much. Is it true, however, to say that she derived an absolute enjoyment from creating havoc, that she took real pleasure in offending and hurting? This has been suggested, by Selina Hastings for one in her biography *Nancy Mitford*, which says that Nancy was 'flattered' by the upset she had caused with 'A Queen of France', and that it had been 'Nancy's intention' to wound Mr Homer A. Thompson with her criticisms of Athens.

This question of intent is important. To go further, there are those who believe that Nancy's 'spiteful side' was perhaps the most significant part of her. Diana Mosley is first among these, and with some cause. The spite is said to derive from frustration; it was the poison that oozed from the wound caused by insufficient love; and it led to Nancy writing her wicked articles, or making remarks such as this extremely silly one about John Wilkes Booth: 'What was the name of that beautiful man who shot Abraham Lincoln?' Or – of course – turning snake-like upon her family.

All of which comes back to the familiar idea that Nancy's life was an emotional vacuum. She tried to deny this but, as time went on and the spaces in her heart became more gaping, her sadness could not help but reveal itself. Her dainty little teases were the means to expel unwanted unhappiness. It was what she had done when, trapped among the rivalries of life at Asthall and Swinbrook, she had forced Diana and Pam to be girl guides, or had told Jessica that with her newly curled hair she looked like 'the ugliest of the Brontë sisters'. It had made her feel better; and if it had made her victims feel worse then that was just too bad. '"Being beastly"', as her friend (*sic*) James Lees-Milne later wrote of her, 'was her favourite sport.' These were only jokes, after all. Nothing mattered so much as a joke.

This 'explanation' of Nancy's character has been fairly generally accepted. The critic Rhoda Koenig, for example, who had previously accused Nancy of being Gaston Palewski's 'tragic, ridiculous hanger-on' (see Chapter 6), would go on to assert, in a *Sunday Times* review of the collected letters, that Nancy had 'more cause for bitterness than could be expended locally'. Her beloved jokes, which were mostly so much 'twittering and sodden fluff and crapping on everything from a great height', were an inevitable waste product: 'While pretending that feelings didn't matter, she showed that they did by taking her unhappiness out on others'. James Lees-Milne felt similarly and gives the impression that Nancy's company was like sitting in a sunny but icy room. In his 1944 diary he recounts lunching in Nancy's 'non-garden', where 'She told me that her upbringing had taught her never to show what she felt. I thought how lamentably my upbringing had failed in this respect, and how too perfectly in her case, for there is a vein of callousness which almost amounts to cruelty.' Emotional crippling leads to teasing: a neat equation with which to solve Nancy's complex personality.

Certainly there was a chill in Nancy's attitude towards her mother, although she believed this to be justified. Then there was her denunciation of Diana during the war, an act that may have been repeated, in different form.

On the 2001 *Omnibus* programme, John Julius Norwich told a very remarkable story. He revealed that some years after the war Nancy had related to him a conversation she had had, with her sister Diana, on the subject of Germany. According to Nancy, Diana still believed that, back in 1939, the Nazis should have been treated as our allies rather than our enemies. 'But darling, seven million Jews!' Nancy had cooed to her sister. 'Oh but darling, it was much the kindest way!' Diana had cooed back.

Now when this story was told on the BBC it created, as may be imagined, a furore among the elderly ex-socialites of Europe. 'I'm very ashamed of myself,' says Lord Norwich, 'because I knew perfectly well that Diana was alive, and Debo was very cross with me, rightly. She wrote to me saying that I know Diana would never have said a thing like that, anybody who believed anything that Nancy said was living in a fool's paradise. So this I have to accept. But it had never struck me to doubt what Nancy said for a second.'

Diana denies the story absolutely. 'Did you hear what John Julius said about me? He wrote me a marvellous letter [a 'groveller', as he calls it, was also published in *The Times*]. But it was terribly libellous, people here say I ought to sue the BBC, not for money but just to get an apology.

'You see it wasn't true . . . But of course it's quite possible that she said it, that's the terrifying thing. Yes it's quite possible. That's where she was, really, rather dangerous. I do just feel that Nancy, and her sayings, and her letters and all that – it's rather like an unexploded bomb. You see she really was rather naughty, she really was. It was quite possible that she would say anything, if she thought it would either amuse or shock. Also she wasn't averse to giving me a bad name . . .'

There seems little doubt that Nancy did tell John Julius Norwich – together with his parents, Duff and Diana Cooper – something along the lines of what was said on *Omnibus*. Lord Norwich would never have invented such a thing, even if the joy of speaking to camera did (as Diana Mosley thinks) cause him to cut loose with his story-telling style. 'If she made that up about Diana then that's pretty malicious . . . I'd love to know what was really said between them.'

Indeed; but a conclusion of sorts has to be drawn, and the conclusion is that Nancy lied. Or, at least, grossly exaggerated. Diana was never afraid of admitting her views about the Nazi regime, but these did not include an endorsement of the 'final solution'. Of course Nancy would never have said what she did had she thought that the story would end up on the BBC; for all the terrible grandeur of its subject matter, hers was a private and social lie, told for the sheer fun of hitting Diana where she was so grotesquely vulnerable. And told, perhaps, because in a way Nancy would not have seen it as a lie.

But – as with the wartime denunciation – it was a remarkable thing for Nancy to do, however much Diana's political sympathies deserved opprobrium. Nancy did have spite in her, and it showed most venomously towards those by whom she felt threatened: her most beautiful sister, her mother. Yet according to Diana she was not above making digs at *all* of her sisters. 'The corollary of her incredible exaggeration, of seeing everything *en rose* – if it was one of her relations she was just the opposite. I used to laugh with my other sisters about it. But it was just her. It was part of her.

'Another thing – I don't think most of her brothers-in-law liked her. That's rather odd, isn't it, because she was great fun. Derek Jackson really hated her. Of course she was rather horrid when they were children to my sister Pam, and I expect that's why Derek disliked her. They really disliked each other. Derek was such fun, and they could have been marvellous together, but they just weren't. And Kit [as Diana called Oswald Mosley] – well. We had this house in Staffordshire, and he just didn't want her there. He was terribly fond of my mother, devoted, and I think he always felt that Nancy was very, very disloyal to her, which of course she was –! He used to say she's very disloyal. He was much more right than he knew, and much more right than I knew.

'And then when we got the Temple [their house at Orsay] she very very often came, and he would have much preferred she hadn't, but I always wanted her. They got on outwardly alright, because of me I suppose, but they must have both been making an effort. I suppose manners –! But as I say he wasn't the only one, because Derek didn't like her. And Esmond [Romilly] of course didn't like anyone, that's different.

'My mother used to say she planted a dart in people . . .' James Lees-Milne used a similar phrase, writing of a 'sharp little barb, barely concealed': for some people Nancy held a faintly repellent quality, as of a cold-blooded reptile dressed in Dior and schooled in the art of epigrammatic gossip. Of course one might say that men such as Jackson and Mosley would never have liked Nancy, knowing as they did that she despised their political affiliations and their rather aggressive masculinity. She saw through them, in fact, and there is nothing that men like less. Indeed it may be that a lot of her 'spite' came from the skewed clarity of perception that could not resist expression. Certainly that was the case with her journalism. It was also true of some of her social *bon mots*, for example her comment upon the writer Rosamond Lehmann's attempts to use spiritualism to contact her dead daughter. 'I said bad luck on the girl. Imagine a heavenly butler saying "the Hon. Mrs Philipps [Lehmann] is on the line again, ma'am" when one is gambolling in a green pasture.'[5] This was a desperately cruel crack, one of the worst instances of Nancy's spite. But she had seen through the lunacy of what Lehmann was doing; and so she could not stop herself.

The 'joke' may have been obscurely linked to Nancy's own childlessness; thus the spite comes back to the personal, to the lack of love in her life. It may even have been the 'splinter of ice' that Graham Greene famously believed to be buried in every writer's heart. But this is not quite right. The coldness in Nancy came and went, like a sudden wind which disappears when the sun emerges.

For all that there were those to whom she was 'chilly and unlikeable' (as her god-daughter Harriet Waugh later put it), there were others who divined the warmth in her. Not least among these is her sister Deborah, who despite her loyalty to Diana says simply: 'I adored her.' Her nephew Alexander understood and loved her – a 'wonderful person to have known' – and Diana, too, is entirely fair in her willingness to praise Nancy's good qualities. 'All my sons were very fond of her. She never showed the spiteful side. She was also very fond of Debo's children. And another nice thing about Nancy, she was generous to the last. If she saw that somebody was poor she'd immediately give them money. There was one couple – very hard-up, I believe she paid for the boy to go to school.' When it came to disinterested kindness, Nancy was exemplary: 'a very nice person indeed', says John Julius Norwich. And in a review of Harold Acton's memoir, Nancy's friend Anthony Powell wrote of how she spent several summers in Venice: 'I can vouch for the fact that her name, mentioned casually in the bar or restaurant of the Torcello hotel, would arouse an immediate reaction of remembrance and affection among the staff.'

Of course it was easy for Nancy to be kind at a distance. Even with Deborah there was sixteen years between them, a space that allowed the rivalries to disperse (imagine if Diana had been Duchess of Devonshire –!). Close up, caught unawares on a sore point, or seized with the sudden desperate desire to hurt, Nancy's warm smile could take on a bright and icy glint. Yet it is impossible to read *The Pursuit of Love*, or her letters to Gaston Palewski – 'I know one's not allowed to say it but I love you' – and not to think that her heart longed, quite desperately, to burn with joyful fires. Impossible not to think that she was cold because she wanted not to be.

And was this merely a shrill frigidity, or was it, as Deborah says, 'absolute courage'? One can take the view that Nancy's life was 'like the story of a real-life Winnie in Beckett's *Happy Days*, buried up to her neck in ruins and a brave, tight, twitchy smile permanently pinned to her face.'[6] Or one can see her, as John Julius Norwich does, as 'one of the bravest women I've ever known. Oh she was brave. I'm sure the misery was there, but she never complained. I never heard a complaint. She could make a good story out of how awful something or somebody was, of course she could – but that wasn't complaining. Those were jokes.'

In September 1955 the magazine *Encounter* published an article by Nancy entitled 'The English Aristocracy'. This contained, within its considerable length, the handful of paragraphs for which she was perhaps best known in her lifetime, and which put forward the theory of U and Non-U language, U being short for – dread word – upper-class. The piece was reprinted a year later by Hamish Hamilton in a book called *Noblesse Oblige*, together with a fond, caustic reply by Evelyn Waugh: 'To the Honble Mrs Peter Rodd On a Very Serious Subject'. 'Dearest Nancy', it begins, 'Were you surprised that your article on the English aristocracy caused such a to-do? I wasn't. I have long revered you as an agitator – agitatrix, agitateuse? – of genius. You have only to publish a few cool reflections on eighteenth-century furniture to set gangs on the prowl through the Faubourg St Germain splashing the walls with "Nancy, go home". In England class distinctions have always roused higher feelings than national honour . . . Was it kind, dear Nancy, to pull their legs?' (Perceptively, Philip Toynbee[7] wrote of this contribution to *Noblesse Oblige* that Waugh's 'primary aim is to show that he knows more about the aristocracy than Miss Mitford does.')

The oddest thing of all about U and Non-U is that the labels –

which did, indeed, cause uproar – were never Nancy's in the first place, but the concept of a philologist named Professor Alan Ross who, at a lunch (Non-U) with Nancy, told her that he was writing an article on sociological linguistics for a Finnish journal. In this he would use an extract from *The Pursuit of Love*, quoting Uncle Matthew as he accuses Fanny of talking about notepaper and mantelpieces (Non-U), instead of writing paper and chimneypieces (U). The idea of this learned, serious and obscure person dealing in such inflammatory material amused Nancy no end, although she claimed that it was Stephen Spender, commissioning her for *Encounter*, who insisted that she brought it all into her article. Indeed, what she called the 'U stuff' does seem slightly dragged in. Her mother told her that the article would have been just as good without it, and she was right. Nancy lists a series of words according to whether they are U or Non-U, giving examples such as 'bike' versus 'cycle' or 'pudding' versus 'sweet', but although she endorses these categorisations ('Silence', she writes, 'is the only possible U-response to . . . the ejaculation of "cheers" before drinking') they actually come straight from Professor Ross. Nancy then moves on to her own thoughts, giving readers a rollicking treatise on the nature of the English Lord, whom she describes as resilient, philistine and 'impervious to a sense of shame'; and this part of the article is much more interesting.

But of course it was U and Non-U that everyone latched on to, it was Nancy who was regarded as its onlie begetter, and the edition of *Encounter* in which her article appeared was an instant and frantic success. 'I went to W.H.S[mith] here yesterday', she told her mother in September 1955, 'manager dashed at me saying all sold out the first day. Heywood who usually sells 20 has sold over 100 last week...' The whole subject grew like a monstrous triffid, entangling English nerves in terrifying questions: are you a snob? and worse, are you common? 'Absolutely fascinating, the reactions to it,' says Alexander Mosley. It was as if some brave soul today were to lay bare the question of equality between the sexes, now similarly festooned with lies and taboos. 'I think in a way,' Mosley continues, 'bringing questions of class home to so many people, and turning it into a sort of game, hastened its demise: it stung at the time, but I think it was antiseptic in a way.'

Which is interesting, and partly true; yet class does still inflame tremendous passions and an article like Nancy's would still cause an anguished furore. It would be different in tone, as it is now the Us rather than the Non-Us who are on the back foot, scattering consonants like confetti in their longing to be loved; but it would not, in essence, be so dissimilar from the national debate of 1955. There would still be intellectual articles like Toynbee's, censuring Nancy for avoiding 'her obvious duty as an analyst to tell us *why* this [Non-U] usage is unspeakable'. There would be jokes, like Nancy's favourite: 'I'm dancing with tears in my eyes 'cos the girl in my arms isn't U.' There would be letters of the kind that she received, such as this: 'My typist is so angry she refuses to type a letter to you'; or this: 'I am descended from Alfred the Great's sister & would like to congratulate you on your splendid stand for people of our sort.' There might even be advertisements like the one in *The Times* for a 'U-type Ski Party'.

Above all, the whole thing would be treated with the utmost seriousness, and it would carry on until everyone was utterly sick of it. 'Can you get over them going *on* with U?' wrote Nancy to Waugh in 1956. Her 1957 BBC television interview began with this excruciating interchange: 'But what I want to talk about is U'; 'But we *are* talking about me.' In 1964 she was invited to translate a novel by Pierre Daninos, entitled *Snobissimo* ('So kind of you to think of me . . .'). And it is not unthinkable that U and Non-U might be dredged up again, were for example Prince William to be seen holding his knife like a pencil.

It did Nancy no favours, in the end. 'The whole thing was complete rubbish,' says her sister Deborah. 'It had started as a joke, and then, you know, nobody could say notepaper [although, as the *Telegraph* delighted in pointing out at the time, Nancy had used that very word in her editing of *The Ladies of Alderley*]. It was just silly. A perfect pest. But it came back to haunt her.' It always would. She was a writer of unusual talent and originality, yet when she died her obituary in the *Telegraph* was headed (inaccurately): 'Nancy Mitford, "U and Non-U" creator, dies at 68'. She was also branded a 'super-snob'. Her own mother was quoted as saying as much, by the BBC interviewer in 1957. And the Audience Research Report after the broadcast could not wait to judge her according to this dread criterion: 'We could do with something more interesting than listening to a snobbish woman airing her views on class distinction', said one viewer, while another offered the thought that 'it is surely definitely Non-U to sniff as often and as audibly as she did'.

More than forty years on, Nancy was still suffering for having dared to say the unsayable. When the BBC adapted her two great novels for a 2001 television series, much of its own publicity centred upon the question of 'why in this age of equality would anyone want to read or watch the semi-biographical adventures of a self-confessed snob?'

Did Nancy really commit the evil crime of snobbery? It is a question that still interests people, although its relevance to her worth as a writer is minimal. Certainly she was the product of her class and upbringing, and she wrote about the society of which she was a product ('Novelists always write about the people they know, don't they?'). This in itself does not, cannot, make her a snob, although the non-logic that so often passes for its opposite suggests that it does, that merely by dealing with the subject of class she was showing herself to approve of it. It is quite obvious that she preferred to be U; funny little asides do give her away. 'A letter from Willie M[augham] saying he can't be U as he says toilet paper', she wrote to Raymond Mortimer: 'Ugh.' Then there were these remarks about Graham Greene's novel *The End of the Affair* (1951), which she had admired, but: 'Oh what a picture of terrible lives. Yet they are all quite rich in the book . . . And Bendrix wrote a novel every year lucky him yet he lives in a terrible bed-sitting room. And all that public house life, like poor people.'[8] (Of course she was also digging at Greene for what she saw as self-conscious slumming.)

There is not a saloon-bar gin and tonic to be had in her novels; yet the point of them, always, is that they show aristocrats to be 'real' people like any others. Even 'The English Aristocracy' never says that she believes that a lord is superior to a commoner. 'It was just a difference of vocabulary, that was the point she was making,' says Alexander Mosley. She admits her hatred of a word such as 'cheers', but equally she says that this is an instinct only, that in itself it means nothing. 'I think she was being honest, yes, that it was just a question of language. At the same time she was very pleased to be on the U side –! But the thing is she was a very intelligent woman, and she could look at her own snobbery clinically.'

Nancy knew what she was, she liked what she was, but she also could see it for *what* it was. 'She was very conscious of her own class,' says John Julius Norwich. 'It *amused* her so much. If it hadn't amused her so much those two great novels wouldn't have been anything like as good as they are. Also, yes, she believed in it. I remember the nearest time she came to being cross with me was when I wrote my first book and she said, "How can you call yourself John Julius Norwich? You're Lord Norwich, or you're John Julius Cooper." She was perfectly right. But that was simply the way things were fifty years ago.

'Nowadays everybody's embarrassed by class. Nancy wasn't. She just saw it as a fact.' And she knew that her class, and her lack of embarrassment about it, were key to her success, and to the fascination that she exerted over her audience. So she went along with it, thus creating the delicious irony of taking a populist stance on her own elitism. A paradox which was, and is, entirely Mitfordian.

Also Mitfordian was the *way* in which Nancy said what she said. In the end it was her style, rather than her substance, that made her an 'agitator of genius'. She was not the only person ever to comment on class, an issue to which almost nobody is truly indifferent. Yet the feeling was, and is, that this burningly interesting question must be handled in a very particular way, with certain assumptions made beforehand and certain things left unsaid. None of which Nancy did. She treated the whole, appallingly delicate subject exactly as she would anything else, placing down words in a clear and childlike way, refusing to infuse them with the correct feelings and to admit the tremendous 'importance' of what was being said.

This drove readers mad; but what *really* incensed – and, of course, delighted – them was the fact that although Nancy obviously meant what she wrote, it was obvious that she was not being wholly serious about it. And it is this, above all, that sent everyone spiralling towards towering heights of solemnity, from where they frowned at the giggling person whose words – apparently mild, yet containing the semantic equivalent of a red-hot chilli pepper – had launched them there.

Before she was cast in this role of Chief Tease, Nancy had once again performed her task of explaining the French to the English in her immaculate little novel *The Blessing*, published in 1951. She wrote it quickly, to judge by her letters in about four months, and as usual towards the end she went away; this time to Violet Hammersley's house on the Isle of Wight, where she was taken 'to the local bridge club & I heard "& of course when I was in London I went to Nancy Mitford's naughty thing" [*The Little Hut*] – wasn't it lovely for me.' In February 1951 she wrote to Gaston Palewski: 'The book gets on. Not quite as quick as I would like, I'm so longing to get back to you.' She finished a month later. Then she sent the book to Evelyn Waugh, to whom it was dedicated, and who proclaimed it 'admirable, deliciously funny, consistent & complete; by far the best of your writings; I do congratulate you with all my heart & thank you for the dedication.'

Not everyone agreed. Indeed the general opinion is that *The Blessing* shows a falling off from its two predecessors: 'it is', wrote the *TLS*, 'perhaps natural that she should have a slight relapse.' Certainly the book is different, neater, set primarily in France although filtered through Englishness; it is less innately ambitious than Nancy's two previous novels but it is, in its way, faultless. There is no Uncle Matthew, no Lady Montdore, none of the wild and magnificent vitality that burst through *The Pursuit of Love*, nor the comedic force that buzzed through *Love in a Cold Climate*; and there are those who think that Nancy wrote best when she was in close communion with the England she knew in her 'blood and bones', rather than taking on the dazzling new world of France. But that is not the point: at least not to those readers who love Nancy for *herself*, and for whom it is the voice, in the end, that does the magic. When the authentic Mitford note is sounding, when those funny, fervent phrases are unrolling, when Nancy is moving through the world of her imagination with all the assurance of which she is capable, resistance is futile. One is reminded, as before, of Muriel Spark, with whom the voice is paramount and who, like Nancy, is both fantastical and realistic: Spark's vision is entirely idiosyncratic and yet she treats with life as it is, describing its good and bad aspects in identical authorial fashion. *The Blessing* may not be what readers most want from Nancy; 'of course it's not really funny like the Uncle M. ones', she wrote to her sister Diana. But it is Nancy still, pure and calm and benevolent, utterly cosy and strangely shocking.

The shock derives from the novel's take on relations between the sexes, which is realistic to the point of cynicism, all the more disturbing for being delivered so lightly. *The Blessing* offers up its hard-won knowledge of life with all the grace of a pretty child handing a bouquet of roses to the Queen, and paints its tough truths in the colours of a Fragonard. People have affairs; other people put up with it; on the whole, the alternatives are even worse: that is what she tells us; and of course tells herself at the same time. If she is explaining France to the English then she is, at the same time, explaining Gaston Palewski to Nancy Mitford.

Charles-Edouard du Valhubert – the Colonel in many ways, including his 'guilty inward laugh' and his habit of singing little snatches of songs – marries Grace, a beautiful English girl with the looks of Diana Mosley and the romantic innocence of Nancy. He loves his wife but he continues to be unfaithful: with the irresistible Albertine, with the pretty little idiot Juliette Novembre de la Ferté and, it is implied, with others also. Grace – who is overwhelmingly in love with her husband – is unable to bear the jealousy and returns to her father, Sir Conrad Allingham, whom the reader expects to take the poor girl's side. But Sir Conrad is a man of the world, French rather than English in his liking for women and love of sleeping with them: a man who understands the nature of other men and tells it as it is. Instead of sympathy Grace gets a pep talk, which has the unmistakable air of Nancy talking to herself. And it jolts the reader: because it treats not with things as they ought to be, but as they are. 'Now he is a man', says Sir Conrad of Charles-Edouard, 'who likes women in the French way of liking them, that is he likes everything about them, including hours of their company and going to bed with them. I suppose you would admit that this is part of his charm for you. But you hardly find a man, or anyhow a young man, with his liking for women who can be faithful to one woman.' When Grace replies that she is, nonetheless, unable to endure the infidelities, her father replies: 'My dear child, I always thought you had a healthy outlook on life, but this is positively morbid. You really must pull yourself together.'

This cold comfort is rather terrifying; but refreshing, too, in the face of confused contemporary maunderings. What Nancy writes is difficult to accept and few women today would dream of doing so; but they would be wrong to dismiss it as *vieux jeu*, inappropriate to the independent female of today. Not so much has changed since Nancy described the pursuit of love as the be-all and end-all of a woman's existence. What *she* does is try to understand how the pursuit of love can end in the achievement of happiness. Nancy sees, all too clearly, what nowadays is denied: that in order to achieve one kind of happiness, other kinds may have to be sacrificed.

So we find, at the end of *The Blessing*, the septuagenarian sex bomb Madame Rocher des Innouïs (a distant literary *cousine* of Amabelle Fortescue in *Christmas Pudding*) visiting Grace in London, and gently telling her, 'my child, it is your duty to return to Paris'. Of Charles-Edouard, she says:

'Picture this unfortunate man, lonely, unhappy, reduced to pursuing the wives of all his friends, forced to go to bed at the most inconvenient times . . . I know the English are fond of duty, it is their great speciality. We all admire you so much for having no black market, but what is the good of no black market if you will not do your duty by your own family, Grace?'

Grace, sick to death of living alone, longing day and night for Charles-Edouard, was unable to conceal from Madame Rocher's experienced eye the happiness these words gave her . . .

Nonetheless Grace asks her aunt-by-marriage how she is supposed to fit happiness into the reality of Juliette and Albertine and, it is again implied, all the others.

'Charles-Edouard was sleeping with you, I suppose? . . . Well then, that's alright. Why not look upon these others as his hobby? . . . Could you not try to see this whole problem rather differently, Grace? More like a Frenchwoman and less like a film star?'

Grace felt that she could, and knew that she longed to, since the different vision was clearly essential if she were to go home to Charles-Edouard.

And nowadays this is heresy, it is frankly impossible, it is contrary to the tenets of the sisterhood and it puts Nancy, firmly, in a lavender-scented box bought only for its charming evocation of a dead era.

Today's women would probably think far more of the Crew, the bohemian English theatre workers who also feature in *The Blessing* (one of Grace's post-Paris suitors, The Captain, owns a theatre). These women think of Grace as a 'spineless creature who, unable to get on with her husband, had run back to her father like a spoilt child. When the various members of the Crew had been unable to get on with their husbands they had struck out proudly on their own, taken rooms near the Deux Magots, hitch-hiked to Lithuania, or stowed away on the Caribbean.'

This sounds far more appropriate for a self-respecting woman. If only it were that simple –! In fact the Crew are wildly satirised as a bunch of bare-footed groupies completely in thrall to The Captain ('they hopped to it at the merest glance from him, emptying ashtrays and bringing more water off the ice'). And few women today would rather be a Crew member, with her 'dusty, blonde hair . . . and bare feet, blue and rather large', than the beautiful Grace, with her 'stiff Paris dresses' and her 'sad, romantic look'.

Nor is Grace's situation easy, for all her appearance of cosseted wealth. Beneath the clean, controlled language there is turmoil; she does not *want* to think of her husband's philandering as a pursuit like 'hunting or racing', she wants him to be with only her, she wants the ideal of love to yield a daily contentment; but that was not the way of the world. Nor is it now. Nancy's stony, stoical philosophy is only irrelevant today because we have chosen to ignore the truths of relations between the sexes, which do not change all that much. Nowadays, when our illusions of love fail us, we move on to construct another set of illusions; but Grace is braver, and tries to live in a way that can hold both romance and reality. What, says Nancy, is the alternative course? That of the Crew members, who strike out for freedom only to end up enslaved again, but with worse clothes? Or of the Bolter, Fanny's feckless mother, who drifts through the novels like a shingle-headed nomad, moving from husband to husband ('eight or nine at least') and ending up with a twenty-two-year-old travel agent?

The Bolter ought to be a sad figure, according to conventional morality. In fact she is fine and at sixty-five looks not a day over forty: 'it was easy to see that her heart had never been involved', writes Nancy, an interesting sideline. As Fanny's husband says: 'Deeply as I disapprove of your mother and her activities I don't think she could be described as unhappy . . . You should try to see things as they are, Fanny.'

Nancy is not making.the tired point that men have affairs and women put up with it, although this is part of her point. She knows quite well that women are also capable of infidelity. Grace has a devoted admirer of her own in *Don't Tell Alfred*; it is assumed that she resists him mainly because he is not quite sexy enough. Fanny speculates as to whether one of her cousins might have gone astray, but dismisses the idea – 'surely good Louisa – oh no, perish the thought!' – not so much on moral grounds but because Louisa 'was incapable of inventing such a wealth of detail to cover up a sin'. This is hard-edged stuff, once again, beneath the smooth veneer.

Nancy's real point is this: it is all very well for the Bolter – who, like Northey, the little fascinator in *Don't Tell Alfred*, is completely unromantic – to have scores of love affairs. Likewise Charles-Edouard de Valhubert, to whom sex really is a sort of recreation. Someone like Linda Radlett, however, whose belief in love is total and whose overwhelming fear is that she might become like the Bolter (whom she tellingly loathes), is very different. Then one has to be realistic about romance, and accept that it is best integrated into the rest of one's life: not easy, as Nancy herself knew. But she gives us a picture of Grace after she has left Charles-Edouard, and although it is extremely funny it is also bleak. Perhaps one ought to think it wrong to show Grace so dependent upon an unfaithful man; but then Nancy did not moralise, she simply showed things as they were.

And she did so with a smiling grasp of reality that the more 'down-to-earth' writer – who scorns her concealing charm and whose plots are concerned with poorer, plainer people – cannot match. It is cruelly accurate to write that Grace was sustained 'by the mental picture of an idealised anglicised Charles-Edouard, whom she was to meet and marry in an incredibly short space of time'. This is just what a woman *would* try to imagine, and it is shattered by the even crueller and more accurate words of Grace's father. 'I'm afraid an ordinary faithful English husband will seem very plain pudding after the extraordinarily fascinating French one you are throwing away so carelessly . . . The fact is women must choose in life what sort of a man it is they do want – whether what is called a good husband . . . or one that really loves women, loves his wife, probably, best and longest, but who also and inevitably feels the need for other relationships with other women.'

So Grace decides; and her decision is vindicated when the Valhuberts reappear, perfectly happy, in *Don't Tell Alfred*. Charles-Edouard is still attractive and his eye still irresistibly roves; but ten years on Grace's attitude has changed. An odd little moment sees her husband sitting on a sofa with Northey, 'laughing very much', while Grace watches 'imperturbably, quizzically, even'. It is as if the idiocy of the philanderer has revealed itself to her. One wonders if Nancy ever looked at Gaston Palewski in this way, as he bounced on assorted Faubourg chaise longues; one cannot but hope that she did.

The Blessing was not well reviewed, although this made no difference to its sales. The time had come to give Nancy what she called 'a beating'; even the *TLS*, usually an intelligent friend, clearly thought she was having an 'off day' and accused the book of lacking a story. In fact *The Blessing* began its life as a plot. It turns upon the desire of the Valhuberts' small son, Sigismond, to keep his parents apart because his life is more amusing this way: each parent tries to outdo the other in giving him things, whilst their various suitors positively knock themselves out for him (Albertine throws a ball in his honour; The Captain, who plans to give him the starring role in his Communist version of *Little Lord Fauntleroy*, blows it when, before proposing to Grace, he sends him off with a shilling rather than a fiver: 'I think he's a bloody bastard, so there', says Sigismond to his mother, who cannot then marry him.)

The strongly schematic plot was untypical of Nancy, and not her invention (she readily confessed as much). It had been dreamed up for her by Alexander Korda[9] (whom her father confused with the Earl of Cawdor). Nancy signed a contract with London Films to turn the idea into a 'full length treatment which in book form may comprise a novel'. At the end of 1949, she wrote to Evelyn Waugh saying, 'Prod is here & has upset me very much by saying . . . Korda has no intention of using my script'; the usual jealous bitchiness. In fact Korda did think Nancy's treatment 'too sophisticated', as she later told Gaston

Palewski. 'Far from being a blow this is a great relief to me, now I can settle down & make it into a novel & not always be thinking of the camera.'

The joke is that *The Blessing* was subsequently made into a film, for which Nancy was paid 'seven million 500 000 francs sò dear dear Colonel I can give you a nice present ("No")'. The 1959 release *Count Your Blessings* starred Deborah Kerr and Rossano Brazzi and according to Nancy was 'so bad I didn't have the heart to see it'.[10] 'Cheerful, ruthless cynicism, not sentimentality, is Miss Mitford's line', ran a perceptive review in *The Times*: 'On the screen, of course, this won't quite do.' Tweeness, instead, was the order of the day. 'Among the victims of the film', said the *Observer*, 'is Maurice Chevalier, as the brat's great-uncle' (an invented character, the Duc de St-Cloud) 'and at any moment one expects him to burst out in song . . .' Nancy was appalled by the casting of Chevalier as a French aristocrat; she thought him far too vulgar (and there was the taint of the collaborator); unfortunately she said so, and had her remarks reported in the *Evening Standard*. She was obliged to grovel to Chevalier who replied, with rather ghastly nobility, saying, '*Chaque fois, Madame, qu'il m'arrive quelque chose de ce genre, je me console toujours en pensant qu'il est arrivé bien pire à des gens beaucoup mieux que moi. Et je m'arrange pour survivre.*'*

Count Your Blessings has evaporated into the land of one showing every twenty years on TCM, so one can only imagine the image of France that it offered (the Duc de St-Cloud, indeed). Of course *The Blessing* put forward a pretty strong image of its own; and it was for this that Nancy's novel was most criticized. 'Where she breaks down', wrote the *TLS*, '. . . is in the strained nature of her "Frenchness". The impossible marquis never actually sings "Auprès de ma Blonde", but he does break into "Malbrouk s'en va t'en guerre" at the slightest provocation . . .

'The fact is that Miss Mitford . . . has fallen into the trap which has caught so many English writers – the illusion that they, and they

---

* 'Every time, Madame, something of this kind happens to me, I console myself by thinking that far worse has happened to far better people. And I manage to survive.'

alone, are specially designed by nature to interpret *l'esprit gaulois*. A course of Stendhal, combined with a resolution to forget every word, for ever, of *Brideshead Revisited*, is perhaps the best corrective.'

This was harsh, wholly inaccurate about the influence of *Brideshead*, and a sure sign that Nancy was not going to get away with swooning girlishly over France the way that she does in *The Blessing*, which does indeed present the country as a repository for all civilised values. France has Charles-Edouard, Albertine, Madame Rocher des Innouïs and her 'great billows of sex'; England has Sigismond's Nanny, who having refused a glorious Provençal lunch asks if the chef can cook her a 'floury potato'.

But England – 'a country of enormous, fair, mad atheists' – is treated with affection (not least by the adorable Madame Rocher, who at a dinner party held for her by Sir Conrad stuns the company with eulogies to 'D.H. Heavens' and 'the Woolworth – oh the joy just to wander in the Woolworth'. She continues: 'I had no time for luncheon as you can imagine, but who cares when you can have a bun and a cup of tea?'). America, however, is merely mocked. When Madame Rocher asks Hector Dexter, the most boring man in the world, 'how, in a country where there are no brothels, do the young men ever learn?' he is too dim even to be shocked. 'We, in the States,' he replies, 'are entirely opposed to physical relations between the sexes outside the cadre of married life.' Nancy's anti-Americanism was an ever-burning flame. It was intensified by her determined hero-worship of de Gaulle, yet the instinct had been there since before the war, when she mocked Jessica for wanting to live in Washington ('Really Susan you Americans . . .'). 'I hate everything that has to do with American civilisation,' she told the *Herald Tribune* in 1957, 'your plastics, your skyscrapers, TV, refrigerators, psycho-analysis and Coca-Cola.' This interview, with Art Buchwald, was not wholly serious. In fact Buchwald was one of (several) Americans whom Nancy adored. At the same time she probably meant every word she said. The American Rhoda Koenig wrote in *The Sunday Times* that: 'Mitford's anti-Americanism was merely the most obvious expression of her unpleasant personality,' a valid opinion. Nevertheless one can also see the force of Nancy's belief that America massively affected European civilisation: one can only thank heaven that she did not live to see the McDonald's on the Champs-Élysées.

Of course *The Blessing* does not describe a factual France. Nancy was in love with her *image* of the country, with the 'light and heat of Provence', with the trick of the Parisian light which can make 'the buildings look as if they are made of opaque, blue glass'. The fervour expressed by Grace is Nancy's own; as Nancy herself knew.

Yet her France *does* have a reality. Balancing romance and reality was Nancy's thing. It is wrong to say, as the *Evening Standard* did in its review, that she was merely providing a 'gentle picture of French high society painted by a well-disposed foreigner', and that this was 'not what Miss Mitford's readers have been brought up to expect'. Critics apparently saw Nancy's two previous novels as satire, and so were disappointed by the girlish love that she bestows upon France. In fact, Nancy was *not* really a satirist. Clear-eyed benevolence is the keynote of her mature writing, and in that sense nothing changed in *The Blessing*: she remained a sophisticate, as well as a woman in love. She grasped the principles as well as the feel of Paris society: she renders its parties just as convincingly as the great dinner at Hampton which opens *Love in a Cold Climate* ('Your descriptions of the Ferté dinner party are quite wonderful – not even exaggerated', wrote Lady Alexandra Haig[11], who moved in similar circles). She conveys the conspiratorial bustle of the French world into which poor simple Grace has fallen: this may not be the absolute truth of how it was, but what does that matter? And it may be a little simplistic to equate English mores (*pace* Sir Conrad Allingham) with innocent romanticism, American mores with a love life conducted in virtual reality, and French mores with worldly practicality. But doing so allowed Nancy to say the things she wanted to say. And the imaginative vitality that she brings to these distinctions is so palpable as to give them reality: the cool, sensual picture she creates of Charles-Edouard and Albertine chatting together ('So! How do you find marriage?'; 'Rather dull, but I rather like it, and I love my wife' . . . 'He got up and locked the door') holds something that is truly French. Artistically true, at least.

Yet the consensus was, and is, that *The Blessing* is less good than its two predecessors. And this judgment does seem connected to the book's 'Frenchness'. The *TLS* thought it naïvely done; more penetratingly, Philip Hensher described Nancy's 'long love affair with France' in *The Blessing* as 'intricate but not deep'. Consequently, although the book is 'excellently done', to him 'it seems a less rooted novel' than the two that went before. This is true, and subtle, but at the same time it raises a question: what *would* Nancy have done next had she not found this new French seam to mine? And – as Hensher implicitly concedes – it does not affect one jot the joy in Nancy's 'marvellous voice, which sounds exactly like someone talking without a moment's notice beforehand'.

In September 1951 Nancy wrote to Hamish Hamilton, saying: 'I know why people (many at least) don't like *The Blessing*. They think all the French characters are stock figures of literature. The trouble is that stock figures of literature (eg the dirty old German professor) exist like anything in real life too . . . I had a terribly nice letter from Mr Maugham [Somerset, that is, who called the book 'extremely shrewd']. He thinks it my best – & he has always lived in France.' She need not have defended herself: 'the public is forking out', as she wrote to Gladwyn Jebb. Clearly her English fans did not mind that Charles-Edouard is an 'impossible marquis'; perhaps they didn't think he was, or they intuited that this wasn't the point. Anyway that was the way they liked their marquises, nonchalant and sexy. Nancy gave them what they wanted, swathed them in the airy silks of her imagination, while all the time stitching away at a tougher, darker fabric. Once again, this was France filtered through Englishness: literally so, when Nanny returns from Paris and starts showing off to her friends. 'Take the shops, dear, they groan with food, just like pre-war . . . animals like elephants. They could have suet every day if they only knew how to make a nice suet pudding. But there is one drawback, nobody there can cook . . .'

The old trick had been pulled; and even the exigent Evelyn Waugh took pleasure in conceding its brilliance. 'You should have seen the genuine schoolgirl delight on *every* face . . . when I brought them the news that you had written a masterpiece', he wrote in April 1951. And in August, more generously yet: 'Reviewers are lazy brutes. They want to say: "Here is another Mitford, sparkling & irresponsible in her own inimitable way." They can't bear to see a writer grow up. They have no influence at all. Everyone I know delights in *The Blessing* and I am constantly buoyed up with pride at the dedication.'

As for what the French thought: one review called *The Blessing* '*un roman d'une elegance rare*'. There may also have been amusement at so much adoration: like Sir Conrad's lover Mrs O'Donovan, Nancy 'belonged to the category of English person ... who can find almost literally nothing to criticise where the French are concerned', and this included not just the *cinq à sept*, the 'rich dark silver' and the *maisons de couture*, but also General de Gaulle, a man who from 1944 onwards did all that he could to be hated by the English. For Nancy, everything that France had to offer was received with a smile. Had Marie Antoinette been French rather than Austrian, she would, as Harold Acton says, almost certainly have been treated with the kindliness bestowed upon Madame de Pompadour.

In *The House of Mitford* it is suggested that this attitude may have 'grated a little' upon the French, 'rather as André Maurois[12] used sometimes to grate on the English; for a prophet can be short of honour not only in his own country, but in one which he has too uncritically adopted.' This book is sometimes hard on Nancy, and offers no particular evidence of its claim. Of course not every French person was as enchanting as Nancy liked to say that they were, and one can imagine the bitchiness that might have been aimed at this bright, somehow vulnerable *Anglaise*, with her girlish enthusiasm and her errant lover. She would have known this, and accepted it as inevitable. At the same time, she never mentions anything of the kind. Aside from the Marie Antoinette controversy, the worst one ever hears is that her French friends considered Fabrice in *The Pursuit of Love* an incredible character – '*je ne marche pas avec Sauveterre*' – mainly because 'no Frenchman would have thrown [Linda's] mink coat away to give her a better one.' She never refers to a quarrel or an unpleasantness; not that she would want to, set as she was upon upholding the belief that, on leaving England, she had escaped 'a sort of brutal island rudeness ... which you never never meet with in France.'

'You know England is getting past a joke', she wrote to Evelyn Waugh in 1949. 'I thought it more terrible than ever when I was there

the other day – everybody so unkind. For instance I went to stay with
my uncle & had to take a station bus from Oxford to Burford. When
we got there I saw my uncle sitting there in his motor & said oh please
stop. "Oh we don't stop there any more" & took me on about 1/4
of a mile, with all my luggage. Now here that simply *couldn't happen*
you know, so much so that when these things overtake me at home I
am so surprised that I almost start to cry.' She continued: 'Have the
English always loved teasing people – I can't help feeling it must be
latent in the character or it wouldn't have come out so strongly . . . Now
the French have a mania for seeing people pleased & happy . . .'. This
sounds, intriguingly, like Nancy describing the two sides of herself.

She maintained contact with English friends, some of whom seem
to have done little to change her opinion of their 'island rudeness'.
Cyril Connolly, told by Evelyn Waugh of Nancy's new 'masterpiece',
is reported to have said: 'Yes. Yes. She keeps at it. I suppose she
is constantly terrified and rightly so by poverty in old age.' Later
Connolly told her that he did not begrudge her success, just as he
would not begrudge a little restaurant that sold good lamb cutlets.
Of course Nancy had mocked Connolly in *The Blessing*, turning him
into the intellectual but lazy Captain, with his left-wing girlfriends
and his love of the high life. It took eighteen months and an effort
from Nancy[13] to heal the breach, although one senses, beyond that, a
niggle that someone he would have considered a lightweight should
be so much better at writing than she ought to be. The jealousy of
men, when it comes to clever women –! or at least to those who are
clever in Nancy's way, which is defiant of category: she was neither
a bluestocking nor a de Vilmorin-style mythologiser of her own wit;
she was simply as talented and intelligent as most of her male friends
but in a wholly feminine way. Peter Rodd – who should have thanked
God for the money that she made – was driven nearly frantic by his
wife's delicious gift. This was partly because of their relationship but
it was also the envy of the failed Balliol man for the female intellectual
savage. Even Gaston Palewski succumbed to jealousy, extraordinary
for a man who so obviously had the upper hand. But how else to
explain the catty little remarks he would throw at her when she read
from her latest writings? *The Blessing*, he said, was 'too slow & had
such dreadful longueurs at the start, & that Nanny must come out as

she was so dull etc etc & I even wondered if H Hamilton would want it'; it is terrible to think how eager she would have been for his praise, and how graceless he was in refusing it. He doubtless resented the fact that she had far more money than he; she was also, at this time, more successful.[14] To his great credit, Evelyn Waugh was completely different in this respect. He treated Nancy's writing purely according to what he saw as its deserts, and was not jealous of her cleverness at all. But then he had no need to be.

Jealous beyond belief, meanwhile, was Violet Trefusis: a writer of sorts but better known as the lover of Vita Sackville-West (and, later, François Mitterrand). Having set up before the war as the English Cultural Ambassadress in Paris, she found Nancy, 'sa grande rivale dans les années 50'[15], a dreadful thorn in her side. But the thorns cut both ways. If Violet ('Auntie') was unhappy about this younger pretender, she still had something Nancy did not: the Légion d'Honneur, given for no good reason in 1950, which she was said to display 'comme un géranium'. This must have been an irritant to Nancy, especially as, according to Harold Acton, Violet's writing was 'no more than an exhibitionist exercise. Unlike Nancy she had a fat independent income.'

Acton cannot hide his dislike for Violet; he calls her 'one of those friends who made one prefer a foe'. Nancy could see another woman as friend and foe at the same time. She and Auntie knew each other well, their Francophilia having created a bond in London – 'Les Françaises Imaginaires', Rebecca West called them – and in Paris they belonged to the same social set. Nancy could not avoid Violet, and in the right mood could relish her, although she was far from delighted when an 'autobiography' entitled Don't Look Round was published in 1953: 'Can you tell me', Nancy asked Acton, with the barely repressed agony of one contemplating an undeserved success, 'why it had what I believe are called "rave notices"???'

Nancy's own suggestion for the book's title was Here Lies Mrs Trefusis. For if Nancy was an exaggerator and an elaborator, Violet was a downright fabricator, claiming for example to be thirtieth in line to the throne (her mother, Alice Keppel, had been the mistress of Edward VII: Violet would hint at her own royal blood). Years later Nancy wrote to Alvilde Lees-Milne with a story that Violet had just told her, of how 'she once had a burning affair with [Count] Ostrorog and got in the family way. I said goodness Violet, where is it? She muttered something about a bumpy taxi . . .' This was irresistible to someone of Nancy's temperament, and explains the perverse pleasure she took in Violet's company. Also they had things in common. As Rebecca West wrote, they were 'both unusually intelligent' and, despite their love of France, they remained intensely English: 'Mrs Trefusis, in the plainest suit by Dior or Cardin, recalled some English opera singer who had specialised in the role of, say, Turandot.'

But Violet lacked what Nancy had in spades – self-discipline – and she could not hide her desire to claw at the pedestal upon which Nancy stood in Paris. She claimed to have had an affair with Gaston Palewski, a story that he sharply kicked into touch: *'étant donné que vous êtes la seule femme à Paris à qui je n'ai jamais fait la cour.'** Later, when Nancy moved to Versailles, Violet was driven mad by the fact that she was not invited to visit: she 'is *déchaînée* [raging] against me', Nancy wrote to Alvilde Lees-Milne. She then reported this conversation: 'N. I say, it's now two years since you wrote to say how vile I am and how everybody hates me. Why all this telephoning all of a sudden?

'V. I'm sorry if I gave offence.

'N. You didn't give offence but you did give me an excuse. Goodbye.'

Violet did in fact pay a last visit to Nancy – 'I can't really keep things up, I mean hates' – then told everybody how ugly she thought the house and everything in it. 'However that's that and I shan't have to see her again.'

Nancy was robust, as people have to be when their lives are dependent upon friends and acquaintances: if one took offence at every remark, one would simply never go out. Nancy was not a sulker. She was delighted to heal the breach with Cyril Connolly, despite his mean-minded criticisms of her book: 'Oh how I love clever people', she wrote to Waugh, giving tidings of this reconciliation. 'Great is my relief – I really minded about Cyril.'

Yet what Nancy really liked was her absorption into French life,

---

* 'Given that you are the only woman in Paris whom I have never tried to seduce.'

which put her at a subtle remove from Trefusis-type behaviour. Living abroad meant liberation to be her best possible self: displacement made her personality more rooted. She could swim in the life that she knew from England, but at the shallow end, without being dragged into its depths. Meanwhile she could lose herself in something else entirely.

She spent holidays, for example, with her 'one really Faubourg friend', the Countess Costa de Beauregard, a half-sister to Violet Hammersley who owned a wonderful eighteenth-century house 'plumb in the battlefield of the Marne'. Although the Valhubert country house in *The Blessing* is in Provence, Nancy was surely describing Fontaines-les-Nonnes, the home of Madame Costa, when she has Grace walk for the first time into 'a huge room, dark and panelled, with a painted ceiling. Furniture was dotted about in it; like shrubs in a desert the pieces seemed to grow where they stood . . . and dotted about among them were human figures. There was an old man painting at an easel, an old lady at a piano playing the Chopin waltz, while another old lady, in the embrasure of a window, was deep in conversation with an ancient priest.' It is a timeless configuration, sunlit and shadowy and infinitely spacious, and one can feel how it would have soothed nerves laid bare by the mad jibes of Violet Trefusis or the jittery affair with Palewski.

Nancy loved to be with old people, especially old ladies (replacement-mothers, as she later suggested); it made her feel secure and comforted to be called 'Child', as she was at Fontaines, where 'nothing has changed for 100 years'[16], where everybody was aged about eighty and where M. le Curé 'has been M. le Curé there since he was 27'. The atmosphere was relaxed, oddly sensual despite Madame Costa's extreme piety (when Nancy was writing her biography of 'the devil' Voltaire[17] she did not dare tell her hostess: 'I smuggle the volumes up to my bedroom like a schoolgirl with *The Green Hat*[18]', she wrote to Harold Acton). The long days were all alike, with variation only in the company at dinner. In England it would probably have bored her to spend the whole of September in the world of 'a Russian play – endless chat, endless leisure, a little plotting, secrets in the charmille', as she described Fontaines in *The Sunday Times*. But this was France, where even boredom and sameness had the power to enliven. Unlike in Chekhov, 'ennui does not exist'.

Of course this was Nancy seeing France *en rose*, as Diana Mosley says. She also stayed at Dolly Radziwill's house at Montredon, near Marseilles: 'Chez la Princesse Radziwill', she headed a 1949 letter to Evelyn Waugh, with the absurdly touching snobbery of a schoolgirl. 'I am here on holiday (holiday from what? as my Nanny used to say) in perfect happiness – boiling heat charming friends & exactly nothing to do except decide at what hour to go down to the rocks & swim.' Yet Diana's memory of Montredon is rather different. 'A few years later I went down there and visited her, and she and the friends lived there in a terrible little cottage, full of mosquitoes, and the field of flowers she had told me about was just sort of dead grass, and when you got down to the bottom of the field you had to cross a terrible main road, with enormous lorries pounding along. When you got over that there was the sea, but there were huge rocks, where people had been to the lavatory on the rocks, and paper floating about, and one didn't feel awfully inclined to go into the sea.

'And it was just unbelievable, how she'd transformed it into a kind of paradise. But I think to her, when she wrote all that about it, it became true.'

Small wonder, then, if some English people were worn down by Nancy's rampant Francophilia. *The House of Mitford* says that Evelyn Waugh 'was not the only person to find Nancy a little irritating on the perfections of France. Sydney and Debo used to tease her on the subject'; this rings true. Francophiles have to be careful. The relationship between England and France renders what they say welcome up to a point, because the English like to see themselves as civilised enough to appreciate French living; beyond that point they are on dangerous ground, because they are saying what many English people believe to be the truth and can't bear to acknowledge: that France might be a better place to live. Then the English superiority-inferiority complex comes rushing forth. Then Nancy receives letters like the one about *The Little Hut*, which told her to go back to her Parisian brothels.

There *is* something schoolgirlish about Nancy's obsession with France. She can become slightly – if sweetly – silly on the subject; she acknowledged as much in her portrayal of Grace de Valhubert, described in *Don't Tell Alfred* as 'Idiot, rolling her r's and dressing up French'. Yet to her friends it may not have been Nancy's love of France that annoyed so much as the blitheness with which it was expressed. Happiness in itself can drive other people mad. 'You have made great friends with a Pole who has introduced you to a number of other Poles,' wrote Waugh in 1952.

You have found some Jews for yourself, such as . . . the lady[19] who gave me caviare & pretended to like painting, filling her drawing room with fine works of art and all the time secretly sipping Picasso in her bed-room. You are the kindest possible hospitaller to your distressed fellow countryman. And you spend long hours with the Harveys talking socialism. This is not the France of Louis XIV or Joan of Arc or Bossuet or the Curé d'Ars. All the great Frenchmen & women would repudiate it. Still less is it the real modern France that fills the world with its self pity.

Of course the French have numerous skills and once had the very purest taste. I am told their music-hall songs are very witty.

Anyway your 'France' is pure fantasy . . .

Which made no difference to Nancy, who would have screamed with laughter over this letter, have seen the truth in it and found it wholly irrelevant. Her France, as Waugh surely understood, was a writer's construct. It was something she dreamed into life with her yearning sophisticate's soul. It was not fairyland, it demanded daily compromise, but it was the place where Nancy could live according to her philosophy. She did not believe that the pursuit of happiness was immoral; if anything, she saw it as the means to morality. 'ONE . . . thinks everybody should have everything & all forms of bliss – the difference between HERE & THERE, really.' Nancy knew, few better, the stoicism required by her epicurean faith; to which she adhered as surely as her friend did to the Catholic Church.

In 1954 she published the finest expression of her love for France, a life of Madame de Pompadour. The idea came from Pamela Berry, who clearly understood the Mitford idiom – 'When will you realise you must write a book about Pompadour? . . . I so ache for it' – and it was brilliant. 'Hamish Ham wants me to do it as a novel & that I won't (can't really)', wrote Nancy to Evelyn Waugh in February 1953, using the solidity of his advice as a sounding board. 'On no account a novel,' he replied. 'Write for the sort of reader who knows Louis XV furniture when she sees it but thinks Louis XV was son of Louis XIV and had his head cut off.'

Waugh had learned to advise according to Nancy's instincts; what he said is what she did; and it worked wonderfully. From the first paragraph, assured and clear to the point of funniness – 'the Duc de Bouillon, wearing a black feather, went out on to the balcony and announced to a waiting crowd, curious but not sad, "Le Roi est mort". He retired into the palace, put on a white feather, came back and announced "Vive le Roi"' – Nancy's readers had the comfortable sense that she knew what she was doing. It has been said, and not just by A.J.P. Taylor, that what she was *really* doing was taking the world of her two best novels and erecting it in the palace of Versailles, casting Fabrice as Louis XV and assorted Radlett girls as Pomp. The similarity between Nancy's novels and her historical biographies (of which she eventually wrote four) is considerable; yet this comes back to the voice, the approach, the divine simplicity with which she ordered her thoughts and opinions. *Madame de Pompadour* does indeed read as easily and astutely as *Love in a Cold Climate*. But this is not because she recast her favourite characters as eighteenth-century French nobility; it is because she continued to use her technique of '*racontez, racontez*', understanding very well that history is still a story to be told.

What she also did – and this was where she revitalised the genre of historical biography, as no writer had since Lytton Strachey[20] – was use her great gift of bringing characters to recognisable life. 'When she gossiped to her friends about Pompadour or Voltaire or Richelieu,' says her nephew Alexander Mosley, 'she wasn't talking about Versailles two hundred years ago. When she gossiped about these things they came alive.' And they *were* alive to her: her ability to perceive motivation, the jealousies or lusts or idiocies that could influence events to an alarmingly disproportionate extent, was just as strong when she considered 'historical personages' as when writing about Linda Radlett, or her own friends. Nancy loved and revered learning, but she had no false awe for the concept of 'history'. She simply saw things as they were, whether in the 1950s or the 1750s. It was inconceivable that there should be a difference. She would make this clear in a 1966 ABC television interview about her Louis XIV biography, *The Sun King*. Her questioner suggests that life at Versailles would have constituted a particularly 'complicated network' of love affairs and intrigues; at which Nancy shrieks (no other word for it) with laughter and says, 'I'm afraid that's life, nothing to do with Versailles, come now – it's only that they had different sorts of names!'

So what brings *Pomp* and its characters to absolute life is the fact that Nancy absolutely saw the life in them all. She also saw herself – 'They were all exactly like ONE, that's the truth!' – but this was wishful thinking as much as anything: she *wanted* to resemble Madame de Pompadour. One can quarrel with some of her interpretations. Raymond Mortimer, who said that the book read 'as if an enchantingly clever woman was pouring out the story to me on the telephone', nonetheless suggested 'that she might not say Louis XV was perfect heaven 3 times on one page'. Nancy does, indeed, exonerate Louis of the charge laid upon him in Cyril Connolly's faintly patronising review, that 'a more lethargic, ungrateful or frivolous monarch has seldom reigned, nor one who took over so prosperous and devoted a nation when he came of age to leave it so impoverished and discontented.' She also acquits Madame de Pompadour on various counts, among them that 'she made permanent use of the secret police' and had what Connolly calls 'an element of cold rancour'. (Connolly is wrong to say that Nancy 'does not mention the rumour that [the Duc de] Choiseul was her lover'; she did, if only to dismiss it.)

What Nancy mainly does, however, is what she always does: by tracing events as they happen, in context, from an intensely personal point of view, she infuses them with an understanding so clear that it bursts forth into benevolence. For example what Connolly calls Pompadour's 'political ambition' becomes, under Nancy's close and convincing inspection, not sinister but rather absurd. She writes of her going off to negotiate the 1756 Treaty of Versailles in 'a bustle of self-importance . . . But how many women in her place would have had the strength of mind to refuse?' Of course a 'serious' historian might find this sort of interpretation irrelevant, and Harold Nicolson wrote that it was 'not history', whatever that means; but the fact is that just because an event – such as the Seven Years War – acquired massive significance, this does not mean that those involved were not also, at the time, subject to less elevated concerns. A perfect example of her understanding is this, on a consequence of the Seven Years War: 'In the nineteenth century the French could not forgive Louis XV for the loss of their colonies, but while it was happening they hardly noticed it.'

And for all her lightness of touch – far harder to achieve than seriousness, just as a soufflé requires more work than a bread pudding – Nancy was an assiduous researcher, fascinated by what she was doing. This was appreciated by one historian at least, Dr Alfred Cobban of London University, who wrote to her: 'he'll bet my reviewers have never read an original 18th century document, or any secondary stuff since Carlyle. Wouldn't they be furious at this news!' The work that she put into *Pompadour* was difficult, and not made easier by her method ('what my old nanny used to call "rockabye"'[21]): 'My system is pathetic, I don't know how to take notes, no French book has an index', she wrote to her friend Billa Harrod in May 1953. 'I have no memory, so I have to read all of every source before writing each sentence. However the result seems rather good, to *me*(!)'

It was an extraordinarily fresh and clever approach to non-fiction: what Evelyn Waugh said of Nancy's journalism, that it would make her 'what is known as a "pioneer"', was really far truer of her historical biographies. *Pompadour* especially has a sense of glorious liberation about it. It seems to have been written empirically, with Nancy thinking at the start that she had no notion of how to do it, and discovering at the end that she had known all along. The deployment of telling little phrases – as when she says that Louis XV felt at ease with the Duc de Choiseul because he 'did not go droning on about things'; or that 'Madame de Pompadour was one of those rare women who know exactly when, and how, to make a scene' – had always been her way of bringing her narratives to life, and this was no different.

She knew that she had taken a risk with its style, but she knew no other successful way in which to write. At first, or so she said, she saw the book as 'Miss Mitford's sober and scholarly work'. Raymond Mortimer shattered this idea by telling her 'I feel that the whole enterprise is questionable' – how pompous – because the style was 'so remote from what had ever been used for biography'. Nancy was rattled by this, as who would not be, and in a letter to Evelyn Waugh she wrote that she had 'nearly *died* on the way' to meet Hamish Hamilton for dinner after sending him the manuscript. 'However, radiant smiles & (verbal) caresses, so the dear girl will see the light of day, Oh the comfort 'tis to me.' Hamilton knew that his prize author[22] had headed in another winner. Despite the thumbing of certain scholarly noses it was received more open-mindedly than might have been expected: it is not accurate to say, as *The House of Mitford* does, that 'reviewers were cold'. The *Telegraph* wrote: 'This is history – authentic history – without tears', a near-perfect summation. And Evelyn Waugh – *cher maître* – understood precisely Nancy's cleverness and originality. As he made clear in a letter from 1959, written about *Voltaire in Love* but equally applicable to *Pompadour*: 'I enjoyed it hugely at the first reading but I didn't appreciate it. You write so deceptively frivolously that one races on chuckling from page to page without noticing the solid structure . . . I can now realise what an achievement of research, selection & arrangement you apparently effortlessly performed. It is a masterly book.'

There are things in *Pompadour* that seem – to a contemporary reader at least – deliberately written to antagonise. 'Madame de Pompadour's excursion into politics will not give much satisfaction to the feminist', she writes; one feels with some pleasure. 'Although she was prettier, better educated, and had a more natural motive for her activities, she was no more successful than those ladies who adorn to-day the *Chambre des Députés* . . . To her, as to most women, politics were a question of personalities.' It is a powerful contradiction – or apparent contradiction – in Nancy that she loved to 'ride my anti feminist hobby horse', while living according to feminist principles. She was the bread-winner in her marriage; she worked almost until the day she died; she made a truly independent existence. *Faute de mieux*, one might say, and some do say. Who knows? What one *does* know is that, despite – or perhaps because of – the fact that she was a successful woman in her own right, she was always at pains to extol old-style femininity. She eulogises Northey, in *Don't Tell Alfred*, as 'the last of the charmers'; and a male character shudders at the 'new ones' who 'make me despair of the female sex'. Alexander Mosley says that Nancy 'held the view that women can exert a great deal of influence behind the scenes, as mistresses, wives, mothers, hostesses'. It is in this capacity – as someone who knew how to handle the King of France for twenty years – that she most admires Madame de Pompadour. It is almost as though Nancy feared that her own cleverness – frankly superior to that of most people, including men – would lead her to be considered 'unfeminine'. Her love life would have given her no cause for confidence on this score. So it is not, perhaps, surprising that she should lay such stress upon the traditional feminine ideal, and should glorify Pompadour for her cleverness in submitting to the King's will while exerting her own, and for being 'the acme of prettiness'.

Prettiness, indeed, is what one remembers most from *Madame de Pompadour*. The book gleams in the mind like a room in the Wallace Collection. One is left with an impression of a ball at the Hôtel de Ville in Paris, whose 'walls were of pink marble and trellis work filled with vine leaves, bunches of grapes and flowers'; of the staircase leading to La Pompadour's rooms at Versailles, 'lacquered by Martin in the bright delicate colours she loved'; of the tiny theatre in the palace 'decorated by Perot and Boucher'; above all of the Marquise herself, an exquisite doll come to life, shell-pink lace at her neck and breast, her cheeks tinged sweetly darker. She suffered ill-health all her life and died with 'her lungs full of water, or pus' at the age of forty-three. Yet to look at her portrait one would never have known that her ruffles and rouge concealed anything but happiness, ease, an ordered contentment with life at its most pleasurable and civilised.

CHAPTER 10

'After this a very great dullness fell upon the Château of Versailles.'

The last line of *Madame de Pompadour*; one of the finest last lines ever written; and after 1957 dullness began to fall upon Nancy also. 'I was sorry to see the end of 1956, which I greatly enjoyed', she wrote to Evelyn Waugh. It was almost as if she had guessed that her enchanted life was about to become more sombre. She had been almost ten years in Rue Monsieur, the boudoir in which her own King could come and find her, although less regularly and devotedly than Louis XV did Pompadour; not an ideal situation but the best that Nancy could hope for, and true to her creed she made the best of it. Then in July 1957 she learned that Gaston Palewski had been appointed French Ambassador to Rome. She was in Venice when she heard the news, and instantly cabled to him: 'O DESESPOIR. O RAGE. O FELICITATIONS. NANCY'.

It was not the end of their affair, but it was never the same again. The appointment enabled Palewski to detach himself, as twenty years earlier Nancy had done from her family. What had kept her going, despite the knowledge that Palewski was '*l'un qui se laisse aimer*', had been the sweet balm of contact: the letters and telephone chats, the lunches and parties at which they were more than likely to see one another. From this, Nancy wove her picture of a love affair. She did not exactly deceive herself, in a way she knew the score all too horribly well, but she managed to make of flimsy stuff something exquisite. In her book she wrote of Louis XV's vast Bourbon sexual appetite, which had frequently to be gratified by court ladies and tarts, saying, 'It is clear that what the King did not want was another Madame de Pompadour; he had already got one, he loved her, was used to her, and she suited him perfectly.' This was perhaps an expression of the hope that she held in her heart, that she was by no means all to Gaston Palewski but that she was something that the others were not.

Which was true, up to a point; as John Julius Norwich says, 'she was the best of Gaston, really.' But she had allowed him to be too sure of her. She had not, as Pompadour had, timed her scenes to perfection. So one finds letters such as this sad little series written in September 1954, not long after the publication of *Madame de Pompadour* in America. Although the reviews of the book were not good – 'they say it seems to have been written by Daisy Ashford' – Nancy received an invitation to work for MGM,[1] for a period of up to six months, at a salary of $6,000 a week. 'I wonder if I'd better do it' – nudge nudge – 'as I have no book in view.'

This was clearly intended to get a reaction out of Palewski; which it did, in a way. He wrote to Nancy, in a tone that he would surely not have used with his other women, to say that he was depressed and exhausted. Although he did not really want her, he did not want her to be independent, and she fell for it immediately. Her alertness to his every mood – few of which he seems to have spared her – was acute, naive, Nancy all over. 'I've been thrown into a turmoil by your letter . . . if you are sad, as I can see you are, & if your prospects are no better I can't go away for months & leave you alone. Or am I no good to you? Oh how I wish I could open you like a book & see what is there. Nobody has ever been such a riddle to me.' This was La Pompadour again, who on her deathbed told the Duc de Choiseul that her lover had been '*indéchiffrable*' [indecipherable] to her. Palewski could never have said this of Nancy, whose heart was laid out for him to walk on; but it was too late now for her to play games, and in a sense her dignity was of a superior kind. All she could do was try to make him happy enough to make her happy also. Which meant, as had always been inevitable, that 'after 2 days of slight hysteria' she decided not to go to America. 'I realised that it's not a question of whether you need me or not – the point is that I can't live without you.' Oh, Nancy.

It was a small sensation when Nancy turned down the MGM deal: mouth agape, the *Telegraph* told its readers that 'Nancy Mitford has rejected one of the largest offers ever made by a film company to an English writer . . . She explained to her friends that she "prefers to stay

in Europe".' Some of these friends – Marie-Laure de Noailles for one
– *'can't* get *over* me refusing all that cash!!' as Nancy wrote to Gaston.
One might say that women are divided into those who would have
been cool enough to go off to America and let the man stew, and those
who would give up something worth having for a man who did not
even really want them. 'Women are divided into two categories', as
Nancy wrote in *Pigeon Pie*, 'those who can deal with the men they are
in love with, and those who cannot.' Few women ever handled their
man less cleverly than Nancy. For all her trickiness she was as sincere
in love as a puppy gazing at its owner. The detachment and deceit of
which she was capable deserted her completely; perhaps this, more
than anything, shows that her nature was warm deep down.

There is something almost unbearable in this would-be sage
outpouring, written to Palewski in 1954. 'You know Colonel you have
let yourself get too depressed & if you go on you will be ill. You've
stayed too long in Paris & life has got out of perspective . . . I worry
about you day & night it's dreadful being able to do nothing, except
worry – that's the worst of this sort of relationship, one is really so
helpless. But do listen to me for once & look after yourself.'

And he listened; especially to the advice about getting away from
Paris. In 1954 his 'prospects' had not looked good, but he had worked
hard throughout the long absence of de Gaulle, and, having been
elected a deputy by the department of the Seine, joined the government
of Edgar Faure in 1956. A year later the greatest prize so far came his
way. He had asked for the post of Ambassador to Rome, and de Gaulle
– making his sole request of the Government during his wilderness
years – obtained it; then took umbrage when in 1958, at the moment
of his return to power, the new Ambassador did not ask to be recalled
('he never recovered his intimate position as adviser', said Palewski's
obituary in *The Times*. De Gaulle had been confirmed in his view that
Palewski was held back by the *mondain* character that had facilitated
his ascent: like so many, he had the defects of his qualities). So instead
of moving triumphantly into government, Monsieur l'Embrasadeur,
as he became known in Rome, was merrily chasing women in the
Palazzo Farnese: missing Paris, but not enough, freed from his erotic
entanglements and from the guilt that he could not help but feel, being
an essentially decent man, towards Nancy.

He was extremely fond of her, after all. It would be wrong to say – as some commentators do – that his one aim, *au fond*, was to evade her ('If a man wants to leave a woman', wrote Nancy in *Voltaire in Love*, 'he can always find ways and means of doing so': completely true). Palewski – a great haver and eater of cake – didn't *not* want to see her, he loved her company, the charm that remained utterly English (*'la bougie anglaise'*). He loved, too, her love for him. Yet it brought with it an unfortunate sense of responsibility, which he found near impossible to deal with. One can see his problem. And it was profoundly intensified by the fact that he had, before his escape to Rome, been conducting a serious love affair with a woman (also married) who lived very close to Nancy.

Sometimes he must have wished he had never gone to that meeting at the Allies Club back in 1942, and lit a flame in the romantic Mrs Rodd that would never burn out (of course it wouldn't, because it was based so much on illusion, because she had written it into indestructible life, because she was passionately imaginative and he was nonchalantly kind). But what to do in the face of a letter like this one, written in January 1956: 'Colonel I see I have offended you & I am very sorry. I beg your pardon. I only understood in the middle of the night as I lay on my b of d thinking furiously that you had abandoned me because being ill bores you [she had flu at the time]. Suddenly I saw with a great jump what it was' – and she goes on to explain, at complicated length, that she believes him to be upset because she has, in some innocuous way, drawn attention to the fact that she gives him more presents than he gives her. 'I must say everybody knows that all the pretty things in my flat were given me by you & it would seem rather unnatural if I never gave you a present. I apologise. But I think it is a little thing to set against 15 years of faithful & unchanging love.' How on earth would a man, accustomed as he was to self-possessed society women, react to this kind of thing? By not reacting at all, one imagines; he would be too terrified of encouraging more of it. Hence Nancy's characterising of his responses to her outpourings: 'I think you are the most good & charming man in the world ("How true that is"). And my life is a desert without you ("I know I know").'

Palewski was a much better man than Peter Rodd, less frustrated in his life and with the almost disinterested niceness of the true sexual

sophisticate. But the two had this much in common, they both treated
Nancy worse for her good behaviour than they would have done had
she been a tough nut, whose feminine malice they were obliged to
respect. 'You are not the sort of woman of whom men are afraid',
the heroine of Anita Brookner's *Hôtel du Lac* is told, the point being
that she would do better if she were: 'modesty and merit are very
poor cards to hold.' Nancy knew this, and when in later life she was
complimented for her character she wailed: 'I don't want to be kind,
I want to be wicked!' Perhaps above all else she was vulnerable; this
tends to unsettle men, for it makes innate demands upon them that
they dislike having to fulfil. Like Charles-Edouard with his wife
Grace, Palewski had no desire to hurt Nancy. At the same time he had
no desire to stop the behaviour that caused the hurt. It was a situation
that he would have been understandably relieved to escape.

'Margaret tells me that Gaston has got his post in Rome', wrote
Evelyn Waugh to Diana Cooper in August 1957. 'True? Is Nancy
desolate? Does one congratulate or condole?' Diana did not bother
to comment on this – 'I've been a state of bent mealancholly [*sic*]', she
replied, which helps explain why Nancy avoided her company in later
life – but Nancy herself was giving spry, terse news of the appointment
to her friends. 'Colonel very pleased with his new job', she wrote to
Waugh at the end of a fan letter ('The shrieks!') about *The Ordeal of
Gilbert Pinfold*. She was reading this book, an account of Waugh's
brief spell of hallucinatory lunacy, when the news about Palewski
reached her: for a moment it may have seemed as if she herself were
going mad. 'The Colonel is off to the Palais Farnese', Nancy wrote
briskly to Violet Hammersley. 'I thought I'd told you . . . He goes in
October after which I shall be as free as air.' Whether she realised
then how bad the parting would be – that she would see Palewski a
couple of times a year, between the end of 1957 and August 1962 – is
impossible to say. Perhaps she thought that she would be able to visit
Rome, although she must have known this was unlikely. At any rate,
and whatever her feelings, the efforts she made to maintain the 'shop
front' were not this time successful: the rumour mill was grinding
over *Le Colonel et l'Anglaise*.

'She goes on saying that everything is going swimmingly with
the Colonel,' wrote her friend Victor Cunard[2] to Billa Harrod in

August 1957, 'but one goes on hearing rumours that the whole thing is breaking up which, from loyalty, one always denies. But my theory is it really is all over bar the shouting, that all her good spirits (or at least most of them) are a bluff and that her almost savage teasing of friends is a sort of safety valve operation. If I am right it is rather pathetic, because if she would only tell one she is unhappy one would do what one could to comfort her.'

Within this concerned kindness was a subterranean probing pleasure, a readiness to light the touchpaper that will set off a sizzling trail of gossip. Nancy adored Cunard, who introduced her to the idea of spending July in Venice (as she did from 1956 to 1970); but she knew his conversation to be, as Harold Acton put it, 'fraught with infectious malice'. (Later she described, with terrible funniness, sitting beside him throughout the summer of 1960, as he lay dying in an Italian hospital: 'I always thought people on their death-beds lay with angelic smiles saying I forgive you – not old Vic who has cooked up every grievance over a friendship of 25 years to fling at my head.'[3]) Cunard's letter to Billa Harrod has been taken as incontrovertible evidence of Nancy's misery, yet one must bear in mind that these were people to whom stories and scandal were meat and drink. Nancy was not the only exaggerator among them, although like her creation Albertine she had turned it into something of an art form.

This is not to say that Victor Cunard was entirely mistaken. Violet Hammersley also noticed Nancy's strained, zinging manner, and even sweet-scented Acton says that 'Nancy had smiled bravely' through the war, but 'ten years later in time of peace her nerves were more easily frayed'. The point is a slightly different one, about lives that are lived – as Nancy's was – in the constant company of friends. However marvellous one's friends may be, their love is rarely pure and disinterested (not that family members don't let one down, but on the whole the relationship is different: both simpler and more complex). Friends are a source of amusement to one another, and this implies that their lives are up for conversational grabs. What happens to one friend is a story to be offered to another. When Nancy had a row with Victor Cunard, as she did in Venice in 1957, this became something to be picked over with Billa Harrod, who would then dissect it with somebody else – this is in the nature of friendship. It is not necessarily malicious; but nor is it a pointer to absolute truth, because it is always entangled in a web of gossip.

No one did this more than Nancy. She completely understood that it was part of friendship: unless friends could be funny and fascinating about one another, like characters in Choderlos de Laclos, then they might as well be in America, or in the land of abstract conversations inhabited by Fanny's fabulously boring son David ('Zen forbids thought') in *Don't Tell Alfred*. Nancy adored gossip, was 'wildly indiscreet', according to Alexander Mosley: 'you couldn't tell her a secret'. Had it been someone other than herself who rowed with Victor Cunard, *she* would have picked it all over afterwards – what? why? who? – with all the greedy delight of someone winkling the meat from a lobster. 'I had it all like a lovely serial story day by day', she wrote to Waugh, of a lurid saga concerning Cyril Connolly and his then mistress, Barbara Skelton[4]: 'oh *did* I enjoy it.' Graham Greene and his mistress Catherine Walston ('I was surprised, having pictured her scruffy Bloomsbury, to see a Ritz vision in dark mink'; 'What a sexy man he must be, Mr Greene'); Diana Cooper ('Honks is starving at Tring. I expect you knew'); and always, always, Connolly ('Boots . . . lost 21 lbs. Well that is a lot for a shortish man. I think it will be the end of him') are all stuffed into the rumour mill by Nancy and Evelyn Waugh, the handle turned and the screams of laughter – part wicked, part joyful, wholly alive – duly produced. 'She was intensely loyal to her friends,' says Alexander Mosley; 'and intensely disloyal.'

So Nancy accepted that this would be her fate also, that *le tout Paris* would lobster-pick over her affair with the new Ambassador to Rome. Yet she remained an innately private person – like Linda Radlett, she both 'told' and withheld – and this is not such a paradox as it seems. When Victor Cunard said that if only Nancy would talk about her sadness her friends would be able to help her (a very modern idea), he misunderstood something fundamental. Nancy saw her social life as a guard against this kind of honesty: if she were to admit her problems to her friends, in anything other than a manner so overt as to constitute another kind of deflection ('oh I simply *die* for the Colonel'), then this would destroy much of the point of having a social life. To her, public and private behaviour were two separate things. 'Even with close friends she maintained a strict reserve about her deepest emotions', as Harold Acton put it. Later, when she became ill, she would prevent people from visiting her because, as Diana Mosley says, 'she used to feel she had to pull herself together, and she couldn't, always.'

Which would be understandable, were it not for the fact that Nancy's friends were more than just jolly acquaintances. They were an enormous part of her life. From the 1950s onwards, they were almost the *whole* of her life.

She had her sisters, of course. It is strange to picture the woman who created the near-mythic entity of 'The Mitfords' surrounded instead by friends; but that was, in fact, a consequence of Nancy's youthful absorption in family. Now she wanted to put them at a remove. At the same time, and at this remove, her sisters remained as important as ever. 'Her family didn't recede,' says Alexander Mosley. She believed absolutely in the Mitford tie. She saw a good deal of Diana, who had moved to France in 1951 and who was probably the person to whom – despite everything – Nancy felt closest, most equal, most mysteriously similar. She exchanged quantities of letters with Jessica in America ('Darling Sooze') and with Deborah ('Dearest Miss'), with whom she frequently stayed; occasionally she saw Pamela. What she also loved was to be visited by the younger generation of Mitfords, like the Mosley boys or Jonathan Guinness, who brought with them all the pleasure of family but without the suffocation. 'Every Sunday for two summers I'd go round to her,' says Alexander Mosley (as a very young man he worked as a travel courier, and would pass through the Gare du Nord on his way back from Spain). 'Have a bath, a terrific lunch and a long chat. I mean, this is an example of her great kindness. Because she was rather spinsterish in her way, and her life was very nicely organised, and I come blundering in . . . she was a wonderful aunt.'

Nancy had not seen Jessica for seventeen years when her sister also came blundering in, on a visit in August 1955 with her new husband, Robert Treuhaft, and two children. This should have been a glorious reunion but Nancy got extremely cold feet ('I'm half delighted, half terrified'[5]) and absconded to stay with Deborah. Meanwhile, the Treuhafts, all unaware, arrived at Rue Monsieur, were admitted by Nancy's maid Marie, and given the strange news that Madame was *chez la duchesse de Devonshire.* Jessica then – as she later told the story – telephoned Nancy: '"Susan!" "Susan!" "Where are you?" "I'm in your flat!" "You beast, that's frightfully expensive!" Crash!!' Later Nancy rang back and the sisters had 'a lovely chat; as Bob said, "on Debo's nickel".'[6]

But Nancy continued to stay away, and fretted about the presence of Jessica and her family in Rue Monsieur. It was as though she imagined Coca-Cola-swilling yanks among her horribly breakable European bibelots: 'Oh dereling oi am in great and terrible despair', she wrote to Diana '. . . the Treuhafts have moved into Rue Mr., and I can't *bear* it.' Of course this was nonsense. 'In fact they behaved perfectly', she told Diana a couple of days later, 'and I think Marie must have thought I'd quite lost my head . . . Well, I had, too!' Nancy returned to Paris and had an enjoyable time with her sister, to whom she gave fifty pounds, pretending that this was payment for books taken years earlier from Jessica's flat (the books had been worth a few shillings). This episode showed with intense clarity the contradictions in Nancy's nature: the disloyalty and the loyalty, the generosity and the mean-spiritedness, the desire both to maintain a distance and to have it infringed.

Jessica had made a sudden disruptive surge into her life; she wanted to be able to cope but couldn't quite do so. Like a domestic animal, Nancy liked what she was used to. And her habitude by this time was the company of friends and enemy-friends: the couple Dolly Radziwill and Mogens Tvede, the beloved old ladies Violet Hammersley and the Countess Costa, the English girls Pamela Berry, Diana Cooper and Violet Trefusis, the clever boys Cyril Connolly, Raymond Mortimer and James Lees-Milne, the delicious homosexuals Harold Acton, Victor Cunard and Mark Ogilvie-Grant (who now lived in Greece), the charmingly normal Billa Harrod, Cynthia Gladwyn and Alvilde Lees-Milne, the exotic Contessas Christiana Brandolini and Anna-Maria Cicogna (with whom Nancy would stay in Venice, in an apartment in the Dorsoduro). Gaston Palewski was *un autre genre,* but above everything else he was Nancy's friend.

These were people whom she knew very well, who shared her belief in the civilising force of society. Dreadful or dull though they may sometimes have been as individuals, as an entity they were solid, united, dedicated to the now near-extinct cause of adult amusement. They were not people who would have brought their children to dinner parties, or talked school catchment areas across the table. They had servants and no television, which helped; but they did strive for wit and elegance, the things that being adult is supposed to signify but no longer really does. Some of them were batty, but at least they didn't mumble miserably into a wine glass about their mortgage.

So Nancy's friendships were satisfying, sometimes very close. With Mark Ogilvie-Grant, who as Diana says 'was really like a brother to her', or the 'old ladies' Mrs Hammersley and Madame Costa, who were almost like mothers, Nancy did have something like the loving certainty of a blood relationship. This was one of her great comforts. Yet with most of these people, with whom she spent a great deal of her life, the connection was different from what one would find in a family. In a way it was much easier, and the affections more easily displayed. Diana tells of how Nancy would rave about the flat owned by Dolly Radziwill and Mogens Tvede in Paris: 'they had one or two nice things in the flat, and they had a little Rubens on an easel which was sort of the nicest thing they had. Well her description of it, you'd think it was Versailles, the Louvre and the Metropolitan rolled into one – because she was so fond of them! If it had been ours, she would have thought nothing of it. I mean Chatsworth, she was supposed to have said that there was nothing beautiful there, and it's just the most beautiful place one's ever seen. She was very funny in those ways.'

Yet the odd implication is that Nancy was more at ease – more herself – with her sisters than with her friends. If the jealousies were deeper, the emotions stronger, they were still more significant and enduring. The bizarre little episode with Jessica shows as much. The fallings-out within the network of friendship happened in a relatively cool way: people got too close and then got fed up, which again is not the kind of thing that happens in families. In 1962, Nancy wrote about Pamela Berry to Evelyn Waugh (with whom, incidentally, her relationship was just about perfect, mainly because they never saw each other): 'I must tell you that I don't love Pam as I used to. She is spoilt . . . her faults are getting worse and she doesn't mellow.' Now Pam and Nancy had once been thick as thieves – 'I say you and Pam Berry have got crushes on each other', Waugh wrote in 1948 – but it was in the nature of friendship that it should not be a till-death-us-do-part affair, that it should allow freedom and change and all the other things that family does not.

Friendship – for which Nancy had a true gift – made both more and fewer demands upon her than family. In a way it was easier; in another way, it was much more tiring, because it demanded the maintenance of the shop front. Nancy believed so overwhelmingly in social standards, in the self-imposed duty to shriek and be shrieked at, in maintaining what John Julius Norwich calls 'her cool, her sparkle', that her friends could never be people with whom she would sit in her nightdress, clutching a cup of tea, and weeping about why the Colonel hadn't telephoned when he said he would, or what is the point of my existence? What, indeed, would have been the point of *that*?

She believed in 'smiling politeness'. It would have been hell to her to row with Victor Cunard or to snap at Mrs Hammersley: that kind of thing was all very well within the family, but with one's friends? Never. It reduced one to the level of a Violet Trefusis, someone who showed their baser nature in a setting designed, as Nancy saw it, to civilise it out of existence: the irony being, of course, that it was precisely Nancy's attempts to conceal her feelings that led to them being revealed. And this she did not like. She was proud. She wanted to be like the Queen in *La Princesse de Clèves*, the book she had translated in 1950, perhaps paying special attention to this sentence: '*Il semblait qu'elle souffrit sans peine l'attachement du Roi pour la Duchesse de Valentinois, et elle n'en témoignait aucune jalousie; mais elle avait une si profonde dissimulation qu'il était difficile de juger de ses sentiments . . .*'*

So it is not so surprising that Nancy realised more and more the value of solitude. She was, wrote Cynthia Gladwyn after her death, 'something of a recluse'. At the same time, and again this is not such a paradox as it seems, she adored company. But rather than lower by the barest inch her social standards, or deprive herself of what she most valued in social contact – its exquisite freedom from sadness

---

* She seemed unworried by the King's attraction to the Duchess of Valentinois, and untroubled by any jealousy about it; but she dissimulated so well that it was difficult to judge how she really felt . . .

and solemnity, its alternative and dazzling reality – she would choose, increasingly, to be alone.

And this: was it *faute de mieux*? Again, who knows? The desire for a quieter, different life sounds an occasional note through her letters, even in the glory days of the early fifties in Rue Monsieur: 'I'm engulfed in – not work exactly – but sort of work & the Paris season, & feel *frantic and overdone*', Nancy wrote to Evelyn Waugh in May 1952, when life was full of fun and success. 'Too many English, telephone all the morning so that I can't get out of bed, all wanting money – three borrowers yesterday & trying to cope with my sketch', my S. Times article *and* a cocktail party for 150 which I give next week for *Blessing* in French. It's too much. I ought to live in the country at this time of year, but then Col? It's too difficult . . .' Yet she would never have dreamed of giving less than her all to any of it. Scarcely a second of her life was lived on auto-pilot. So remarks like the one to Waugh, about wanting to slip off the merry-go-round, are perfectly understandable; and not to be taken too seriously. Her exhaustion was only what lay, like a tired and happy puppy, on the other side of her buoyancy.

As time went on, however – as she grew older, and the exuberance that had sustained her for ten magnificent years began to drain away – then Nancy was revealed as someone for whom solitude was the natural state. She still went out a lot, but sometimes it was a relief not to: 'No dearest I can't go to a ball even for you', she wrote to Waugh in 1956, in reply to an invitation to his daughter's coming-out dance. 'Ce n'est plus de mon âge & I've no wish to make a guy of myself.'

She was in her fifties by then, although Harold Acton makes constant reference to her ageless appearance and her freedom from illness: 'When I asked her to recommend a Parisian doctor she replied with a faint air of disgust that she had never needed one.' Nancy had a disciplined physicality, utterly natural to her: she was the kind of woman who would spend her days walking about Paris, skittering lightly through her beloved streets, rather than sitting slumped in what she would have called a 'motor'. The reverse of this was that she would also spend long mornings in bed, reading, writing letters, waiting for stamina to flood back into her; it was the same principle as solitude between social engagements. She was physically insubstantial, as unfurnished as a yearling, and what flesh there was dropped away very easily; she also had the lowest blood pressure 'for my age anyone has ever had – & I faint in the morning continually', as she told Evelyn Waugh. At the same time she had a slightly febrile energy; and a tensile toughness, as though her body held within it a steel armature, which had kept her going through the war and kept her young in Paris.

The only real sign of ageing was eye strain, which began in the early 1950s ('I seem to be going blind – can't read all day as I used to'[8]) and was eventually a great problem: 'I am truly very much handicapped now by my eyes being so poorly', she wrote to Waugh in 1960. She also grew lined ('I should love to have my face ironed'[9]), partly no doubt because she relished ninety-degree heat: 'boiling sun oh the bliss'. But this in no way detracted from her attractiveness, which had always lain in her debonair aspect rather than in pulchritude; as her 1966 television appearance shows, her spry and restless elegance was still there at an age when most women have succumbed either to gravity or the knife. Her love of clothes was undiminished and always would be (she is wearing what looks like a Dior on television, smart as you like and *sleeveless*, quite something at the age of sixty-one). Nor did she fear growing old. 'The Col is 50 & *minds*. I've never minded any of the terrible ages that have overtaken me so don't quite understand', she wrote to Waugh in 1951. Of course she was aware of age, as who is not: in 1957 she would write of Voltaire: 'I see him as *old* at 54 and to me 54 *is* old although I'm nearly it.' But she had too little vanity to worry about physical changes. Nor was she insecure in that way; she found it funny, if anything, that she had been urged to wear more make-up by Harold Acton, Raymond Mortimer and Cecil Beaton (the Three Weird Sisters) and that after an attempt to dye her hair she had been asked by her hairdresser: '*Mais qu'est-ce que ce curieux reflet vert?*' Eventually she did rid herself of the grey: 'Have had my hair dyed boot black', she wrote to her mother, '& look *lovely.*'

By the mid-1950s she was starting to slow up, all the same. For ten years or so she had lived on the sheer miraculous thrill of being in France, where the smallest routine moment – the cup of real coffee, the cheerful sound of 'bonjour Madame' instead of the mumbled 'good morning', the emergence from the silent streets around Rue Monsieur on to the wider bustling world of the Boulevard Raspail – had been separate, alive, its every detail lit from within. Now, although the joy of France was as real and strong as ever, the magical fires were burning less brightly. She was getting older; it was as simple as that; and it was part of the joy of Nancy that it had taken her so long to do it.

And so she confronted the square, grey salon at Rue Monsieur, and for a few more years she was contented to be alone there. It was not what she had thought would happen; few people do; but as what she had always known became finally clear, that Gaston Palewski would never marry her, so she began to accept solitude. Occasionally she would throw out this sort of remark – 'Oh how I wish I knew some rich millionaire, it's a thing one needs as one gets older' – and probably, somewhere beneath the joke, she meant it. She never stopped worrying about money although she had plenty. And the thought of being alone at what she called THE END may have occasionally frightened her into thoughts of marriage. But deep down Nancy realised that she was not that kind of woman. 'Nancy, in her heart of hearts, was . . . a bachelor', wrote Harold Acton: it is the most striking sentence of his memoir, and it cuts straight through – as perhaps it needed another bachelor to do – all the triteness of 'oh poor Nancy, the *sadness* of her lonely life'.

'Yes I think Harold was quite right,' says Diana. 'I think she was very happy on her own, and in the end she realised that. She loved people in and out, but didn't really want someone living in the house, you know. I think she was, yes, a natural bachelor.' Debo: 'I don't think she was *ever* lonely.'

Nancy was not the type of woman that she celebrated in her books, who knew how to handle their female destiny. She had wanted to be such a woman: like Coco Chanel she would probably have said that the greatest achievement for any woman was '*être aimée*'. And one might say that she could have achieved this had she only been a better picker of men: that a string of sheerest bad luck had taken her to this solitary place, this bachelor's life.

She would probably not have agreed. She thought that people had more control over their lives than that. Her hysterectomy, of course, had been out of her hands, and it affected – how could it not? – the way she thereafter viewed her life. As often as not, however, what seems like fate is directed by a subliminal choice; or an overt choice, as when Nancy went bravely marching upon Paris at the end of the war, in pursuit of a man whom she knew in her heart could not be captured.

'I wonder if we are all as exactly like ourselves as Voltaire was from the beginning to the end of his life?' she would later ask. One wonders how she would have answered that for herself. Had she always, inevitably, been moving towards life in France? She would not have realised it, of course, as a girl dreaming of love or a wife dreaming of happiness. Nancy had believed in the fulfilment of her female destiny – like her sad twin Jean Rhys, whose exquisite ghost shadowed her along the Left Bank – only to find that she had mysteriously become a writer instead, that the wrong turns of her life had brought her to the right place, that however much this was *faute de mieux* it was also what had been meant.

Nancy's was a writer's life: she was, as Debo said, 'The French Lady Writer'. Yet her temperament was and was not that of an artist. She did and did not detach herself. She did not just imagine; she tried to live what she imagined. She did not just write *Madame de Pompadour*, its world acquired a here-and-now reality for her. The Paris with its new *faubourgs*, where the nobility built their 'pale honey colour' houses and their gardens 'full, in summer, of orange trees and oleander'; Versailles, with its rooms 'crammed to bursting point' and the sound outside the vast windows of 'the King's hunt in the forest': she dreamed these back into life. No wonder she hated finishing the book: 'The trouble is my imagination won't switch off all of THEM at Versailles,' she told Raymond Mortimer almost six months after completion. 'I haven't got them out of my system.' Such was the nature of her artistry. She created her glorious construct of France, through which the spirit of the eighteenth century shimmered; and it did not just infuse her books, it penetrated her life as well. 'She lived as closely to that ideal as she could,' says Alexander Mosley. 'A lovely life, a delightful life.' And that was what she had wanted, what she strived for: *that* was her achievement.

'Most pleasure comes from illusions', she quoted in *Voltaire in Love*, 'and he who has lost them is seldom happy.' After *Pompadour*, a different kind of reality would start to move into Nancy's life. Like 'the poor Marquise', overtaken by the humiliation of her failed role in the Seven Years War, and by the congestion that crept remorselessly through her lungs, Nancy would find the Fragonard colours of her life begin to shadow. But she would cling to her vision of 'a civilised, decorous, beautiful way of living' (Alexander Mosley), and to her philosophy of joy and jokes, which would sustain this brave woman through the encroachment of the great dullness.

The world of *Voltaire in Love*, published in 1957, was as cleverly delineated as that of *Madame de Pompadour*, but it was less intensely a part of her own. This was Nancy's first truly grown-up book. It is marvellous stuff, once again, and she herself thought it her best; yet it has a different quality from the books that had gone before. For the first time, one feels the weight of professionalism upon her. 'How difficult it is to write & in the end what is the aim?' She wrote this in a letter to Evelyn Waugh; a sure sign that she was now doing it for a living.

The research that went into her exposition of the love affair between Voltaire and Emilie, Marquise du Châtelet – 'not an ordinary love. They were not ordinary people' – is truly scholarly in its refusal to treat with anything but meticulously recorded fact. There are no slurrings over, no guesses unless they are admitted to be such, no flights of fancy. There are opinions, of course, but that is different, and anyway they do not take quite so much of the 'Louis XV was really rather a duck'[10] form. *Voltaire in Love* and its successors, *The Sun King*, published in 1966, and *Frederick the Great*, published in 1970, are works of unusual intelligence. They have all Nancy's worldly yet childlike clarity: like *Pompadour*, they are characterised by her grasp of human nature, its influence upon grand 'historical' events. But they are also, somehow, adult books. They do not bubble with the feeling that here are new worlds to be written about; they do not have that quick breath of creativity, that delighted sense of daring, that *love*, in fact, which infuses every sentence of the first four books that Nancy wrote after the war. They are readable, but they are not, like the others, *infinitely* readable; and this can only be because some spark in the author, some spellbinding glee in the discovery of what she was capable of doing, has been replaced by the knowledge of what she can do; and that it is her destiny – her sole destiny – to get on with it.

'I'm in a very bad way', she wrote to Raymond Mortimer, in April 1956 – 'simply cannot work. What can it be, it's not like me. I've cleared the decks to any extent . . . and then I sit playing the wireless & gazing sadly at *La jeunesse de Voltaire* & other tomes & simply can't get on. Of course I'm sure really in my heart that Voltaire is too unattractive – il manque ce côté poètique de Dear Good [Louis XV] & du Châtelet is even worse. I can't say they bore me exactly but they don't inspire me. I don't know whether to go pegging on or chuck the whole thing?'

Things got better, of course; it would be a odd writer who did not know this feeling of Nancy's, this sudden terrible urge, as Harold Pinter once put it, 'to go out and buy a 40 watt lightbulb'. But there remained a distance between Nancy and the characters she wrote about, and she found this difficult to overcome. 'Colonel Voltaire perhaps', she wrote to Waugh, asking him to think of a title – 'really no they aren't very much alike & even I can't make them. As for Emily heaven preserve ONE from being like her' (an interesting aside. The Marquise was an extremely intelligent woman whom Nancy defended as 'miles above' the average; yet she could not bear any implication that this cleverness made Emilie less than feminine in other ways).

It is too simple to say that Nancy could only bring characters to life when she identified with them. Lady Montdore was essentially a fictional creation, who strode light years clear of her factual origins, and no character has ever been more stupendously alive than she. Nonetheless Nancy knew exactly what she was doing with her. She was not of Lady Montdore's world, but she knew it through and through. When the world was not one that she understood with her instinct, and she had instead to use her intellect, her rampaging vitality was naturally quietened.

With Voltaire and Emilie, who lived together in his country house at Cirey, working in their separate quarters – she at her scientific and mathematical books, he at whatever piece of coruscating literature was engaging him at the time – Nancy had to start pretty much from scratch, and it is infinitely to her credit that she fought her way into this semi-lit world and gave it reality. She had touched upon Voltaire before, in *Madame de Pompadour*, where it must be said that he springs into instant life in a way that he does not in *Voltaire in Love*. Impressionistic little asides ('Voltaire, always at his insufferable worst with the King') were what Nancy shone at, and this she could do in the earlier book. As Evelyn Waugh had said to her, however, a writer must be allowed to grow up. And it is astonishing to think that within the uncertain upper-class girl, who had shown off her small facility for modish jokes in *Highland Fling* and had been published chiefly because she was pretty and posh, lay this truly accomplished woman, who thirty years on would be exchanging ideas with the academic Theodore Besterman, whose life's work was the study of Voltaire (as well as editing vast numbers of letters, Besterman wrote a biography published in 1969). If this is auto-didactism, then there is a good deal to be said for it.

Nancy's correspondence with Besterman is a complete joy to read, and remarkably instructive about what she had become by 1956: industrious, incisive, rigorous. The amusing thing is that each clearly thought the other misguided in their opinions, and that it was *they* who understood Voltaire while the other was missing the point. ('Can you imagine', Nancy wrote to Diana, 'giving your life to Voltaire without having one ray of sense of humour?') At the same time there is a mutual respect, although beneath the politeness not much mutual liking, at least not at first: 'Besterman is a very odd creature', Nancy wrote to her mother in April 1957. 'I've seldom disliked anybody so much, & yet he is NOBLE. In spite of the fact that he himself is to write a life of Voltaire he has let me see all the new letters which entirely change the story & which he could easily have kept dark . . . It must have been a temptation – I don't know that I, in his place, would have behaved so well.' Nancy was up against the kind of person she had not dealt with before: a disinterested scholar, to whom suppressing a fact would have been a kind of crime. She was, in a sense, better equipped than he to write about Voltaire, because she understood what he could not, the incongruities of human behaviour. She was better equipped, indeed, because she would have been tempted not to show the new letters: exactly the kind of temptation that Voltaire himself would have felt, and very likely given in to. Yet Besterman brought something out in Nancy that might not otherwise have emerged. It was not just that he showed her the letters (which concern an important love affair of Voltaire's, with his niece Madame Denis, and were crucial to her book). It was that he revealed the intense and absorbing joy of scholarship, which in his naïve way he simply assumed her to feel; so much so that she *did* feel it, and lost her fretful doubts about the whole enterprise. She disagreed with him about almost everything. But in a strange way it was he who brought her book to life.

As soon as Besterman replies to her first, slightly nervous letter, saying that he will lend his help, she is off: 'I really long for a *good gossip* about them all!' she writes, which must have frightened the life out of him. As for what she would have thought, when she asked him to translate Voltaire's phrase '*Vous me l'avez tuée*' and he offered 'Man, you've done 'er': one can only imagine. But he begins to send her the letters that he has already edited ('it is like coming into a lighted room' she wrote to him when the first book arrived, although after a while she would be exhausted by the way these exceedingly expensive volumes kept arriving: 'ruin stares me in the face (not to speak of having to move into a larger flat)'. Then the correspondence begins in fascinated earnest.

On Nancy's side much of it is, indeed, gossip, conducted at the most intelligent level and leavened with spoonfuls of the honeyed, faintly ruthless Mitford charm: 'Oh oh *no* he would *never* have written of Em as ma femme. This is a joke about one of the neighbours . . . oh do agree . . .' she wrote in early 1957; and in May: 'You can't say the love affair had *ordinary* physical foundations . . . They (she and V) slept together of course but that wasn't the basis. Do admit.' Knowing Besterman's near worship of the all-too-human Voltaire she could not resist a tease, and sent this postcard in March: 'Would you say the letters to Mme Denis read like the pornographic outpourings of an old & impotent man? That's what I guess he *was*.' (Back came Besterman's instant reply: 'Yes I felt pornographic ravings would bring an answer by return of post . . .')

What also comes across is Nancy's agonised absorption in her work, the like of which one suspects she had never yet known. In March 1957 she is deep in the book – 'I've bitten off more than I can chew', she flaps to Besterman – and asking for help as and when she needs it. This he gives, in the noble manner that managed to irritate her so much. For example she writes in a panic about the misdating in her book of the new letters: 'You will understand', he ponderously replies, 'why I was so anxious for you not to see the letters until I had dated them.' Panic is barely suppressed in Nancy at this time – 'More & more overworked & flustered' reads a straggly postscript to one letter – and she is horribly indecisive about whether or not to visit Besterman in Geneva: 'The *calme* of total paralysis having descended upon me.' She does visit, is ill and very bored ('I go home today thank goodness', she wrote to her mother in April), but no doubt would have felt that she had not done right by her book, had she not made the effort.

Then, in a letter dated 3 May, she writes to Besterman: 'I was sitting up in bed writing the book when suddenly I finished it!' An extraordinary sensation; and a beautiful one. Whereas finishing *Madame de Pompadour* had been an exquisite wrench, there was nothing but relief in getting shot of Voltaire and his hideous complexities, as it were finally solving him (she hadn't, of course, and went on discussing him for years with Besterman; but by then he was no longer her problem).

She wrote to her mother a couple of weeks after finishing: 'Travail & labour both come from words meaning torture & I'm afraid it generally is.' The book had been desperately hard, not least because her eyes had played up madly – 'I realised last night that I have had a perpetual headache for a whole year' – and because she had been writing the book at the same time as assimilating new material for it. Also, and although she was almost bilingual by this time, it would surely have been more relaxing to read sources in English, rather than to deal continually with niggling questions of translation (she and Besterman exchanged several letters on the meaning of Voltaire's not very important phrase 'voyage de Versailles': 'we seem to be divided by de', Nancy wrote in the end, somewhat shattered by what she clearly saw as Besterman's exigent obtuseness).

One goggles, frankly, at how far Nancy pushed herself with this book – much, much further than *Madame de Pompadour*, which itself had been more taxing than it appeared. Her abilities were revealed by necessity rather than intention: did she, indeed, know how hard it was going to be? Perhaps one should not be so full of amazed admiration – other people write fine historical biographies, after all – but there is something about *her* that inspires it: she was so game, so untutored, so unprepared. Her tremendous natural talents were so remote, really, from this kind of work. She brought them to bear upon it, and through them brought her historical books to life, yet she did so with humility: charm, she knew, was useful, but it was not a substitute for knowing one's stuff.

One imagines her, at her desk or in her bed, where she liked to write for the warmth, outwardly as correct as ever (impossible to think of her slobbing around in a dressing-gown and eating out of a tin), papers strewn about her impeccable person, endless books marked with endless reminder slips, her hands flicking to and fro, searching for a reference then picking up her pen, her eyes painful and screwed, her ear waiting always for a telephone call (*'ma chère Nancy . . .'*), her mind cluttered as one of Pompadour's rooms at Versailles yet remaining, despite it all, clear and bright. What a clever, clever girl; and, as with her friend Noël Coward[11] – in whom she had instantly found a kindred spirit – what grit lay beneath the veneer. They had real substance, these brittle jokers, these entertainers, these weavers of fantasy who knew so much more of life than many a 'serious' writer; how odd that they should be dismissed as lightweights, purely because of the obligation that they felt to hide their efforts: because they felt it bad manners, as much as anything, to let their public ever guess how hard they had worked.

But the reviews did take her seriously, on the whole; no doubt more so than they would today, when the leap from *Noblesse Oblige* to scholarly biography would be a bit too much to take (as if Ian McEwan had suddenly written a joke book). Nevertheless the *Manchester Guardian* could not resist a puritanical mention of the 'stately homes' in which Nancy had written *Voltaire in Love*. In fact, as she told Besterman, these were 'a tiny pub near Venice, a 2 roomed cottage at Hyères and a small château in Seine et Marne': U and Non-U was still rearing its head, jangling its cap and bells at Nancy's reputation. But her book was admired by Bertrand Russell and Harold Nicolson – exigent critics both – and positively adored by Evelyn Waugh, who wrote to praise Nancy's 'unique gift of making the reader feel physically in the presence of your characters'. He went on to say that 'the book should correct two popular heresies 1) Cinema-born, that only beautiful people enjoy fucking 2) Spender-born, that the arts flourish best in a liberal society.'

Meanwhile Theodore Besterman was behaving with utter correctness towards the whirlwind that had blown so violently around his precious manor. Although he complained that he had had 'little acknowledgment' in the reviews (which he was entitled to have expected) he retained his disinterested, essentially benevolent attitude toward Nancy, and by late 1957 she had come to appreciate it. He, in his turn, seems to have fallen *sous le charme*. Their letters grew into expressions of dry fondness, and were about more than just Voltaire; although the presence of '*our friend*' continued to prance elusively through them. What Besterman thought of Nancy's book is a mystery; certainly she didn't think much of his; and what she wrote to him in 1961, after he had sent her the first chapter, is intriguing, firstly in that she dared to do it but also because it sketches her author's philosophy.

But for what public do you write? . . . I think you MUST prune. Remember the old boy himself said 'if you want to bore the public tell it everything' . . . Just an example of what I mean: . . . Richelieu – all you say perfectly true, but he was screamingly funny, that's why they all forgave everything.

There – I'm really very impertinent . . . I'm only thinking of the book as a work of art – it's awfully important to keep your eye on the whole wood & not describe minutely every tree . . .

A couple of weeks later, she continues:

No no Theodore you must not give up. We all (said she presumptuously) have to overcome difficulties when writing any sort of book even dotty ones like mine . . . Only you mustn't confound the letters, which tell all, & the book which tells the essential.

Nancy later confessed (to Peter Quennell) that she found Besterman's biography 'fascinating' but fundamentally wrong: 'It is written with Voltaire himself considered as the only reliable source & without a scrap of fun. The old boy, if he reads it in the Elysian Fields, must be surprised at the way all his wickedness is not only justified but positively sanctified . . .' But these two were such different people, it was inevitable that they would see Voltaire as two different people also. And Nancy found a real satisfaction in having Besterman's solid, irreproachable, unworldly mind to bounce off. Although she was about the least boring person who ever lived, her passions easily became obsessions that not everyone could share; and it gave her intense pleasure to pick them over in what was, indeed, a highly elevated form of gossip. She continued to do it pretty much until she died, taxing Besterman up to THE END with her thoughts on the relationship between Voltaire and Frederick the Great, and on Frederick himself. 'Of course B . . . is absurdly unfair to F & compares him to Hitler', she wrote to Peter Quennell; and then, to Besterman himself: 'But surely Hitler's philosophy was bolstered up by cruelty & the suppression of freedom, two things Frederick abominated? Certainly he was not always true to his ideals – are any of us?'

Besterman wrote in 1970 to tell Nancy how much he had enjoyed *Frederick the Great*. 'Thank you very much for your kind and praising letter', she replied, before launching for the last time into a small flurry of opinions about Voltaire. 'I can't help thinking that he used Frederick too much & loved him not enough', she wrote; an opinion that may have contained other, more personal thoughts. At the end of her letter Nancy says that she hopes to see Besterman in London, but it does not happen. In fact they met only a couple of times. Which was of no importance at all; the friendships that she conducted by letter – the one with Evelyn Waugh being by far the most important – were Nancy's most perfect relationships.

In late 1957, when *Voltaire in Love* had just been published, Nancy wrote to Besterman to take him to task over his interpretation of Voltaire's relationship with his niece. 'Mme Denis. If she was really so much to Voltaire how could he have left her for two whole years?'

For this was the moment when Gaston Palewski left for Rome; and

Nancy was left with her finished book, her intellectual triumphs and a Rue Monsieur no longer painfully enlivened by her lover's sensual, bustling and – of late – occasional presence. She was left, too, without a husband: a strange thing to happen at such a time, that Peter Rodd should agree at last to the divorce that he had resisted for so long.

He had been living a rackety life. In 1953 Nancy reported to Evelyn Waugh that he was on a yacht 'usually tied up at Golfe Juan. He is a perfectly happy human being and the idol of the local population there. He looks exactly like some ancient pirate – bone thin, pitch black, white hair & beard & dressed in literal rags . . . Just at the moment I am on cool terms with the old boy because a form which he must sign in 2 places so that I can recover about £3000 in tax rebate, has just come back after 18 *months* signed in *one* place. It's almost too much to bear . . .' Nancy's success had struck a blow at Peter; while she sailed ever more triumphantly through the civilised world, he abnegated himself from it. It is Basil Seal, from *Black Mischief*, whom he is said to resemble among Waugh's characters, yet there is also a distinct touch of Sebastian Flyte, the beautiful blond boy who cuts adrift from his failure to live up to himself, moves to Morocco, and spends his days drunk, wrecked, not unhappy.

But Peter was not quite done with yet; and by the end of 1957 he had found a new woman. The divorce, Nancy wrote to Theodore Besterman, was 'in aid of Peter marrying some nice rich person . . . I'm all for it.' Besterman had written to offer sympathy after newspapers reported the proceedings; right up to the end, Nancy's marriage was leading her into farcical situations. 'The fact is that 4 judges refused to hear the case because they said they knew me (old dancers I suppose – I had no idea I knew 4 judges!) . . . It all went through yesterday with no trouble.' She must have wished that it had gone through ten years earlier, when she first moved to Rue Monsieur; possibly she had regrets about the whole business, although it had really dragged on too long for that kind of emotion. Above all, Nancy was surely glad that it was over. The long-drawn-out ambivalence of her situation had been symbolised in a funny little feature of her letters to Besterman, some of which are signed 'Mitford' and some 'Rodd': 'Rodd or Mitford absolutely indiscriminately', she told her correspondent, who was clearly bemused as to correct usage – 'I'm equally used to both.' But on a postcard sent in March 1957 she crossed out THE HON. MRS RODD, printed at the top, and wrote 'Nancy Mitford' instead. Perhaps, by then, she had heard about the 'nice rich person'?

It was not edifying, this behaviour of Peter's. Yet Nancy seems to have felt no rancour towards a man who had, on far too many occasions, caused her humiliation, suffering, the anguish of uncertainty. 'He does more damage than a bomb', she said, and meant it; but she also meant it when she said 'old Prod is good at heart'. Remarkably, after such a bad marriage, she retained a kind of fondness for him. Perhaps the relationship had never contained the feelings that lead to hatred. 'It may be necessary to have him certified', wrote Waugh in 1954, when Peter was threatening to sue Ed Stanley (for what he saw as an offensive literary portrait) and Waugh (for his review of the book[12] in which this was contained). 'Do you mind particularly?' To which Nancy replied: 'No doubt Prod is a little bit mad, but that's no reason to mock him & be unkind.'

Her husband had been unkind, however. Nancy had every reason to bear a grudge for his refusal to give her a divorce at the end of the war – an act of selfishness, or weakness, or malice, or all of the above, that had stifled Nancy's enjoyment of her best years with Palewski. Yet it may have been that Peter, without wanting to, had done Nancy a favour by hanging around Rue Monsieur in the late 1940s. The fact of her marriage protected her against another fact: that, even if she had been free, Palewski would not have married her. Peter's presence gave Nancy a beautiful cast-iron explanation for almost anything that went wrong with her lover. Had she and Palewski been able to do as they pleased, it would soon have become clear that what pleased him was not what pleased her. And this grim truth would have been hard to bear, lying like a shadow across her sunlit world.

Perhaps in some obscure way Nancy recognised this, and so did not blame Peter for clinging on: he was her alibi, in the Case of the Unwanted Englishwoman. Nor did she blame him for trying to make her feel guilty, even though his own infidelities had been many and careless. Being the sort of woman she was, Nancy always agonised a little over her marriage. 'I feel very sad about Prod & of course remorse', she wrote when he died in 1968. 'But I couldn't live with him.'

As might have been predicted Peter did not marry again. He continued to drift through his shiftless life, living in Rome after his yacht sank, ending up finally in Malta; humble, dependent upon hand-outs still, Sebastian Flyte at last. Nancy continued to feel a kind of sad responsibility for him. She sent him the odd cheque, and wrote to him up until the end; he died with one of her letters in his hand.

Her divorce had not been a trauma for Nancy; she was tougher than that ('I was looking forward to my day in court') and it had little real significance. But it represented a dismantling of the life she had known. So too did the death of her father, aged eighty, in March 1958.

At the end of the previous year she had paid an extended visit to England, and visited Lord Redesdale for the last time. 'I loathe going there,' she wrote to Besterman, 'it fills me with nervous terror, but I must see my relations who are getting too old to come and see me here.' So she made the journey to Northumberland and Redesdale Cottage, which 'stands in the coldest valley in the north'.[13]

It was a depressing place, but it was the choice that Lord Redesdale had grimly made for himself, the life he had loved with such fierce, bewildered passion having ended with the outbreak of war. 'It is sad', wrote Nancy to Waugh, in reply to a letter of condolence on her father's death, 'but the odd, violent, attractive man he used to be had already gone except for an occasional flash. He was so weak & so very deaf . . .' Two years later she brought him back to life in her last novel, *Don't Tell Alfred*. It must have hurt to conjure Uncle Matthew again – 'it went to my heart to see him now, stiff and slow in his movements' – but Nancy was, yes, tough in some ways, and she knew that in a problematical book she could not leave out such a winner of a character (as he now was to her). Nonetheless the Uncle Matthew of *Don't Tell Alfred* is a diminution of his earlier self. Not in any obvious way; although one has a faint sense that Nancy is basing him upon her own caricature, rather than his reality. But he is still tremendously funny, with his passion for cocktail parties ('don't you have them in Paris?'). He still has the life of 'an old lion', which her father had in fact given up without much of a fight. He is shown gamely going along with the youthful craze for music, so ridiculed in the book as a whole: 'He's not much to look at', says Uncle Matthew, of the pop star with whom he has shared a ride to the British Embassy, 'and his clothes would frighten the birds, but I'm bound to tell you he whacks merry hell out of that guitar. We had tunes all the way here.' His vitality is compared with that of the young characters, and it measures up gloriously ('I'll go and sit down for a few minutes, then I'll be ready for anything').

So it is all there; but the context has changed so much – the life of Alconleigh is so long gone – that Uncle Matthew can only seem displaced and *déraciné*, using as he does every scrap of his resilience to recreate his own world, so solid yet so besieged, within London, Paris, places that are alien to him. 'Such men . . . would not have been themselves had they not always been kings in their own little castles', Fanny says to herself. 'Their kind is vanishing as surely as the peasants, the horses and the avenues, to be replaced, like them, by something less picturesque, more utilitarian.' Unclé Matthew is splendid still, but he is almost unbearably poignant, and all the more so when compared with the quenched reality of Lord Redesdale. Towards the end of *Don't Tell Alfred* he takes his leave of the Embassy, of the book, of Nancy, in a brisk and wholly characteristic exchange: '"I shan't come and disturb you in the morning, Fanny – I know you've never been much use before seven and I want to be off at half-past five. Many thanks . . ."

'"Come again," I said.'

But Uncle Matthew was gone.

The odd thing, perhaps, is that the loss of her mother in 1963 caused Nancy more pain. Not straightforward sadness, as with Lord Redesdale, but something more complex and intense. With her father, although they had seen each other infrequently since her move to France, she had the certain knowledge that there had been love between them, that despite the eccentric flourishes of their relationship it had been fond and warm; she also had the deep satisfaction of having captured this in print, and having given him the great gift of his mythical self. So there was no unfinished business, no residual guilt nor fury in Nancy; only sorrow for what David's life had become, and that so big and vital a man should have ended, as she wrote to Jessica in America, as a box of ashes carried into Swinbrook church: 'in the sort of parcel *he* used to bring back from London, rich thick brown paper & incredibly neat knots . . . Alas one's life.'

With Lady Redesdale, however, the sense of unfinished business grew ever more pressing. The knowledge that her mother's life had been desperate since the outbreak of war did not mitigate her dislike one jot. If anything, the sense that Sydney was entitled to sympathy made her all the more determined not to give it; it was a childlike reaction, and compelling evidence of the 'chill' that could blow through Nancy's heart.

During the happy years of Rue Monsieur she did not give Sydney much real thought. She wrote funny, sharp letters, full of news and jokes. She felt sorry about Unity and the separation from Lord Redesdale, also when Sydney contracted Parkinson's disease; but she was dealing with her mother at the delicious, bubbling remove that had liberated her into happiness and put her in a good temper for ten years, so it was easy to be nice.

Yet as the sparkling tide of her life began to recede, revealing the dark stony rocks beneath, so Nancy returned to the theme of 'My Mother, the Ice Queen'. She channelled into the figure of Sydney a good deal of frustration. In 1962 the 'Mothering the Mitfords' essay was published in *The Sunday Times*, after which Sydney wrote to Nancy, saying: 'It seemed when I read it that everything I had ever done for any of you had turned out wrong and badly, a terrible thought, and can't be remedied now.' Desperately sad; although within this is a delicate sense of someone fingering the guilt that Nancy was undoubtedly – and furiously – feeling. 'Oh what a bad mother I have been, I'm so sorry, what can I do' is a good line and not, one suspects, something that Sydney actually believed.

Most of the Mitfords took Sydney at her own valuation: the other girls did not share Nancy's uncontrollable antipathy. But it is interesting that their father – whom Nancy resembled closely in some ways (more hot blooded than the rest?) – had also moved instinctively away from his wife. The Redesdales still corresponded and they saw each other occasionally, but that was all. It would surely have been better for David had he spent his last years with Sydney, certainly less horribly lonely if they had lived together after the death of Unity in 1948; yet he did not want it. He preferred instead that she should be on Inch Kenneth with her goats, and he in his icebox cottage with the safe stuffed full of firelighters, remote from each other and from life.

Extraordinary, that these two glamorous, characterful people should have ended this way; and all the more so when one thinks of the sure, devoted, unchanging love between the Alconleighs in *The Pursuit of Love*, which has a timeless truth, and which in fact no longer existed at the time that Nancy wrote of it.

At the end, however, there was a kind of *rapprochement*. Sydney visited her husband at his bedside for his eightieth birthday, not long before he died, and according to Diana: 'they seemed to have gone back twenty years to happy days before the tragedies. She sat with him for hours, Debo and I going in and out . . .'[14] Perhaps David remembered the sombre, sensual girl whom he had worshipped, for whom he had bought a peach every Friday evening and with whom he had created this family, these Mitford girls, whose terrifying vitality had brought such quantities of tragedy, joy, shame, triumph.

For Sydney, her girls would bring her more pain before she died: not just Nancy's essay but Jessica's *Hons and Rebels*, published in 1960 and perpetuating to the point of extreme exaggeration the image, started by Nancy, of Sydney as a vague semi-nutter with Christian Scientist views on health. 'Doubtless the author realises how "supremely unpleasant" she makes her family appear', wrote Diana to the *TLS*, emphasising that the portraits of the Redesdales were 'grotesque . . . meant to amuse, rather than to be "wise", "loyal" or "truthful".' Nancy wrote to Jessica, praising the book but saying: 'A slightly cold wind to the heart perhaps – you don't seem very fond of anybody but I suppose the purpose is to make the Swinbrook world seem horrible, to explain why you ran away from it . . .' Sydney would no doubt have smiled at the thought of Nancy accusing her sister of coldness. Yet the difference is there, albeit a subtle one: Jessica's detachment was cheerful and considered, it was a rational act on her part to portray her family as Exhibit U in the Swinbrook museum. With Nancy, despite the control with which she wielded her icicle pen, coldness was not innate in her: it was her way of dealing with blazing emotion.

And she suffered for her mother when she arrived at Inch Kenneth in May 1963, along with all the sisters except Jessica, having been told that Sydney's illness had moved into a critical stage. She was eighty-three; it was not unexpected; yet she fought it off, and in a way that aroused a helplessly characteristic reaction in Nancy. 'Here it goes on & poor Muv is getting so fed up', she wrote to Jessica. 'She scolds us now for "dragging her back from the grave – what for?" But all we have done is give her a little water when she asks which isn't exactly dragging . . .'

More gently, Nancy wrote to Mark Ogilvie-Grant. 'Muv is failing – we are all here – it is very poignant . . . Two days ago she seemed to be going – she said perhaps, who knows, Tom & Bobo & said goodbye to everybody & said if there are things in my will you don't like please alter it. I said but we should go to prison! & she laughed. (She laughs as she always has . . .)' Eleven days later the prolonged scene – the beautiful middle-aged girls drifting around their mother's bedroom, 'half the time in tears & the other half shrieking', their faces perhaps becoming indistinguishable to Sydney – came to an end. 'We took my mother over the water to Mull on a marvellous evening, 8pm, with the bagpipes wailing away, it was very beautiful', Nancy wrote to Evelyn Waugh. It reads like a moment of healing, but it did not last. For the rest of her own life Nancy brooded and agonised over her relationship with Sydney, planning the autobiography that would tell all; a sad, silly thing for so clever and clear-eyed a woman to do, but if the life that she craved was to run its pure and sparkling course, then it needed, more and more, the dark wastegrounds on its banks.

Gaston Palewski had written to Nancy on Inch Kenneth, offering his sympathy (he had met Lady Redesdale – who knew of her daughter's love for the Colonel – and had pronounced her enchantingly patrician when, at their first meal together in 1947, she picked out the truffles from her omelette and left them at the side of her plate). Nancy replied very sombrely. 'I have a feeling nothing really *nice* will ever happen again in my life, things will just go from bad to worse, leading to old age & death.'

Her tone with him was different now. It was wary, as if a terrible hurt had been done to her; she had forgiven, just, but forgetting was utterly out of the question. And she *had* been hurt, to a degree that made the skirt-chasing behaviour of the post-war years look as harmless as a schoolboy's hand in a biscuit barrel.

She had been right to intuit that the posting to Rome (her

unluckiest city; one remembers her honeymoon) would change her relationship with Palewski for ever. What she had not imagined was what she heard in 1961, when she returned from a visit to the Colonel's 'pal-exquis'. The married Frenchwoman – Nancy's near neighbour – with whom he had been having an affair had given birth to his son. The gossip was all over Paris. One hardly dares to think of how Nancy was told the news: at a party, over a glass of champagne? Gleefully? Pityingly? She must have known of this other woman's existence, and would probably have found the thought of her just about bearable; she was used to it, after all. Whether she knew how seriously he took the affair is another story. Her one fear had always been that her lover would meet a woman who was not just an alternative to her, but all things to him. And although she had steeled herself – not least through telling the women in her novels how to cope with infidelity – it is one thing, in a love affair, to be prepared for what one expects. But the unexpected is another thing altogether; and this was a blow that had come out of nowhere.

A cruel blow, too, in the form that it took. Nothing could have hurt Nancy more than to learn that Gaston's other lover was capable of doing what she was not: bearing a child. Of course she was hardly going to fall pregnant at fifty-six (oddly enough, it was at this age that she had, as she put it, 'that utterly boring and pointless curse for the last time'[15]). But the wound of the hysterectomy – and of the miscarriages that had preceded it – would always remain open, and she no doubt tormented herself with the thought of how things might have been, had she been capable of conceiving at the start of her relationship with Palewski. These would not have been logical thoughts. For some time now Nancy had known that she would not marry the Colonel; in her more honest moments she may have recognised that such a marriage would not have been really happy, or even what she wanted. She also knew that children would, for her, have been a mixed blessing. She had known a great happiness that had nothing to do with such things, that had come to her not in spite of freedom, but because of it.

Nonetheless the thought of another woman having Palewski's son would have touched a deep, raw place; it is a near-sickening notion, in fact; and the calmly pompous way in which Palewski wrote to Nancy about '*le petit et gentil element nouveau*' in his life (ensuring that she accepted it with grace, else she would have been attacking the baby rather than his father) would only have probed the wound further. 'Old age & death, what a prospect for us all', she had written to Harold Acton in 1953 – 'and we have no sons to soften them for us when our turn comes.' The tone was lighter then; ten years on she would have felt her words more deeply, and envied Palewski this barely deserved gift from life.

He, meanwhile, was safely in Rome – perhaps just as well for his future parental prospects – and blithely skating over the whole business. He had wanted a son, but he had no intention of marrying the child's mother; indeed he was still willing to go on having and eating as much cake as possible. '*La grande affection que je vous porte n'a en rien diminué*',[16] he wrote to Nancy. She, however, knew that the child had changed things irrevocably; if only in the sense that Palewski was now tied in a way that he had never – most comfortingly for her – been before. 'I wake up in the night & think of your new situation & I *mind*', she wrote in 1962. One year on, the immovable facts – and the buried longings that they stirred up – had become no easier to bear.

The breach was supposed to be healed, all was now supposed to be what Nancy called 'au mieux' between them. Yet in 1962 a letter of Nancy's makes clear that Gaston was indeed detaching himself, just as he had said he wouldn't. Nancy wrote to him more coldly than she would ever have done in the old days, when he would bounce merrily into the Rue Monsieur and demand 'What are the news?' before sweeping her to bed, and testing to the full the ninety copper springs. Her 1962 letter concerned the fact that Palewski had accused her of speaking about him to a journalist. It was a mean thing to have said, impelled by casual disdain for her feelings, and in his more judicious mind he must have known that Nancy, a lady through and through, would never have done it. 'I am most careful never to speak of you. If people say what does Gaston think I say he never talks politics with me & I hardly see him (too true).' Then she goes on, and in a tone she had never used to him before: 'I am all the same a respectable person.

'I always thought you would stand by me whatever happened. You seem only to blame me – it's wrong of you. If I'm supposed to have given an interview I think it should be denied, but I am paralysed by not knowing exactly & by your silence.'

This was bad enough, especially as Gaston did not reply directly to the letter; in July it got worse. Nancy was staying at the Countess Cicogna's flat in Venice when she read in a newspaper of Palewski's imminent marriage. It was only a gossip item, completely false in fact; and somehow one senses that Nancy herself was not convinced of its truth, but used it to say a few things that she thought he should hear. 'But you always said you would tell me – I quite understand not telling because almost too difficult', she wrote. 'All the same I find it odd of you, after a month's silence, to write comme si rien n'était [as if nothing had happened] & ask how I am. I am very sad & also do not know what to do with myself. I can't live in Paris where I miss you more than anywhere . . . So I feel perplexed I must say . . .' What she no doubt wanted was to tell him that he was a complete bastard, but as with the letter written to Hamish St Clair-Erskine when he had broken off their 'engagement', Nancy did not want to look bad in the Colonel's eyes. Rather she wanted him to *feel* bad. But the key line in the letter does indeed ask the unanswerable of this opaque, kindly, selfish man: 'The question is, too, what have I ever been in your life . . . I've never understood.'

A couple of weeks later Nancy wrote to him in a far more friendly, almost normal tone. Around this time Palewski was recalled to Paris, to serve in the government of his old protégé Georges Pompidou as Minister for Scientific Research. So things were back, in a sense, on a stable footing. Nancy knew more or less where she was; not least because she knew where *he* was. But she bravely made the effort to detach herself; she worked hard, she travelled to stay with Deborah at Chatsworth or Lismore Castle in Ireland, she went to Tripoli and Istanbul (which she loved: 'until one has seen this place one hasn't lived'), she spent her regular holidays at Fontaines and in Venice, and she did not, as before, write continually to beg Palewski to join her. Eventually she moved away from Paris and bought a house at Versailles. She had no choice but to accept that their love affair would never be the same again, and did so stoically, remembering that courage is not courage unless it wears a bright smile.

So the moment would never now come when Palewski entered her grey salon at Rue Monsieur and said, as Fabrice du Sauveterre says to Linda: 'I came to tell you that I love you.' Perhaps this explains why the romance of *The Pursuit of Love*, with its bursting happiness and dying rose fragrance, is reprised in Nancy's last novel as something slightly different. In *Don't Tell Alfred*, a conversation between Fanny and Charles-Edouard de Valhubert gives us the more worldly view of Linda and Fabrice's 'great great love':

'Poor Fabrice! He was the most charming person I have ever known, by very far.'

'So was my cousin Linda.'

'Le coquin! You say he hid her in Paris for months and nobody had any idea of it.'

'She wasn't divorced. Besides, she was terrified that her parents would find out.'

'Yes . . . Also I think Fabrice had somebody else – another reason for secrecy. Always these complications!'

Fanny does not react to this, implying that she is completely unshocked by it; yet the reader, poor thing, is not. It feels like an act of near cruelty on Nancy's part, to take that deathless love and, with a casual snap of her fingers, turn it into just another Parisian *liaison*. One senses that it gave her pleasure to do so, pleasure of a satisfying and destructive kind, like tearing to shreds a book of beautiful sonnets given by a faithless lover. Which was exactly what she was doing, in fact.

Don't Tell Alfred, published in 1960, is an unloved novel; even its creator was not very enthused by it. 'I've just written the last words of my book', she told Evelyn Waugh. 'It's not good.' She had thought herself incapable of writing another novel: 'what can I write now?' she asked Theodore Besterman after finishing with Voltaire. 'No good saying a novel, I can't any more.' Perhaps she was thinking of the preface she had written in 1950 (and was rewriting ten years later) about the author of *La Princesse de Clèves*: 'Madame de Lafayette went on writing novels, but her characters never again came to life. At last she seems to have realised this herself; she gave up fiction.'

The consensus is that Nancy should have done the same, that after *The Blessing* she should have stuck to historical biography (although her sales remained high as ever, 50,000 for *Don't Tell Alfred* in the first two months). 'Poor Nancy, I thought when I read it,' says John Julius Norwich: *'It's gone.'* The book was not really about anything. It was just a series of incidents set in the British Embassy, peopled with old favourites – Fanny and Uncle Matthew and the Valhuberts – who were wheeled out like nonagenarian film stars on Oscar night. Nancy frequently said how hard it was to think of plots: 'lacking in creative talent', she said of herself, which was true in one way (she was not an inventor) and false in another (she was an intensely creative interpreter). 'Isn't it agony thinking of things for *them* to do', she had written to Anthony Powell[17] in 1951, 'So unfair too the way Dickens & Co could use opening graveyards, long lost wanderers, & illegitimacy & so on, all closed to us!'

Don't Tell Alfred is indeed unburdened by plot: it meanders along, lightly steered by the ever-satisfying Fanny, and touches amusingly upon the elegant fatuities of French politics (governments formed in the morning and dissolved by evening, which is pretty much what the Fourth Republic was like). Nancy is steeped by now in essence of France, as cosily bedded down as a potted geranium. From her position in the courtyard she views the world that she loves, and tells her relaxed, inconsequential tale. *Et c'est tout.*

But the novel is a little underrated. It contains some highly prescient thought: about the encroachment of America upon the world of European civilisation, about the threat to adult values from the worship of youth culture. And it is written in the Mitfordian voice, clear and benevolent, although devoid by now of romantic idealism. The young heroine, Northey, is an exquisite little tough nut: 'an Arch-shit', according to Christopher Sykes[18], who refused to believe that she was not sleeping with every man in the book (Nancy's original plan). Innocent though Northey is ('I don't hug'), she retains the sentimental, invulnerable aspect of a successful young courtesan, with money in the *Bourse* and a baby badger in her back garden. This is a book in which love is everywhere but has no real power. 'Silly old love', Fanny says to herself; 'bother it.'

This is the book's charm and interest, but commentators seized greedily upon its more 'newsworthy' features: for instance the fictionalized rivalry (dead some thirteen years by then) between the Coopers and the Harveys at the British Embassy. '"Is there any resemblance"', Nancy was forcefully asked by the *Evening Standard*[19], '"between the dragonfly brilliance and beauty of Lady Leone and Lady Diana Duff Cooper . . . ?" Smiling silence.' The interviewer then told Nancy that her depiction of youth culture was dreadful. 'I felt obliged to inform her that . . . although they might have done so when Miss Mitford was a debutante, disc idols no longer "croon" . . . "Oh dear, how silly of me!" she remarked. "I wanted to examine the impact of today's younger generation on people like me. I did try to get it right . . . on a station bookstall I saw a paper called *Disc*, and bought it and enjoyed it very much".'

Nancy does get her young people wrong, so much so that it is unintentionally funny; not something she had managed before. The pop star, Yanky Fonzy, is a stunningly unconvincing creation ('we must keep up the tempo. Where are the kids now?'), as if Noël Coward had created the role of a Hoxton Brit artist ('what a terribly, terribly dirty bed'). One is reminded of what Nancy said about Jane Austen and Siberian peasants. She had used Diana Mosley's sons, Max and Alexander, as her guide: Alexander is the model for Fanny's travel-courier son Basil. But clearly she had not listened very carefully (Alexander never said, for example, of his courier activities, 'I'm the boy wot packs in the meat': a truly Bestermaniac phrase). 'The jargon was so wrong,' he says now. 'Wrong wrong wrong!'

In fact the youth culture in *Don't Tell Alfred* is only really there to show the superiority of the pleasures of adulthood, which is as beautifully depicted as ever; but reviewers latched on to this dreadful failure of Nancy's, and used it to characterise her as 'in no good sense, middle-aged'. 'She goes in for a lot of headshaking – half despondent, half irritable – over the younger generation', said a review in the *Guardian*. Nancy was often accused of hating the new, and she did rail against such things as the despoliation of Venice, the belief that 'London, at least from an architectural point of view, has become a branch of New York', the 'ugliness and mechanisation of modern times' and, later, the Paris *événements* ('Having said how much they [the rioting students] despised everything in life, especially money, they keenly gave the numbers of their postal accounts so that we could hurry out and send them some'[20]).

'I really think that the world today is worse not better? and getting worse all the time?' Nancy wrote in 1966. But these were genuine, one might say justifiable, opinions. They were not an inevitable adjunct to the ageing process; nor were they, as has often been said, evidence of her belief that Progress is Non-U. She had some sympathy with youth, battling its way through the tangled banalities of a world that it supposedly owned: 'young men must suffer when they think that, however much they may protest as students, their future is bounded by office walls, their fame spurs them in vain while the laurels go to pop singers', she wrote in 1968.[21] This was wise, and remains so. Nancy felt alienated from the young, but she also pitied them: 'When we were young every country still had its own architecture and customs and food. Can you ever forget the first sight of Italy?' wrote Nancy in Don't Tell Alfred, speaking her own thoughts through Charles-Edouard de Valhubert. 'But ... our children never saw that world ... There is an immense gap between us and them, caused by unshared experience. Never in history have the past and the present been so different.' Of course Nancy believed that the past was preferable. But it is belittling to say that her stance was purely reactionary. Her view of life required the past to be kept intact; in her own head at least.

A more percipient review of Don't Tell Alfred appeared in the TLS in October 1960. It was probably the most interesting review Nancy ever received, amounting to an assessment of her authorial worth.

'To most of her readers', it said,

the world she describes is as remote as the Mato Grosso, and a great deal more attractive; and where the art of the novel is concerned a certain aristocratic off-handedness may well seem to them as appropriate as it is to the passions and velleities of Miss Mitford's characters. And yet there is, among her admirers, a small and captious minority which insists, when it can get a hearing, that she does not quite do herself justice. They deplore, in short, that one so well equipped to become our foremost writer of serious comedy should fob us off ... with something not far above ramshackle farce ...

Consider her initial advantages: she has a sense of phrase which is, on occasion, marvellously acute . . . She is exceptionally observant . . . She has the magician's art of making people want to read on . . . She has a fine sense of place; and when she is on her best form she can put a human being before us, with just a stroke or two . . .

Against this, she has two characteristics which, though honourable in life, are something of a handicap to a professional novelist. Fundamentally she is reticent, and does not care to intrude too closely upon her characters; and she is not at all malicious. The two together stand for a complete absence of that killer's instinct which is indispensable to the serious novelist. Such a novelist would have forced all Miss Mitford's characters out into the open, with no loss of comic effect. What is now left vague would have been made plain; and we should not feel, as we do now, that Miss Mitford vouchsafes to her public only a part of her true self. There is finer metal in her than is allowed to ring out in *Don't Tell Alfred*.

To which one can only say: '*Discuss*'. Nancy herself was invited to do so, in her 1966 television interview. She deliberately slightly misunderstood what she was being asked, and terrorised her questioner in the process. On the question of reticence, she said: 'It must be a fault of my own, I mean it's nothing to do with my upbringing.' But did she stand too far away from her characters, did she lack the killer instinct? 'Because they're caricatures? They're not exactly caricatures are they? No, I don't think so. I think it's how people are. I don't – no, I don't quite believe that criticism. I see that it's always made.' As for her lack of malice: 'My friends think I'm terribly malicious! . . . Do you think my novels are . . . somebody said they had a soft centre, do you find that? Cedric and Lady Montdore I think I've been quite hard, serious, quite cruel about, no?'

In other words: in Nancy's own view, she wrote the way she did because that was the way that she wrote. This is the question that engaged Evelyn Waugh when she produced her first little masterpiece, *The Pursuit of Love*, and fifteen years later engaged the *TLS* reviewer of *Don't Tell Alfred*. Would she have been a better novelist if she had 'tried harder', gone in further, cut the charm, looked beyond the worlds that she knew and, more importantly, loved? Were her historical biographies better books than her novels, because although she could still use her tricks she was forced into greater rigour? Or was she, as a novelist, the complete item? Would trying harder have taken the edge off her voice, like a singer who practises so many scales that the performance itself becomes perfect, polished and slightly dull? Might she – had she plunged deeper – have lost that strange, tremulous, artless artistry, which sprang as much from her relationship with her life as with her work? One wonders. One thinks so.

Which is not to say that her last two books, *The Sun King* and *Frederick the Great*, were not 'superior' works to *Don't Tell Alfred*: they were superbly done, and when Nancy herself said of *The Sun King* (to Deborah) that 'No more readable book has ever been written in my view!!!!!' she had a point. She chatted about it quite fascinatingly in a companion programme to the 1966 interview, entitled *Nancy Mitford's Versailles*. And, as she talked, one saw the workings of her talent: saw how what reads as the brilliant idiosyncrasy of her mind springs from its absolute clarity.

For example, as she said of Louis XIV: 'he organised things so that everyone was always on the verge of being a little bit late for something – there was never time to plot!' And instantly the court of Versailles comes to life; the reality of her vision switches the imagination on to full power; one sees the great dresses rustling along endless corridors, the proud noblemen reduced to the state of schoolchildren trying to beat the bell for the start of lessons; and one is absorbed in the immediacy of what Nancy saw. Absorbed in her instinctive honesty, direct to the point of funniness. 'I haven't come to much conclusion about what Louis XIV was like,' she told her interviewer, who seemed a little thrown by such frankness. 'So what do you do?' 'Well I've said, here one doesn't know.'

This was her gift: the same gift, really, in every one of her eight post-war books; and, in different form, in her magnificent letters. One can take the opening of *The Pursuit of Love*, written in early 1945:

There is a photograph in existence of Aunt Sadie and her six children sitting round the tea-table at Alconleigh. The table is situated, as it was, is now, and ever shall be, in the hall, in front of an open fire full of logs. Over the chimney-piece plainly visible in the photograph, hangs an entrenching tool, with which, in 1915, Uncle Matthew had whacked to death eight Germans one by one as they crawled out of a dug-out. It is still covered in blood and hairs.

One can take some of the last lines of *Frederick the Great*, written twenty-five years later:

On 15 August he started to work, as usual, at 5 am. The next day he did not wake until 11 am and then tried in vain to give orders to a weeping general. All that day he was dying in his chair. He asked his reader for a chapter of Voltaire's *Précis du Siècle de Louis XV*, but he could not listen to it. Towards the evening he went to sleep again. He awoke at midnight and told the servants to throw a quilt over his dog who was shivering with cold.

And one can take sentences, almost at random, from any of the books in between: 'Lady Montdore, who resented death, clearly thought it most inconsiderate of her sister-in-law to break up their little circle so suddenly'; ' "Ravi de vous voir, ma chère Grace", he said, kissing her hand in his rapid way'; 'Few women would have been so magnanimous, but Madame de Pompadour knew her own worth, she suffered neither from an inferiority nor a superiority complex, she saw herself as she was and on the whole she approved of what she saw'; 'David and Dawn had gone to share a bowl of rice with a friend – they could never say they were dining out, like anybody else'; 'Voltaire's real interest was in the human race, past, present and to come'; 'Louis XIV fell in love with Versailles and Louise de la Vallière at the same time; Versailles was the love of his life'.

And one finds, with a mysterious and satisfying pleasure, that these sentences form a pattern, almost a poem: for all that they trace the changes and movements in Nancy's writing they are entirely and joyfully of a piece: to read them is like looking at the six faces of the Mitford girls and seeing their certain and indissoluble bond. Such is the strength of Nancy's voice. Such was her gift of seeing and imagining with equal intensity. Such was the communion between what she wrote and what she lived.

CHAPTER 11

In 1967 Nancy left Rue Monsieur and moved to a little house at Versailles. And one wonders if she did so because, having written Versailles into life in *Madame de Pompadour* and *The Sun King*, she had fallen in love again.

As a girl she had begun to create her image of Paris, and it had sustained her as surely as meat and drink, had made her happier than anything in the world had ever done. But now, writing as she was about Versailles, lost as she was in what she called the atmosphere of 'an enormous and rather terrifying house party'[1], at which she no doubt thought she would have acquitted herself rather well, she wanted to live anew the reality of what she imagined. Versailles began to take over from Paris; in it she found the purest distillation of all that she loved about France, and life. It was, to her, an absolutely real fantasy. 'I do love Versailles I would like to live here & will when old I mean older', she wrote to her friend Billa Harrod in 1953 during the writing of *Pompadour*.

Thereafter, according to mood, she occasionally returned to the idea of buying herself a house there. 'Went to see the little house at Versailles that I've been hatching for years', she told Violet Hammersley in January 1958 (perhaps Nancy had some intoxicating idea of Palewski coming back to Paris, beating at the door of Rue Monsieur and being told with quiet finality, '*Madame est partie, Monsieur le Colonel*'). 'I think it's now definitely for sale & I shall soon have to decide. Oh goodness!' Two years later she wrote to Jessica that the house had 'fallen through – I am very sorry'. But the thought that she might one day move there lay inside her head, glittering as the château, green and shadowy as le petit Trianon, comforting, as thoughts of a new life always are.

The choice to go to Versailles was easy enough to understand: she was in love with what she had written about it. But her reasons for deciding at last to turn her vague dream into reality, which she did towards the end of 1966, were rather more complex. There was a practical consideration, the uncertain (and expensive) lease on her flat. 'In the Rue Monsieur', says Diana, 'there was a count and countess owned it, and they had five children. Well, in France you can't really get a tenant out, but if it's for your own child then you more or less can. And with Nancy – I mean she was so good in those ways, they'd only have to hint that they wanted it for one of their children and she'd have given it up. That was one reason.

'The other was the garden. You see the garden at Rue Monsieur was completely dark, nothing would grow. She had her geraniums in the yard . . . But she was longing for this *champ-fleuri* that she had in her mind.' Nancy had been brought up a countrywoman. The occasional refrain of 'I long & long & *long* to live quietly in Provence' should not perhaps be taken too seriously, but she did crave air and flowers and birdsong ('an occasional nightingale' was what she hoped to hear in heaven). What she had loved when growing up, as she wrote to Evelyn Waugh in 1964, was 'the suburbs – I always thought they would be the place to live in (any of them in those days) with their pretty little houses buried in lilac & often a paddock or stables like the real country. I hated the real country (boredom) but always longed for fresh air & trees.' The suburbs, to Waugh, were there to be snobbish about (viz. *Scoop*, and Lord Copper's country mansion in East Finchley), and it is possible that Nancy was teasing him a little. Yet it is not hard to see the attraction to someone of her temperament, which liked things controlled and calm and pleasant; nor to see that Versailles (hardly Ealing) would have presented itself as one of the more glamorous examples of suburbia.

There were other, vaguer reasons for leaving Paris. As she approached and passed the age of sixty, Nancy felt that the flame of her life was dimming. The natural instinct towards smiling affirmation was turning, towards sombreness: '*où sont les neiges d'antan?*' 'I think the world is getting horrider more & more quickly. I intend to buy a house in Versailles when I can find one ... I can't always live in a town, not even Paris.'[2] What had once filled her with ecstatic energy could now dance demonically upon her nerves. The sound of children playing outside her window caused her to say: 'When I see [in the paper] fillette dans le coma depuis 4 jours I do so wish it could be all the children in this courtyard.' She had always loved to 'spend the long, hot evenings in my courtyard', reading as the air became 'full of swifts chasing in and out of the houses'.[3] So infantile screams would indeed be an irritant. But hoping – as she wrote in a *Sunday Times* column – for the children to be struck with 'eight mild attacks of laryngitis' was a long way from thinking of comas.

This, again, was mood-related – it is dangerous to extrapolate a state of mind from a throwaway remark – and in 1965 Nancy was still capable of writing to Evelyn Waugh: 'I'm so sorry you are low in spirits. Why don't you come here to have a change? Of course *I* always think one can't be very low in Paris ... !' In fact Nancy's letters from the mid-1960s are as spikily good-natured as ever. She did not move to Versailles – only half an hour from Paris, after all – in the spirit of a poor old lady settling into Sunny Bank Retirement Home. What she probably thought was that the day-to-day happiness she craved would be rediscovered – assured – if she made this change, got her garden, sat in the sun and wrote and dreamed of the Bourbon family up the road.

For there were sadnesses in her life now. Some were quite desperate; and however much she fought to shake off their cold clutch it was impossible ever to be rid of it. 'It's the dropping off of perches', says Aunt Sadie in *Love in a Cold Climate*. 'I've always dreaded when that begins. Soon we shall all have gone – oh well, never mind.' There had been deaths before, of course: 'We must think of Robert [Byron] and Tom [Mitford] today', Nancy wrote to Evelyn Waugh on All Saints' Day 1962 – 'those are the ones I miss the most. It will be nice to see them again, rather soon now.' But the process that Aunt Sadie describes had really begun, for Nancy, with the death of her father in 1958. Once started, it continued with a quiet, remorseless rhythm before which she could only bow her head, giving in and not giving in. She described in 1966 her annual visit to Venice, at which her friends were 'pleased, I think, to see one but the number is terribly diminished.

I had a long talk with Vittorio the bagnino which consisted in him reciting the names of the dead and me saying Oh Vittorio every now and then and crying. It's Victor one misses so much . . .'

Victor Cunard had died in 1960. Then Lady Redesdale in 1963; Violet Hammersley in 1964 ('I've now seen the pathetic last post card saying please tell Nancy I am very ill indeed & can't write'[4]); and Eddy Sackville-West in 1965 ('O dear, I *mind*. Monsewer'[5]). Peter Rodd died of an embolism in 1968, while Nancy was in Venice. Diana saw her walking along the Zattere 'dressed in *black*': a strange and solitary image.

But it was 1966, the year she decided to go to Versailles, that brought loss upon loss. 'All these blows makes one's own end more supportable, there is that to be said.'[6] The Countess Costa de Beauregard died, along with the lovely life at Fontaines that seemed not to have changed for one hundred years; so too did Dolly Radziwill, probably Nancy's closest Parisian friend; and so, in April, did Evelyn Waugh, to whose wife she wrote: 'Oh Laura I am so miserable. I loved Evelyn I really think the best of all my friends . . . As for you, what *can* one say? . . . For him, one can only say he did hate the modern world, which does not become more liveable every day. (It is always my consolation for the death of my brother Tom, how much he would have hated it) . . .' Not long afterwards Nancy talked about Waugh in her television interview. 'Probably my greatest friend I ever had, and I probably admired his work more than anybody else's. What nobody ever remembers about Evelyn is everything with him was jokes. Everything. That's what none of the people who wrote about him seem to have taken into account at all.' Fewer people were getting the joke anymore; the world, as Nancy saw it, was becoming both more serious and more ridiculous. '*C'est à ne rien comprendre*. I shall bury my head like an ostrich at Versailles.'[7]

The loss of that perfect relationship with Waugh – a man who always got the joke, except about Catholicism – was terrible to Nancy. It caught at her writer's self, as well as the self that loved Waugh as a friend. There is a real case for saying that the letters between these two elicited from each their best writing: relaxed to the point of being absurdist, funny to the point of lawlessness. Waugh responded to something in Nancy that no one else seems *quite* to have seen. Despite his pose of treating her as an equal-cum-idiot, he grew to appreciate what she could do as a writer; he regarded her with an absolute respect and understanding perhaps unique among her literary friends and he, more than anyone, probed the deepest nerves of her fantastical humour. Every single one of Nancy's letters is brilliant and readable, but those to Waugh have an extra energy, as if they are making constant little delighted leaps ahead of their own inventiveness: 'The great excitement of the week', she wrote to him in typical vein, back in heavenly 1948, 'has been the death of Pierre Collé, aged 38, of overeating. He *literally* burst . . . then somebody – the restaurateurs probably, had the bright idea of putting it about that it *wasn't only eating*, that he'd had a child at the age of 15 & furthermore that he'd been *too much in aeroplanes* lately.'

Later, in 1961, she had written in all sincerity to quiz him – and tease him – on the subject of the afterlife:

You know *death* – (my brother Tom aged 3 said once Grandfather, you know *adultery* –).

Well, one dies, is buried & rises again & is judged. What happens then between death & the end of the world? Are we what the French would call en liberté provisoire? Do we sleep? But I'm always hearing people say he's in a better place *now* or he knows *now* this that or the other. Do elucidate . . .

Death again . . . If we go to heaven first, then have the resurrection of the body (like finding your motor after a party) & then have the court martial & then go to hell that seems awfully disappointing?

Oh DO TELL.

Which he did, soberly and exhaustively ('No you haven't quite got it right'); living without him must have been so dreary. They had never had a speck of romantic interest in each other, and when they met after Nancy's move to France the occasion ('I die for it') was generally a disappointment, but the love between them was real and alive and utterly *sui generis*. 'People say to me does he love anyone, I say yes He loves *me*.'

Waugh's last letter to her was subdued. 'It is a long time since I wrote to you; so long that I do not know [in fact it was just a month]. I keep getting the news that I am dying and drug-soaked. Not true.'

But the tone was also characteristic.

> M. Bowra's autobiography[8] will be a great disappointment to
> people like Lady Pamela [Berry] who read only for malicious
> gossip. It is really very soft & dull. He said you and I had sexual
> connexions. I explained to him that it was not so & he expunged
> the offending passage.
>   Love E.

Five weeks later Waugh was dead of a heart attack, aged sixty-two. 'Oh
Evil', said Nancy, 'when has one been so sad?' There was no possible
comfort for the loss of Evelyn Waugh, because there was no substitute:
he was wholly individual and thus wholly irreplaceable: there was only
a blank space on the breakfast tray where his letters had once been,
regularly now for twenty years. Compared with such a relationship,
one of the great literary friendships of the twentieth century, 'sexual
connexions' had a lot to live up to.

They did not, of course. Not for Nancy. And here was another
reason why she left Paris for Versailles: *the* reason, according to some.
Her relationship with Gaston Palewski had reached an impasse,
indeed had been at one since he went to Rome. The days of running
back and forth from Rue Monsieur to Rue Bonaparte, of the sudden
telephone summons ('*je vous dérange?*'; '*pas du tout*'), of the delicious
confabs with Marie as to what they might concoct that night for
dinner *à deux*, of the strung-out hours of anguish pierced by sudden
ecstasy; they were over, they would never return. Rather than sitting
there minding about it, why not move?

Nancy knew perfectly well the state of play with the Colonel and,
as with Peter Rodd, she bore him no malice whatsoever. Really he
deserved none; he had simply done what he wanted, pursued his
own happiness, in a way that made it hard for Nancy to pursue hers.
Had he been less fond of her, or handled her with less practised grace,
then she might have found it in her to break the habit of love. But he
did not want to lose her, and she did not want to *want* to lose him. In a
novel she would have made no moral judgment upon him, nor indeed
upon herself: it was just one of those things, beautifully sad, the way
of the world, and she would have portrayed it as such.

Because they were polite and civilised people, with a real affection for each other, the love affair managed to ease itself into friendship. If she suffered about this then one would not have known it. 'Tomorrow is Colonel's party', she wrote cheerfully to Debo in 1966; 'Much agony and ex: about what to wear – I'm all right if it's fine & done for if not. Must flee now . . .' Perhaps there was a relief, in no longer striving to cope with feelings that she knew to be inappropriate. Yet it was an ending all the same, a relinquishing inimical to her nature, to give up on the image of love she had created for Fabrice and Linda, and for herself.

But the thought of the move to Versailles thrilled Nancy. All her girlish passion came flooding back into her sixty-two-year-old body as she dreamed of her garden, her own home, the château around the corner. She gave bubbling paeans to her removal men, whom she must have charmed into near-insensibility: 'They were so adorable – we parted in silence & tears & ENORMOUS tips.'⁹ The smiling tone, first heard in her voice when she moved to Paris in 1945, was firmly back in place; she was ready to find joy once more in the daily consolations of normality. To Alvilde Lees-Milne she wrote: 'All goes swimmingly so far – my neighbours are perfect, sensible and kind, the sort of neighbours one dreams of.' To Deborah: 'Everything to do with the house is made easy and delightful on account of the great sweetness of all concerned . . . You'll have to tell me how to sow grass. Isn't it exciting?' Making a bonfire – 'oh how enjoyable', watching 'rooks flying home', seeing the servant next door 'shutting the shutters. I never saw such a dear old face, like olden times': all these small pleasures gathered themselves together inside Nancy's susceptible soul and lifted her into a state of buoyancy: the state she craved. 'Goodness I long to move.'

And yet. Three weeks later she wrote this, to Mark Ogilvie-Grant: 'I move next week, a week today. Feel as if I were dying.'

For if ever Nancy's imagination was working overtime, it was now. How she had become euphoric about her move to 4 Rue d'Artois at Versailles is one of the great mysteries of her life. Why she moved there is probably the greatest mystery of all. On first seeing the house, one cannot actually believe that this is right; only the plaque outside

that bears her name can convince one that it is, that the magical
Nancy Mitford, who as a girl had been sheltered within a vast baronial
Gloucestershire manor the colour of old gold, who had stepped out
to debutante dances from a Knightsbridge mansion the size of a
hotel, who had conquered Paris from an elegant apartment in the
impeccable 7ème, should have come to end her days in what looks
like an elongated dirty white slum, an ugly peeling rectangular box,
eighteenth century but without a single redeeming bit of prettiness,
stuck between houses on an insignificant street that might be in a
different country, a different world, from the château a bare mile away.
What was she thinking of? Did she believe that she was participating
in some timeless image of French life, making herself a part of these
simple silent streets, with their little grey church around the corner,
the workaday shops nearby, the motor repair shop opposite? Was this
what she wanted, or thought she wanted, after twenty years of the
city and its glittering demands? Was it reassuring to be surrounded
by symbols of 'olden times', by a life that seemed not to have changed,
as Paris in the 1960s was surely changing? Or did Nancy, in some
resigned part of herself, recognise that the yellowing house with the
garden full of birdsong was her resting place, that halfway up the Rue
d'Artois was the end of the road?

Ever polite, Harold Acton writes in his memoir that the house 'was
much prettier in her mind's eye than in reality. Its façade on the street
was unassuming but its interior was adaptable, and she proceeded
to arrange the rooms with discriminating taste . . . For Nancy, the
garden behind the house was the cynosure.'

'When I showed the house to Harold, soon after she died,' says
Diana, 'he couldn't believe it, because he'd had her description. He
said is this really the house? I said yes. Is that the garden? Yes. And he
couldn't get over it.'

It was more than that, however, more than the fact that Nancy
– despite her considerable wealth – had chosen to live in this almost
wilfully plain and provincial home. It was the sense – acknowledged
only obliquely, as in the letter to Mark Ogilvie-Grant – of being in
exile from her own life. She had come to Versailles on what was really
a whim: impelled by a vision that had not in fact existed for two
hundred years. She had left what she knew, the life she had made for

herself with courage and hard work and good fortune; she had done so for reasons that were partly logical and partly obscure; they were not good enough to justify this sudden wrenching change.

But Nancy being Nancy, the brief black moment passed; and she turned her face resolutely to the sun. 'I like the house very much in fact I love it', she wrote to her sister Pamela. 'Yesterday we planted about ten rose trees, two wistaria, two jasmine and other climbers. The walls are old and real, which is by no means always the case at Versailles, and covered with plants growing out of them. Marie is loving it here.' And then she wrote to Mark, as if to cover up – apologise, even – for her sudden lapse into terror: 'I shall never regret coming here I'm sure: at present I'm in a state of wild happiness and if one feels like that in January, what will April bring?'

'It was not – very nice, honestly, the house,' says Debo. 'No – it wasn't really. But she invested it with a sort of glamour. It was perfect, and the blackbirds were perfect, and the cat was a perfect pest, and the poppies were wonderful, and she didn't notice when all the grass went dead. No, she could do that.'

And she could be so touching in the determination to be happy; and in the pleasure that she began to find in flowers and birds, hedgehogs and tortoises. 'Her garden', wrote Acton, 'drew her gently back into the world of children's fairy tales.' It is like at the end of *The Pursuit of Love*, when Linda lies in the Hons' Cupboard waiting for Fabrice, wrapped in a mink coat with her dog beside her, 'reading fairy stories'. Although Nancy's life was now punctuated by seemly, mature activities like listening to the BBC, or writing letters to newspapers, or gardening of a sort, she was also returning to the recessed world of childhood. She longed for a dog, or a rabbit; she wrote that 'My grass is rather tufty so I pretend to be a cow & pluck it with a grazing motion.' It is strange to read of her concern for her tortoise in winter, or her curiosity as to what kind of bird it is who 'honours me all the time and is so pretty' while, in the great grown world outside, *The Sun King* was blazing away at the top of the best-seller list, being praised in cabinet by none other than General de Gaulle and selling 350,000 copies in the five years after publication ('CAN you tell me why?'[10]).

She had not completely turned her back on public life. A 1968 interview with the *Sunday Express* suggested that she had: 'I won't go out to dinner parties any more. Boredom is one thing I cannot put up with. Oh, how I've suffered from the boredom of dinner parties! And from all the fuss of getting one's hair done and getting into a long dress and hiring a car . . . I find myself getting more and more like my father and mother. My father never in his life went out to dinner.' In truth, however, she had one elegant foot still planted in the Faubourg. She visited Paris regularly and received her friends for parties; she dined at the British Embassy with the new ambassador Christopher Soames ('I predict TOTAL SUCCESS'[11]); she saw Palewski from time to time ('I remain your Excellency's humble & obedient servant'[12]); she was in close contact, as ever, with Diana at Orsay; and she was busy with work, fan mail, interviews, the lot.

She was an absolute success by now: unassailable, totemic, 'La Reine Soleil' as she was called in the *Sunday Telegraph*. Her name was constantly in the newspapers. 'Nancy Mitford is moving into a three-bedroom house at Versailles'; 'Mr Justice Stamp heard allegations that considerable parts of a book called *Madame de Pompadour* by Nancy Mitford had been plagiarised'[13]; 'Imagine Nancy Mitford on the shilling counter! Yet that is where I found yesterday a quite presentable hard-backed copy of *The Pursuit of Love*.' Her books were broadcast on the radio.[14] Nancy wrote to the adapter of *Love in a Cold Climate*, aired on *Woman's Hour* in 1969, to say 'I only hope the person who reads it won't "put in too much expression"': a telling concern.

She was interviewed by the *Observer*, a fascinating article in which she was allowed simply to deliver her thoughts about love: 'To fall in love you have to be in the state of mind for it to take, like a disease. You have to be very much wanting it, expecting it. Then if you see anyone and he is at all attractive you are ready to start all the strange imaginings, ready to run around indulging all his most selfish whims. You imagine he has such extraordinary qualities and at the same time you do know partly that he can't quite be like that in reality. There are always those two feelings together.' Such good sense is reassuring even now to read; and according to Nancy was positively gobbled up by her questioner, Mrs Green ('Well it seems all the young people in England are in despair about Love & Mrs Green described this despair so vividly with such a wealth of realism & detail that I soon saw she too was in despair', she wrote to Deborah in 1968. 'She says they all talk non stop about WHAT WENT WRONG? For hours & hours about WWW? I said but how do they have time – I thought they all had jobs? . . .'). How enchantingly robust it all sounds; and how one envies Mrs Green her audience with Nancy.

By the time of this article, in April 1968, Nancy's words were hung upon by many more than just Mrs Green. Her following was immense: the publication of *The Sun King* in 1966 had pushed her into a wider sphere. The book was the perfect vehicle for her mature style. There was no better subject than Louis XIV and Versailles for Nancy to pull off her trick of filtering France through Englishness; she did it stunningly, juggling the myriad glittering balls of the Bourbon family with a conjuror's ease, imparting to the whole enterprise an air of contented relaxation ('Each time [Louis XIV]'s eye slid down this river on the map he was annoyed to be reminded of little Holland'; 'Colbert had one unexpectedly romantic side to his nature: he was a snob'). The result was another example of the theory, or truth, that the best books work on two levels.

On the one hand, Nancy dealt acutely with the king's reign and the role played within it by Versailles. She, like Louis, was obsessively in love with the place, and her love informed and lubricated her book; but she did not describe it as fairyland; she saw, as Bossuet[15] had said, that 'it carried within it the seeds of its own destruction'. She could understand Colbert: 'He hated Versailles, but he alone was capable of producing the enormous sums of money which it swallowed and as soon as he saw that the King was determined to live there he bowed to the inevitable and began to think of ways in which the house could be made to further French commerce'. Her book had grit and perceptiveness, and most reviews treated it accordingly. In *The Sunday Times*, the fond but exigent Raymond Mortimer (whose letters had become substitutes for Waugh's), asked himself if Nancy could 'cope with Louis XIV, so formal, so formidable, and in the second half of his life so earnest in his piety?' She had, thought Mortimer, fudged the fraught subject of Jansenism. Yet in reply to his own question he wrote: 'A decided "yes" is the answer . . .'

On the other hand, *The Sun King* was the kind of book that could be bought for other, less elevated reasons. It was what Nancy called 'one of those picture books which Americans like': a coffee-table book in fact, produced with Hamish Hamilton by a publisher named George Rainbird, who had invented the concept. Nancy hated the idea at first. 'I shall make more money but of course nobody will read it', she had written to Evelyn Waugh in 1964. Like the reviewer in *The Times*, for whom the large colour plates were 'rather crudely done', her instinct was to back off. She came round when Rainbird told her 'he got orders for 100,000 copies at Frankfurt book fair wh, at 3 gns, seems more than promising.'

And so Nancy acquired a yet greater public: not just General de Gaulle but the entire, desperate, please-God-give-me-an-idea Christmas-stocking brigade. Back in 1945, at the end of a hard day in the bookshop Heywood Hill, she had written to Evelyn Waugh that 'two quite separate people came in & asked me to think of a book for the Duke of Beaufort "he *never* reads you know". If somebody could write a book for people who never read they would make a fortune.' *Et voilà*: Nancy had pulled off one more trick.

She continued to work, although she was far too rich to need to. 'I am driven to write', she told the *Sunday Telegraph*, 'by two things: impecuniousness [*sic*] and boredom'. The problem with her eyes had eased – would come and go for the rest of her life – so she seized upon the respite and busied herself. She rewrote a script for a musical of *The Pursuit of Love* ('dialogue terrible'), which opened at the Bristol Old Vic and got no further ('A journalist said to me who is G. Palewski & why did you dedicate your book to him? I said a Frenchman I knew in the war who gave me a hand with street names & so on' . . .[16]). She reviewed the republished Mapp and Lucia books by E.F. Benson: 'No writer nowadays would allow Georgie to do his embroidery and dye his hair and wear his little cape and sit four hours chatting with Lucia and playing celestial Mozartino, without hinting at Boys in the background.' She wrote a marvellous essay ('I've been pegging away for three weeks & seem to be no further forward') on Carlyle's biography of Frederick the Great: 'Unfortunately he [Carlyle] found much that was not grandly true of Frederick; much that he would have liked, but was too honest, to ignore, and much that he failed to understand.'

Her interest in Frederick had derived, in the first instance, from 'his sparring matches with Voltaire'. Then she wanted to write about the man himself: a massive undertaking, which she began in 1968. Possibly she was impelled by what she saw as the magnificent wrongness of Carlyle, who for Nancy was 'at odds with the epoch ... the arts of the eighteenth century were vacant oblivion [to Carlyle], and its enlightenment eternal night.' Nancy may have a 'wrongness' of her own about Frederick, however. There is a slight sense, in her biography, that she is striving for a point of identification: that she has fallen for Frederick chiefly because of his love of France, because he 'wrote and thought and dreamed in French': like ONE. 'It seems to me his reign, after Frederick William's [his brutal father], is into a Watteau out of a Rembrandt', she wrote to Raymond Mortimer, thus revealing her bias. Nonetheless her book is a remarkable achievement; the finest of all in a sense, for in it she took on the enemy, the man who brought about the possibility of a united Germany, for heaven's sake. *Pace* the friendship with Voltaire, her knowledge of the Seven Years War, this was unknown territory. Rainbird, she wrote, 'groans at the prospect & longs for Catherine the Great ... I'm dreadfully afraid the English only like books about Mary Q of S & Marie Antoinette & that new ground won't go down – specially German ground.'

One realises just how daring, how confident in her abilities, how eager to push herself Nancy had become by the end of her career (and one thinks again of *Highland Fling*; who would have believed it possible?) The idea that Catherine the Great was her ideal subject was to misunderstand her. Rather it was to misunderstand what she wanted to be, the ambition she had, at the age of almost sixty-three, to develop as a writer. 'I think if I could bring off this book & if it had the same enormous public as *The Sun King* [which of course it did not] it might do a little good from a European point of view. English people regard F the G as a sort of Hitler I believe.'[17]

She did not see him that way. Nonetheless she was tackling a world that was not just new but in many ways alien (ironically she was helped by Diana's knowledge of German; her sister translated some letters and the book was dedicated to her: 'she never dedicated to any of the sisters except that,' Diana says. 'It's a lovely book I think'). She fought her way past her easy understanding of Frederick's Francophilia, his funniness, his friendship with Voltaire; she sought instead an overview; and she achieved it. It was difficult and that, for her, was the point. As has been said, Nancy was a brave woman.

In late 1968, as she was just getting to grips with her new house and book, Nancy felt a pain in her left leg. 'From November she was saying oh, my leg hurts,' says Diana. It seemed innocuous; like her poor eyesight a reminder, to be accepted with good grace, that she had taken 'one more step towards THE END'. She would have seen it as such. But in fact the pain in her leg was a different sign. It said that the slow encroachment of shadows, the seemly movement into old age, the chance to find resignation and peace, was not to be Nancy's fate: for her, as for the world of Versailles, it would be the sudden fall of a great dullness.

'In '69 she wasn't well,' says Diana. 'And our own doctor, Dumas, felt her tummy and felt something.' He did not tell Nancy much about his findings, simply said that she should rest in bed while awaiting tests. So in March 1969 she was lying there obediently, 'stuffed with drugs', waiting for this unaccustomed pain to pass – as it surely would – when she received a visit from Gaston Palewski. 'Hallo Colonel, I've got cancer', was her not-very-serious greeting. This put him off his stroke. He had come to tell her that he was about to get married.

Having funked it he was forced to return the next day, as there was to be an announcement in *Le Figaro*. This time Nancy was given the news. Palewski, *le célibataire par excellence*, who had once said of marriage that it was '*une terre promise vers laquelle on se promène lentement*', had reached the promised land. At the age of sixty-eight he had become engaged to Violette de Talleyrand-Périgord: extremely rich, recently divorced, and his intended prey for some time now. The marriage was to take place almost immediately, on 20 March 1969.

Was it a shock to Nancy? She had expected it for so long that probably, paradoxically, it was; by 1969 it had come to seem as though it would never happen. What made it worse was that the Colonel's surprises always had an element of refined cruelty to them. His argument had always been that he could not, for the sake of his career, marry a divorcée, and a Protestant one at that; this in itself was ludicrous, as the perceived 'taint' of divorce could hardly have been worse, in the eyes of de Gaulle, than the very real taint of Palewski's obsessive womanising. But by 1969 his political career was over, and he was free to do as he liked. So what he did, with all speed, was become engaged: not to Nancy, but to another divorced Protestant (albeit one with an exceptionally beautiful château, Le Marais).

Of course Palewski was under no obligation to marry Nancy just because it would have been nice for her, because his constant company in her later years would have brought a quiet flame to light her life. As usual, he could not be blamed for the hurt he had caused to her, although there is something quite awful about the way in which he did it. How *could* Palewski have come sidling into Nancy's bedroom and presented her – no doubt in a manner full of due honour and respect – with this sneaky *fait accompli*? And yet, why should he not have done? What did he owe her? It was not his fault that he was stoking the physical pain that had begun its remorseless creep through Nancy's body.

It has been suggested that her illness was connected to Palewski's news: that his marriage brought it on, or made it worse, or removed her will to fight it. The BBC *Omnibus* took this line and, according to Rhoda Koenig in *The Sunday Times*, Nancy 'died soon after reading that [Palewski] was married'.

This, of course, is the ultimate expression of the idea that all the buried sorrows and frustrations had somehow to be released: that over the years they had emerged in glinting little dribs and drabs, as flurries of spite, as lethal teases, as darting attacks; but that now, as Nancy realised that the pursuit of love had led only to failure, so the agony poured out of her in a poisonous stream that flooded her body with pain. How convincing and schematic that sounds; and how insulting, somehow. Nancy would not have thought much of it – she never went in for fitting theories on to life, like lids on to jars that are slightly the wrong size – and her relations did not either. 'Well, no,' says Diana, 'she was ill already when Gaston got married. No that wasn't fair' (to either Nancy or Palewski). Alexander Mosley is even more robust: 'Nonsense.'

That Palewski should have got married when Nancy fell ill was nothing more nor less than our old friend, coincidence. Nor was it the only sorrow that she suffered at this time: Mark Ogilvie-Grant died from cancer of the oesophagus in February of that terrible year ('even

you', Waugh would have scolded, 'cannot say blissful blissful 1969'). In
her last letter to Mark she had written: 'I had a dream. Robert [Byron]
rang up from Paris & said he was alive & coming down by the next
train . . .' The deaths were starting to overwhelm her. 'Oh the Reaper',
she wrote to Cecil Beaton. Yet what the Colonel had done stirred up a
different kind of pain, compounded of betrayal and humiliation and
impotence, spiced to burning point with a sense of having been the
worst kind of fool for twenty-five years. Nancy could do nothing but
lie there in her silent bedroom, on her own small wheel of fire, and
submit to it all. In April 1969 she wrote a letter full of honesty and
obfuscation to Deborah (by now her most cherished correspondent):

Colonel (married) has just been. He makes that face – 'it's all too silly'. He's
to go on living rue Bonaparte . . .

  Well I did the tests, it was like a horror-comic. No meal, but much
worse, a large jug full of liquid was injected taking 10 minutes . . . Then
they kept on leaving me naked in pitch darkness which at first
I thought was to reduce me to obedience but after a while I realised
they were developing the photographs in a kitchen sink next door
like children with a Brownie . . . The snaps have just arrived & lumpling is
terrifying simply huge. I wonder if it's my twin brother (it has happened
I believe) little old Lord Redesdale shrieking away . . . hope he can cook.

And for bravery of that kind one can forgive, very easily indeed, these
feminine digs at poor harmless Madame Violette Palewski, which
Nancy sewed firmly into a subsequent letter to Alvilde Lees-Milne:

She's a sort of dead person, an anti-person, always very amiable but with
no apparent reason for being on this earth. He's to go on living in the Rue
Bonaparte & the Marais at weekends.

  My health drags on the same . . .

By this time the other Mitford girls were sensing the presence of
danger and, like loyal animals, had begun to close around Nancy's bed.
'Woman [Pam] was wonderful', she wrote to her friend Viscountess
Mersey in April, from the Clinique Georges Bizet in Paris. 'Somebody
told me I ought to have a companion for my tortoise so she went out &

got one . . . As for Elle [Deborah] one can't help noticing that she only comes when there are wills in the wind – when I see that large black plastic bag & large, welling with croc tears, blue eyes I shall know I've had it. Saint [Diana] says she will be here throughout which is too good & holy. In short my sisters are perfect not that I doubted it.'

What they knew, and Nancy did not, was that the operation in Paris had found 'an enormous tumour', says Diana, 'which was partly on the liver' (the advanced nature of this cancer does raise the question of whether Nancy was feeling ill before November 1968, and had not wanted to admit it).

Debo stayed with me at the Temple [the Mosleys' house at Orsay] for the operation. We were all day at the hospital and then two days running we could not get hold of the surgeon. And I said to the sister: we must be allowed, as the family, to see the surgeon and find out what the prognosis is. 'Il est parti, Madame, non il est parti ∴.': so. So I think Kit said you must, you must ask the surgeon to ring up tonight, and we gave the number.

I can see us now. We were sitting at the Temple, out of doors, it was a lovely evening and – telephone. And it was the surgeon. And he said: 'I'm afraid it was cancer'. 'Oh'. He said, 'she might live two months, or it might be three, but it's gone up into her liver, and although I took the tumour out there are sort of little bits in the liver, and I took as much liver as I could away but I had to leave some.'

So I went back to Kit and Debo, and we began to cry. I think we cried for about three days. And we kept going to see Nancy and pretending we were cheerful, and she was saying 'I'm terribly well! The pain has quite gone!', and all that. And we had been told two or three months.

Neither Diana nor Deborah was willing to say this to Nancy; although Jessica (who visited France that summer), schooled in the American way of Total Honesty, thought they were wrong: 'She said we ought to have told her,' says Diana. 'But you see she was really a nervous person, I think it would have been an awful mistake myself.' Of course this was true. Above all Nancy required her illusions. Had she been waiting for the hangman she would have sought to believe in an eleventh-hour reprieve; this was not much different.

It created a problem, however. In the scheme of things it seemed unimportant, yet Diana understood that it was anything but. After her operation Nancy had restarted work on *Frederick the Great*, but in a desultory way: 'N says she has got on so well with the book that there is absolutely no hurry', Diana wrote to Debo. 'This kills one with guilt, in case finally she reproaches & says I *could* have gone quicker & finished if I'd known. So I have got a plot to ask the man they all like at Rainbird to ask her as a great favour to let them have it sooner – telling him why.' Thus it was that Nancy wrote to her friend Joy Law (who had done the Rainbird picture research for *The Sun King*), saying that she really had to get cracking with *Frederick*: 'it seems Hamilton have got a poor list for '71.'

As it happened, Jessica was proved wrong, as was the surgeon, for in fact the operation upon Nancy's cancer was completely successful. She did not have two or three months to live. And she managed – as she would surely not have done, had she expected to die at any moment – to visit Germany (with Pam and the Laws) in October 1969 and collect material for her book. She finished soon afterwards.

She suffered pain throughout 1969, sometimes very badly, as in June when she said 'I've had to chuck Venice.' Then in July she was 'better every day – no more bed at all in fact, it is *made*, with its cover . . . went to the hairdresser and walked there and back (only 100 yards, but still).'[18] And in August she wrote:

I'm really cured though I get sort of growing pains which are nasty but bearable. The lump which they carved out (benign like Bossuet) had nothing to do with the back, it was just an extra treat discovered by some busybody while examining me . . .

Frederick whizzes. I sit in the garden scribbling, without specs on account of the brilliant light . . .[19]

As Harold Acton wrote, 'her obsession with Frederick was almost analgesic': the sheer massiveness of the subject kept her going. There is something almost perversely courageous about a woman who writes the most difficult book of her life when her life became most difficult. Even if she did feel a little better by late 1969, believed herself essentially cured, it was still a defiant act of will to go plodding round East Germany and Potsdam in order to recreate Frederick's Prussian

campaigns. Most people would have given it a miss, stayed in bed
with E.F. Benson, written a biography of Mistinguett instead. Nancy's
desire to push on with this serious work suggests a complex inner
bargain: if she resisted the temptation not to write the book, she need
not acknowledge the terrible thing that might stop her. Also there was
something liberating in the work. 'I suppose a cavalry charge must
be the nearest thing to heaven on this earth', she wrote to Raymond
Mortimer. Nancy had a thick vein of steel that had little to do with
her French love of prettiness and *politesse*, that was robust, austere,
almost masculine. It was this unexpected side to her character that led
her to write a long essay on Captain Scott, 'A Bad Time', published in
her collection *The Water Beetle*, which with old-fashioned schoolboy
respect told of male camaraderie, courage half-embarrassed by its own
nobility, excruciating physical hardships. And then, in *Frederick the
Great*, the battle strategies of the Seven Years War are analysed with
an eye so cool, so impersonal, so truly *interested* that one would never
imagine it could delight itself with Dior and Fragonard ('my favourite
painter, the pink bottoms I think are what one can't resist'[20]). Writing
about Frederick freed Nancy's imagination in a way that things closer
to home might not have done at this time: 'I would like to be a pretty
young General and gallop over Europe with Frederick the Great &
never have another ache or pain . . .'.[21]

And although it is probably just another coincidence, when Nancy
finished writing the pain almost instantly returned: 'lancinating,
ghoulish', as Acton puts it. 'She would just sit up in bed and cry with
it', says Deborah, to whom Nancy wrote in January 1970:

Pain killers. If one has a perpetual pain this is what happens. They kill
it. They also give you a headache, make you stupid & stop you going to
the loo. Then after about 4 hours the pain comes back & as well you have
got a headache & can't go to the loo & feel like death as well as having the
pain . . .

If I weren't afraid of it not working & permanently ruining my brain
what there is of it I would have tried to take an overdose of something ages
ago because I would much much sooner be dead than have this awful pain
all the time.

One wonders if it would have been better had Nancy only had three months to live after her operation. Not that she would have agreed. There was Frederick, for one thing, and anyway she had not lost her hope of being cured. Indeed she was planning her next book, a life of Clemenceau: 'He's everything I like – a man of action + intellectual + joker + plenty of documentation (oh yes indeed!)' she told Raymond Mortimer. But in April the illness exerted its iron grip again. She was in the Hôpital Rothschild in Paris:

cast on my book, no pillow, unable to write & almost unable to read, with, as fellow, the wife of a vigneron from Champagne (and I don't mean Odette Pol-Roger!) She refused a chink of window & indeed had to have heavy linoleum curtains drawn over it & DID all night, into a pot between our beds never emptied or covered! Oh Raymond! . . . Colonel came unexpectedly & found them wheeling me back & was so appalled that he told Diana she must get me out . . .

The problem, as Diana says, was that 'they never properly diagnosed her'. Or perhaps this was not such a bad thing? At least not knowing left Nancy with hope ('You may say I long for death well yes, but I long even more to be cured'[22]). At the Rothschild hospital Diana was told that cancer would show up in the tests; 'so when she'd done her awful ten days or whatever it was, Kit and I went to see the head doctor and I said, have you found anything in your microscope? He said: *il y a rien de méchant*. So how can you square that? I used to say to a great friend of mine, it *must* be cancer – and he'd say, of course it must. But they couldn't find it!

'And the old GP at Chatsworth said to Debo, you know, if she'd been an old poor woman and just had one doctor, she'd probably have been a lot better looked after.' In fact Nancy saw thirty-seven doctors, between the time of her first illness and her death four and a half years later. 'She was kept going from pillar to post. Kit would say oh, she must go to London, they're so clever there – and then the London ones were hopeless – you know, it was really awful. I'm sure we didn't do very well. But we did whatever seemed right at the moment.'

In a way, Nancy knew it all already. In *The Sun King* she had displayed an absolute contempt for doctors and their inability to diagnose, cure or save: Fagon, the court doctor, she called the 'killer of princes'. She also wrote:

It is not a very reassuring reflection that in another two hundred and fifty years present day doctors may seem to our descendants as barbarous as Fagon and his colleagues seem to us. The fashionable doctors...stood then as they do now, in admiration of their own science. As now, they talked as if illness and death were mastered...In those days, terrifying in black robes and bonnets, they bled the patient; now, terrifying in white robes and masks, they pump blood into him. The result is the same: the strong live; the weak, after much suffering and expense, both of spirit and of money, die.

The self-possessed clarity of this passage is almost unbearable; all too soon Nancy herself would be at the mercy of these purveyors of 'one worthless formula and another', these thirty-seven men who would take their tests and eventually work out that she was suffering from Hodgkin's disease, or cancer of the lymph glands, said to cause one of the worst two or three pains known to man.[23] Her scepticism about the medical profession, which pervades The Sun King like the stench of disinfectant, was prescient. So too was her description of Louis XIV's own ending. 'His death was long and dreadful and conducted, like his life, with perfect self-control.'

For Nancy's bravery did not falter: the brightness that she had looked for at Versailles had been snuffed, but she continued to flicker with a trembling, determined vitality as the pain ripped through her. 'I've always felt the great importance of getting into the right set at once on arrival in Heaven', she wrote to Raymond Mortimer in October 1970. 'I used to think the Holland House lot would suit me – now I'm not so sure...The thing is, one must be careful in a new place not to get into uncongenial company. Let's make for the same objective – what do you think?' Although Evelyn Waugh wouldn't have thought much of it, Nancy did have a religious sensibility; it bore no relation to any recognised creed, but was connected to her belief that people should strive, and be allowed, to be as happy as possible, and should strive to allow others the same happiness. That a religion might make demands against happiness she found absurd; contrary to God's intention. She saw through the hysterical sacrifices made by Julia in *Brideshead Revisited* ('the God I believe in ... likes people to be happy', Nancy wrote to Waugh) and by Sarah, in Graham Greene's *The End of the Affair*, who renounces her lover having promised God that she will do so if he survives a bomb blast. 'The only thing I couldn't swallow was that she could give up her lover like that ... without having something to put in his place. I know that subconsciously she had something but I don't feel that that's enough ...' Nancy wrote to Waugh. 'The fact that you can write of G. Greene's heroine that "subconsciously she had something" is evidence of worse than defective education.' But Nancy had no time for what she saw as grandiosity. Happiness was too precious a thing to be hurled into an ideal, a concept, that would simply eat it up to no good purpose: *that*, to her, was an act of immorality.

Her life, from 1970 until she died more than three years later, was something close to torture. Its comfortlessness is almost beyond imagining – this wrecked woman lying desperately on the bed in her strange house, so remote somehow from the life that might have brought consolation; her poor skeleton of a body – she weighed around six stone – shaken by tumultuous earthquakes of pain that she was barely able to contain; her head fogged with drugs but fighting for a lucidity that nonetheless brought terror and loneliness, or a frank disbelief that this could now be her life, or thoughts of the Colonel making love to Violette, or memories of the smiles of dead friends, or images of a past life in which Tom and Unity ran lively as puppies and her father cracked his stock-whips outside the windows at Asthall – it was beyond endurance, and yet Nancy endured it, and sought with all she had left in her for joy and jokes, in which she still believed. Even then she would not have exchanged this torture for the two or three months of life that had been assigned to her in 1969. 'Odd as it may seem I get a lot of happiness,' she said. This was her religion: it had a reality, a concreteness, above all an effect upon those who saw it, that went way beyond dramatic abstract gestures.

'Do go on praying', she wrote to her friend Tom Driberg – 'I will let you know what happens'. But, she continued, 'I used to believe so unshakeably in God but I can't any more – or at least ... I feel, like Frederick the Great, that He takes no notice of individuals.' In truth her faith had always been elsewhere: in the possibilities of life itself, in its irreducible gift. And now comfort would be found in the same place as ever: in Nancy herself, in the philosophy that she was called upon now, as never before, to try to live. Two Parisian friends had once taken her to jovial task, because she always described them as 'shrieking' over some joke or other. 'If we were being taken off in a tumbril you would say we were roaring with laughter –!' said her friends. 'Well you probably would be', was Nancy's reply. 'There is always something to laugh at.'

But Nancy's comfort lay also in illusions: 'he who has lost them is seldom happy', she had quoted in *Voltaire in Love*. She had faith, still, in her recovery. She would have found it as hard as anyone to believe that this was happening to her, that her life would never again be more than this dark square of racking pain, that the only respite would be death; she would *not*, in fact, have believed it, and her letters trace a desperate graph that pushes, over and over, up towards hope. 'Very much better', she wrote to Jessica in April 1971, 'cured by an Honest Injun after nameless useless horrors had been perpetrated by the Faculty here. I had: a lumbar puncture AGONY, a major operation AGONY, deep rays SICK & FAINT for a fortnight . . . Anyway I feel much better.' This complicated rigmarole of treatments, by the Fagons of a London hospital, cost around £3,000. It was reported in the *Evening Standard* that Nancy had been 'laid up for the last two years with a bad back', news that produced vast quantities of get-well letters. Six weeks later the pain was as bad as ever before: 'I don't think agony is too strong', she told Raymond Mortimer. 'So I read & read as you may imagine . . .

'Oh Raymond what is to become of me? Colonel says Cécile de R[othschild] pique une depression nerveuse. I say give her a pain in her leg for a week & she'll soon snap out of that. Never has the world seemed more beautiful & agreeable to me than it does now . . .'

She took pleasure, still, in the world outside her window: her *champ-fleuri* garden full of animals and birdsong, in whose beauty she longed to believe, else why was she not still in Paris? Yet this was one of the most pitiable illusions of all. Nancy's dream had been of a cultivated wilderness. She had a horror of the kind of 'lady watercolourist's heaven' described in *The Pursuit of Love* and, says Diana, 'she despised the idea of a lawn. But of course it became a disaster. So sad looking!' Nancy's garden became 'an unkempt jungle'[24]. Any hint of cultivation was smothered beneath tussocks of grass with hay growing out of them; purple cabbage heads poked through the undergrowth. From the bedroom window, however, the garden could be the colour-dotted tangle of Nancy's dreams. As Linda had done from her flat high over Paris, she could watch as 'the skeleton tree-tops began to fill out, they acquired a pinkish tinge, which gradually changed to golden-green'. She could hear the birds. She became absorbed in the activities of some blue tits, 'all in a perpetual rage like an English family on holiday', and nursed a blackbird with a torn wing for two days. 'Fearful drama going on about the blackbirds' nest which has been half blown down while two vile cats sit gazing at it . . . There are still only eggs so it will be a fortnight before the birdies fly', she wrote to Alvilde Lees-Milne. 'I wish you could see the garden now there is this explosion of roses, really wonderful because of the mixture of colours, one forgets how divine it is . . .'

A few days later she wrote again, to tell Alvilde that 'Hassan put his curly head among the roses and announced three half-fledged babies but I dread the day when they fly.' Hassan, a sweet-natured Moroccan boy, had replaced Nancy's beloved Marie, one of the great friends of her life rather than a servant, who stayed with her until 1969. She was then in her seventies, and Nancy wrote that she 'is so affected seeing me like this that it makes her ill, so I'm sending her home to *prendre sa retraite*.' Hassan was a good cook – not that this was much use to Nancy by then – and sought constant small pleasures for his employer: 'he found one of my hedgehogs & brought it in & so on – you know, the sort of person one can do with.' Yet for all his kindness, he was no efficient Normandy housewife; and one has to think that Nancy's sufferings would have been eased by Marie's bustling presence. Her rigorous standards would have imparted a bright cheerfulness, reminding Nancy of a life that was not merely an unpunctuated scream of misery but had its small, sane, civilised routines. As it was, with these props removed, Rue d'Artois became something of a lost house, pervaded by a slow and creeping squalor. 'Hassan had no idea of how to clean anything,' says Diana. 'Nancy had a big bedroom and a big bathroom which was lovely. But the other bath – I think it was poor Woman [Pam] who found out – it was grey, the whole thing. Nobody knows how dirty that house was, it used to worry Woman terribly.' This was the responsibility of the *femme de ménage*, Madame Guimant – 'this scrappy lot of servants costs me £3,000 a year' – who from Diana's account was a poor replacement for Marie; nonetheless Nancy left her 'quite a lot of money'.

But Hassan ('My good Moor') did at least care about Nancy, and this was her comfort, sometimes useless, always essential: that there were people who cared. Her sisters had become rocks. The unsentimental Mitford bond was unbreakable as ever. Diana drove to Versailles constantly. Her relationship with Nancy had not always been easy: her husband had never liked her; the differences between them were more than evident, even though Diana did not at this time know of Nancy's great betrayal during the war; but all that was irrelevant, their closeness was a transcendent thing, and so Diana visited almost every day. 'I used to stand outside the front door and think, what am I going to find? Sometimes agony, and sometimes very high spirits, you know [which may on occasion have been due to the brandy that Nancy – never a drinker – would take to dull the pain]. But she longed for One, and she longed for Pam.'

Pamela was then living in Switzerland, from where she would come to stay; again, the relationship between these two sisters had been difficult, and Pam had much to forgive; again, this was irrelevant. True to form, indeed reassuringly so, Nancy was still 'not always very kind. Sometimes she was longing for her, and then after a bit she got bored. And Woman used to feel well, I've come all this way – I really felt sorry for them both. But she was awfully good, Woman was. Awfully good.' When Nancy felt very ill it was Pamela's pale, soothing presence that she craved.

Deborah, meanwhile, was in constant touch and Jessica made three visits. Her account of the last of these – in a letter to Debo – gives a sense of the fractious horror of pain, the way in which its power, that of a petty and pointless tyrant, can make sympathy hard to give:

Her eyes filled with tears & she said 'everyone says there are masses of roses in the garden, *why* doesn't anyone bring them up here?' So I said I'll dash and get some . . . So N. in cuttingest tones said, 'I see your life doesn't contain much art and grace'. Too true perhaps, but *Hen!* So I got lots more and put 'em round. Nancy: 'I can't think why you didn't get them earlier, you've nothing else to do.' In other words I think she's rather taken against me . . .

To her husband, Jessica wrote: 'As you know we've always been slightly arms-length in contrast with Nancy/Debo, Nancy/Diana or even Nancy/Woman, so it's one of those things where, most likely, one can't do anything right . . .' It was probably true that Jessica would bring the least comfort to Nancy, and feel the least urgency to be with her. Yet Nancy's pitiful snaps, as of a dying Pekinese, were only incidentally aimed at her sister. They were screams, pleas, fury aimed at the pain that pranced through her body with untiring steps, waving its armoury of knives and corkscrews, its fiendish energy gaining ever more strength from her suffering. Jessica was not the issue; nor were Nancy's words to her. Of course a jibe like the 'art and grace' one was in character, but then Nancy was no saint and had never been one: she was simply learning how to die, as Madame de Pompadour had, 'with a courage rare for either sex'.

But the pain ground her down; and it was not always attractive. 'Since living – well, not actually living, co-existing – with Hassan', she wrote to Raymond Mortimer, 'my view of le tiers monde is greatly modified. He is a dear soul but the thought of giving him a vote makes me shriek.' Five years earlier she would have resisted that kind of thing. If she had thought it she would also have thought her way past it; but now, with death clutching at her, she frankly could not be bothered to fight her prejudices. With such remarks she reverted to type, became the kind of person that she had dedicated her life to not being. Nor was it the sum of her opinion about Hassan, of whom she was in fact deeply fond (the last words she ever wrote, in a letter to Palewski, were 'Hassan has been too wonderful'). But it was part of a pattern, the same pattern that was making her turn over in her mind the autobiography that she wanted to write and never would, that *J'accuse* letter directed at her mother.

She could rarely face her friends. Their concern was of course immense. No doubt they found it almost impossible to grasp that the seemingly ageless Nancy should, at the very height of her success, have been felled thus, stripped of her civilised accoutrements and reduced to the gowned anonymity of the hospital patient: it would have been one of those disasters that takes a long time to become real. Nancy herself would have been amazed, had she heard the news. Friends were desperate to help, although sometimes this desire irritated rather than comforted. 'Cynthia [Gladwyn] is the limit', she wrote to Heywood Hill in 1971 –

though all is *so* kindly meant. First she ordered me to drive to the other side of Paris, an hour at least each way, to see a faith healer. As the smallest movement hurts you may imagine what this would have done to me. I wriggled out of that whereupon I get a perfectly raving letter from an RC priest in London (medal enclosed)[25] saying that C had begged him to do what he could for me . . . Meanwhile the Almighty, thinking no doubt that all this was going too far, decided to give me a booster & I had some appalling days . . .

Yet when she felt relatively well, or hopeful, she would still try to see friends. Back in 1970 she had gone to Venice for the last time – Diana saw her off in a wheelchair – and she even spoke of buying a flat there, which implies faith in a cure. Those who saw her seem to have known better: Harold Acton wrote that 'when she moved one pretended to look in another direction', and John Julius Norwich saw her 'lying on a sofa, looking like death. And I only talked to her for five minutes, and I got the feeling that that was actually enough.' This was what she could not bear; failing to relish her social obligations had always destroyed the point of them and, as she would later write to Raymond Mortimer, 'I'm not one of those heroes (do they really exist?) who can be in agony without letting anybody see it, I've had to stop people from coming here it's too depressing.'

But this – as she must have known – was because exile to Versailles had brought so much of her familiar life to an end. 'People would ring up and say could they come,' says Diana, 'and she always said no. And she loved company really, and I used to say don't say no, let them come, and she'd say I can't. They'll come all this way, and then I might have to say they must go away again, I'm in too much pain. Well, it was very thoughtful, but it was really rather a mistake. If it had been Rue Monsieur they'd have looked in the yard, and if someone had said go away they'd have gone away again.'

.   Gaston Palewski, however, visited several times a week. This required an answering effort from Nancy, but one imagines that she would have had it no other way. 'I used to think I wish he'd come,' says Diana, 'and then I'd almost wish he hadn't, do you know what I mean? He tired her quite, because she'd always try to think of things to amuse him, you know. It was quite a drama really.' Although it should not be, illness is a humiliation: a solitary business in a sense, especially to a woman as proud as Nancy. No doubt she was still, in her extremis, worrying about whether the Colonel was worried about her, or whether the sight of her agony was causing him pain. Nevertheless his presence was saying something essential, that her love for him had had significance. He was not merely impelled by guilt, although there may have been a bit of that. Nor was he a saint: at the last lunch party she ever gave, in 1972, when he would have known the importance to her of his presence, he was still making Nancy anxious in the familiar old way – 'Col in a hurry was annoyed by the delays', she wrote – because the food was taking too long in coming.

Yet his great fondness for her was real and solid, as his love had never been: as undeniable now to Nancy as her physical torments. '*Il n'y a pas d'amour, il n'y a que des preuves d'amour*':[26] it was true of affection also, and the proofs were there, day upon day, in the quiet sound of his little spaniel padding about the house, in the feel of his eyes fixed upon her, sparkling and compassionate, in the practised touch of his hand. 'For a few days the King hardly left her room', Nancy had written when she described the death of Madame de Pompadour at Versailles: this, too, had acquired a kind of reality.

Towards the very end there was a further proof, when Palewski helped to get Nancy the Légion d'Honneur that she had longed for. It was awarded in 1972 (the CBE followed soon after). '... you may imagine', she wrote to James Lees-Milne, who had sent congratulations, 'that I am delighted to have been given the only honour I have ever coveted.'

In April 1972 Gaston Palewski came to the ugly white house at Versailles to make Nancy a Chevalier of the Légion d'Honneur. She could barely walk that day, but Diana helped her down the stairs – a child could have carried her – and she stood while the love of her old life pinned the decoration to her dress. The tears poured down her face. It would have been a fitting end to the story; but Nancy still had a year to live, and although it would be filled with horror and agony, moments of 'a pain like the end of the world', she did not yet want to die.

'Various jokes keep one going', Nancy wrote to Jessica in August 1972. They were not necessarily funny; 'unsuccoured', as Diana puts it; but the belief in them remained essential. For instance, at Nancy's final lunch party at Rue d'Artois, Cyril Connolly had done 'that thing I call rude of, as if one's entrée were sure to be uneatable, bringing plover's eggs from Hediard. They were raw.' She was furious, and to Anthony Powell she wrote: 'I shall never ask him here again.' But when she returned to her almost-vanished self she said that she would laugh for the rest of her life at the image of Cyril's plump, sad, voluptuary's face covered with exploded yolk.

By 1972 she knew at last what was wrong with her; although she must have already guessed that it was cancer. 'These boys alone diagnosed what I have got', she wrote to Palewski from the Nuffield Hospital in London, where she had previously had an agonising and ultimately useless operation to relieve a fused vertebra. To learn that she had Hodgkin's disease was, one would think, like hearing a death sentence confirmed. Yet Nancy was still waiting for the warder to bring the reprieve: her extraordinary life force flared again, and she turned the deadly certainty of her diagnosis into a reason for optimism. If they finally knew what it was, then they could surely get on and do something about it? 'I'm *quite quite* sure now they will cure me & you know how sceptical I had become.'

When she returned to France, however, she wrote a letter to one of her doctors that took a different tone: 'From a medical point of view I must point out that I've been twice to London now in the hopes of being cured of a vile pain which for 4½ years has made my life unbearable. It still does . . . That is why I ask if in your view & that of Dr Hanham I've got it for life? I've never been so bad or at least worse . . .'

Still she fought, however. She wrote letters to friends, her writing looking shrunken and childish on the page. Books were her salvation; she clung to the words as if they were lighting the way to sanity, devoured Trollope and Isherwood and Gibbon (who 'fills the gaps'): 'How glad I am not to be one of those kids who can't read.' She had, by now, a nurse 'of the lowest class', as she told Raymond Mortimer: 'I feel like a refined Prussian officer who has been picked up on the battlefield.' The nurse cost £10 a day – unbelievably, Nancy continued to fret about money – but had become an absolute necessity. She now needed someone to help her eat the little pieces of cheese, prepared by Hassan, that had become her sole sustenance; she could not wash herself, and she required daily injections of morphine: the needles themselves were agony, so close was she now to the bone. She also took vast quantities of painkillers smuggled in from England (French doctors, 'shockingly behindhand in matters of pain control',[27] would not give unlimited supplies): a final, precious service from her friends. The nurse helped with the pain but in other ways she was, according to Nancy at least, a 'horrid old Gamp', who would give 'two sharp blows with the brushes' if asked to brush her hair: 'the bed-pan is an all-in wrestling match at which I am, screaming with pain, the loser & as for washing, one is the kitchen floor', she wrote to Cynthia Gladwyn: her phrases still sang with Mitfordian life as her body shrivelled into nothingness. In the night, she told James Lees-Milne, 'I long for Blor or Marie.'

Her last, supreme act of courage was to see death as the greatest joke of all: like her friends in the tumbrils, to defy and accept it with roars of laughter. 'It's very curious, dying, & would have many a drôle amusing & charming side were it not for the pain wh the drs try in vain to control', she wrote to Lees-Milne in May 1973. 'Debo was here for some days – the PRESENCE is so delightful. We had screams over the Will & the Dame [Alvilde]'s share. "But she'll be furious if she only gets *that*".' And maybe, yes, one does hear the shrieks in the bedroom at Rue d'Artois, as if it were the chilly top floor at Asthall, outside whose windows lay a patiently waiting churchyard.

By June, the pain had won its battle with Nancy. There was nothing of her left, no body, no consolation. '*Je veux me dépêcher*,' Jessica heard her whisper into the ear of her doctor. '*Je souffre comme je n'avais pas imaginé*', she wrote to Gaston Palewski, in her last letter. '*Je pense et j'espère mourir . . . Vous ne savez pas.*' Then a faint but familiar note sounded, from the blissful anguished days of Rue Monsieur: 'My telephone doesn't seem to work or else you don't hear & that upsets me so I hate being telephoned to. The pain *is so bad* I can't think of organising things & can hardly write at all, & if you don't hear the telephone it makes things so difficult . . .'

Elusive as ever, the Colonel; yet throughout his life he retained the felicitous touch of the *homme à femmes*, and three weeks after receiving this letter, on the morning of 30 June 1973, he had what he later called 'a premonition that I must see her'.[28] So he drove to the faded white house once more, inside which lay a barely conscious Nancy, and ran up the stairs to her bedroom. ('Oh! Fabrice – *on vous attend si longtemps.*' '*Comme c'est gentil.*') It may have been that she heard the bark of Palewski's spaniel, but it seems that Nancy smiled when he took her hand. ('She lay back, and all was light and warmth.')

A few hours later Nancy died. 'That was', said the Colonel, 'our last meeting.'

'You will be a wonderful old lady', Linda is told in *The Pursuit of Love*. But Linda dies. She is not the sort of person who dies; like her creator she had in her an infinite supply of life, of hope, of joy; but Nancy, too, was struck by the same casual irony. She too would have been a wonderful old lady. And the way her life ended is hard to contemplate.

She was cremated at Père-Lachaise, so she did in a sense fulfil her desire to rest, like Napoleon, '*parmi ce peuple que j'ai si bien aimé*'. Then she was brought to her other home, at Swinbrook, where her ashes were buried next to her sister Unity. The funeral was held on 9 July, on a beautiful day, 'sunny with clouds which rendered the Windrush landscape blue', as James Lees-Milne wrote in his diaries. The *beau monde*, much of it now worn and tired, made its way up the tiny flight of steep steps that take one from the country road to the churchyard, streamed past the graves of Lord and Lady Redesdale, and crowded into the little church in the calm, quiet, beating heart of England. There, in front of the assembled configuration of drooping black hats and sombre faces, of Diana, Deborah and Pamela with their heads swathed in tight black scarves, of the ghosts of Tom and

Unity and Nancy's many dead friends, 'raised on a small blue velvet covering', was a 'tiny, common little wooden box, one foot by one foot, containing all that is left of Nance.'

But the Swinbrook grave does not contain Nancy. It holds the still, silent part of her. Her voice spills out and over it, light and sparkling as the Windrush on a sunlit day, flowing away from the stone mole on the tomb; into the glittering world of another reality.

NOTES

Chapter 1

1 This story was told by the Duchess of Devonshire during a BBC *Omnibus* programme about Nancy, broadcast in 2001.

2 David Mitford's father, Bertram, was created first Baron Redesdale in 1902 (this extinct title had been revived for him). David did not become heir to the title until his older brother, Clement, was killed in the First World War in 1916.

3 Unless specified otherwise, all quotations from Lady Mosley are from conversation with the author.

4 'Decca' was a family nickname for Nancy's sister Jessica.

5 Notwithstanding Sydney's misgivings this essay was published, along with thirteen others by Nancy, in a collection called *The Water Beetle* (Hamish Hamilton, 1962). In the book the essay has the title 'Blor'.

6 Unless specified otherwise, all quotations from the Duchess of Devonshire are from conversation with the author.

7 In a letter to Diana, 29 July 1946, Nancy wrote of a meeting with Sydney's sister Weenie, in which it was implied by her aunt that Nancy had 'gone to the bad' (by that time her marriage was over and she was having an affair in Paris). 'If I have become what they all regard as wicked, *that* is Muv's fault because if I had had a family there would have been no Col [her lover] & that's quite certain. But I can't say that . . .'

8 From *The House of Mitford*, by Jonathan Guinness with Catherine Guinness.

9 Clementine's daughter, Mary Soames, ended the speculation about her mother's parentage in 2002. Notwithstanding Clementine's so-called resemblance to David Mitford, her father was named by Lady Soames to be Captain Bay Middleton, another of Blanche's lovers. The dashing Captain Middleton died in a riding accident when Clementine was a young girl.

10 In *The House of Mitford*.

11 In an interview for ABC TV's *Tempo*, broadcast in 1966.
12 In his book *Ancient as the Hills: Diaries 1973–1974*, James Lees-Milne records that shortly after Nancy's death he was asked by her publishers, Hamish Hamilton, to write her biography. He told them that he had several reservations: 'The chief one was that I did not admire Nancy's prose style; never had. They took this badly and were, I could see, amazed . . .' (In the end no formal biography was written at this time; instead Harold Acton published his memoir of Nancy, chiefly made up of her own letters, in 1975.)

Chapter 2

1 The word 'Hons' (whose 'h' is pronounced) became resonant within the Mitford family: according to Jessica's *Hons and Rebels* it originated as a derivation of 'Hens', which she and Deborah kept when young. Of course it also – annoyingly, to some – meant 'Honourable', the title held by the Mitford children. Evelyn Waugh refers to Nancy and her sisters as 'Hons' in this sense. But they themselves would use it as a natural term of approval for anyone they liked, as when Linda says of Davey Warbeck (Aunt Emily's husband in *The Pursuit of Love)* that he 'seems a terrific Hon'. Conversely someone nasty could be a 'Counter-Hon'.
2 In a radio talk given in 1946 for the BBC programme *Women's Magazine.*
3 Nancy's article 'The English Aristocracy', published in *Encounter* in 1955, contained the famous 'U and Non-U' theory which categorised the way people spoke as either 'Upper-class' or 'Non-Upper-class'. It caused a furore. Waugh's 'Open Letter', which constituted a reply of sorts to Nancy's article, appeared in *Encounter* in December 1955. Both essays were published in 1956 in *Noblesse Oblige: An Enquiry into the Identifiable Characteristics of the English Aristocracy* ('I think the book should have a pompous name', wrote Waugh to Nancy).
4 From *Unity Mitford: A Quest* by David Pryce-Jones.
5 All quotations from Alexander Mosley are from conversation with the author.
6 Quoted in *The House of Mitford.*
7 From a letter to Nancy's friend Robert Byron, 18 September 1931.
8 This story was told in the 1980 BBC documentary *Nancy Mitford: A Portrait by Her Sisters.*
9 Quoted in the 1980 BBC documentary.
10 From *A Life of Contrasts* by Diana Mosley.
11 Ibid.
12 From a letter to Evelyn Waugh, 31 January 1951.
13 In an interview with David Pryce-Jones.
14 In the 1946 BBC radio broadcast.
15 This story was told in *The Sunday Times* in an article by Julian Jebb,

published to coincide with the broadcasting of his 1980 BBC film.

16 Quoted by Diana in the 1980 BBC documentary.

17 In a letter to Nancy describing a book by Cyril Connolly, *The Unquiet Grave*, in which Connolly reflected upon his past and his beliefs, Waugh wrote: 'There was a large blank in my acquaintance with Cyril which must I suppose have been a deformative period in his life.'

18 From an interview in *Unity Mitford: A Quest*.

19 In the 1980 BBC documentary.

20 Raymond Mortimer (1895–1980) credited himself with having taught Nancy the difference between a comma and a semi-colon ('. . . Raymond says he can teach grammar & if I put him up in the Continental with a suite on the Tuileries gardens he will teach me in return, so I'm considering it', wrote Nancy to Evelyn Waugh in 1950). A highly literate man who worked as a critic and editor, Mortimer became a good friend to Nancy after she moved to France and a precious one at the end of her life.

21 During the mid-1930s, as Unity began to espouse Fascism with ever greater fervour, Nancy would almost always begin letters to her with this kind of phrase.

22 Quoted in *Unity Mitford: A Quest*.

Chapter 3

1 From a letter to Lady Redesdale, 8 April 1922.

2 In the 1966 interview for ABC Television's *Tempo*.

3 From a letter to Robert Byron, 18 September 1931.

4 Diana was married for the first time, to Bryan Guinness, at just eighteen, Jessica married Esmond Romilly aged nineteen, and Deborah was twenty when she married Lord Andrew Cavendish. Pamela, on the other hand, was twenty-eight at her wedding to Derek Jackson; Unity never married.

5 In fact Esmond was rumoured to be more than that: 'everyone knows Esmond is Winston's son', Nancy once said to Jessica, who apparently also believed this to be true. If so, it would mean that Churchill had had an affair with his wife's sister Nellie, who was the daughter of the naughty Mitford aunt, Blanche Hozier.

6 In an essay entitled 'My Friend Evelyn Waugh', published in *Arts et Loisirs* after Waugh's death.

7 Quoted in *The Brideshead Generation* by Humphrey Carpenter.

8 From a letter to Tom Mitford, 27 November 1926.

9 From a letter to Mark Ogilvie-Grant, 20 June 1932. Randolph Churchill made passes at everyone, hence the hilarity. He remained a friend of sorts all Nancy's life, although she later wrote: 'There is *nothing* to be said for Randolph . . .'

10 Sir Oz was Nancy's nickname for Mosley. Later she also called him Sir Ogre.

11 All quotations from Viscount Norwich are from conversation with the author.

12 Cyril Connolly (1903–1974) was a dear friend of Nancy's, although the butt of many of the jokes in her correspondence with Evelyn Waugh. The intense seriousness with which Connolly took himself, his writing and his complicated love life is probably what set them both off. Connolly founded the literary magazine *Horizon*, was an elegant critic and had an absolute belief in the importance of art and literature, but produced only one failed novel (*The Rock Pool*, 1936). He always, in fact, threatened to do more than he actually achieved. Perhaps he spent too much time worrying about his contemporaries, his three wives and his self-image; it is not surprising that he was admired by Kenneth Tynan, who similarly promised great things at Oxford and ended up tightly bound within his own incestuous artistic circle. In an essay on Connolly – 'a part for Charles Laughton at his driest and least expostulatory' – Tynan wrote that 'it is difficult to leave his company without feeling determined to repel all forms of literary prostitution, a determination which can lead to inertia': a clever *aperçu*. In her more worldly and childlike way Nancy said something similar when she satirised Connolly, in *The Blessing*, as a man of high ideals let down by his own flabby nature; the portrait was accurate enough to cause great offence.

13 From a letter to Evelyn Waugh, 30 September 1950.

14 From a letter to Mark Ogilvie-Grant, 22 January 1932.

15 Ibid.

16 From *Brian Howard: A Portrait of a Failure*, edited by Marie-Jacqueline Lancaster.

17 From a letter to Tom Mitford, May 1929.

18 *The Little Hut*, by André Roussin, was translated by Nancy, directed by Peter Brook and starred Robert Morley. It opened at the Lyric Theatre in August 1950. The play was set, said *The Times* review: 'On a desert island so wittily exotic it might have been designed by Mr Oliver Messel – which has, in fact, been designed by Messel . . .'

19 From a letter to Waugh's wife, Laura, 11 April 1966.

20 In the 1966 television interview.

21 In the 1980 BBC documentary.

22 In the 1966 television interview.

23 Ibid.

24 From a letter to Mark Ogilvie-Grant, 10 March 1930.

25 From a letter to Mark Ogilvie-Grant, 15 March 1931.

26 The phrase is from Philip Hensher's introduction to the Penguin Classics edition of *Love in a Cold Climate and Other Novels*, published 2000.

27 Indeed Nancy later viewed Hamish with some affection, but as an absolute nuisance and idiot. The two saw each other occasionally. In a 1958 letter to

Mark Ogilvie-Grant she described how Hamish had dropped in to her Paris flat: 'he is *so* silly. He was sitting here – I said now I advise you to go and catch the train. Oh no, it would mean waiting at the station. So he misses the train. Two expensive taxis, a telephone call to Bourgogne, and another night in an hotel, and another taxi in the morning. Made me cross. Quite a fiver I guess . . .' Amazingly, Hamish visited Nancy at the end of her life and said to her: 'we would have been married now for thirty years.' To which her reaction, as expressed in a 1972 letter to Deborah, was: 'Help!!'

28 Maurice Bowra, Oxford don and later Vice-Chancellor of Oxford University. Despite Hamish's attempts to claim Bowra for himself, he was in fact a good friend of Nancy's.

29 From a letter to Mark Ogilvie-Grant, 10 December 1930.

30 Rosemary Hope-Vere, a friend of Nancy's.

Chapter 4

1 From *Love from Nancy: The Letters of Nancy Mitford*, edited by Charlotte Mosley.

2 In *Diana Mosley: A Life*, by Jan Dalley, the author writes of Oswald Mosley: 'His engagement diary for 6 January 1933 reads: "Lunch Cim [his wife]; Baba 4.15; Dine D[iana] . . ."'

3 Milly the dog was named, in full, Lady Effie Millington-Drake, after an acquaintance of the Mitfords. 'Do you remember', Nancy wrote to her mother in 1947, 'once when [Milly] was going to be "married" [that is, mated] Monica Winterton bought an awful little wedding cake & sent it to Lady E M D at Blomfield, & the shop most officiously sent it instead to her real address with Mon's card saying "Best wishes for your future from us both" . . .'

4 From a letter to Evelyn Waugh, 23 October 1952.

5 From a letter to Deborah, 1933.

6 In 1949 Nancy wrote to Evelyn Waugh that she did *not* like the Elweses – 'you I believe do' – but it was not uncommon to find her dancing between opinions of people in this way.

7 From a letter to Evelyn Waugh, 25 July 1955.

8 *Der Stürmer* was edited by the rabidly anti-Semitic Julius Streicher.

9 The 'two old ladies' were Nancy and Diana, whose great friend was an 'old gentleman' based upon Mark Ogilvie-Grant. For some reason Nancy always put Mark into a 'curly butter-coloured wig' when she wrote about him: he appears in it again as the character Sir Ivor King in *Pigeon Pie*.

10 The Stanley family was that of David Mitford's grandmother, Lady Airlie (1830–1921), who before her marriage was Henrietta Blanche Stanley.

11 Nancy herself *did* go to Russia in 1954 and wrote a wonderful essay, 'Diary of a Visit to Russia, 1954', which was published in *The Water Beetle*. To

Evelyn Waugh she wrote on her return in June 1954: 'Oh Russia *was* fascinating. So much more beautiful than I'd expected for one thing . . . I saw a lady from the State publishing house. I said to her "how many copies would a best-selling novel sell?" She replied 150 million. "Goodness" I said "I can't wait to come and live here . . . What is the name of the novel which has sold 150 millions?" "Well there is The Testing of the Steel – &, of course, Cement". By this time I was distinctly giggly. They are just like Americans just as I knew they would be . . .'

12 In the 1966 television interview.

13 Pamela's way of expressing herself was so absolutely earthbound as to become, perversely, as fantastical as that of Nancy. Once, during a wordgame played at Swinbrook by Nancy and her aesthete friends, while everybody was offering extravagant and glamorous words such as 'chrysoprase', Pam shouted the word 'fish'. 'My dear!' said Brian Howard to Nancy. 'Your sister is *macabre*.'

Chapter 5

1 From a letter to Violet Hammersley, 15 September 1939.

2 Violet Hammersley (1877–1964) was one of Nancy's closest friends, despite the great age difference which made them more like mother and daughter ('Horror-Child' was what Nancy was often called by Mrs Hammersley; Nancy called her 'the Widow'). The two women corresponded frequently. Diana considers that some of what Nancy wrote in her letters to Mrs Hammersley – specifically on the subject of Lady Redesdale – was 'the most awful lies'. But Nancy was not lying when she told Mrs Hammersley that Sydney supported Hitler; nor did Mrs Hammersley think that she was. 'You Mitfords like dictators,' she once said, 'I don't.'

Mrs Hammersley, who had been left a rich widow then lost most of her money, was of an eccentric character and appearance in which Nancy took great delight. Although it did not mitigate one jot the affection and respect in which she held her, Nancy created a delicious caricature of her friend – as gloomy, self-obsessed and demanding – that featured in many of her letters, such as this written during the war: 'When the Wid wakes up in the morning her first thought is how does she feel (herself) how did she sleep & her second thought *will she get any MEAT*? . . . She longs for meat so terribly that she can't look at the sheep on the downs, she *craves* their legs . . .'

.3 This phrase was the title of a book by Apsley Cherry Garrard, a member of the expedition to the South Pole led by Captain Scott. Nancy was fascinated by this to the point of obsession: James Lees-Milne, in his diary for 1942, recorded that she 'is mad about the Antarctic Expedition and has collected every book about it she can lay her hands on'. Later she would write an essay about Scott, published in *The Water Beetle* under the title 'A Bad Time': 'I don't quite know why I have felt the need to write down this well-known story, making myself cry twice . . .'

4 Pamela Churchill (1920–1997) later Hayward, later Harriman, married extremely successfully for status and became a dazzling hostess in Washington. She was a woman of the kind that Nancy admires in her novels: clever in a wholly feminine way, ravishingly attractive, powerful without ever being humourless or sexless. Her last *coup* was to be appointed US Ambassador to Paris by Bill Clinton.

5 Lady Pamela Berry (1914–1982) was a highly attractive woman, a hostess of renown, whose husband, Michael Berry (later Baron Hartwell), became editor-in-chief of the *Daily Telegraph*. Both Nancy and Evelyn Waugh delighted in her charm and verve in the post-war years but, again for both, this fondness wore thin after a while: 'Pam joins Randolph [Churchill] among the legion of the damned', Waugh wrote of her in 1962, after she had betrayed a private conversation with Waugh by using it in the *Telegraph*.

6 From a letter to Evelyn Waugh, 25 November 1951.

7 From a 1962 review of *The Water Beetle*. In this teasing, prickly and perceptive *Sunday Telegraph* essay Waugh wrote of Nancy: 'Her conventions are of her own devising; she attributes them to a world of her own imagination . . . But her essential quality is that she can write.'

8 From a letter to Jessica, 7 October 1940.

9 Quoted by Diana in the 1980 BBC documentary, *Nancy Mitford: A Portrait by her Sisters*.

10 Gladwyn Jebb, later Baron Gladwyn, was a distinguished diplomat and appointed Ambassador to France in 1954. He and his wife Cynthia had known Nancy before the war – 'I'm in love with Gladwyn', she wrote, not wholly seriously, in a letter from 1936 – and the friendship grew when all three were living in Paris. Lady Gladwyn wrote a charming appreciation of Nancy after her death: 'A happy memory springs to mind of Nancy at a party, entrancing with a beautiful arrangement of roses and ribbons round her neck such as the great Mistress [Madame de Pompadour] wore . . .'

11 This was Diana's striking, opening remark in the 2001 BBC *Omnibus* programme about Nancy.

12 From a letter to Violet Hammersley, 20 December 1940.

13 From a *Sunday Telegraph* interview, published 2002.

14 From Jan Dalley's biography of Diana.

Chapter 6

1 Billa (Wilhelmine) was a friend of Nancy's from the early 1930s and is said to have contributed to the character of Fanny, narrator of three of Nancy's novels. Like Fanny, Billa was happily married to a don: Roy was University

Lecturer in Economics at Oxford, where the Harrods lived.

2 This was an especially favoured Mitford joke, which came from Diana's time in prison: according to her husband's autobiography, *My Life*, she had said, 'It was still lovely to wake up in the morning and feel one was lovely *One*.' In 1948 Nancy wrote a letter to Diana saying that John Julius Norwich (then aged nineteen) 'nearly died when I told him about Isn't it *bliss* to be ONE'.

3 From Waugh's review of *The Water Beetle*.

4 Diana had four sons: Jonathan and Desmond Guinness, and Alexander and Max Mosley. Deborah had three children: Lady Emma Cavendish (now Tennant), Peregrine, now the Duke of Devonshire, and Lady Sophia Cavendish (now Topley).

5 Deborah's son was always known as Stoker, after a family friend named Adrian Stokes.

6 In a review of Nancy's collected letters.

7 In the index to *The Letters of Evelyn Waugh and Nancy Mitford*, there are twenty-one entries under 'Waugh, Harriet Mary; presents from NM'.

8 From a *Spectator* review of Nancy's collected letters, written by her friend Alastair Forbes. In fact this wonderfully amusing article is more like a brief and idiosyncratic memoir of Nancy's life, complete with several mentions of the part played in it by Forbes himself. 'I was naturally rather pleased to read . . . that, in a 1947 letter to her sister Diana, Nancy had written: "I really love Ali Forbes and so does the Col [her lover, Gaston Palewski, was also a good friend of Forbes]. I think he is the only clever young man I know with a heart . . ."'

9 Nancy's sister-in-law, Gloria Elwes.

10 From a letter to Violet Hammersley, 26 December 1940.

11 Osbert Lancaster, who would later illustrate *Noblesse Oblige* and *The Water Beetle*, was best known as cartoonist on the *Daily Express* and creator of Maudie Littlehampton, glorious snob and would-be social barometer. Nancy wrote to Lancaster praising Maudie: 'Oh she is lovely . . . and then of course she is always right about everything.' Maudie in her turn devoured *Noblesse Oblige* and, in Lancaster's collected cartoons for 1957, was depicted eating off her knife saying: 'Oh, to hell with Nancy Mitford! What I always say is – if it's ME it's U!'

12 From Harold Acton's *Memoir*.

13 So Deborah described her sister's instinct towards fidelity, in the 1980 BBC documentary *Nancy Mitford: A Portrait by Her Sisters*.

14 West Wycombe Park was the home of Nancy's friends Sir John and Lady Helen Dashwood. Nancy called Helen 'Hell Bags' and indeed she was disliked by many people (James Lees-Milne referred in his diaries to her 'extraordinarily unadult character'). Nevertheless it was to West Wycombe that Nancy went to recuperate after her hysterectomy: this would have been

wonderfully comfortable, and agreeably full of friends like Cecil Beaton, Eddy Sackville-West and Lees-Milne himself. During the war the Dashwoods were allowed to run West Wycombe with all its servants, the deal with the authorities being that the house would be filled with evacuees: 'strangely enough nearly all of them friends of Helen's', wrote Selina Hastings in her biography of Nancy.

15 From the letter to Diana, 22 November 1941, written by Nancy from her hospital bed (Charlotte Mosley, editor of Nancy's collected letters, adds that this letter was 'passed by prison censor 28/11/41': Diana had then been in Holloway for seventeen months).

16 From a letter to Diana, 28 November 1942.

17 The brothers of Dame Edith Sitwell, with whom they formed a fey, somewhat self-mythologising but civilised triumvirate: the Sitwells all wrote (Osbert no less than five volumes of autobiography), while Edith was very much in the tradition of the grand, rich, literary lioness. 'Every magazine has six pages of pictures of them headed "The Fabulous Sitwells"', Evelyn Waugh wrote to Nancy, from New York, in 1948. 'They have hired the Philharmonic Orchestra . . . to play while they recite poetry. Goodness how they are enjoying it. I said "Is Sachie joining you?" "Alas. Sachie is High Sheriff of His County and therefore unable to leave the United Kingdom."'

18 This nickname for Connolly has been attributed to Virginia Woolf, but Nancy and Evelyn Waugh certainly picked it up and ran with it (indeed Waugh called it 'our joke'). The very word 'Boots' seems to have set them off. In 1954 Nancy began a letter to Waugh with this:

> 'Since Bonny-boots is dead
> That so divinely
> Could foot it & toot it
> (Oh he did it finely)
> Say, lusty lads, who now shall
> Bonny-boot it?

I found this in a book of English madrigals – are you shrieking?'

19 The 14th Baron Berners (1883–1950) was the model for the refined, shrewd and urbane Lord Merlin in *The Pursuit of Love*. Lord Merlin's exquisite house full of Watteaus and dyed pigeons, his two black whippets with their diamond necklaces, his aesthetic sensibility and love of practical jokes – these attributes were all those of Gerald Berners, as was the incongruity that placed Lord Merlin slap bang in the middle of rugged Gloucestershire hunting country, with Uncle Matthew as his nearest neighbour. Lord Berners's own house, Faringdon in Oxfordshire, was similarly close to the Mitfords.

A writer, painter and musician, Gerald Berners was originally a friend of

Diana's, and was one of those homosexuals who, as she now says, were 'God's gift to women like Nancy and me.' He also had the guts, insouciance and loyalty to stick by Diana when she was sent to Holloway ('Are you burrowing under your cell with a teaspoon?' he wrote to her on the day of her arrest). Then he became close to Nancy also, and Faringdon provided her with a glorious oasis in wartime. A year before his death she dedicated *Love in a Cold Climate* to her friend.

20 Lady Cunard and Lady Colefax were the two great London hostesses of the war years, by which time both were in their seventies. Their styles contrasted a good deal. Emerald (*née* Maud) Cunard was a rich American: James Lees-Milne described in his diaries one of her parties at the Dorchester, into which she 'darted like a bird of paradise . . . we dined off expensive, pretentious food which lacked the necessary refinements of good cooking.' Lady Colefax, on the other hand, he described as 'totally without ostentation. Because she is quite poor and inhabits a small house this is not allowed to interfere with her mode of living. She gets people just the same . . .'

21 From a letter to Diana, 28 November 1942.

22 From James Lees-Milne's diary, 17 June 1944.

23 As described by Diana to the editor of Nancy's collected letters.

24 *The Unquiet Grave*, a book of reflections by Connolly upon his life and beliefs, was published in 1944 and reviewed unkindly by Waugh the following year.

25 James Lees-Milne recorded in his 1943 diary taking Lady Anne Hill, wife of Heywood, to lunch 'in order to plead with her that they raise Nancy's salary'. Anne 'explained laughingly that whereas Nancy got paid £3 10s. od. she only got £2 10s. od.; that the shop barely paid its way . . .'

26 These were a wartime invention, selling food like stuffed heart at extremely low prices.

27 Journalist and biographer Harold Nicolson, married to Vita Sackville-West (more famous for her lesbian love affair with Violet Trefusis), was a friend of sorts, although he and Nancy were not mad about each other. In her editing of Nancy's letters, Charlotte Mosley quotes this from Nicolson's diary: 'She is essentially not an intellectual and there is a sort of Roedean hoydenishness about her which I dislike' (this quotation was used in a biography of Nicolson by James Lees-Milne, who although fonder of Nancy held a not dissimilar view of her). But civilities were maintained between Nicolson and Nancy. In 1957 he reviewed her book about Voltaire favourably, even though he disapproved of what he saw as its immorality. And in 1963 she asked to be released from a lucrative contract to write a book about the Congress of Vienna, having read Nicolson's own book on the subject and found it to be unimprovable.

28 From his review of Nancy's collected letters in the *Spectator*.

29 From a description of the clever seductress Albertine in *The Blessing*.

30 This is Selina Hastings's word; elsewhere in her biography, however, she writes that Nancy felt for Palewski 'a deep and overwhelming physical attraction'.

31 With the *Observer* in 1968.

32 Nicholas Mosley, son of Oswald and his first wife Cynthia, had recently published *Natalie Natalia*.

33 Lady Diana Cooper (1892–1986) was one of the greatest beauties of the twentieth century: among the women of London only she and Clementine Churchill were said to have had faces that could launch a thousand ships. Diana married the politician (later British Ambassador in Paris) Duff Cooper, and was the mother of John Julius Norwich. She was a close friend of Evelyn Waugh and their correspondence – collected in *Mr Wu & Mrs Stitch*, edited by Diana's granddaughter Artemis Cooper – was extensive, although it lacked the relaxed exhilaration, the sheer cleverness of the letters between Waugh and Nancy. For her part Nancy was fond of Diana and initially dazzled by her, although she seems later to have found her slightly wearing: neither Diana's tendency towards melancholia nor her dislike of France were to Nancy's taste.

34 The phrase is Winston Churchill's.

35 The Hon. Daphne Vivian, later Fielding, was married at the time to Viscount Weymouth.

36 Alastair Forbes has robustly refuted what he called 'Osbert's silly lie' on a couple of occasions, including in his *Spectator* review of Nancy's letters: 'dear Osbert, with his clothes modelled on Max Beerbohm's, his voice on Maurice Bowra's and his complexion on Gaston's, was quite capable of wanting to cut a figure at table by questioning the absent Gaston's courage and blaming it on the absent Ali . . .' Forbes then describes watching, in June 1944, the first V1 bomb to fly over London, in the company of a totally unfazed Palewski. 'We calmly discussed the possible effect on the course of the war of the new weapon before parting, Gaston it seems to Nancy's arms and I to mind-your-own-business . . .'

37 From *Paris After the Liberation: 1944–1949*, by Antony Beevor and Artemis Cooper.

38 Violet Keppel (1894–1972), described in Charlotte Mosley's droll editor's notes thus: 'Minor novelist. Married Denys Trefusis in 1919. Eloped several times with Vita Sackville-West.' Violet moved to Paris a little before Nancy – where the two women moved in very similar circles – and thus viewed Nancy (younger, funnier, infinitely more talented) as something of a threatening interloper. Nonetheless the two exerted a certain fascination upon one another, as will be seen in Chapter 9.

39 Later married to James Lees-Milne, and a good friend of Nancy's.

40 In an essay published in *House & Garden*.

41 'I had tea with Nancy in her garden', James Lees-Milne recorded in his 1944 diary, 'which is a wilderness of rank grass and chickens . . .'

42 His *mother* was a girlfriend of Gaston Palewski's –!

Chapter 7

1 From a letter to Lady Redesdale, 24 September 1944.

2 Instead Heywood Hill engaged a man named Handasyde Buchanan ('Handy'), who became a partner in the shop and married Nancy's co-worker Mollie Friese-Greene.

3 From a letter to Evelyn Waugh, 17 January 1945.

4 From a letter to Evelyn Waugh, 22 December 1944.

5 From a letter to Violet Hammersley, 29 January 1949.

6 This story is told by a character in *Frost in May*, by Antonia White.

7 'Evelyn's letter *pure wickedness*, not fun at all', Nancy wrote to Mrs Hammersley after Waugh had attacked her behaviour with Palewski. 'I wrote & said you are supposed to be fond of me, you should be glad that I am happy. He replied I am fond of you, very, & that is why I am not glad . . .'

8 This point is made in Selina Hastings's biography of Evelyn Waugh.

9 From a letter to Lady Redesdale, 8 June 1945.

10 Waugh had written that Cedric talked exactly like the Radlett girls: 'I can just accept Polly speaking exactly like Linda – but Cedric is a Parisian pansy. Oliver Messel doesn't talk like Debo.' Nancy made some adjustments, and phrases such as 'solidarity between working girls', which Cedric says to Fanny, are not exactly Debo-speak (the young Deborah's authentic voice is apparently that of Northey in *Don't Tell Alfred*: 'you are *lucky* to be so kind'). Cedric *does* talk like a Radlett, but in a voice distinctly spiked with camp; as when he tells Lady Montdore that she must sleep in a face mask: 'you mustn't telephone until you've removed it with the remover, because you know how if you telephone smilelessly you sound cross, and if it happened to be *One* on the other end, *One* couldn't bear that.'

11 Nancy called the Jacob et d'Angleterre 'Heath's hotel', in reference to the murder committed in 1946 by Neville Heath in a then low-rent Notting Hill hotel. The trial of Heath, a handsome sexual psychopath, was a *cause célèbre* after the war: 'Diana says shall we be 2 of the not-so-young women who fight their way into the courtroom', Nancy wrote to Evelyn Waugh. '*Think* of the papers next day!'

12 Quoted in Philip Ziegler's biography of Diana Cooper (Hamish Hamilton, 1981).

13 An article in *Le Figaro* in 2001, by Stéphane Denis, reviewed Jan Dalley's biography of Diana Mosley, and mentioned having met Nancy at Fontainebleau '*chez des amis de mes parents. Elle avait eu une liaison avec Gaston Palewski, qui était très coureur* [one who runs after women] . . .'

14 Peter and Dominick Elwes were the nephews of Peter Rodd. In her letters Nancy wrote fascinatingly about Dominick, comparing him with her husband, as when in 1952 she wrote to Evelyn Waugh that he 'came to see me – it all took me back to my early married life – the looks, the get-rich-quick line of talk. Only whereas old Prod is good at heart I feel this boy is really bad . . . I skilfully parried the question of an advance which loomed throughout the interview.' A member of the Lord Lucan gambling set, Dominick committed suicide in 1975.

Chapter 8

1 In a programme called *At Home*, an interview with Nancy at Rue Monsieur. 'I saw Debo last week', Waugh wrote to Nancy in March 1957. 'I feel it my duty to tell you that she is spreading a very damaging story about you: that you have allowed yourself to be photographed by the Television. Of course I don't believe it, nor does anyone who knows and loves you . . .'

2 From a letter to Evelyn Waugh, 7 January 1946.

3 In a 1970 *Daily Express* interview.

4 From a letter to Raymond Mortimer, 24 April 1971.

5 From a letter to Diana Mosley, 12 April 1946.

6 This of course was old francs, of which there were one hundred to the new 'franc lourd' (introduced on 1 January 1959): a sizeable win to have missed, all the same.

7 From a letter to Harold Acton, November 1947.

8 Waugh described in his diary for 1945 a visit from Nancy to his home, Piers Court: 'A mild winter; sunshine half the day . . . Nancy came for the weekend and remained seated by the fire for two days.'

9 A Danish architect and painter who married Nancy's close friend, Princess Dolly Radziwill.

10 'Chimneypiece': U, as opposed to 'mantelpiece': Non-U, was one of the notorious distinctions made in Nancy's essay *The English Aristocracy*, and earlier by Uncle Matthew in *The Pursuit of Love*. When *Pigeon Pie* was republished in 1951 she wrote to Evelyn Waugh: 'I've given it a brush up (I say it's *full* of mirrors mantelpieces handbags etc don't tell my public or I'm done for) . . .'

11 The description is Michael Ratcliffe's, in a review of Harold Acton's *Memoir*.

12 Chevalier had performed for the Germans during the war.

13 From a letter to Diana Mosley, 15 June 1946.

14 The nickname 'Honks' was one that Nancy had invented for Diana Mosley, and that segued into usage for the other Diana: Evelyn Waugh seems always to have loved employing the private Mitford language.

15 Sir Henry 'Chips' Channon, who became an MP and married (like Diana Mosley) into the extremely rich Guinness family, loved European society as

perhaps only someone born in America can. His diaries were published posthumously in 1967 to a great sensation, but Nancy wrote to Gaston Palewski, 'you can't think how vile & spiteful & silly it is . . . you are in the index as J-P Palewski & when one turns to the page there you aren't . . .'

16 From a letter to Theodore Besterman, 19 September 1957.

17 The model for worldly, health-obsessed Davey Warbeck, stepfather to Fanny, who appears in The Pursuit of Love, Love in a Cold Climate and Don't Tell Alfred. The Hon. Edward Sackville-West, who became 5th Baron Sackville in 1962, was a novelist and music critic, and greatly adored by Nancy: 'I'm glad you love him, so do I', she wrote to Evelyn Waugh. This affection is palpable in the portrait of Davey, an irresistible character who is utterly at home with the Radletts, which is to say the Mitfords.

Davey's fascination with food and his insides may have come partly from Nancy's uncle Geoff, brother to Lady Redesdale, who believed in whole foods plainly cooked, and produced without artificial fertilisers ('murdered foods', he called those). Davey Warbeck has, in his bedroom at home, 'a picture of a grain of wheat (magnified, naturally) which shows the germ', and he refuses to eat shepherd's pie on the grounds that it contains 'twice-cooked meat . . . it imposes a fearful strain on the juices'. But Davey's other characteristics – his hypochondria, his sophistication, his intellectualism, his knowledge of all gossip ('That was the heaven of Davey'), his understanding of France, his innate goodness spiked with realism about human nature – are very much Eddy Sackville-West; although it might be said that Davey is, too, very much his own man. 'Pam Berry [was] full of keys to explain who everyone was, which I always find an infuriating sort of appreciation, don't you?' wrote Evelyn Waugh to Nancy about The Blessing. In her mature years, Nancy's novels were more than mere romans à clef.

18 Quoted in Philip Ziegler's Diana Cooper.

19 Born Marguerite Decazes, daughter of a French duke and an American heiress, thus well placed to be a central part of Paris society and to be unusually well dressed. Married the Hon. Reginald Fellowes. Before writing Madame de Pompadour, Nancy would tell Evelyn Waugh that she saw 'Pomp' as being like Daisy, but this was the sort of thing she would say at the start of books, perhaps as a kind of reassurance to herself that she understood her characters. In fact, once again, Madame de Pompadour is very much her own woman.

20 From a letter to Diana Mosley, 25 May 1948.

21 It has been suggested that Nancy's Gaullism was her equivalent of Jessica's Communism, and Unity and Diana's Fascism. The House of Mitford makes the point that: 'Under the influence of her love for [Palewski], Nancy became . . . as blindly pro-French as Unity had been pro-German, and in an equally partisan way. That is, she was unable to see that there was any other

form of French patriotism than Gaullism . . .' This is a good point, for – as with her sisters – Nancy's political passion was bound up with the passion she felt for the man who espoused it. Had it not been for Palewski, the Englishwoman in her might have felt an absolute loathing for de Gaulle, so rude to darling Winston when he ought to have been so grateful.

However, the comparison falters quite quickly. With Nancy's sisters, the political passion had a real and obdurate life outside the passion for their men. Not so with her. Although she was not a political idiot, as she has sometimes been portrayed, it is hard to see Nancy's Gaullism as much more than a passion acquired to please Palewski; in 1952, when she was fed up with hearing about de Gaulle's perfections, she wrote very firmly to her lover: 'The Gen: is not God . . .'

22 From a letter to Diana Mosley, 26 July 1948.

23 Jessica married US attorney Robert Treuhaft in 1943.

24 In his introduction to the 2000 Penguin Classics edition of *The Pursuit of Love, Love in a Cold Climate* and *The Blessing*.

25 Peter Quennell was a distinguished editor and reviewer, who thought highly of Nancy's writing: 'Counter Hon Quennell behaved well about *Love* in his *Daily Mail*', wrote Waugh to Nancy in 1946 (Waugh disliked Quennell, hence the Mitfordian epithet).

Chapter 9

1 From a letter to Heywood Hill, 13 March 1954.

2 Sir Hugh was an amateur historian who began writing to Nancy after the publication of *Madame de Pompadour*; although the two never met, they continued to exchange letters until Nancy's death.

3 George Rainbird's publishing firm conceived the 'coffee-table book' and published Nancy's *The Sun King* and *Frederick the Great*.

4 From a letter to Evelyn Waugh, 15 September 1953.

5 Quoted in Selina Hastings's biography of Rosamond Lehmann.

6 From Hilary Spurling's review of Selina Hastings's biography.

7 Novelist and critic: in a review of Harold Acton's *Memoir*, he made the acute remark that the stuff of Nancy's humour was not – as it is usually assumed to be – 'polished wit', but was more like 'high buffoonery'.

8 From a letter to Evelyn Waugh, 12 September 1951.

9 Korda was a film producer and director of great renown: among much else he put Laurence Olivier and Vivien Leigh together on screen in *Lady Hamilton* and produced *The Third Man*.

10 As she told the *Sunday Telegraph*.

11 Daughter of Earl Haig; Nancy sent her letter praising *The Blessing* nto her publisher Hamish Hamilton 'just to show you that really it *is* all true'.

12 Writer (notably of *Ariel*, a life of Shelley), some-time supporter of the Vichy government and, according to Nancy, 'a particularly horrible human being'.

13 'When I was in London I made up my quarrel with Cyril', Nancy wrote to Evelyn Waugh in December 1953. '. . . I was desperate for an opening. Bobbie Helpmann, next to me, said "Do you know who I miss most in the world? Constant [Lambert]". I could see Cyril was listening, & I said to him "Do you know who *I* miss most in the world? You". And he melted . . .'

14 After a time in the wilderness Palewski was elected a Deputy in 1951 by the department of the Seine, and in 1953 became vice-president of the Assemblée nationale.

15 From *Une Passion Inachevée: Violet Trefusis* by Antoine d'Arjuzon.

16 From a letter to Evelyn Waugh, 30 September 1950.

17 Six years after the book was published, one of the priests who visited Fontaines-les-Nonnes asked for Nancy's *Voltaire in Love*. 'I said to Mme Costa what should I put as a dedicace? She said perhaps nothing – I'm afraid if you do it will be very compromising for him after his death; you are (in English) such a beautiful young (sic) lady . . .' (To Evelyn Waugh, 26 October 1963.)

18 By Michael Arlen, a thrillingly over-written novel about a fallen woman that caused a sensation in the 1920s.

19 This was Vicomtesse Marie-Laure de Noailles: as Charlotte Mosley put it in Nancy's collected letters, 'friend of the Surrealists'. In Nancy's version of the party that Waugh describes, she wrote this to Pamela Berry: 'I took [Evelyn] to see Marie-Laure & he said afterwards "While I was looking at that lady's pictures I found a Picasso so I've hidden it. They won't find it again for months I hope". He really *is* a leetle bit mad isn't he . . .'

20 Lady Antonia Fraser, writing in the *Evening Standard* after Nancy's death: 'In any examination of the remorseless process by which historical and biographical sales have soared since 1950, she must be regarded as an important if not central figure.' In her turn, Nancy was an admirer of Lady Antonia's books.

21 Nancy drawled this strange phrase at the start of the ABC television programme about Versailles and *The Sun King*.

22 Nancy Mitford and Raymond Chandler were in fact Hamish Hamilton's stars at this time: an unlikely coupling.

Chapter 10

1 Nancy had been asked to work on the final script for a film called *Mary Anne*, based on a novel by Daphne du Maurier.

2 Cunard (1898–1960) was a lifelong friend of Nancy's, another of the homosexuals who were, as Diana says, 'god's gift'; although in Victor Cunard's case with a distinct touch of the diabolical about him. He lived in

Venice much of his life and, after his death, Nancy found it painful to return. 'I miss him so much I almost wonder if I wasn't in love with him. It's the jokes of course . . .' At the time of his death Cunard had been 'in the middle' of writing Nancy's own obituary (somewhat prematurely, as she was aged only fifty-five). He had also exchanged many letters with her whose dazzle and fun can only be guessed at, as they were burned by his brother Edward: 'you have burned a fortune', he was told, when he strode into a Venetian lunch party and announced to Nancy what he had done.

3   From a letter to Mark Ogilvie-Grant, 1960.

4   Eventually Connolly married glamorous Miss Skelton – the 'Conk' (concubine), as Nancy and Waugh called her – although he found her rather hot to handle. She had previously been the mistress of King Farouk of Egypt; during her marriage to Connolly she went back and forth between him and the publisher George Weidenfeld (whom she then married); and finally married Derek Jackson, ex-husband of Pamela Mitford. Evelyn Waugh wrote to Nancy in 1950 asking: 'Why can't one's friends marry *nice* girls?' to which she replied: 'I call them the insect-women oh aren't they horrible & so mal-elevées. I mean Cyril brought Miss S to a v. small cocktail party I had & she sat & read a book! Then my brother in law Jackson turned up . . .'

5   From a letter to Evelyn Waugh, 2 August 1955.

6   Jessica told this story, with every appearance of great good humour, during the 1980 BBC documentary *Nancy Mitford: A Portrait by Her Sisters*.

7   The sketch was for a charity revue, to which Violet Trefusis also contributed: 'Mine is too lovely; the daughter of un vieux duc who becomes a man and wins the Tour de France. The duc doesn't turn a hair', Nancy wrote to Harold Acton. She continued in familiar vein, knowing that Acton would love it: 'Violet has retired to Florence to write hers, in the company of two professional dramaturges . . .'

8   From a letter to Evelyn Waugh, 16 June 1952.

9   From a letter to Katherine, Viscountess Mersey, 16 March 1970.

10 The phrase is from John Julius Norwich.

11 In his diaries, Noël Coward referred to an evening in 1960 spent at Jamie (Hamish) Hamilton's: 'Nancy Mitford, Debo Devonshire, Diana Cooper, Harold Nicolson, etc.: very civilised and charming and an irrefutable proof that, in spite of the "modern trend", genuinely witty and educated conversation can *still* take place.'

12 Lord Stanley had written a book called *Sea Peace* which contained a portrait of Peter. In his review of the book in *Time and Tide*, Waugh wrote: ' "Prod" has an element of genius which Lord Stanley quite misses in casting him in a P.G. Wodehouse part and in crediting him with a desire to please which is most unfamiliar . . .'

13 The phrase was used by the journalist Nancy Spain, in a 1953 radio

broadcast describing a visit to interview Nancy at Redesdale Cottage (she was then on tour with *The Little Hut*). 'I have been *reading*', Nancy said, 'for a life of Madame de Pompadour I hope to write. I don't know. I get so cold when I'm writing.'

14 From Diana Mosley's A *Life of Contrasts*.

15 From a letter to Jessica, 8 March 1968. 'Re the Change. I never had it.'

16 Nancy was always 'vous' to Palewski; this was not so much a deliberate coldness, more a respectful courtesy. Charles-Edouard de Valhubert addresses Grace as 'vous' in *The Blessing*.

17 In a deliciously succinct quote from a letter written in January 1958 to Violet Hammersley, Nancy described having visited Powell, L.P. Hartley (Leslie) and Evelyn Waugh over the holiday season. 'My visits to the major novelists were very successful. The food of all 3 about equal (not good). Leslie had the warmest house & warmest heart, Evelyn by far the coldest house & Tony Powell the coldest heart but the most fascinating chats and a pate de foie gras . . .

'I find all these writers take themselves very seriously & Tony Powell speaks of *Punch*, of which he is literary editor, as though it were an important vehicle of intellectual opinion . . .'

18 'Xopher' was an old friend of Nancy's from the days of the Swinbrook Sewers. A scriptwriter and producer for the BBC, he also wrote a biography of Evelyn Waugh. At the end of her life he advised Nancy to accept the CBE she was offered: 'I'd never heard of CBE but I'm told it's a good sort . . .'

19 The author of this article, the *Standard*'s Paris correspondent Sam White, was extremely full of himself for having penetrated the roman a clef mystery of Nancy's new novel. Little did he know. He himself was portrayed as the low-life journalist Amyas Mockbar, who plagues the lives of Fanny and Alfred with ludicrous stories: I WALK WITH THE SCREAMING TEN THOUSAND, he writes, when an apparent riot takes place outside the Embassy (in fact it is a crowd of teenagers waiting for a jazz concert). Nancy was spot-on in her parody of White's style, so much so that he wanted to sue but was dissuaded by Lord Beaverbrook. After an uncomfortable moment, Nancy had achieved what she wanted: revenge upon White for printing her unflattering remarks about Maurice Chevalier made during the filming of *Count Your Blessings*.

20 This was from 'A Revolutionary Diary' published in 1968 in the *Spectator*. The tone, perceived to be reactionary, annoyed certain readers: 'There is no bread in the house but I have found some cake and would like Miss Mitford's permission to eat it', wrote the party-going mouth organist Larry Adler in a letter to the magazine.

21 From an article entitled 'Views' published in the *Listener*.

Chapter 11

1   As described by Nancy in her 1966 television interview about *The Sun King*.

2   From a letter to Sir Hugh Jackson, 4 April 1966; he would have agreed whole-heartedly.

3   From *The Sunday Times*, 30 July 1950.

4   From a letter to Deborah, 30 January 1964.

5   From a letter to Deborah, 9 July 1965.

6   From a letter to Anthony Powell, 28 May 1966.

7   From a letter to Sir Hugh Jackson, 4 August 1966.

8   Bowra's book was entitled *Memories 1898–1939*.

9   From a letter to Sir Hugh Jackson, 29 January 1967.

10   From a letter to Raymond Mortimer, 19 December 1971.

11   From a letter to Deborah, 28 September 1968.

12   From a letter to Palewski, 8 October 1967.

13   A writer named Ian McInnes was said to have plagiarised 'large parts' of *Pompadour* in a book called *Painter, King and Pompadour*. Nancy won her legal action against McInnes, his publishers and printers in February 1966, and was awarded £100 damages and costs.

14   *Love in a Cold Climate* was both suggested and read by Prunella Scales, who no doubt understood very well the need for restraint. 'It was partly that [over-expressiveness] I minded so much when they read *The Pursuit of Love*', Nancy wrote to the BBC, referring to an adaptation done in 1963. In 1974 *Pursuit* was done again on the radio, this time as a rather freely interpreted drama. It contains additions such as the characters Celia Debenham, Bunty Fairweather and Hugo de Vrees, and begins with Uncle Matthew listening to Galli-Curci and shouting at his dogs Sebastian and Rudolph ('stop chewing that antimacassar').

     The same adapter also dramatised *The Sun King*: in 1972, when she was very ill, Nancy wrote him 'a charming scrawl saying she has gone through the scripts & (quote) "nothing seems to be out of place. It *must* have been a job".' What she thought of his adaptation of *Pompadour* – dramatised as a three-part series called *The King's Favourite* – is unrecorded, however. One wonders whether she would have approved this exchange, for example, between Pomp and the King: 'I have never been happier, Your Majesty'; 'You must not call me "Your Majesty". This is the night for changing names. You must call me Louis . . .'

15   Jacques Bénigne Bossuet, Bishop of Meaux, whose sermons were one of the great literary achievements of Louis XIV's reign.

16   From a letter to Deborah, 21 April 1967.

17   From a letter to Valentine Lawford (a good friend of Nancy's who lived with the photographer Horst), 23 February 1968. At the end of the letter Nancy commends Lawford for his ambition to write a history of the Thirty

Years War: 'I shall call you Father Courage, it's the bravest thing I ever heard.'

18 From a letter to Sir Hugh Jackson, 20 July 1969.

19 From a letter to Sir Hugh Jackson, 10 August 1969.

20 From a letter to Evelyn Waugh, 14 April 1949.

21 From a letter to Sir Hugh Jackson, 30 April 1970.

22 From a letter to Raymond Mortimer, 10 October 1970.

23 'The very worst', Nancy wrote to James Lees-Milne in 1972, 'is something on your face called tic douloureux. Bags not having that as well –!'

24 As it was described by the *Sunday Express* interviewer who visited Nancy in 1968.

25 The 'medal' had its funny side, being a scapular of the kind worn by Marie Antoinette at her trial. 'What a great and not only charming woman she was!' wrote the priest in his accompanying letter to Nancy.

26 Said, famously, by Proust.

27 So an indignant Alastair Forbes wrote in his *Spectator* review of Nancy's letters.

28 This was said by Palewski (unnamed then, except as 'The Colonel') in the 1980 BBC documentary *Nancy Mitford: A Portrait by Her Sisters.*

SELECT BIBLIOGRAPHY

ACTON, Harold, *Nancy Mitford: A Memoir*, Hamish Hamilton, 1975

BARROW, Andrew, *Gossip 1920–1970*, Hamish Hamilton, 1978

BEEVOR, Antony and ARTEMIS COOPER, *Paris After the Liberation: 1944–1949*, Hamish Hamilton, 1994

CARPENTER, Humphrey, *The Brideshead Generation*, Houghton Mifflin, 1989

COOPER, Artemis (ed), *Mr Wu & Mrs Stitch: The Letters of Evelyn Waugh and Diana Cooper*, Hodder & Stoughton, 1991

DALLEY, Jan, *Diana Mosley: A Life*, Faber and Faber, 1999

D'ARJUZON, Antoine, *Une Passion Inachevée: Violet Trefusis*, Perrin, 2001

DAVIE, Michael (ed), *The Diaries of Evelyn Waugh*, Weidenfeld & Nicolson, 1976

GUINNESS, Jonathan with Catherine Guinness, *The House of Mitford*, Hutchinson, 1984

HASTINGS, Selina, *Evelyn Waugh: A Biography*, Sinclair-Stevenson, 1994

HASTINGS, Selina, *Nancy Mitford*, Hamish Hamilton, 1985

HASTINGS, Selina, *Rosamond Lehmann*, Chatto & Windus, 2002

JAMES, Robert Rhodes (ed), *Chips: The Diaries of Sir Henry Channon*, Phoenix Press, 1996

LANCASTER, Marie-Jacqueline, *Brian Howard: Portrait of a Failure*, Timeless Press, 2005

LEES-MILNE, James, *Ancestral Voices & Prophesying Peace*, Chatto & Windus, 1975

LEES-MILNE, James, *Ancient as the Hills*, John Murray, 1997

LEES-MILNE, James, *Another Self,* John Murray, 1998

LOVELL, Mary S., *The Mitford Girls*, Little, Brown, 2001

MITFORD, Jessica, *Hons and Rebels*, Gollancz, 1960

MOSLEY, Diana, *A Life of Contrasts*, Hamish Hamilton, 1977

MOSLEY, Diana, *Loved Ones*, Sidgwick & Jackson, 1985

PRYCE-JONES, David, *Unity Mitford: A Quest*, Weidenfeld & Nicolson, 1976

RHYS, Jean, *Good Morning, Midnight*, André Deutsch, 1967

RHYS, Jean, *Quartet*, Penguin, 2000
RHYS, Jean, *Smile, Please*, André Deutsch, 1979
TOYNBEE, Philip, *Friends Apart*, Sidgwick & Jackson, 1980
TYNAN, Kenneth, *Profiles*, Perennial, 1990
WAUGH, Evelyn, *Brideshead Revisited*, Longman, 1968
WAUGH, Evelyn, *Vile Bodies*, Methuen, 1930
ZIEGLER, Philip, *Diana Cooper*, Hamish Hamilton, 1981

By Nancy Mitford

Books

Highland Fling, Thornton Butterworth, 1931
Christmas Pudding, Thornton Butterworth, 1932
Wigs on the Green, Thornton Butterworth, 1935
Pigeon Pie, Hamish Hamilton, 1940
The Pursuit of Love, Hamish Hamilton, 1945
Love in a Cold Climate, Hamish Hamilton, 1949
Madame de Pompadour, Hamish Hamilton, 1954
Voltaire in Love, Hamish Hamilton, 1957
Don't Tell Alfred, Hamish Hamilton, 1960
The Water Beetle, Hamish Hamilton, 1962
The Sun King, Hamish Hamilton, 1966
Frederick the Great, Hamish Hamilton, 1970

Edited by Nancy Mitford

The Ladies of Alderley, Chapman and Hall, 1938
The Stanleys of Alderley, Chapman and Hall, 1939

Translations

The Princesse de Clèves (from Madame de Lafayette), Euphorion Books, 1950
The Little Hut (from André Roussin), 1951

Contributed to

Noblesse Oblige, Hamish Hamilton, 1956

Collected Letters and Journalism

Love from Nancy: The Letters of Nancy Mitford, edited by Charlotte Mosley, Hodder & Stoughton, 1993
The Letters of Nancy Mitford and Evelyn Waugh, edited by Charlotte Mosley, Hodder & Stoughton, 1996
A Talent to Annoy: Nancy Mitford's Essays, Journalism and Reviews 1929–1968, edited by Charlotte Mosley, Hamish Hamilton, 1986

INDEX

Murray, Pauline and Basil 229
Murray, Venetia 229
Mussolini, Benito 121

*Nancy Mitford: A Portrait by Her
    Sisters* (TV) 27
Nancy Mitford's Versailles (TV) 348
Nicolson, Harold 185, 306, 331
Norwich, John Julius: comment on
    NM 79, 96, 171, 194, 213, 266,
    279, 283, 287; and Hamish St
    Clair-Erskine 94; and Peter Rodd
    100, 103, 104; NM's homes 113,
    227; on Palewski 190–1, 195,
    222–3, 311; *Omnibus* controversy
    196, 279–81, 372; NM's final
    illness 377
Nuffield Hospital, NM at 398–9

O'Neill, Mary ('Middy') 75
Observer 294, 359
Ogilvie, Clementine, Lady
    see Mitford, Clementine
Ogilvie-Grant, Mark: close
    friendship with NM 82, 259;
    and correspondence 85, 87, 92,
    95–6, 97, 100, 107, 108, 157–8,
    163, 267, 364–5; war years 181,
    218
Oliver, Vic 239
Olivier, Laurence 252
Omnibus (TV): 196, 279–80, 364

Palewski, Gaston ('Col'): love affair
    with NM 79, 184–87, 189–92,
    193–96, 197, 200, 202, 213–23,
    242–4, 257, 288, 299–300; war
    work 186–7, 197; as NM's muse
    (*The Pursuit of Love*) 212–14;
    post-war political work 220–2,
    225, 312–13, 342; cooling of affair
    with NM 259–61, 311–14; alleged
    affair with Violet Trefusis 301;

made French Ambassador to
    Rome 310, 311–14; end of
    relationship with NM 339–42,
    355–6; birth of illegitimate son
    340–1; marriage 342, 363–5;
    NM's final illness and death
    377–8, 380
Palewski, Violette (née Talleyrand-
    Périgord; wife of Gaston
    Palewski) 363, 365
Penguin (publishers) 245, 273
Père-Lachaise cemetery: NM's
    cremation 380
Peter (NM's dog) 45
Peters, A.D. (NM's literary agent)
    241, 270
Petite Hutte, La (Roussin; adapt.
    NM) 274–6, 303
Philipps, Hon. Mrs *see* Lehmann,
    Rosamund
Pinter, Harold 326
Pompidou, Georges 342
Powell, Anthony 39, 282, 344, 378
Pryce-Jones, David: *Unity Mitford:
    A Quest* 16, 28, 45, 50, 56, 65,
    73–4, 141
Pursuit of Love, The: BBC TV 243;
    Bristol Old Vic (musical) 361

Quennell, Peter 267, 332

Rachel (NM's horse) 44
Radice, Betty 273
Radziwill, Princess Dolly 255, 303,
    318, 319, 353
Rainbird, George (publisher) 274,
    361, 362, 367
Ratular (Unity's pet rat) 45
Redé, Baron Alexis de 254
Redesdale Cottage (David Mitford's
    final home) 262, 335
Renard, Marie (NM's maid) 251,
    317–18, 373–4

PICTURE CREDITS